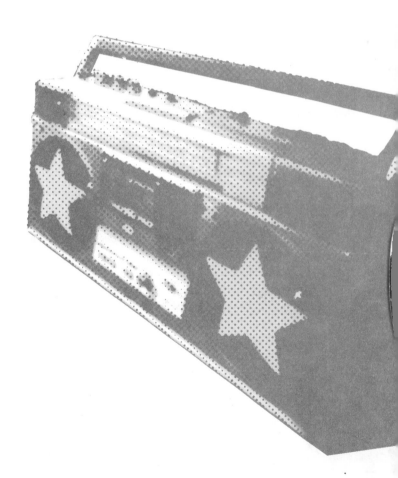

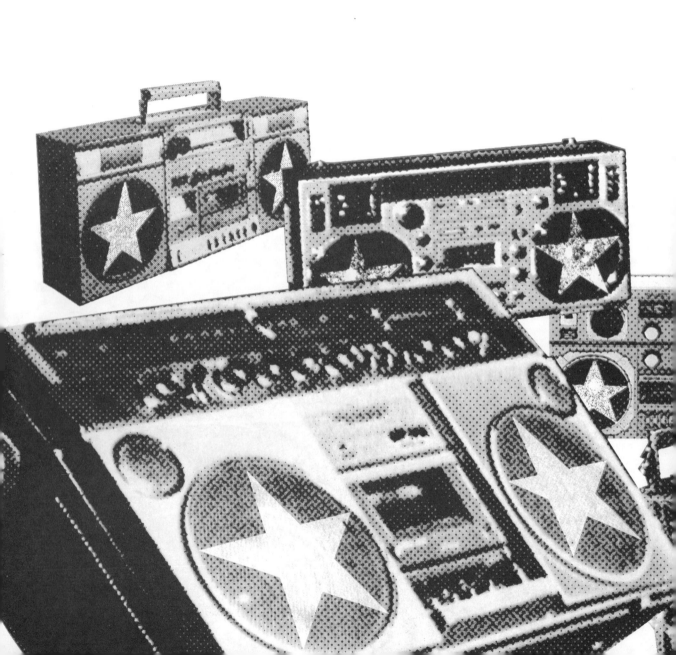

egotrip's™
BOOK OF RAP LISTS

BY SACHA JENKINS, ELLIOTT WILSON, CHAIRMAN MAO, GABRIEL ALVAREZ & BRENT ROLLINS

St. Martin's Griffin New York

Design by Brent Rollins.
Cover photograph by Louis Gisone.

Photo credits:
Bill Adler: pg. 116
B+: pgs. 51, 73, 88, 162, 185, 295
Henry Chalfant: pgs. 22, 56, 80, 86, 123
Josh Cheuse: pg. 135
Rachelle Clinton: pgs. 98, 113, 262, 269
Andréa M. Duncan: pg. 302
Talib Haq (Wadeva Images): pg. 18
Ben Higa: pg. 88
Dorothy Low: pg. 147
Ricky Powell: pg. 84

Additional photos on pgs. 79, 204, 240, 283 courtesy of Adler Archives.

Flyer on pg. 89 courtesy of Ben Higa's private collection.
Flyers on pgs. 28, 29 courtesy of Toshio Kajiwara's private collection.

Cover key on pg. 342 by (((s))).
Illustration on pg. 297 reproduced courtesy of Tommy Boy Records.

ISBN 0-312-24298-0

10 9 8 7 6 5 4 3 2

To Matt Reid,
Thank You For Showing Us That
Everything Is Dooable.

TABLE OF CONTENTS.

TABLE OF CONTENTS.

10 Logos Haze Wishes He Had Created.

10 Cool Stickers.

Rappers Who Attended Manhattan's High School Of Art & Design.

Artsy Types Who've Made Contributions To Hip Hop.

13 Comic Book–Inspired Jacket Designs.

Little Known Design Trivia.

Art Ideas That Didn't Make The Cut.

Personalities Pictured On The Cover Of A Tribe Called Quest's
   Midnight Marauders.

Film...180

Noreaga's Favorite Cinematic Love Stories.

Hollywood Types On Rap's Bozack.

26 Feature Film Cameos By Rappers.

34 Rap Song Titles Based On Movie Titles.

29 Rap Album Titles Based On Movie Titles.

Rap-Related Career Highlights Of Hollywood Hot Boy, Ice Cube.

Film-Inspired Rap Names.

Music Videos Based On Movies.

20 Rap Theme Songs To Non-Rap Films.

Rap Movie Soundtracks That Don't Suck.

Sampled Movie Dialogue Quiz.

Debi Mazar Recounts 6 Close Encounters With Hip Hop In The '80s.

Rap Logos Based On *The Godfather*.

The *ego trip* Oscars.

Cheddar...192

Money Ain't A Thang.

Rappers Who've Made *Forbes* Magazine's Annual
   Highest-Paid Entertainers List.

Rappers Who Have Declared Bankruptcy.

7 Costly-Ass Artists To Sample.

It All Comes Down To Money.

Rap Artists Who've Owned Their Own.

Most Expensive Hip Hop Records.

20 Invaluable Songs About Money.

Rap Personalities Who Admit To Having Worked At Food Chains.

Things Rappers Spend Their Money On.

Sports...200

D.M.C.'s All-NFL Dream Team.

14 Great Lyrical References For The Real Players.

Rappers Who've Assisted The World's Tallest Emcee.

Rappers Who Ball (Well).

15 Pro Hoopsters Who Rap (Badly).

Legendary Ballers Mentioned On Hurt 'Em Bad's "NBA Rap."

Legendary Ballers Mentioned On Kurtis Blow's "Basketball."

'70s Baseball Players Who Get Shouted Out On
   "Two Brothers With Checks (San Francisco, Harvey)."

Negro League Baseball Players, Teams & Personalities
   Mentioned In "Saga Of Dandy, The Devil & Day."

Inspectah Deck Picks His Favorite Professional Wrestlers Of All-Time.

Nuthin' But The Very Best Tyson Lyrical References.

When Rap & Sports Collide.

12 Sports Lyrics That Lose.

In Full Gear...210

Models On Rap's Bozack.

Hip Hop's Greatest Sweater References Of All-Time.

Items De La Soul Dismisses On "Take It Off."

Rappers & Their Signature Accessories.

Rappers Who Have Been Photographed In The Buff Or In Their Drawers.

Tattoos That Make An Impression.

You Gotta Reckon With Fashion.

Products Slick Rick Plugs In "La Di Da Di."

Leave My Jheri Curl Alone.

Good Hair.

Cock-Diesel Rap Dudes.

Short But Funky.

6 Feet High & Rising.

Skinny & Proud.

Rap Heavyweights (Literally).

TABLE OF CONTENTS.

Monkeylove.

This book would not have been possible without the love, support and good grooming of our families, loved ones, life-long friends and, believe it or not, our enemies (eat shit and die!).

We also wish to extend our undying gratitude to *ego trip*'s co-founder Henry Chalfant, our live-ass editor, Dana Albarella, as well as the following hamburger helpers:

Amir Abdullah, Bryan Adams @ FAB Communications, Cey Adams @ The Drawing Board, Abby Addis, Bill Adler @ Mouth Almighty, Afu-Ra, AJ Scratch, Maria Alamillo @ Warner Bros., Alchemist, Harry Allen, A-1 Records, Stretch Armstrong, Babu, Baby Paul, Miguel Baguer @ Columbia, Meegan Barnes @ Femme Arsenal, Malik Bellamy @ Thugged Out Entertainment, Beni B @ ABB, Debi Bensinger @ Interscope, Noah Callahan-Bever, Big Boi, Big Daddy Kane, Big Punisher, Big Shug, Billy Jam, Biz Markie, Black Star, Blak Shawn @ Rawkus, Betsy Bolte @ No Limit, Theola Borden @ Jive, Jared Boxx, B+, Brian Brater @ Rawkus, Shawn Brauch @ Pen & Pixel, David Bry @ *Vibe*, Erin Burke, Greg Burke @ Elektra, Kevin Burke, Ayana Byrd @ *Rolling Stone*, Jamie Cadwell, David Calderly @ Gee Street/V2, Cappadonna, Hope Carr, Matt Carter, DJ Cash Money, Vanessa Ceballos @ Loud, Cee-Lo, Chris Chambers @ Interscope, Josh Cheuse, Chuck D, Jennifer Clay @ Skechers U.S.A., Rachelle Clinton, DJ C-Los, Lyor Cohen, Chris Connelly @ MTV News, Cormega, Don Cornelius, Rob Corrigan, Count Chocula, Craig B, Daddy-O, DB's, Dead Prez, De La Soul, Del The Funkeé Homosapien, Nate Denver, Nina Diaz @ MTV, D.M.C., Doctor Dré, The Dubwiser, Andréa M. Duncan, Dyme, DJ Eclipse, Electric Boogaloos, El-P, Eminem, EMZ @ Stimulated, Michael Engelaan, Express @ Supermen Productions, DJ Evil Dee, Fat Beats, Fat Joe, Melissa Ferstl @ Pen & Pixel, Jonathan P. Fine, Stu Fine @ Wild Pitch, Jana Fleishman @ Elektra, Herman Flores @ *Industry Insider*, Freddie Foxxx, Aaron Fuchs @ Tuff City, Funkmaster Flex, Nick Gamma @ Jive, Jeff Gandel @ Tuff City, Bobbito Garcia, Starlite Gentry, Brian Gilmore @ Loud, Gimme Gimme Records, Louis Gisone, Max Glazer, Lea Goldman @ *Forbes*, Michael A. Gonzales, Belgica Gonzalez, Karen R. Good, Abélla Gomez Gotay, Greg Nice, Guru, Talib Haq, Stephen Harrigan, Carter Harris @ *Vibe*, Anthony Harrison, Darcie Hayashi, Haze @ Hyperformance, Ebon Heath @ (((stereotype))), Heather B., Grace Heck @ Relativity, Dave Helm, Haitian Mike Heron @ Hydra, Ben Higa, Lauryn Hill, Selwyn Seyfu Hinds @ *The Source*, Danny Hoch, Sarah K. Honda, Chris Houghton, Inspectah Deck, Molly Jackel, Elon D. Johnson, Julio G @ 92.3 The Beat, Toshio Kajiwara, Dennis Kane, Kaves, Rob Kenner, Zuhairah Khaldun @ Tommy Boy, Kid Capri, KLC, Paul, Carol & Sunshine Kleinberg, Kool Keith, Kool Moe Dee, Kool DJ Red Alert, Krayzie Bone, kris ex, Anne Kristoff @ Elektra, Jeremy Larner @ JL Entertainment, Christian Lantry, Laze-E-Laze, Lisa Leone, Sheena

ACKNOWLEDGEMENTS.

Lester, Joe Levy @ *Rolling Stone*, Miles Marshall Lewis, Valerie Lewis @ MCA, Alan Light @ *Spin*, Chris Lighty, Amy Linden, Aaron Lockenfaura @ Famous Artists, Lootpack, Jeff Lorez, Dorothy Low Photography, Greg Mack, Mac Mall, Jeannine Magno @ Cornerstone, Nadia Majid @ Double XXposure, Chaka Malik, Risa Malkinson, Bönz Malone, Marley Marl, Rachel Marsh, Marlo Martin, Angie Martinez, Kimmy Mason @ Jive, Yasushi Matsuda, Debi Mazar, Maze, Amhalise Mbolo, Donna McCleer, Iain McNee @ Tape Kingz, Alexander Mejia @ Virgin, Mia X, Sia Michel, Tracey Miller, Mills from Zulu Nation, DJ Mister Cee, M.O.P., Rigoberto Morales @ *The Source*, Alejandro Morales, Jr., Aimee Morris @ Gee Street, Patrick Moxey, Mr. Complex, Mr. Len, Mr. Magic, Mr. Serv On, Mr. Walt, Mr. Wiggles, Aurelio Santos Muñoz, Musolini, Jarret Myer @ Rawkus, Nikki @ Asti Management, Ninety-9, Noreaga, Diana Oberlander, Noa Ochi @ Loud, Maureen O'Connor @ Rogers & Cowan, Minya Oh @ *Vibe*, Keisha Orange @ No Limit, Jackie Osae-Asare @ Columbia, Kim Osorio, Jay Papke @ Pawnshop Press, Peanut Butter Wolf, Gabrielle Peluso @ Def Jam, Alison Pember @ London, Percee P, John Perez, Barbara Pescolido @ No Limit, Pharoahe Monch, Phase 2, Phat Gary @ Empire Management, www.platform.net, Ricky Powell, DJ Premier, Prince Paul, R.A. The Rugged Man, Shaheem Reid @ *Vibe*, Peter Relic @ *Vibe*, Rhettmatic, Lorraine Robertson @ La Face, Brian Robinson @ Tommy Boy, Chris Rock, A Kid Called Roots, Aldo Rosati, Danté Ross, Shabaam Sahdeeq, Saviour @ Alphanumeric, Shani Saxon @ *Teen People*, Scaramanga, Christine Schaar, Schoolly D, Heidi Schuessler, Andy Schwartz @ Epic, Sen Dog, MC Serch, Shazam, Jon Shecter @ Game, Russell Simmons, Zenobia Simmons @ Penalty, Sir Mix-A-Lot, Slick Rick, Danyel Smith, Will Socolov @ Freeze, Paul Sommerstein, The Sound Library, Mark Spear @ Songwriter Services, Special K (Awesome Two), Dorothy Stefanski @ *Rap Pages*, Bill Stephney, DJ Steve D, Georges Sulmers @ Raw Shack, Cathy Symeonidis @ Def Jam, Taheem @ Loud, Tash, Teflon, Rob "Reef" Tewlow, Michele Thorne @ (((stereotype))), Jean Tirebuck @ *Blues & Soul*, Vikki Tobak, Tomika @ Du Boi Management, Dave Tompkins, Too Poetic, Too $hort, Julio C.Trejo @ Priority, Jasmine Vega @ Virgin, Cristina Verán, Konstantin Vilenchitz, Jennifer Vogelmann @ Will, Monty Wan, Wendy Washington @ Universal, Bill Weinstein, Richard Weissman, Wendy @ The Cleaver Company, Carl "Real Niggas Do Real Things" Weston @ Graf Core, Will @ Flip, Felicia A. Williams @ *The Source*, "Fly" Ty Williams, Monica Williamson, Tim Willis, Wise, Douglas Wolk, Howard Wuelfing @ Columbia, Xzibit, Zhou Dao-Yi, DJ Git Zimmerman, Christie Z-Pabón @ DMC.

Special big 'em up shout-outs to all *ego trip* contributors and fans past and present. One of us equals many of us. Foe life.

Ted Bawno's Forward Foreword.

It's been a long road traveled. Rumors of my death have been greatly exaggerated. Oh, by the way, for those who don't know—hi, my name is . . . Theodore Aloysius Bawno. But you can call me "Ted." (And if your name is Angie Dickinson, you can call me anytime, sunshine.)

I am the original P.E.—Publisher Extraordinaire. And I'm number one, baby. My mighty hard-rockin' rap magazine, *ego trip*, is the definitive, arrogant voice of musical truth. What does this mean? It means that there are so many non-kosher slabs of perfect-bound dead trees that scream beats, rhymes and lifestyle, but ain't really sayin' jack-squat.

Me? My team? Big dogs—like my dear, late pal, "The Yankee Clipper," Joe DiMaggio, and his great championship teams of the '40s. Everyone else? Geeky, pen-holding, dollar-and-a-dream-having cracker barrel crackers (yeah, I might be white, but I'm on the Black hand side, ya smell me?). They're riding the whimsical tradewinds of my ghetto Bible like a junkie with a $10 habit on one of those coin-operated kiddie pony rides that you find in front of your local take-out Chinese restaurant. Sure, those might seem like good vibrations, but the truth comes from a special place.

You know, I was recently shot. And I've been in this damn print game for well over 45 years. I started out delivering papers in Hackensack, New Jersey—yeah, that's publishing right there. I know it from the ground up. Anyway, I've been shot and I'm alive today. I've never been spiritual, but

BAWNO.

now I realize that things happen for a reason (and that oranges are little candies from God).

The bottom line is this: no matter what the competition says, no matter how they spin it, no matter what they do, what they do, what they do . . . they're all BITERS. Every last lost one. They've all taken from what *ego trip*'s created. That's the truth. And hip hop don't like biters. And God don't like ugly.

So here we are. Movies, clothing, rap. Lots of money out there. Lots of stories to be told. Lots of facts to be shared with you good people, the people I love (because you love to spend). You're here because you fancy yourselves as rap know-it-alls. Know this: you don't know shit! You're here because you're ignorant! But you're not alone. The world has starved for a tome of rap knowledge such as this for far too long. Time's up, kemosabe.

I promise that you'll have a grand ol' time absorbing the precious jewels that my monkey academy worked so hard to put together. From the times Afrika Bambaataa treated his Zulu Nation parishioners to White Castle burgers to the unmasking of the real person depicted in the Public Enemy logo to Kool Keith's favorite places to massage Mr. Frisky in public, this is *ego trip's Book Of Rap Lists*—an event. A motherfunking rap phenomenon. I know you're glad to be a part of it.

Excelsior!
Theodore Aloysius Bawno
Cayman Islands
July 4, 1999

P.S. SCOREKEEPERS BE ADVISED: My staff wanted you nitpickers to know that December 31, 1998, was the cut-off date for the information you are about to bless yourselves with. Millennium watchers prepare for the literary sequel, *Volume 2 . . . In Ted's Lifetime*, coming soon! (God, I love the dough—how much you'll never know.)

FOUND

ATION.

PLAID IN FULL: Run-D.M.C.'s first gig ever at Disco Fever, Bronx, New York, 1983.

★ let us start from the beginning at the top of the li

STILL #1:
Important Firsts.

1. **First hip hop DJ:** Kool Herc

2. **Location of Kool Herc's first party:** 1520 Sedgewick Avenue, Bronx, NY, 1973

3. **First emcee:** Coke La Rock

4. **First recorded rap song:** "King Tim III (Personality Jock)"—Fatback (Spring, 1979)

5. **First recorded rap hit:** "Rapper's Delight"—Sugarhill Gang (Sugar Hill, 1979)

6. **First hip hop radio show:** *Mr. Magic's Disco Showcase*, WHBI 105.9 FM, New York City, circa 1979

7. **First rap artist signed to a major label:** Kurtis Blow (Mercury)

8. **First rap group signed to a major label:** Fearless Four (Elektra)

9. **First rap album on CD:** *King Of Rock*—Run-D.M.C. (Profile, 1984)

10. **First rap double album:** *He's The DJ, I'm The Rapper*—DJ Jazzy Jeff & The Fresh Prince (Jive, 1988)

11. **First rap double CD:** *Master P Presents Down South Hustlers*—Various Artists (No Limit, 1995)

12. **First rap LP to receive an Explicit Lyrics Warning sticker:** *Move Somthin*—2 Live Crew (Luke Skyywalker, 1988)

13. **First rap artist to release two albums on the same day:** DJ Magic Mike—*Bass The Final Frontier*; *This Is How It Should Be Done* (Magic, 1993)

14. **First artist to reach #1 with two albums in the same year:** DMX—*It's Dark And Hell Is Hot*; *Flesh Of My Flesh, Blood Of My Blood* (Def Jam, 1998)

15. **First Hollywood feature film to feature b-boying:** *Flashdance* (Rock Steady Crew) (Paramount, 1983)

16. **First rap artist to make a national TV appearance:** Kurtis Blow on *Soul Train*, October, 1980

17. **First rap group to make a national TV appearance:** Funky 4 + 1 on NBC's *Saturday Night Live*, February, 1981

18. **First major network news program to document hip hop:** ABC's *20/20*, July, 1981

19. **First music video TV show dedicated to hip hop:** *Video Music Box* featuring Ralph McDaniels & Lionel Martin, WNYC, New York City, April, 1984

THEY GOT A BOX OF NEWPORTS & PUMA SWEATS:
First Hip Hop Signees To 22 Renowned Labels.

1. Afrika Bambaataa: Tommy Boy
2. Biz Markie: Prism
3. Cheba: Ruffhouse
4. Craig Mack: Bad Boy
5. Eazy-E: Priority
6. Fearless Four: Elektra
7. Gang Starr: Wild Pitch
8. Funky 4 + 1: Enjoy
9. Heavy D: Uptown
10. Kurtis Blow: Mercury
11. LL Cool J: Def Jam
12. Lonnie Love (b/k/a Mr. Hyde): Profile
13. Master O.C. & Krazy Eddie: Next Plateau
14. The Real Untouchables (b/k/a TRU): No Limit
15. The Rose Family: Rawkus
16. MC Shan: Cold Chillin'
17. Smooth Rhyme Criminals: Suave House
18. The Sounds Of JHS 126 Brooklyn: Sleeping Bag
19. Tung Twista: Loud
20. U.T.F.O.: Select
21. Vertical Lines featuring Phase 2: Tuff City
22. Whodini: Jive

Lauryn Hill's Greatest Musical Influences.*

1. Nina Simone
2. Al Green
3. Stevie Wonder
4. Aretha Franklin

*In no particular order.

Refugee Camp All-Superstar Lauryn Hill is the first lady of hip hop. She can sing, rap, dance, write and produce, and she's got five (count 'em) Grammy Awards to her credit. And she's got so much soul, she only listens to old music.

Afrika Bambaataa's *Blues & Soul* List.*

The August 1988 edition of England's *Blues & Soul* magazine featured a profile of Afrika Bambaataa in which the hip hop godfather presented an extensive list of important old school breakbeat records. This list was the first published record of breakbeat information to ever hit Europe, thus it set off a continent-wide beat-hunting craze for nations of aspiring hip hop DJs that lasted for years. Collect 'em all!

1. "Apache"—Incredible Bongo Band (Pride, 1973)
2. "Jam On The Groove"—Ralph MacDonald (TK, 1976)
3. "Theme From *Star Wars*"—Dave Matthews (CTI, 1977)
4. "Catch A Groove"—Juice (Greedy, 1976)
5. "Reach Out In The Darkness"—Friend & Lover (Verve, 1968)
6. "Minimum Wage"—Rock 'N Roll**
7. "Give It Up Or Turn It Loose"—James Brown (King, 1969)
8. "Get Up I Feel Like Being A Sex Machine"—James Brown (King, 1969)
9. "Sing A Simple Song"—Sly & The Family Stone (Epic, 1969)
10. "You're The One"—Little Sister (Stoneflower, 1970)
11. "It's Just Begun"—Jimmy Castor Bunch (RCA, 1972)
12. "Dance To The Drummer's Beat"—Herman Kelly & Life (TK, 1976)
13. "Scorpio"—Dennis Coffey (Sussex, 1971)
14. "Ride Sally Ride"—Dennis Coffey (Sussex, 1972)
15. "Son Of Scorpio"—Dennis Coffey (Sussex, 1972)
16. *Willie Dynamite* Soundtrack—J.J. Johnson & Various Artists (MCA, 1974)
17. "Take Me To The Mardi Gras"—Bob James (CTI, 1975)
18. "Let A Woman Be A Woman (Let A Man Be A Man)"—Dyke & The Blazers (Original Sound, 1969)
19. "Funky Broadway"—Dyke & The Blazers (Original Sound, 1967)
20. "The Champ"—The Mohawks (Cotillion, 1968)
21. "Tramp"—Otis Redding & Carla Thomas (Stax, 1967)
22. "Groove To Get Down"—T-Connection (TK, 1977)
23. "Get Off Your Ass And Jam"—Funkadelic (Westbound, 1975)
24. "Give The Drummer Some"—Little Milton**
25. "Get On The Good Foot"—James Brown (Polydor, 1972)
26. "Funky Drummer"—James Brown (King, 1970)
27. "Keep On Doin' What You're Doin'"—Bobby Byrd (Brownstone, 1971)
28. "I Know You Got Soul"—Bobby Byrd (King, 1971)
29. "Think (About It)"—Lyn Collins (People, 1972)
30. "It's My Thing"—Marva Whitney (King, 1969)
31. "Get Up, Get Into It, Get Involved"—James Brown (King, 1970)
32. "Honky Tonk Women"—Rolling Stones (London, 1969)
33. "Hot Stuff"—Rolling Stones (Rolling Stones, 1976)
34. "Dance To The Music"—Sly & The Family Stone (Epic, 1968)
35. "Family Affair"—Sly & The Family Stone (Epic, 1971)
36. "Jam"—Grand Central Station (Warner Bros., 1975)
37. "Joyous"—Pleasure (Fantasy, 1976)
38. "Rock Creek Park"—The Blackbyrds (Fantasy, 1976)
39. "Happy Music"—The Blackbyrds (Fantasy, 1975)
40. "Africano"—Earth Wind & Fire (Columbia, 1975)
41. "Shining Star"—Earth Wind & Fire (Columbia, 1975)
42. "Power"—Earth Wind & Fire (Columbia, 1972)
43. "Ring My Bell"—Anita Ward (TK, 1979)
44. "The Funk Is On"—Instant Funk (Salsoul, 1980)
45. "Funky Stuff"—Kool & The Gang (De-Lite, 1973)
46. "Jungle Boogie"—Kool & The Gang (De-Lite, 1973)
47. "Flashlight"—Parliament (Casablanca, 1977)
48. "More Bounce To The Ounce"—Zapp (Warner Bros., 1980)
49. "Dancin' Kid"—Disco Tex & The Sex-O-Lettes (Chelsea, 1976)
50. "The Breakdown"—Rufus Thomas (Stax, 1972)
51. "Do The Funky Penguin"—Rufus Thomas (Stax, 1972)
52. "Shakara"—Fela Ransome Kuti (Editions Makossa, 1974)
53. "Brother Green (The Disco King)"—Roy Ayers Ubiquity (Polydor, 1975)
54. "Lonesome Cowboy"—Roy Ayers Ubiquity (Polydor, 1976)
55. "Yellow Sunshine"—Yellow Sunshine (Gamble, 1973)

*In no particular order.
**These records either don't exist or are so rare that only Bam has them. If you happen to stumble upon these recordings, please contact us immediately. Operators are standing by.

RAP MUSIC, WHICH STARTED ON THE STREETS AND IN THE PARKS OF NEW YORK CITY, HAS HAD A POSITIVE INFLUENCE ON THE TASTES AND ASPIRATIONS OF TODAY'S YOUTH.

THROUGH THE RAP MUSIC INDUSTRY THE YOUTH OF TODAY CAN IDENTIFY WITH THE EXAMPLE OF SUCCESSFUL AND SUPPORTIVE CELEBRITIES, AND BE ENCOURAGED TO DEDICATE THEIR OWN TIME AND TALENT TO SELF DEVELOPMENT AND SERVICE TO THEIR COMMUNITIES.

NOW, THEREFORE, I, EDWARD I. KOCH, MAYOR OF THE CITY OF NEW YORK, DO HEREBY PROCLAIM MAY 3, 1985, TO BE

"RAP MUSIC DAY"

IN NEW YORK CITY.

IN WITNESS WHEREOF I HAVE HEREUNTO SET MY HAND AND CAUSED THE SEAL OF THE CITY OF NEW YORK TO BE AFFIXED.

MAYOR, THE CITY OF NEW YORK

SUCK MY KOCH: A New York kingpin shows rap some love.

WE'RE ON OUR OWN DICK:
Rap Celebrates Itself.

1. "Ego Trippin' (Part Two)"—De La Soul (Tommy Boy, 1993)
2. "Going Way Back"—Just-Ice (Fresh, 1987)
3. "Hip Hop"—Jigmastas (Beyond Real, 1996)
4. "Hip Hop"—LL Cool J (Def Jam, 1995)
5. "Hip Hop Hooray"—Naughty By Nature (Tommy Boy, 1993)
6. "Hip Hop It Is Kind Of Different"—Tone-Lōc (Delicious Vinyl, 1991)
7. "Hip Hop Music"—Groove B Chill (A&M, 1990)
8. "Hip Hop vs. Rap"—KRS-One (Jive, 1993)
9. "I Don't Like Rock 'N Roll"—Schoolly D (Jive, 1988)
10. "i used to love h.e.r."—Common (Relativity, 1994)
11. "Living In The World Of Hip Hop"—MC Shan (Cold Chillin', 1987)
12. "Manifesto"—Talib Kweli (Rawkus, 1998)
13. "The Meaning"—The High & Mighty (Eastern Conference, 1997)
14. "Old School"—2Pac (Interscope, 1995)
15. "Rap Is Here To Stay"—Spyder-D (Profile, 1985)
16. "Return Of The B-Boy"—The Pharcyde (Delicious Vinyl, 1992)
17. "South Bronx"—Boogie Down Productions (B-Boy, 1986)
18. "They Used To Do It Out In The Park"—MC Shan (Cold Chillin', 1988)
19. "This Is Called Hip Hop"—Q.B.C. (Capitol, 1988)
20. "Wheelz Of Steel"—OutKast (LaFace, 1996)

Kool DJ Red Alert's Essential Old School DJ Round-Up.*

1. **Kool Herc**

If you're talking about the mid '70s, you're talking about relief from the gang days and relief from how people were living in fear in the South Bronx. People came out to enjoy parties, a lot of them never knew about coming downtown or to midtown to clubs. They stayed up in their area. When Herc came here from Kingston, Jamaica, all he knew about from back home was toasting and dubbing—what eventually became rapping and mixing. He expressed his own way of playing music. He studied a lot of alternative type records, certain rock records, records that people would never have in mind to dance to or relate to—a Baby Huey or a Babe Ruth or certain LP cuts such as "'T' Plays It Cool" off of Marvin Gaye's *Trouble Man*.

At that time, nobody knew what these beats were. Herc was known for washing off the labels and changing the labels onto other records. People would come over and look at it and go, "Oh, that's that record!" And if they'd go to the store thinking they had that record, they got the wrong record.

Herc also introduced the very first emcee by the name of Coke La Rock. Coke La Rock was only saying certain phrases like, "You rock and you don't stop" or "Rock on, my mellow." Herc would also get on the mic and he would say various

*In no particular order.

phrases. As he was introducing his sense of music, all of the elements of the culture were built around it: the lingo, the style of clothing—the whole awareness of what it was like growing up in the South Bronx at that particular time.

2.   **Afrika Bambaataa**
The people that were coming to hear, dance to and enjoy Herc are some of the old schoolers who became DJs later on—people like Bam. Bam discovered hip hop in his own way. He was influenced by winning a trip to Africa when he was in school and from that he learned about the culture and everything. When he came back, his mother bought him a set of turntables. Bam started to introduce his own style of music—similar to Herc's—but he brought it out in the Afrocentric style and within the neighborhood of Bronx River.

Bam had females and males down with him and he called them Shaka Zulu Queens and Shaka Zulu Kings. Bam was the type of person who, no matter if you were a DJ or an emcee, if he liked you, he'd put you on. One time there used to be three DJs and 10 emcees down with him. Everybody said, "Bam, you got too many!" But Bam did not care. It was in his heart. They were who he

STEEL WHEELS: Park-jamming at the Patterson Housing Projects, Bronx, New York, mid-'80s.

loved and this is what he loved to do. I remember up in the center, if we only made a certain amount of money at a party, he'd go send my man, Monk (rest in peace), and a couple of friends to White Castle and we all had White Castle. That's how it was with Bam.

And Bam was the master of records. He had all the different styles that everybody just grooved to. It was funny because at one time, Bam and Herc didn't get along with each other. I remember when Herc brought it upon himself to play in Bronx River and the plug got pulled. They said, "You steppin' in this house?" It got deep at one point, B!

3. **Disco King Mario**
Herc was known for the respect he got for his sound system. At that time, the major amplifier was called the MacIntosh. If you had a MacIntosh, you were well respected. People didn't care about the speakers or the turntables or nothing. It was that amp that gave you that respect. There were only two people who had that amp: Kool Herc, and then later on, my man, Disco King Mario (rest in peace).

I consider Mario one of the pioneer DJs at that time. The funny part about it was that Disco King Mario and Bam worked a lot of the same sections within the Soundview part of the Bronx. There was a gym at Junior High School 123, and you had the big divider in the gym separating one side of the gym from the other. Mario and Bam used to play at the same time. Disco King Mario had the sound system. But Bam had the records and the emcees.

4. **Grandmaster Flash**
On the West side of the Bronx you had Herc and on the other side you had Bam. Flash was somewhere up around the middle area. I remember when scratching came out, people used to go, *zoom-zoom, zoom-zoom*, and that's all it was. You were hearing the same basic chopping. But Flash was very fast in cutting. Cutting was perfected by Flash and later by many other DJs. He took it to another level. Flash started seeing how fast he could catch the movement from one record into another, decreasing the number of bars he spun back on. And that's what he started being known for.

5. **Grand Wizard Theodore**
I remember hearing Mean Gene and Flash playing together before Flash's sideman, Disco B, came along. Gene didn't play that much. But when Flash and Gene broke up there was some dispute. That's when Gene started bigging up his brother, Theodore.

While I think Flash is the first person I seen spinning back a record instead of dropping the needle, Theodore was the person I always saw dropping needles. Dropping nee-

dles like a muthafucka! Theodore was also known for the "back door" thing. The "back door" is bringing the beat in a second before the other record. In the past, you saw DJs with doubles backspinning on the one. But Theodore took it back—b-boom!

He was a short little muthafucka who'd be standing on top of a milkcrate, bending over and just catching it. Theodore formed the L Brothers with his brothers, Mean Gene and Claudio Livingston. Theodore was the flashiest person out of the three because he was the smallest, youngest and most appealing. So they always showcased him. And he would rock. Oh my God!

6. **Jazzy Jay**
My cousin, Jazzy, moved up to the Bronx after I taught him the basics and he got his own set. But Jazzy wasn't on with Bam yet because Bam already had two DJs—Sinbad and Zombu. Since Disco King Mario didn't have his own turntables and had heard so much about Jazzy, Mario said, "Yo, come on over and join me." Jazzy let Mario use his turntables, then Mario had Jazzy checking to see the titles of Bam's records. Jazzy eventually acknowledged that Mario was jerking him around.

Bam said to Jazzy, "Yo man, I'm cuttin' off one of my DJs, you come over." I guess Bam felt he needed to step up. Jazzy was the new "flashy" DJ. He was another little guy standing on top of a milkcrate, getting low over the records and cutting it up. And later Bam asked Jazzy about me. I wasn't really playing that much because I wasn't into cutting, I was more into mixing. For me, the highlight of the evening was standing right next to Jazzy and watching him play. Bam would warm it up, Jazzy would rock it on and at the end of the night I'd play a couple of records. Me and Jazzy knew how the records looked and we knew where to put the needle. But we still don't know the names of the records after all this time. There's still a whole bunch of different beats that Bam got that nobody knows.

Jazzy was also known for building speakers in high school. He was the first one to build the big, double scoop Collins. And then, little by little, he kept building speakers until we had a massive sound system.

7. **Grandmixer D.ST**
One thing you could always say about Zulu was Zulu had some DJs. D.ST had a very unique style to himself. The way he showcased his talent when he was mixing was very sharp. To a tee.

8. **Whiz Kid**
Whiz Kid had an unorthodox style of cutting and everybody

FOUNDATION.

wondered how he did that shit. You had to really listen to the way he cut as compared to the others. He put a little rhythm style to it. If you hear a basic bass player and then you hear someone like a Larry Graham comin' in and puttin' a little extra to it, you'll be like, "Ooh, that shit sound even doper!" That's what it was with Whiz. It's like he was talkin' with his shit.

9. **Afrika Islam**
Afrika Islam had a crew called the Mayberry Crew that was from out of Parkchester. It was him, this guy named Kid Vicious and a guy that moved out to the West Coast and got down with Ice-T named Donald D. They were Islam's emcees. Aside from that, Jazzy used to play with Islam too. Islam was another one who was sharp with his shit. He was known as being the Son of Bambaataa and that's how he got the title.

10. **Breakout**
Breakout was known for cuttin' up for the Funky Four. DJ Baron was his sideman. Their section was further up in the Bronx, like up in the Gun Hill area. Breakout and the Funky Four had a very unique routine to the music from *Gilligan's Island* which was very well known.

11. **Charlie Chase**
I don't remember which emcees were with Charlie Chase and Tony Tone at first. But eventually they formed together to become the Cold Crush Brothers with them two as the DJs. Tony Tone was at the side of Chase. He could play, but he wasn't playing that much. Chase was known not for rocking a party, but for being a show DJ for Cold Crush, keeping everything on beat, keeping it on time, keeping everybody stepping and moving.

12. **AJ Scratch**
AJ was known for playing at the Moore House Center, E. R. Moore Projects. AJ was also known for cutting up. He used to play in combination with Kenny G and Lovebug Starski. AJ was holding his own.

13. **Johnny Thunderbird**
He was known in Harlem. He wasn't into hip hop, but he DJ-ed disco, R&B and that sort of music and influenced certain people on how to rock a party in that style. One person who learned under him was . . .

14. **Lovebug Starski**
I gotta give a lot of respect to Starski. He learned to combine the elements of playing hip hop, R&B and disco. He became a party rocker. He was a person who knew how to handle crowd participation—mixing and vibing with the mic at the same time. He could play for an older crowd, he could play for a younger crowd. He had that sense and ability to please a crowd whether he was playing in the Bronx or in Harlem. He could go hip hop, he could go the other way. He was good.

I remember when Lovebug and DJ Smokey—another good DJ from the past—used to DJ in Burger King on Prospect Avenue. They used to close Burger King and a night it was a disco. That was hip hop, baby.

15. **Hollywood**
He was another person who learned under Johnny Thunderbird's influence. Hollywood came up around the same way as Pete DJ Jones, a disco DJ who played down in midtown Manhattan in the clubs and who also came up to the Bronx and had a good following. Also a part of this scene were people such as Junebug (rest in peace), man Reggie Wells and Eddie Cheeba. Their hip hop was directed toward that disco crowd. And while they were playing this club called 371 that was in the Bronx off Webster Avenue, you had Flash, Bam or the L Brothers playing for a younger crowd that was either in a center or a hall. It was hip hop, but in different segments.

People such as Russell Simmons, who was a promoter at that point while going to City College, acknowledged what these people in the 371 crew were doing. After hearing about all these people, he started bringing them downtown, playing clubs like the Hotel Diplomat and other big spots.

16. **Grandmaster Flowers**
Grandmaster Flowers was a well respected disco DJ from out in Brooklyn. Flowers was known as having one of the best sound systems there ever has been. They told me that he used to bring it to Manhattan in Central Park around the section called the Fountain. They'd say when he turned it on, you heard that sucker from afar and he knew how to mix his ass off. And I think that's where Flash got the title "Grandmaster" from. Flowers had it in a disco mode. Flash took it in a hip hop mode. Grandmaster Flowers, rest in peace.

A vital member of Afrika Bambaataa's Zulu Nation, the legendary Kool DJ Red Alert has gone from rocking New York City block parties and clubs to recording with his own group, The Jazzy 5 ("Jazzy Sensation"), to becoming a Gotham radio mainstay. Now in his 17th year on the air, he can currently be heard daily on two separate shows on NYC's WQHT 97.1 FM. Yeeeeeeeeessssssss!!!

Guru's 11 Voices Of Inspiration.

1. Anita Baker
2. Barry White
3. Louis Farrakhan
4. Rakim
5. Martin Luther King, Jr.
6. Patricia Elam, Esq. (My older sister)
7. James Brown
8. The Notorious B.I.G.
9. James Earl Jones
10. James Cagney
11. 2Pac

Guru has been the irrepressible and unmistakable voice of hip hop's most revered underground music merchants, Gang Starr, since day one. And as the Ill Kid's 1994 composition states, it's "Mostly Tha Voice" that gets you bucked. So you best protect ya neck and your larynx.

Most Disappointing Debut Rap LPs.

1. ***Can-I-Bus*—Canibus (Universal, 1998)**
After a year of well-received guest vocal appearances and a rhyme tussle with LL from which he emerged remarkably unscathed, Canibus released an LP that succumbed far too easily to freshman mistakes: pretentious song concepts, monotonous performances and disgraceful production choices. *Can-I-Bust* was more like it.

2. ***The Firm The Album*—Nas, Foxy Brown, AZ & Nature (Aftermath, 1997)**
When it was announced that rap luminaries Nas, Foxy Brown, AZ and QB verbal sniper, Cormega, had collectively signed with Dr. Dre's new, post-Death Row label, rap audiences anticipated an album on par with "Affirmative Action"—the quartet's sparkling debut from Nas' *It Was Written*. Somewhere along the way, Mega was replaced by Nature, Dre produced only one track (the album's best song, "Phone Tap") and *The Firm*'s underworld musical edge went decidedly corporate. Unimaginative, slick pop pap like "Firm Biz," "Five Minutes To Flush" and "Hardcore" were conference room rap muzak.

3. ***Down To Earth*—Monie Love (Warner Bros., 1990)**
U.K.-born Monie was being hailed as the newest princess of the Native Tongues' posse after her showstopping guest appearances on De La Soul's "Buddy" remix and Queen Latifah's "Ladies First." Who, then, could have anticipated *Down To Earth*'s misconceived mish-mash of nouveau-club rap and hip house?

4. ***Soul On Ice*—Ras Kass (Priority, 1996)**
For years, the West Coast rap intelligentsia had been singing the praises of Ras' stinging punchlines and compositional scope. What they didn't mention was his wretched taste in beats.

5. ***No Pressure*—Erick Sermon (Def Jam, 1993)**
6. ***Shadē Business*—PMD (PMD, 1994)**
In the wake of EPMD's devastating break-up came these two underwhelming solo efforts, which achingly demonstrated that the group was much more than the sum of its parts. Strictly disappointing.

7. ***Project: Funk Da World*—Craig Mack (Bad Boy, 1994)**
The undeniable bump of the "Flava In Ya Ear" single left da world ill-prepared for this album of decidedly unfunky songs. Most ironic song title? "Makin' Moves With Puff." It would be Craig's first and last dance with the Puffster.

8. ***Regulate . . . The G Funk Era*—Warren G (Def Jam, 1994)**
Based on his contributions to *The Chronic*, Dr. Dre's protegé was touted as Cali's next important production auteur. But the generic, middle-of-the-road musical politeness of Warren's *Era* bore closer comparisons to another musical G—Kenny.

9. ***Doe Or Die*—AZ (EMI, 1995)**
Before the Firm debacle, Nas' vocal foil from "Life's A Bitch" proved rather un-unique on his debut—a lackluster collection of ghetto narratives that fell far short of his popular partner's street poetry.

10. ***Money, Power & Respect*—The Lox (Bad Boy, 1998)**
Bad Boy's supposed return to the streets was to be epitomized by this Yonkers, NY trio. Aside from the compelling title track, what we got were vapid observations on the thugged-out glamorous life over more re-used loops and breakbeats.

FOUNDATION.

15 Artists Who Debuted As Guests.

1. **Biz Markie: "Def Fresh Crew"
   —Roxanne Shanté (Pop Art, 1986)**
   The inhuman orchestra's beatbox rendition of the Meow Mix cat food jingle is one
   of hip hop's great recorded moments.

2. **Sean "Puffy" Combs: "Dolly My Baby
   (Bad Boy Extended Mix)"—Super Cat
   also featuring 3rd Eye, The Notorious
   B.I.G. & Mary J. Blige (Columbia, 1993)**
   Thankfully, Puff Poppa never resuscitated
   the freaky, hyper-grimy flow he displayed
   on his debut. Headz in the Hamptons
   weren't ready for the shit he got.

3. **Cam'Ron: "8 Iz Enuff"—Big L also fea-
   turing Terra, McGruff, Buddah Bless,
   Twan, Trooper J & Mike Boogie
   (Columbia, 1995)**
   No, Killa Kam (as he was then known)
   didn't rhyme over the TV theme song to
   Dick Van Patten's hour-long family dram-
   edy. But, hey, there's an idea.

4. **Del The Funkeé Homosapien: "Turn Off
   The Radio"—Ice Cube (Priority, 1990)**
   At the conclusion of Cube's classic anti-
   airwave anthem, his Funkeé cousin
   calls in with a special announcement: "I
   just called to say, 'Fuck the radio!'"

5. **Hurricane G: "Tonight's Da Night"
   —Redman (Def Jam, 1992)**
   Who could forget this *mami* with attitude's agitated urging after Reggie's
   false start? "Yo, yo, Redman! Man, what
   the fuck, man? Get off that punk
   smooth shit, get on that rough shit—you
   know how we do!"

6. **Jay-Z: "Hawaiian Sophie"—The Jaz
   (EMI, 1989)**
   Jigga plays hype man to his Marcy
   Projects pal on this touching tale of
   Pacific Island love.

7. **The Lady Of Rage: "Total Chaos" &
   "The Winds Too Def To Die"—L.A.
   Posse (Atlantic, 1991)**
   Death Row's first Lady was "discovered"
   by Dr. Dre off of these guest debuts.

8. **Lil' Kim: "#!*@ Me" interlude, *Ready To
   Die*—The Notorious B.I.G. (Bad Boy, 1994)**
   That's not just any random chick
   Biggie's making whoopee with—that's
   Junior M.A.F.I.A.'s own Big Momma!

9. **The Lox: "Set It Off"—Main Source
   also featuring Lotto & Shaqueen (Wild
   Pitch, 1994)**
   A pre-Bad Boy Jadakiss and Sheek join
   forces with a post-Large Professor Sir
   Scratch and K-Cut.

10. **The Notorious B.I.G.: "A Buncha
    Niggas"—Heavy D also featuring 3rd
    Eye, Guru, Rob-O & Busta Rhymes
    (Uptown, 1992)**
    The future of Bad Boy's funk made his
    inauspicious first appearance in the
    middle of this random line-up.

11. **DJ Premier: "I Keep The Crowd
    Listening"—Lord Finesse & DJ Mike
    Smooth (Wild Pitch, 1990)**
    Preem's voice is heard for the first time on
    record introducing the Funky Man.

12. **Q-Tip: "The Promo"—Jungle Brothers
    (Idlers, 1988)**
    The first in a long line of consummate
    Abstract performances.

13. **Souls Of Mischief & Casual: "Burnt"
    —Del The Funkée Homosapien
    (Elektra, 1991)**
    Oaktown rhyme snipers blazed through
    this frenetic first foray.

14. **Sweet Tee: "One For The Treble
    (Fresh)"—Davy DMX (Tuff City, 1984)**
    The Q-borough princess known for "It's My
    Beat" and "It's Like That, Y'all" made her
    debut as the cockney-accented rap chick
    exhorting Davy to rock on.

15. **2Pac: "Same Song"—Digital
    Underground (Tommy Boy, 1990)**
    A D.U. dancer at the time, 'Pac proved he
    could bust a rhyme as well as a move in
    his world premiere. Who knew thug par-
    adise was just around the corner?

10 Weak Debut Singles By Major Rap Performers.

1. "Advance"
   —Scott La Rock &
   The Celebrity Three (b/k/a
   Boogie Down Productions)
   (Street Beat, 1985)

2. "Boof Baf"—Fugees
   (Ruffhouse, 1994)

3. "Born Loser"—DMX
   (Ruff Ryders, 1993)

4. "Come Do Me"
   —The Genius
   (Cold Chillin', 1991)

5. "Crime"
   —Masters Of Ceremony
   (M-Low, 1985)*

6. "Description Of A Fool"
   —A Tribe Called Quest
   (Jive, 1989)

7. "The Lesson"—Gang Starr
   (Wild Pitch, 1987)

8. "Lies"—Spectrum City
   (b/k/a Public Enemy)
   (Vanguard, 1984)

9. "Ooh I Love You,
   Rakeem"—Prince Rakeem
   (b/k/a RZA)
   (Tommy Boy, 1991)

10. "To Give You Love"
    —Ultramagnetic MC's
    (Diamond International,
    1986)

*Grand Puba's first record-
ed group.

12 Funky Fresh Old School Flyers.

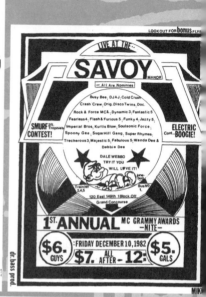

FOUNDATION.

28 ego trip's book of rap lists. ★ it's you they never hire, you're never on flyers...

(two sided)

DÉJÀ VU:
'90s Rap Hits That Lifted Their Hooks From '80s Classics.

1. **"Award Tour"—A Tribe Called Quest featuring Trugoy (De La Soul) (Jive, 1993)**
   ORIGIN: "Hobo (Scratch)"—Malcolm McLaren & The World Famous Supreme Team (Island, 1982)

2. **"4, 3, 2, 1"—LL Cool J featuring Method Man, Redman, Canibus & DMX (Def Jam, 1997)**
   ORIGIN: "We Rap More Mellow"—The Younger Generation (Brass, 1979)*

3. **"Hypnotize"—The Notorious B.I.G. (Bad Boy, 1997)**
   ORIGIN: "La Di Da Di"—Doug E. Fresh & MC Ricky D (b/k/a Slick Rick) (Reality, 1985)

4. **"If I Ruled The World"—Nas featuring Lauryn Hill (Columbia, 1996)**
   ORIGIN: "If I Ruled The World"—Kurtis Blow (Warner Bros., 1985)

5. **"Keep Their Heads Ringin'"—Dr. Dre (Priority, 1995)**
   ORIGIN: "Funk You Up"—Sequence (Sugar Hill, 1980)

6. **"Make 'Em Say Unngh!"—Master P featuring Fiend, Silkk The Shocker, Mia X & Mystikal (No Limit, 1998)**
   ORIGIN: "Funkbox Party"—Masterdon Committee (Enjoy, 1982)

7. **"New York, New York"—Tha Dogg Pound featuring Snoop Doggy Dogg (Death Row, 1995);**
   "L.A., L.A."—Capone-N-Noreaga featuring Mobb Deep & Tragedy (25 To Life, 1996)
   ORIGIN: "New York, New York"—Grandmaster Flash & The Furious Five (Sugar Hill, 1983)

8. **"Puerto Rico"—Frankie Cutlass (Hoody, 1994)**
   ORIGIN: *Live Convention '82* side 1—Grand Wizard Theodore & The Fantastic Five (Disco Wax, 1982)

9. **"Re-Definition"—Black Star (Rawkus, 1998)**
   ORIGIN: "Stop The Violence"—Boogie Down Productions (Jive, 1988)

10. **"This DJ"—Warren G (Def Jam, 1994)**
    ORIGIN: "Adventures Of Super Rhyme (Rap)"—Jimmy Spicer (Dazz, 1980)

11. **"Wooh Hah!! Got You All In Check"—Busta Rhymes (Elektra, 1996)**
    ORIGIN: "8th Wonder"—Sugarhill Gang (Sugar Hill, 1980)

12. **"Zoom"—Dr. Dre & LL Cool J (Interscope, 1998)**
    ORIGIN: "Get Retarded"—MC EZ & Troup (Fresh, 1988)

*Not from the '80s, but definitely a classic.

FOUNDATION.

RENEGADES OF FUNK:
Pioneering DJs Of Uncle Jam's Army.

1. Bleeps
2. Bobcat
3. Doctor Rock
4. Dr. Dre
5. Egyptian Lover
6. Iceberg
7. Mr. Prince
8. DJ Pooh
9. Unknown

Founded by Rodger Clayton (a/k/a Uncle Jam), Uncle Jam's Army was greater Los Angeles' most-fabled and longest-running throwdown of the early '80s.

Billy Jam Names The Essential West Coast Old School Rap Joints.

1. "Gigolo Rapp"—Disco Daddy & Captain Rapp (Rappers Rapp Disco, 1981)
2. "NBA Rap"—Hurt 'Em Bad (Groove Time, 1982)
3. "Rappin Partee Groove"—Rappers Rapp Group (Rappers Rapp Disco, 1982)
4. "Sexy Baby"—Darkstar (AVI, 1982)
5. "Tainted Love"—Excalibur (AVI, 1982)
6. "West Coast Poplock"—Ronnie Hudson (Magic Disc, 1982)
7. "Bad Times (I Can't Stand It)"—Captain Rapp (Magic Disc, 1983)
8. "The Coldest Rap"—Ice-T (Magic Disc, 1983)
9. "Dial-A-Freak" b/w "Yes, Yes, Yes"—Uncle Jam's Army (JDC, 1983)
10. "Egypt, Egypt"—Egyptian Lover (Egyptian Empire, 1983)
11. "Erotic City Rapp"—King MC & DJ Flash (DJ Flash, 1983)
12. "Radio Activity Rapp"—MC Fosty & Lovin' C. (Magic Disc, 1983)
13. "State Of Shock Rapp"—King MC & DJ Flash (DJ Flash, 1983)
14. "Body Rock"—Ice-T (Electrobeat, 1984)
15. "Rough Cut"—Kid Frost (Electrobeat, 1984)
16. "Techno Scratch"—Knights Of The Turntables (JDC, 1984)
17. "We Like Ugly Women"—Bobby Jimmy & The Critters (Rapsur, 1984)
18. "Batterram"—Toddy Tee (Evejim, 1985)
19. "Beverly Hills Cop"—The Future MC's (DJ Flash, 1985)
20. "Big Butt"—Bobby Jimmy & The Critters (Rapsur, 1985)
21. "Calling On The Dream Team"—The L.A. Dream Team (Dream Team, 1985)
22. "808 Beats"—The Unknown DJ (Techno Hop, 1985)
23. "Hittin' Hard"—DJ Flash (Flash, 1985)
24. "In The House"—The L.A. Dream Team (Dream Team, 1985)
25. "Juice"—The World Class Wrekin' Cru (Kru'-Cut, 1985)
26. "M.P.G. Rap (A Tribute To Marvin Gaye)"—The Triple Threat Three (Saturn, 1985)
27. "Revelation"—2 Live Crew (Macola, 1985)
28. "Rockberry Jam"—The L.A. Dream Team (Dream Team, 1985)
29. "Slice"—The World Class Wrekin' Cru (Kru'-Cut, 1985)
30. "Terminator"—Kid Frost (Electrobeat, 1985)
31. "2 Live"—2 Live Crew (Macola, 1985)
32. "The Alezby Inn"—Egyptian Lover (Egyptian Empire, 1986)
33. "Everlasting Bass"—Rodney O & Joe Cooley (Egyptian Empire, 1986)
34. "Freak-A-Holic"—Egyptian Lover (Egyptian Empire, 1986)
35. "Roaches"—Bobby Jimmy & The Critters (Macola, 1986)
36. "Rumors"—Timex Social Club (Macola, 1986)
37. "6 'N The Mornin'"—Ice-T (Techno Hop, 1986)
38. "Give Me The Mic"—Rodney O & Joe Cooley (Egyptian Empire, 1987)
39. "Supersonic"—J.J. Fad (Dream Team, 1987)
40. "Feel My Bass"—DJ Matrix (Bad Boy, 1988)

Outspoken rap renegade Billy Jam is an accomplished hip hop journalist and radio DJ who resides in the Bay Area. For further enlightenment on the West Coast heritage, contact the muthafuckin' man at billyjam@aol.com.

FOUNDATION.

Too $hort's 10 Secrets To Longevity.

Stay True To The Streets.
Just to break a rap or R&B act in the market now you gotta spend millions of dollars before the shit even drops. I never spent that much makin' a Too $hort album—on marketing, videos, everything combined. I still feel the same way. Fuck the commercial world. Fuck radio. Fuck video. You never seen me sittin' on a couch wit' Donnie Simpson and Rachel. They never invited me like, "Say, come here and be on BET." You never got up in the mornin' watchin' MTV and seen Bill Bellamy sittin' there talkin' to me. I don't do that shit.

Stay On Top Of Your Business.
You won't last in this business if you don't keep your money in your own bank account. I don't care who you get to run your finances. I don't care if it's your wife. If you don't take care of your personal finances, sooner or later, your money will be theirs.

Remain Down-To-Earth.
Just deal wit' people in a cool lil' manner. Cuz there's a lot of different people you have to deal with, sometimes all in the same day—like one minute, it's a reporter, next thing you know here's a magazine photographer, next thing you know here's a CEO at Time Warner or some shit. You gotta watch how you burn your bridges, too. Cuz I seen so many people in 10 years go from receptionist to executive.

Don't Dis Your Fans.
That's a big no-no. Don't ever be like, "Get the fuck out my face!" Or, "Hell no, you can't have an autograph!" If you come up to me and say, "$hort, man, I got all your shit. Can I take a picture wit' you?" I'll take a picture wit' you. I'll have a short lil' conversation wit' you just because you came at me properly wit' no static.

Don't Stop Rappin' Or Workin'.
Every year throughout this whole career, I've set aside two or three months when I'm in the studio makin' records. Even those times where I'm not makin' an album, I still make songs. The rule is, "Don't let the fans have too much time in between albums." Because when you think you're on some new-and-improved shit, something new-and-improved really is comin'. Fans will forget about your ass.

Choose The Right Music.
When I picked the tracks that I would rap to, I would always think, "Is this the kind of beat that a Too $hort fan wants to hear?" Not, "Do I like it?"

7. Keep A Sense Of Humor.
Instead of just throwin' sex and "I'm a pimp" down everybody's throat, you gotta always put some humor in it. If you're a real Too $hort fan, you know that.

8. Tour Extensively.
Arenas are very rare for rap and there's people out there who'll never pay $35 to see you at Madison Square Garden. But they will go to the night club that's not too far from where they live and pay $20 to see you. Get in these clubs, man, I'm tellin' you. You make a livin' off that shit. And go everywhere. Stay in lil' theaters and shit where the promoter can make some money and the fans can see a good show. No, it's not all the explosions and props and lights, but it's rap.

For rappers to not tour is a rip-off. If you can't rock the crowd, go practice doin' some high school lunchtime shows or somethin'. You gotta have stage skills.

9. Have Fun.
Instead of bein' mad at the label, mad at the road manager, mad at your girlfriend, mad at fuckin' everything all the time, you gotta have fun wit' it—even when you're stressin' about just hangin' in there. I got that from one of the original members of The Dramatics. He told me, "Don't look back when it's over and say, 'Damn, I forgot to have fun.'"

10. Do What You Do Best.
You'll never read me in an interview bein' quoted as sayin', "Oh, this album is on some new shit." Basically, it's always the same shit. If you say I did nuthin' else, you can say, "Too $hort was the one that got everybody sayin', 'Beeyotch!'" So when I'm gone, there's still dozens of records out there with different people sayin' it in different ways. That's my contribution. I gave that word to hip hop.

Sir Too $hort is a one-man hip hop institution. For 16 years, this fanatic of the B-word has become world famous for freaky tales like "Blow Job Betty," "Invasion Of The Flat Booty Bitches" and "I'm A Player." He will be here forever.

LYR

Greatest Emcees Of All-Time.

1. KRS-One
2. Rakim
3. LL Cool J
4. Chuck D
5. Slick Rick
6. Ice Cube
7. The Notorious B.I.G.
8. Kool G Rap
9. Big Daddy Kane
10. Grandmaster Caz
11. Kool Moe Dee
12. Grandmaster Melle Mel
13. Jay-Z
14. Redman
15. Lauryn Hill
16. Nas
17. Snoop Doggy Dogg
18. Scarface
19. Kool Keith
20. 2Pac

GET YA RHYME RIGHT:
14 Lyrical *Faux Pas.*

1. **"Bad To The Bone"—Kool G Rap & DJ Polo (Cold Chillin', 1990)**
Blinded by the color green, a pimped-out G Rap kicked this ethnically confused lyric: "Sleeping in sheets that's made of satin with one of my money-makin' honeys/ She's mixed, Spanish and Latin." Hmmm . . . a good combination.

2. **"Blackman In Effect"—Boogie Down Productions (Jive, 1990)**
The Teacher sets off his fourth LP with the 18-wheeler-D.W.I.-grammatical pile-up, "Wake up! Take the pillow from your head and put a book in it!" See how he sounds? A little unrational . . . oops!

3. **"Full Cooperation"—Def Squad (Def Jam, 1998)**
All brothas do look alike. So when Keith Murray warned, "I'm gonna get you sucker like Damon Wayans," we know he really meant D's older sibling, fallen late-night chat host, Keenan Ivory. Or was it Shawn, Marlon or Tito? Who cares.

4. **"Funky For You"—Nice & Smooth (Fresh, 1989)**
The honor for most infamous rap *faux pas* of all time goes to Boogie Down revisionist jazz historian Greg Nice for his opening line—"Ay yo, Dizzy Gillespie plays the sax"—on Nice & Smooth's party starter. Although the late, great trumpet-playing bebop pioneer John Birks Gillespie (a/k/a "Da Original Mr. Cheeks") was, in fact, capable of playing the saxophone in his spare time, Greg didn't find out until later when he was twisting L's with New Kids On The Block.

5. **"Just Rhymin' With Biz"—Big Daddy Kane featuring Biz Markie (Prism', 1987)**
If Biz "watched *Star Wars* just to see Yoda," he must have sat in the theater for three years. It wasn't until the film's sequel, *The Empire Strikes Back*, that the old sage alien fuck, Yoda, finally made his celluloid debut. Peace, Frank Oz.

6. **"King Of Rock"—Run-D.M.C. (Profile, 1985)**
The Kings from Queens may have bridged rap and rock but they unintentionally brought a morbid angle to pop music mathematics when they rhymed, "There's three of us, but we're not the Beatles," in 1985—a little more than four years after John Lennon's death. Later, Run confessed that he believed the Fab Four were a trio all along.

7. **"Knick Knack Patty Wack"—EPMD featuring K-Solo (Fresh, 1989)**
Central Islip, Long Island spelling bee champ, K-Solo, stumbled in his first opportunity to shine on the mic by bungling the line, "F-L-Y like a B-R-I-D in the S-K-Y." But he's still B-A-D in our book—the one in your H-A-N-D-S.

LYRICS.

8. **"Live!!!"—Onyx (Def Jam, 1995)**
Notable for Sticky's redundant observation, "We shoot niggas every day daily." We heard you the first time, when you said it first.

9. **"Make 'Em Pay"—Gang Starr featuring Krumb Snatcha (Noo Trybe, 1998)**
Boston's rhyme slasher, Krumb Snatcha, had his corporate pizza chains confused with the lyric, "Like Pizza Hut I gotta stay Noided." As pie-lovers worldwide already know, The Noid represents Domino's, rap dude.

10. **"Makin' A Name For Ourselves"—Common featuring Canibus (Relativity, 1997)**
This C&C music factory couldn't keep its books straight when delivering the hook, "I'm your worst nightmare squared/ That's times two for those who aren't mathematically aware." Count them out.

11. **"1, 2 Pass It"—D&D All-Stars (Arista, 1995)**
KRS-One comes with another messy reference sure to be banned from TV: "The aroma reaches up to my nostril, I get hostile/ Your lyrics are stiff like David Koppel." Maybe he meant Ted Letterman.

12. **"Punks Jump Up To Get Beat Down"—Brand Nubian (Elektra, 1992)**
"Black prodigy since the age of 20," boasts Sadat X, evidently unaware that at the double decade mark, he was a little old for the gifted child title.

13. **"The Set Up"—Nas featuring Havoc (Mobb Deep) (Columbia, 1996)**
"QB since 1933," Nas Escobar announces at the outset of this song in dedication to his beloved home, the Queensbridge Housing Projects. Not only did Nas drop science, he also dropped History (class). Queensbridge was, in fact, opened to the public in 1939.

14. **"What's Next"—Warren G featuring Mr. Malik (Def Jam, 1994)**
The G-Child not only rhymes like one—frequently sprinkling his songs with nursery limericks—but he also apparently spells like one. On his first LP, Warren uttered the lyric, "What's next?/ What's N-X-E-T?" Warren, geez!

12 Songs Slick Rick Wishes He Had Written.

1. "Do You Want To Know A Secret?" —The Beatles (Capitol, 1964)
2. "Hey Mr. D.J."—Zhané (Motown, 1993)
3. "J.Beez Comin' Through"—Jungle Brothers (Warner Bros., 1989)
4. "Hello Stranger"—Barbara Lewis (Atlantic, 1963)
5. "He's So Fine"—The Chiffons (Laurie, 1963)
6. "My Way"—Frank Sinatra (Reprise, 1969)
7. "Shook Ones Pt. II"—Mobb Deep (Loud, 1995)
8. "Take Five"—The Dave Brubeck Quartet (Columbia, 1960)
9. "Theme From *Mahogany* (Do You Know Where You're Going To)"—Diana Ross (Motown, 1975)
10. "Venus"—Frankie Avalon (Chancellor, 1959)*
11. "Walk On By"—Dionne Warwick (Scepter, 1964)
12. "When A Man Loves A Woman"—Percy Sledge (Atlantic, 1966)

*Though Frankie's rendition is the first and best known, Rick prefers the version performed by Johnny Mathis (Columbia, 1968).

When it comes to creating some of hip hop's greatest lyrical compositions (i.e., "La Di Da Di," "Children's Story" and "Mona Lisa"), Slick Rick The Ruler has no equal. Bow down, crumbsnatchers. The stories he's written, you wish you could.

13 Tongue-Twisting Talents.

1. Bone Thugs-N-Harmony
2. Common
3. Das EFX
4. Do Or Die
5. Fu-Schnickens
6. Jay-Z
7. The Jaz
8. Freestyle Fellowship
9. Three 6 Mafia
10. Treach (Naughty By Natutre)
11. Treacherous Three
12. Twista
13. Wise Intelligent

Rappers Who Use The Same Lyrics On Two Different Songs.

1. **Chill Rob G**
   "Let The Words Flow"—Chill Rob G (Wild Pitch, 1989) & "The Power"—Chill Rob G (Wild Pitch, 1989)

2. **Diamond D**
   "I Got Planz"—Scientifik featuring Diamond D (Definite, 1994) & "5 Fingas Of Death"—Diamond D featuring Big L, Lord Finesse, AG & Fat Joe (Mercury, 1997)

3. **The Genius & RZA**
   "Words From A Genius"—The Genius (Cold Chillin', 1991) & "Severe Punishment"—Wu-Tang Clan (Loud, 1997)

4. **Ghostface Killah**
   "This Is For The Lover In You (Puffy's Extended Face To Face Remix)"—Babyface featuring Ghostface Killah (Epic promo, 1996) & "Visionz"—Wu-Tang Clan (Loud, 1997)

5. **Grandmaster Melle Mel**
   "Superappin'"—Grandmaster Flash & The Furious Five (Enjoy, 1979) & "The Message"—Grandmaster Flash & The Furious Five (Sugar Hill, 1982)

6. **Guru**
   "Fed Up (Remix)"—House Of Pain featuring Guru (Tommy Boy, 1996) & "You Know My Steez"—Gang Starr (Noo Trybe, 1998)

7. **Havoc**
   "Set It"—PHD featuring Hostyle, Solo, Havoc, Slinger, KL & Reecey (Tuff City, 1994) & "Right Back At You"—Mobb Deep featuring Ghostface Killah & Raekwon (Loud, 1995)

8. **Ice Cube**
   "Get The Fist"—Get The Fist Movement featuring King Tee, Yo Yo, MC Eiht, B-Real, J-Dee (Da Lench Mob), Kam, Threat & Ice Cube (Mercury, 1992) & "We Had To Tear This Mutha Up"—Ice Cube (Priority, 1992)

9. **KRS-One**
   "Bronx Tale"—Fat Joe featuring KRS-One (Relativity, 1995) & "No Gimmicks"—Lord Finesse featuring KRS-One (Penalty, 1995)

10. **Lord Finesse**
    "Da Graveyard"—Big L featuring Lord Finesse, Microphone Nut, Jay-Z, Party Arty & Grand Daddy I.U. (Columbia, 1995) & "Check The Method"—Lord Finesse (Funky Man, 1996)

11. **Ol' Dirty Bastard**
    "Brooklyn Zoo II (Tiger Crane)"—Ol' Dirty Bastard featuring Ghostface Killah (Elektra, 1995) & "Damage"—Ol' Dirty Bastard featuring The Genius (Elektra, 1995)

12. **Tomahawk Funk**
    "Hypest From Cypress"—Mellow Man Ace featuring Krazy D, Chief T (b/k/a Tomahawk Funk) & Sen Dog (Capitol, 1992) & "Here I Am"—Funkdoobiest (Immortal, 1993)

SO WAT CHA SAYIN'?
8 Songs With Notoriously Unintelligible Lyrics.

1. **"Electric Relaxation"—A Tribe Called Quest (Jive, 1993)**
The drowned-out hook was hotly contested even years after the song's release. The actual line—"Relax yourself girl/ Please settle down"—is a lot simpler than what most people thought.

2. **"It's My Thing"—EPMD (Fresh, 1988)**
When mush-mouthed Erick Sermon lets loose, "The mind is weary floatin' like a dove/ Sweatin' a thing like if *you* was makin' love," it sounds like he's saying, "*Jews* makin' love."

3. **"It Takes Two"—Rob Base & DJ E-Z Rock (Profile, 1988)**
The line, "Don't smoke buddha/ Can't stand *cess*, yes" was mistakenly interpreted by happy, dancing white people as, "Can't stand sex."

4. **"Knowledge Me"—Original Concept (Def Jam, 1986)**
The intro and hook are actually, "Knowledge me—aw, man." Not, "Knowledge me—amen," as commonly thought.

5. **"My Philosophy"—Boogie Down Productions (Jive, 1988)**
KRS-One finishes the first verse with the line, "I'll be back, but for now just *seckle*!" His use of the Jamaican slang is commonly mistaken for "settle."

6. **"So What'cha Want"—Beastie Boys (Grand Royal, 1992)**
Go back and check out Adrock's line, " . . . You're eating crazy cheese like you would think I'm from Paris," and see if it doesn't sound like, "You're eatin' crazy chicken like a nigga from Paris."

7. **"Sucker MC's"—Run-D.M.C. (Profile, 1983)**
The famous conclusion—"When the beats commence"—is erroneously repeated as "When the beats come in" by many rap fans.

8. **"Zulu War Chant"—Afrika Bambaataa Presents Time Zone (Planet Rock, 1992)**
This club classic's murky main call-and-response refrain—"Zulu! *Gestapo*!"—is frequently mistaken as any number of different chants—among them, "Zulu! Can't stop our flow!" The curious routine (sampled from the live version of Grandmaster Flash & The Furious Five's "Flash To The Beat") is a call for Zulu Nation allegiance inspired by the literal definition of the German word—"a secret police organization employing underhanded and terrorist methods against persons suspected of disloyalty."

25 Intriguing (Parenthetical) Hip Hop Thoughts.

1. "Dedication (Bitch Or A Hoe)"—RBL Posse (In-A-Minute, 1994)
2. "The Enema (Live At The White House)" —Paris (Scarface, 1992)
3. "Gangsta (Put Me Down)"—Geto Boys (Rap-A-Lot, 1998)
4. "Get At Me (Call Me)"—The Comrads (Street Life, 1997)
5. "Gimme, Dat (Woy)"—Boogie Down Productions (Jive, 1989)
6. "Go Down (But Don't Bite It)"—The Real Roxanne (Select, 1992)
7. "A Groove (This Is What U Rap 2)"—The Jaz (EMI, 1990)
8. "If I Ruled The World (Imagine That)" —Nas featuring Lauryn Hill (Columbia, 1996)
9. "If It Ain't One Thing It's Annuddah (Bruddah)" —Fat Boys (Tin Pan Apple, 1989)
10. "I'm A Ugly Nigga (So What)"—Biz Markie (Cold Chillin', 1993)
11. "Last Night (I Had A Long Talk With Myself)" —Whodini (Jive, 1986)
12. "Let The Good Times Roll (Nickel Bag)" —Arabian Prince (Orpheus, 1989)
13. "Mathematics (Esta Loca)"—Noreaga (Penalty, 1998)
14. "Medley For A 'V' (The Pussy Medley)" —DJ Quik (Profile, 1998)
15. "Music Appreciation (Sweet Music)" —Boogiemonsters (Pendulum, 1994)
16. "Out On Parole (Time To Flip)" —Almighty RSO (RCA, 1994)
17. "Pieces Of A (Black) Man"—AZ (Noo Trybe, 1998)
18. "Rhythm (Devoted To The Art Of Moving Butts)" —A Tribe Called Quest (Jive, 1990)
19. "Rock The Girl, Gee (Every Inch)" —Too Nice (Arista, 1989)
20. "Same Ol' Thang (Everyday)"—Yo Yo (EastWest, 1996)
21. "Same White Bitch (Got You Strung Out On Cane)"—Schoolly D (Jive, 1988)
22. "(So Far) The Ghetto's Been Good To Me" —YZ (Livin' Large, 1993)
23. "Story (Pinky In The Twat)" —The Beatnuts (Relativity, 1993)
24. "Twinkle Twinkle (I'm Not A Star)" —DJ Jazzy Jeff & The Fresh Prince (Jive, 1993)
25. "(You Ain't Just A Fool) You's An Old Fool" —Spoonie Gee (Tuff City, 1988)

Hard-Hitting Homophobic Lyrics.

1. "I Got Cha Opin"—Black Moon (Nervous, 1993)
   Buckshot: "Straight from the floors of Hell feel the flame/ You faggot-ass, I heard your nickname's Blaine."

2. "Meet The G That Killed Me" —Public Enemy (Def Jam, 1990)
   Chuck D: "Man to man, I don't know if they can/ From what I know the parts don't fit—ahh shit!"

3. "Pass The Gat"—Brand Nubian (Elektra, 1992)
   Sadat X: "Shoot a faggot in the back for acting like that."

4. "Pimpin' Ain't Easy"—Big Daddy Kane featuring Nice & Smooth (Cold Chillin', 1989)
   Kane: "The Big Daddy law is anti-faggot— that means no homosexuality/What's in my pants will make you see reality."

5. "Ten Crack Commandments" —The Notorious B.I.G. (Bad Boy, 1997)
   "Money and blood don't mix/ Like two dicks and no bitch."

6. "Truly Yours"—Kool G Rap & DJ Polo (Cold Chillin', 1988)
   "A sex disease was as common as TB, but gays today get VD in 3-D/ And that is called AIDS in case you didn't know."

7. "Watch The Sound"—Fat Joe featuring Grand Puba & Diamond D (Relativity, 1993)
   Grand Puba: "It's the God and I still bag chicks/ Make the girls feel happy like a faggot with a bag of dicks."

8. "Whatchu Lookin' At"—Audio Two (First Priority, 1990)
   Milk: "Word to Giz, I hate faggots/ They living in the Village like meat on some maggots."

9. "Ya Bad Chubbs"—Chubb Rock featuring Hitman Howie Tee (Select, 1989)
   "A homo is a no-no, but you know I'll smack a faggot/ Boy, you gotta see me, I'm rich like Jimmy Swaggart."

HEY LADIES:
16 Memorable Misogynistic Rap Music Moments.

1. **"Ain't No Fun (If The Homies Can't Have None)"—Snoop Doggy Dogg featuring Nate Dogg, Kurupt & Warren G (Death Row, 1993)**
   A true lyrical gang bang.

2. **"Bitches Ain't Shit"—Dr. Dre featuring Tha Dogg Pound, Snoop Doggy Dogg & Jewell (Death Row, 1992)**
   They don't love dem hoes. Really doe.

3. **"The Bitch Sucks Dick"—Too $hort (75 Girls, 1985)**
   She swallowed it.

4. **"Blac Vagina Finda"—Onyx (Def Jam, 1993)**
   There's obviously no shame in these horny baldheads' game when they spit, "Praise the Lord cuz even nuns get stuck."

5. **"Boo Boo Heads"—Del The Funkeé Homosapien (Elektra, 1993)**
   Dumb girl blues.

6. **"Domestic Violence"—RZA As Bobby Digital featuring Jamie Sommers (Gee Street, 1998)**
   "Girl, I'll slave trade your ass like Kizzy Kinte," is just one of the insults hurled in this tense discourse between a man and his wife.

7. **"If We All Fuck"—Tha Dogg Pound featuring Snoop Doggy Dogg (Death Row, 1995)**
   Gang bangin' on wax, Pt. II.

8. **"One Less Bitch"—N.W.A (Ruthless, 1991)**
   Pimpin' *really* ain't easy.

9. **"Problemz"—Street Smartz (Tru Criminal, 1996)**
   How do you mend a broken heart? "Deal with it, be real with it/ And if your ex give the ass, you should still hit it."

10. **"Pussy Ain't Shit"—Funkdoobiest (Immortal, 1995)**
    The "P" is free . . . to be criticized.

11. **"Talk Like Sex"—Kool G Rap & DJ Polo (Cold Chillin', 1990)**
    Hip hop misogyny's *pièce de résistance*.

12. **"We Want Some Pussy!!"—2 Live Crew (Luke Skyywalker, 1986)**
    Hello, kitty.

13. **"Wildflower"—Ghostface Killah (Razor Sharp, 1996)**
    Love don't live here anymore.

14. **"Wonders In Da Bed"—YG'z (Reprise, 1993)**
    Key lyric: "I wanna fuck, I wanna fuck, I wanna fuck/ Bitch, drop your drawers, let this nigga bust a nut." Never no time for foreplay.

15. **"You Can't Fade Me"—Ice Cube (Priority, 1990)**
    Accused of knocking up the "neighborhood hussy," Cube learns a valuable lesson: protect yourself before you wreck yourself.

16. **"You Wanna Fuck Her"—MC Ren (Ruthless, 1993)**
    Ain't nothin' goin' on but the Ren's misogyny.

Lyrics That Hurt People's Feelings.

1. "Ah Yeah"—KRS-One (Avatar, 1996)
   "Every President we ever had lied/ You know, I'm kinda glad Nixon died."

2. "Clan In Da Front"—Wu-Tang Clan (Loud, 1993)
   The Genius: "The bitch caught a fitz like Geraldine Ferraro, who's full of sorrow/ Cuz the ho didn't win, but the sun will still come out tomorrow."

3. "Epilogue"—Diamond D (Mercury, 1997)
   "All you fake emcees you know the deal/ I carve up your face and now you look like Seal, a-ight."

4. "Fight The Power"—Public Enemy (Motown, 1989)
   Chuck D: "Elvis was a hero to most but he never meant shit to me/ You see, straight out racist the sucker was simple and plain—motherfuck him and John Wayne."

5. "Freestyle Rhymes"—Chino XL (American, 1996)
   "Your career is like George Burns/ I can't believe you ain't dead yet."

6. "The Funkiest"—Funkdoobiest (Immortal, 1993)
   Son Doobie: "The crazy ill Hitler who performs like a fiddler/ I'm ill like The Riddler—fuck a Bette Midler."

7. "How Do U Want It"—2Pac featuring K-Ci & Jojo (Death Row, 1996)
   "C. DeLores Tucker, you's a muthafucka/ Instead of tryin' to help a nigga, you destroy a brother."

8. "I'll Wax Anybody"—Tim Dog (Ruffhouse, 1991)
   "I'm def, don't take me lightly/ Fuck Eddie Murphy, I'm rollin' with Spike Lee."

9. "I Need Some Pussy"—Willie D (Rap-A-Lot, 1989)
   "I'm so damn horny tonight for snatch/ That I'd fuck Whoopi Goldberg's ugly ass."

10. "It's All About The Benjamins (Remix)"—Puff Daddy featuring The Lox, Lil' Kim & The Notorious B.I.G. (Bad Boy, 1997)
    Sheek: "Player, you mad false/ Acting hard when you as pussy as RuPaul."

11. "Let Me Ride"—Dr. Dre (Death Row, 1992)
    "So won't you just walk on by cuz I'm too hard to lift/ And no, this ain't Aerosmith."

12. "Represent"—Show & AG (Payday, 1992)
    AG: "Styles will vary, they won't carry over/ Don't fuck wit' no devil, I'd rather marry Oprah—yeah, you got it, I'm pro-Black."

13. "Return Of The Crooklyn Dodgers"—Crooklyn Dodgers '95 (MCA, 1995)
    Chubb Rock: "You watch Channel Zero with that bitch Barbara Walters/ She'll have you believe Blacks invented crack."

14. "Rollin'"—Redman (Def Jam, 1996)
    "Pick me as your senator/ Take the love from your battlefield, son, fuck Pat Benatar!"

15. "Soul Food"—Goodie Mob (LaFace, 1995)
    T-Mo: "They know they making it hard on the yard/ Fuck Chris Darden, fuck Marcia Clark."

16. "Steppin' It Up"—A Tribe Called Quest featuring Busta Rhymes & Redman (Jive, 1998)
    Redman: "Funk Doc gets the money/ And best believe I went through more trees than Sonny [Bono]."

17. "3 Card Molly"—Xzibit featuring Ras Kass & Saafir (Loud, 1998)
    Xzibit: "Picture yourself crushing Xzibit with your tough talk/ That's like Christopher Reeves doing the Crip walk."

18. "Unrational"—Art Of Origin (American, 1993)
    Chino XL (once again): "In the bottomless pit, I spit hate from my tongue/ I'm throwin' that ass out the window like Eric Clapton's son."

Some Hot-Ass Song Title Acronyms.

1. "A.F.D." (ASS FOR DAYS)—DOMINO (OUTBURST, 1993)
2. "B.I.B.L.E." (BASIC INSTRUCTIONS BEFORE LEAVING EARTH)—THE GENIUS FEATURING KILLAH PRIEST (GEFFEN, 1995) 3. "BORN 2 B.R.E.E.D." (BUILD RELATIONSHIPS WHERE EDUCATION AND ENLIGHTENMENT DOMINATE)—MONIE LOVE (WARNER BROS., 1993) 4. "C.I.A." (CRACK IN AMERICA)—DONALD D (SIRE, 1991) 5. "D.I.Y.M." (DICK IN YOUR MOUTH)—RED HOT LOVER TONE (SELECT, 1992) 6. "F.A.G." (FAKE ASS GANGSTA)—M.O.P. (SELECT, 1994) 7. "F.A.L.A." (FUCK AROUND LAY AROUND)—GANG STARR FEATURING BIG SHUG (CHRYSALIS, 1994) 8. "F.F.F.F." (FIND 'EM, FEEL 'EM, FUCK 'EM & FORGET 'EM)—DOUBLE XX POSSE (BIG BEAT, 1995) 9. "GIRLS L.G.B.N.A.F." (LET'S GET BUTT NAKED AND FUCK)—ICE-T (SIRE, 1988) 10. "H.A.A." (HERE'S ANOTHER ASSHOLE)—BLACK SHEEP (MERCURY, 1995) 11. "I USED TO LOVE H.E.R." (HIP HOP IN ITS ESSENCE FOR REAL)—COMMON (RELATIVITY, 1994) 12. "LIVE AT THE O.M.N.I." (ONE MILLION NIGGAS INSIDE)—GOODIE MOB (LAFACE, 1995) 13. "L.L.O.L.M." (LIP LOCK ON LOVE MACHINE)—LUKE (LUKE, 1993) 14. "A MESSAGE TO THE B.A.N." (BITCH

LYRICS.

ASS NIGGA)—CHUBB ROCK (SELECT, 1992) 15. "M.N.O.H.P." (MORTUARY NOTE ON HIS PAGER)—RBL POSSE (IN-A-MINUTE, 1994) 16. "N.O.R.E." (NIGGAS ON THE RUN EATING)—NOREAGA (PENALTY, 1998) 17. "O.P.P." (OTHER PEOPLE'S PROPERTY)—NAUGHTY BY NATURE (TOMMY BOY, 1991) 18. "P.B.E." (POWERFUL, BEAUTIFUL, EXCELLENT)—JOHN FORTÉ (RUFFHOUSE, 1998) 19. "P.S.K. WHAT DOES IT MEAN?" (PARK SIDE KILLERS)—SCHOOLLY D (SCHOOLLY D, 1985) 20. "P.W.A." (PUSSY WEED ALCOHOL)—5TH WARD BOYZ FEATURING DEVIN & WILLIE D (RAP-A-LOT, 1997) 21. "R.E.A.L.I.T.Y." (RHYMES EQUAL ACTUAL LIFE IN THE YOUTH)—KRS-ONE (JIVE, 1995) 22. "SFNU" (STILL FUCKING NIGGAS UP)—MC BREED (ICHIBAN, 1995) 23. "S.K.I.T.S." (SHORTIES KAUGHT IN THE SYSTEM)—LORD FINESSE (MAD SOUNDS, 1994) 24. "T.O.N.Y." (TOP OF NEW YORK)—CAPONE-N-NOREAGA FEATUR-ING TRAGEDY (PENALTY, 1997) 25. "T.R.O.Y." (THEY REMINISCE OVER YOU)—PETE ROCK & CL SMOOTH (ELEKTRA, 1992) 26. "W.G.O.N.R.S." (WHAT'S GOING ON IN OUR SOCIETY)—BIG DADDY KANE (MCA, 1994)

THEY WRITE THE SONGS:
Certified Ghostwriters.

1. **Grandmaster Caz**
Cold Crush Brother and old school legend wrote Big Bank Hank's verse on "Rapper's Delight" and Biz's "A Thing Named Kim."

2. **Run-D.M.C.**
Composed "Slow And Low" and "Paul Revere" for the Beastie Boys.

3. **LL Cool J**
In addition to MC Lyte's verse on the Stop The Violence Movement's "Self-Destruction," Uncle L wrote "Can You Rock It Like This" for Run-D.M.C. when he was only 16-years-old.

4. **Hurby "Luv Bug" Azor**
Salt-N-Pepa's longtime mentor was the driving force behind most of the group's biggest early hits, writing "The Showstoppa (Is Stupid Fresh)," "Push It," "My Mic Sounds Nice" and "Tramp."

5. **Big Daddy Kane**
The Juice Crew's in-house songwriter penned the majority of rhymes for Biz Markie's classic *Goin' Off* LP, as well as Roxanne Shanté's "Have A Nice Day" and "Go On Girl."

6. **Ice Cube**
Eazy-E's "Boyz-N-The Hood" and the N.W.A classics "Dope Man," "8-Ball" and "Express Yourself" are amongst his best known lyrical creations.

7. **Young MC**
Wrote Tone-Lōc's frathouse hits "Wild Thing" and "Funky Cold Medina" while an undergrad at USC.

8. **The D.O.C.**
Though official writing credits don't always necessarily reflect the extent of his penmanship, the N.W.A-associate picked up much of the lyrical duties after Ice Cube's departure from the group on *Efil4zaggin*, and later, on Dr. Dre's *The Chronic* and MC Breed's *Funkafied*.

9. **Del The Funkeé Homosapien**
Co-wrote Ice Cube's "Jackin' For Beats" and Yo Yo's "Stompin' To Tha 90's" and "Ain't Nobody Better."

10. **Jermaine Dupri**
The Atlanta mega-producer not only produced and conceived kiddie-sensations Kris Kross, but he also wrote all of their lyrics. Unbelievable.

11. **Grand Puba**
Was responsible for virtually all of Pete Rock's lyrics on both Pete Rock & CL Smooth's *All Souled Out* EP and *Mecca And The Soul Brother* LP.

12. **Sauce Money**
Puff Daddy's Biggie homage, "I'll Be Missing You," was composed by Marcy Projects' own. The Brooklynite's also written rhymes for Shaquille O'Neal, but don't hold that against him.

13. **Jay-Z**
Authored Foxy Brown's "Get Me Home" and "I'll Be," Queen Pen's "All My Love" and Bugs Bunny's "Buggin'" from the *Space Jam* soundtrack. And for the right price, he'll even make your shit tighter.

LYRICS.

Kool Moe Dee's Rap Report Card.

On the inner sleeve of his second solo album, *How Ya Like Me Now* (Jive, 1987), old school legend Kool Moe Dee turned the tables on his rapping peers by delivering a critical breakdown of what it took to be a great emcee.

REPORT CARD	VOCABULARY	ARTICULATION	CREATIVITY	ORIGINALITY	VERSATILITY	VOICE	RECORDS	STAGE PRESENCE	STICKING TO THEMES	INNOVATING RHYTHMS		
Kool Moe Dee	10	10	10	10	9	10	8	8	10	10	95	A+
Melle Mel	10	9	10	10	9	10	8	10	10	9	95	A+
Grand Master Caz	9	10	10	10	10	9	7	10	10	9	94	A+
L.L. Cool J	10	10	9	6	10	9	9	10	9	8	90	A
T. La Rock	10	10	10	9	8	9	8	7	10	9	90	A
Rakim	8	10	10	9	8	10	10	7	9	10	91	A
KRS One	7	9	9	10	9	9	9	9	10	9	90	A
Spoonie G	7	8	9	9	8	9	9	7	9	7	82	B
M.C. Shan	7	9	9	9	9	7	9	8	9	7	83	B
Doug E. Fresh	7	9	10	10	9	8	9	10	9	9	86	B+
Bizmark	7	7	9	8	8	9	9	9	9	9	93	B
Kurtis Blow	7	7	7	8	9	9	9	9	9	7	81	B
Just Ice	9	8	8	9	8	8	8	7	8	9	82	B
Run DMC	6	9	8	8	7	8	10	10	9	7	82	B
Fat Boys	6	8	8	9	8	8	8	9	10	7	81	B
Whodini	7	8	9	9	9	8	9	9	10	8	86	B+
Beastie Boys	6	7	7	6	6	6	8	8	10	6	70	C
UTFO	7	9	9	9	9	9	8	10	9	10	89	B+
Heavy D & the Boyz	7	9	8	8	8	8	8	10	9	8	83	B
Boogie Boys	7	8	8	8	8	7	8	7	8	8	77	C+
Ultra Magnetic	10	7	8	8	8	7	8	7	8	9	80	B
Public Enemy	7	9	8	9	8	9	8	7	8	7	80	B
Stetsasonic	9	7	9	9	8	7	8	9	8	8	82	B
Grandmaster Flash and the Furious Five	9	8	7	10	7	8	7	9	9	7	81	B
Jazzy Jeff and the Fresh Prince	8	9	10	10	9	8	8	10	9	7	88	B+

Kool Moe Dee Rates The Rappers Of Today.

Now, 12 years later, history repeats itself as old school legend Kool Moe Dee delivers a critical breakdown of what it still takes to be a great emcee. You didn't think he could do it again—another evaluation! The joke's on you, Jack!

REPORT CARD

	VOCABULARY	ARTICULATION	CREATIVITY	ORIGINALITY	VERSATILITY	VOICE	RECORDS	STAGE PRESENCE	STICKING TO THEMES	INNOVATING RHYTHMS		
JAY Z	7	9	9	8	7	8	10	6	9	9	82	B
DMX	7	9	8	10	7	10	9	10	9	10	89	B+
MASTER P	6	7	7	10	7	8	7	7	9	8	76	C+
BIG PUN	8	7	8	8	8	8	9	8	9	9	82	B
SNOOP	7	8	9	10	9	9	9	8	9	9	87	B+
NAS	10	8	8	8	9	8	8	8	9	8	84	B
CORRUPT	10	9	8	8	9	8	7	9	9	9	86	B+
Lauryn Hill	10	10	10	10	10	10	9	9	9	10	97	A+
Redman	10	9	9	10	8	9	8	9	8	9	89	B+
Keith Murry	10	9	9	9	9	9	8	9	9	8	89	B+
Ice Cube	9	9	9	9	9	9	9	9	9	7	88	B+
Too Short	7	8	7	8	6	8	8	8	9	7	76	C+
Black Thought	10	9	9	9	8	8	8	8	9	9	87	B+
Most Def	10	9	9	8	8	8	8	8	9	8	85	B+
Buster	9	8	10	10	9	9	10	10	8	10	93	A
TREACH	9	9	9	10	9	8	9	9	9	10	90	A
Methon man	9	9	9	9	9	10	9	9	8	10	91	A
Raekwon	9	8	9	9	8	8	9	8	8	9	86	B+
Common	10	9	9	8	8	8	8	8	10	9	87	B+
Ras Kas	10	9	9	8	8	8	8	8	10	8	88	B+
Biggie	9	9	10	9	9	10	10	9	10	10	95	A+
2nd PAC	9	10	10	9	10	9	9	9	10	8	93	A
MASE	7	7	9	8	8	8	9	7	8	7	79	C+
PUFFY	7	8	8	7	8	8	10	9	8	7	80	B
CANIBUS	10	9	9	9	8	8	7	8	9	8	85	B+
Buck Shot	9	9	8	9	8	8	8	8	8	8	83	B
FOXY	8	9	8	8	8	8	9	9	8	7	82	B
Lil Kim	8	9	8	8	8	6	9	9	8	8	83	B
Mac 10	8	9	8	9	8	8	8	9	8	8	83	B
Sticky Fingas	9	8	9	10	9	9	8	9	8	9	88	B+
Mystical	9	9	10	10	8	9	8	9	8	10	90	A

LYRICS.

SAY WHAT?
Famous Last Words.

1. **"Express Yourself"—N.W.A (Ruthless, 1988)**
"Yo, I don't smoke weed or cess/ Cuz it's known to give a brother brain damage," the good Dr. Dre rhymed on Niggaz Wit' Attitude's most positive recording ever. After leaving Ruthless four years later, Dre apparently bumped his head and switched it on 'em. The new prescription: *The Chronic.*

2. **"Welcome To The Terrordome"—Public Enemy (Def Jam, 1989)**
"Never be a brother like me go solo," Chuck D stated on hip hop's last great single of the '80s. We still don't believe he went for delf. Check 1996's *Autobiography Of Mistachuck* for the noise brought *á la carte.*

3. **"Bonafied Funk"—Brand New Heavies featuring Main Source (Delicious Vinyl, 1992)**
"Main Source forever/ Crews gotta get more clever—whatever," Large Professor declared of he and his Canadian partners, Sir Scratch and K-Cut (a/k/a Los McKenzie Brothers—take off, eh!). Shortly after the song's release, the trio broke like atoms.

4. **"Deeez Nuuuts"—Dr. Dre (Death Row, 1992)**
"Peep out my manuscript/ You see that it's a must I drop gangsta shit," professed Dre. After leaving Death Row four years later, he apparently had a change of heart. The Aftermath: "Been There Done That."

5. **"Who Killed Jane"—EPMD (Def Jam, 1992)**
In part four of the "Jane" series, Parrish's murder suspect character shoots Erick's racist cop character at the song's conclusion. Might this have been the first sign that all was not well between Mic Doc and E Double? Ooooohhh . . .

6. **"Ain't No Stoppin' This"—LL Cool J (Def Jam, 1993)**
"I guess I need a TV show to get mine/ But I don't feel like kissin' no director's behind," vowed Uncle L. We don't know if LL smooched any butt, but he sure as hell picked up some dirty drawers playing the housekeeper on his sitcom, *In The House.* Ann B. Davis, hold your dome.

7. **"Runnin'"—2Pac featuring Thug Life & The Notorious B.I.G. (Mergela, 1995)**
"Don't say you never heard of me/ 'Til they murder me—I'm a legend," Tupac rhymed in '94 on this track originally intended for Thug Life's *Volume 1* LP. (It would later appear on the Million Man March compilation album, *One Million Strong.*) In death, this remains the truest shit he ever wrote.

8. **"Zealots"—Fugees (Ruffhouse, 1996)**
"Kill the notion of biting and recycling/ And calling it your own creation," bemoaned Wyclef Jean on this number from *The Score*—a multi-zillion selling album who's biggest hits were cover versions of songs by Roberta Flack and Bob Marley.

9. **"You're Nobody (Til Somebody Kills You)"—The Notorious B.I.G. (Bad Boy, 1997)**
"You could be the shit, flash the fattest 5, have the biggest dick/ But when your shell get hit, you ain't worth spit—just a memory," the pride of Bed-Stuy reflected. Sorry Biggie, but we disagree. We'll always love Big Poppa.

10. **"Children's Story"—Black Star (Rawkus, 1998)**
Mos Def and Talib Kweli's critique of beatjacking practices is itself an unabashed conceptual re-write of Slick Rick's classic of the same name. This from the same group who jacked the beat for BDP's "The 'P' Is Free" on its single, "Definition." Bite your native tongues.

HONORABLE MENTION: The skit preceeding "Lodi Dodi" on Snoop Doggy Dogg's *Doggystyle* is a houseparty scene in which Daz Dillinger makes disparaging and eerie reference to Eazy-E and his Ruthless cohorts as "Buster-ass HIV pussy-havin' muthafuckas." Answers Dre, "Eazy come, Eazy . . ." before a gunshot blast ends the conversation. Two years later Eazy would die after announcing his contraction of the AIDS virus.

DJs

5 Records That Changed Funkmaster Flex's Life.

1. **The first record I ever bought:**
   "One For The Treble (Fresh)"—Davy DMX (Tuff City, 1984)

2. **The first record I ever stole:**
   "Impeach The President"—The Honey Drippers (Alaga, 1973)

3. **The first record I ever scratched:**
   "Get Into The Mix"—DJ Divine (West End, 1983)

4. **The first record I ever got for free:**
   "Beat Box"—Art Of Noise (ZTT, 1983)

5. **The first song I ever spun at a club:**
   "Let The Music Play"—Shannon (Emergency, 1983)

The official Big Dog in the land of big dogs, DJ Funkmaster Flex is the reigning kingpin of New York rap radio. He currently holds it down on WQHT, 97.1 FM, six nights a week and has released three gold albums—Funkmaster Flex Presents The Mix Tape: 60 Minutes Of Funk Volumes 1, 2 & 3. (Insert explosion here.)

GIVE THE MAN BEHIND THE WHEELS SOME CREDIT: 25 Compelling Homages To The DJ.

1. "AJ Scratch"—Kurtis Blow (Mercury, 1984)
2. "Aladdin's On A Rampage"—Low Profile (Priority, 1989)
3. "All Night"—Tha Alkaholiks (Loud, 1997)
4. "Cooley High"—Rodney O & Joe Cooley (Egyptian Empire, 1988)
5. "Cool V's Tribute To Scratching"—Biz Markie (Cold Chillin', 1988)
6. "Daddy Rich In The Land Of 1210"—3rd Bass (Def Jam, 1991)
7. "Girls Love The Way He Spins"—Grandmaster Flash (Elektra, 1985)
8. "Go Cut Creator Go"—LL Cool J (Def Jam, 1987)
9. "He Cuts So Fresh"—Marley Marl featuring MC Shan (Uptown, 1987)
10. "He's My DJ (Red Alert)"—Sparky D (Nia, 1985)
11. "Hey DJ"—The World Famous Supreme Team (Island, 1984)
12. "Hot Day Is Burnin'"—Grandmaster Hot Day & The Imperial Wizard (Tuff City, 1988)
13. "Jam Master Jay"—Run-D.M.C. (Profile, 1983)
14. "King Kut"—Word Of Mouth featuring DJ Cheese (Beauty & The Beat, 1985)
15. "The Magnificent Jazzy Jeff"—DJ Jazzy Jeff & The Fresh Prince (Word Up, 1986)
16. "Marley Marl Scratch"—Marley Marl featuring MC Shan (Nia, 1985)
17. "Mister Cee's Master Plan"—Big Daddy Kane (Cold Chillin', 1988)
18. "Mr. Muhammad"—A Tribe Called Quest (Jive, 1990)
19. "Peter Piper"—Run-D.M.C. (Profile, 1986)
20. "Play That Beat Mr. DJ"—G.L.O.B.E. & Whiz Kid (Tommy Boy, 1983)
21. "Red Alert Is A Great Man"—MC Mitchski (Ski, 1987)
22. "Scratch Bring It Back (Part 2-Mic Doc)"—EPMD (Def Jam, 1992)
23. "Spinderella's Not A Fella (But A Girl DJ)"—Salt-N-Pepa (Next Plateau, 1988)
24. "Terminator X To The Edge of Panic"—Public Enemy (Def Jam, 1988)
25. "Three MC's And One DJ"—Beastie Boys (Grand Royal, 1998)

BACKSPINNERS TAKE NOTE: "Eric B. Is President"—Eric B. & Rakim (Zakia, 1986) was omitted because producer Marley Marl reputedly performed half of the cuts on the record.

DJs.

D'YA LIKE SCRATCHIN'?
25 Deadly DJ Cuts.

1. "The Adventures Of Grandmaster Flash On The Wheels Of Steel"—Grandmaster Flash (Sugar Hill, 1981)
2. "Behold The Detonator"—Tuff Crew (Warlock, 1989)
3. "Contract On A World Love Jam"—Public Enemy (Def Jam, 1990)
4. "Hip Hop Dancers' Theme"—DJ Jazzy Jeff & The Fresh Prince (Jive, 1988)
5. "Itz Krack"—Schoolly D (Schoolly D, 1987)
6. "Jazzy On The Mix"—Busy Bee (Strong City, 1988)
7. "Jazzy's In The House"—DJ Jazzy Jeff & The Fresh Prince (Jive, 1988)
8. "King Goes Solo"—Movement Ex (Columbia, 1990)
9. "King Of The Beats"—Mantronix (Capitol, 1988)
10. "DJ K La Boss"—EPMD (Fresh, 1988)
11. "Play That Beat Mr. DJ (Lesson 1: The Payoff Mix)" b/w "Lesson 2: The James Brown Mix" & "Lesson 3: The History Of Hip Hop"—Double Dee & Steinski (Tommy Boy promo, 1985)
12. "Lesson 4"—DJ Shadow (Hollywood BASIC promo, 1991)
13. "Mega Mix 2 (Why Is It Fresh?)"—Grandmixer D.ST (Celluloid, 1984)
14. "Mr. Mixx On The Mix!"—2 Live Crew (Luke Skyywalker, 1986)
15. "The Music Maker"—Cash Money & Marvelous (Sleeping Bag, 1988)
16. "One For The Treble (Fresh)"—Davy DMX (Tuff City, 1984)
17. "Pam's Song"—The Coup (Wild Pitch, 1993)
18. "DJ Premier In Deep Concentration"—Gang Starr (Wild Pitch, 1989)
19. "Pure Skill"—Alliance (First Priority, 1988)
20. "Rockin' Music"—Steady B (Jive, 1987)
21. "Scratchin' To The Funk"—Dr. Funkenstein (b/k/a DJ Cash Money) (Soundmaker, 1985)
22. "T.D.S. Scratch Reaction"—T.D.S. Mob (Race, 1989)
23. "What I Like (Scratch Version)"—2 Live Crew (Fresh Beat, 1985)
24. "Who Is This?"—Three Times Dope (Arista, 1988)
25. "You're Gonna Get Yours (Terminator X Getaway Version)"—Public Enemy (Def Jam, 1987)

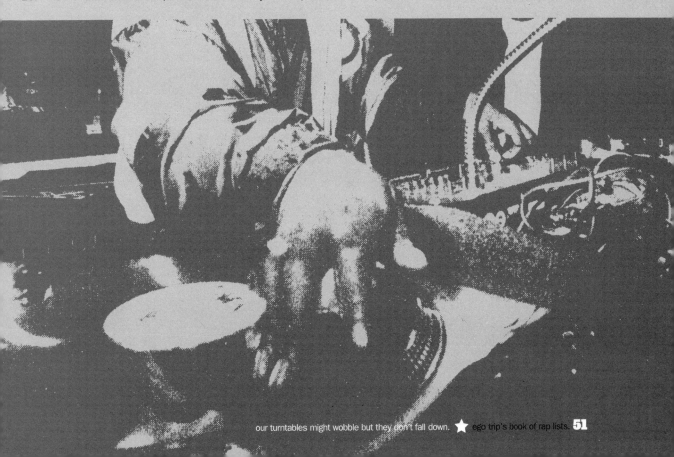

THE COOLEST CUT-UPS IN CAMP:
Dave Tompkins' Top 20 Modern DJ Tracks.

1. "Invasion Of The Octopus People"—Invisibl Skratch Piklz (Bomb, 1995)
2. "Captain Splatter Patty"—Mr. Dibbs (4 Ways To Rock, 1998)
3. "Tricks 'N Treats"—Kid Koala (Ninja Tune promo, 1996)
4. "Hardcore (Instrumental) Hip Hop"—DJ Shadow (SoleSides, 1996)
5. "Lesson 4: The Radio"—Cut Chemist (Bomb, 1995)
6. "Lesson 6: The Lecture"—Cut Chemist (Om, 1997)
7. "Shiggar Fraggar"—The Shiggar Fraggar Show Starring The Invisibl Skratch Piklz (Hip Hop Slam, 1998)
8. "Radar Frees Tibet"—Radar (Om, 1997)
9. "Entropy"—DJ Shadow (SoleSides, 1993)
10. "Number Song (Cut Chemist Party Mix)"—DJ Shadow (Mo' Wax, 1997)
11. "Unidentifried Decomposed Essential"—Mix Master Mike (Funk Octopus, 1996)
12. "Turntablism"—D Stiles, Babu & Melo-D (Comprehension, 1995)

DJ Cash Money's Favorite Scratch Inventions.

1. **The Babiggaba's**
   The name came because it would sound like "b-bigga-bigga-brrr, b-bigga-bigga-brrr." I seen D.ST do a similar scratch to this but what I did was try it without using the fader. Then I started using the fader and created a whole different sound. I could do more creative things with that type of scratch than with any other.

2. **The Transformer**
   There was a guy named DJ Spinbad from Philadelphia who would chop the sound of a record while bringing it back. What I did was make the sound much longer and rhythmic so it would sound like a *Transformer* cartoon. New York cats are claiming it and all this other stuff. They need to stop it because this originated from me.

3. **The Drag Scratch**
   Accidentally created when I turned the turntable off and made a dragging sound.

4. **Doubling And Tripling**
   Using the two turntables so that the record repeats the same words two and three times.

5. **The Shiver**
   If you were to look at my hand while I was doing this one, it would look like it was standing still. I put my finger on the record and just go, "Brrrrrrrrrr." It's all in the wrist.

6. **The Stutter Scratch**
   Makin' a record stutter so it sounds like a sampler being triggered.

13. "Ode To Sucker DJs"—Babu (Bomb, 1995)
14. "Rock Star"—Z-Trip (Bomb, 1997)
15. "Rob Swift vs. Rahzel"—Soulful Fruit (Stones Throw, 1997)
16. "Bear Witness"—Dr. Octagon featuring Q-Bert (Bulk, 1995)
17. "Course Of Action"—Scratch Perverts (Om, 1998)
18. "Raida's Theme"—X-ecutioners (Asphodel, 1997)
19. "Man Or Myth"—Faust (Bomb, 1998)
20. "Judeas Transmission"—Mr. Dibbs (Dog Day, 1998)

Respected journalist Dave Tompkins has written for Spin, Vibe *and* The Source *but still has nothing better to do than listen to these in sounds from way out. Nevertheless, he's our favorite know-it-all supercracker from North Kakalaka.*

7. **The Breakdown**
Breaking down the individual words of a record. I do this one on "Rock The Bells" all the time.

8. **Money In The Middle**
On this one, I put the fader in the middle and just go back and forth on the turntables at the same time like, "Cash-cash-cash-c-c-c-cash-cash-mo-mo-mo-m-m-m-money."

9. **The Up & Down I Get Around**
Using the cross fader and the ups and downs at the same time.

10. **The R2D2**
I do this one on Whistle's "(Nothing Serious) Just Buggin'." I turn the turntable off, push the record a little bit back and forth and use the fader to make the sound come in and out until it sounds just like R2D2.

11. **The Andy Griffith**
Also created by accident while I was transforming on Whistle. The theme from the *Andy Griffith Show* is classic.

12. **The Pee-Wee Herman Scratch**
Another one I perform on "Rock The Bells": "Hard as he-e-e-e-eh-eh-eh-ell" transformed to the Pee-Wee Herman (b/k/a "Tequila") melody. Pee-Wee was the man at that time, you know.

There are two kinds of DJs in the world—turntablists and those that rock parties. The legendary Cash Money is that unique combination of both. When not touring the world displaying his talents, the green-eyed brother may be found in his hometown of Philadelphia, PA.

13 Rappers Recognized For Their DJ Skills.

1. Bahamadia (p/k/a "DJ Toni Tee")
2. Big Daddy Kane (began as Roxanne Shanté's DJ)
3. Biz Markie
4. Grandmaster Caz
5. King Tee
6. Kurtis Blow
7. Lord Finesse
8. Mixmaster Spade
9. Q-Tip
10. DJ Quik
11. Redman
12. Run (a/k/a DJ Run, p/k/a "Son Of Kurtis Blow")
13. Schoolly D

14 Historical DJ-On-The-Mic Milestones.

1. **"That's The Joint"—AJ Scratch (Diamond, 1980)**
Old school pioneer AJ's disco fluid solo single owes an obvious stylistic debt to his future partner Kurtis Blow's "The Breaks." It featured such archaic couplets as, "I'm the flyest, dopest DJ you're ever gonna see/ Just look up here on the stage, baby doll, I'm talkin' about little ol' me!" Thankfully, cutmaster Kurt didn't hold this performance against Kool AJ, who became the subject of a loving homage on Blow's 1984 banger, "AJ Scratch."

2. **"That's Life"—Cutmaster D.C. (Airport, 1984)**
A surprisingly decent piece of post-"The Message" social commentary that commenced the BK spinner's career. A haunting synth melody adds potency to hard knock life details like, "Riding on the subway, yo, something's wrong/ I can't hardly breathe—it's piss ammonia strong." No sleep 'til Brooklyn.

3. **"Home Of Hip Hop"—Grandmixer D.ST (Celluloid, 1985)**
Tired of all the attention being thrown the way of Queens newcomers like Run-D.M.C. and LL Cool J, the Bronx grandmixer composed this history lesson about his home borough. While the guitars and vocoders are a little on the *Miami Vice* side, D.ST's enthusiastic, Busy Bee-like vocal performance and still-relevant lyrics shine like the tint off his wraparound Terminator shades: "Today and tomorrow is the hip hop era, new jacks trying to monopolize—deceiving the public's eyes about they're the ones who started the show/ Ask them about hip hop, they don't know."

4. **"Funky Beat"—Whodini (Jive, 1986)**
Grandmaster Dee started out strong with his rhyming spotlight—"Last Fresh Fest I was rockin' 'Good Times'/ This Fresh Fest I'm bustin' out rhymes"—before mangling his infamous kicker—"I rock the beat because it is fresh/ And the other DJs know that I am—def!" Thus, Dee proved that mixing records with your tongue on cross country stadium tours can do irreparable damage to your rapping abilities.

5. **"Do Or Die Bed-Sty"—Divine Sounds (Reality, 1986)**
DS's 2 Bigg DJ, Mike Music, was able to reclaim respect for both fat DJs and DJs with fat rhymes: "Sucker DJs, I call y'all—don't like it, wanna battle, just gimme a call/ I'm cuttin' and scratchin' so damn precise—Machete's what they call me, but my name is Mike!"

6. **"Puttin' On The Hits"—Latee & DJ Mark (b/k/a 45 King) (Wild Pitch, 1987)**
Mark wasn't lying when he rhymed, "Part time rappers, emcees beware—do the industry a favor, find a new career/ Cuz I'm better than half of you." This B-side of "This Cut's Got Flavor" (from which Latifah's Flavor Unit got its name) would provide the first in an impressive series of funky forums for Mark to flex his highly underrated microphone techniques.

7. **"All You MC's"—Super Lover Cee & Casanova Rud (Elektra, 1988)**
Ironically enough, it was a song that accused other *rappers* of biting that provided Casanova Rud's chance to shine on the solo vocal tip. "MC Rud is in effect, you will give respect/ Bow your head and honor the rhymes that I connect," he flows in a dexterous verbal display that gives his partner a run for his money.

8. **"Nice & Smooth"—Nice & Smooth (Fresh, 1989)**
The Awesome Two's bespectacled DJing half, Teddy Ted, got more than a little stupid when he spat, "Get a little mellow, then say hello to a fly booty that's

DJs

dressed in yellow/ I'm a mack laddy in a brown caddie, been around the world freakin' fly girls—call me 'Daddy.'" Ooh, Teddy Ted!

9. **"Pause"—Run-D.M.C. (Profile, 1989)**
"Pause" represented a watershed moment in Run-D.M.C.'s career for three significant reasons. First, it inaugurated the trio's newly upscale fashion sense (a/k/a the "Back From The Mall"-look). Second, it displayed their first awkward handling of the then-burgeoning New Jack Swing phenomenon. Third, it represented Jam Master Jay's first test to become an emcee. He failed. Attempting to introduce the "Pause" dance as well as big up his homie that supplied the song's Teddy Riley–like keyboard embellishments, Jay's lyrical uzi jammed: "It's simple just like stop and go—you can Pause whether fast or slow/ Participate, but you all get down—here's a solo from my homeboy Stanley Brown!"

10. **"Do It Like A G.O."—Geto Boys (Rap-A-Lot, 1989)**
The first classic edition of the GB's comin' through featured some well-placed racial aggression from their original, light-skinded musical anchor, DJ Ready Red: "Bitch, motherfuck the KKK/ Wearin' dresses and shit—what the fuck is they gay?" Fight the muthafuckin' power.

11. **"Afro Connections At A Hi 5 (In The Eyes Of The Hoodlum)"—De La Soul (Tommy Boy, 1991)**
P.A. Maseo is the unexpected highlight of one of De La's greatest underacknowledged tracks. Baby Huey even rips the coveted final vocal slot behind Pos and Trugoy thanks to some fresh, fly, wild and bold, couture-informed verbals: "My jeans are brand new with 12 more/ In the closet with my silk and velour."

12. **"Give It Here"—Kid 'N Play (Select, 1991)**
Chris 'N Chris (a/k/a D. Original Kris Kross) finally relinquished a few bars to their DJ, Wizard M.E., to vocally rip on the group's long-forgotten third LP, *Face The Nation*. "I'm not talkin' 'bout the KP law," bragged M.E. "A blizzard from the Wizard is one hell of a storm." He blew us away.

13. **"This Boy Is Smooth"—DJ Jazzy Jeff & The Fresh Prince (Jive, 1991)**
Jeff's botched vocal cameo provides palpable evidence as to why Will Smith kept him on the turntables all those years: "Yo, I'm the J-A double Z—Jazzy," he managed before flubbing his flow with what we can only decipher as, "the smooth with self and smooth and I had to be/ Known, acknowledged and recognized as the king of the groove." All the people who can't rhyme be quiet.

14. **"This Is What You Came Here For"—Kid Capri featuring TJ Swan (Cold Chillin', 1991)**
Uptown's Midnight Rocker/Chief Bootknocka toned things down for this lost quiet storm rap jewel—an absurdly macked-out track complete with TJ Swan's Michael Jackson-isms. Between boasts that his girl massages him while he's sipping Dom P, Capri has never sounded this laid back: "Rap lord with a twist, I promise you this/ That I'm bad on the mic, double bad on the mix."

18 Songs Kid Capri Appears On.*

1. "Back It Up"—Grand Puba (Elektra, 1992)
2. "Brown Skin Woman"—KRS-One (Jive, 1992)
3. "Busy's Revenge"—Busy Bee (Pandisc, 1992)
4. "Family Got To Get Busy"—H.E.A.L. Project also featuring Salt-N-Pepa, Kool Moe Dee, Grand Daddy I.U., Ms. Melodie, Ziggy Marley, D.M.C., KRS-One, Chuck D, Doug E. Fresh & Kool DJ Red Alert (Edutainer, 1991)
5. "Fiesta"—Noreaga (Penalty, 1998)
6. "Heal Yourself"—H.E.A.L. Project also featuring Harmony, Big Daddy Kane, Freddie Foxxx, LL Cool J, MC Lyte, Queen Latifah, KRS-One, Ms. Melodie, D.M.C. & Jam Master Jay (Edutainer, 1991)
7. "Hip Hop Is . . ."—Kid Capri, Kidd Creole (Furious Five) & Ecstacy (Whodini) (from *The Show* Soundtrack—Def Jam, 1995)
8. "Ill Na Na"—Foxy Brown (Def Jam, 1997)
9. "Intro"—Diamond D (Mercury, 1997)
10. "Keep It Movin' Intro"—Ill Al Skratch (Mercury, 1997)
11. "Da Kid Himself"—Lord Finesse (Penalty, 1995)
12. "The Original Way"—Boogie Down Productions (Jive, 1992)
13. "Party Groove"—Show & AG (Showbiz, 1991)
14. "Put It On"—Big L (Columbia, 1995)
15. "Silence Of The Lambs (Remix)"—Show & AG (Payday, 1992)
16. "Soul Clap"—Show & AG (Showbiz, 1991)
17. "Stop Frontin'"—KRS-One (Jive, 1992)
18. "Walk On By"—Fat Joe featuring Charli Baltimore (Big Beat, 1998)

*Excludes songs that appear on Capri's two albums, *The Tape* (Cold Chillin', 1991) and *Soundtrack To The Streets* (Columbia, 1998), but cop them.

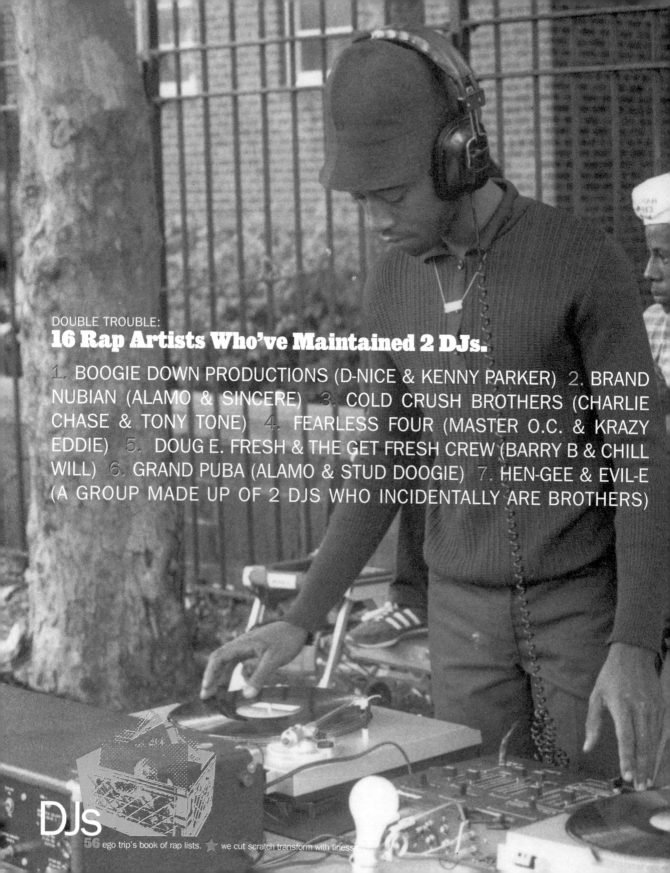

DOUBLE TROUBLE:
16 Rap Artists Who've Maintained 2 DJs.

1. BOOGIE DOWN PRODUCTIONS (D-NICE & KENNY PARKER) 2. BRAND NUBIAN (ALAMO & SINCERE) 3. COLD CRUSH BROTHERS (CHARLIE CHASE & TONY TONE) 4. FEARLESS FOUR (MASTER O.C. & KRAZY EDDIE) 5. DOUG E. FRESH & THE GET FRESH CREW (BARRY B & CHILL WILL) 6. GRAND PUBA (ALAMO & STUD DOOGIE) 7. HEN-GEE & EVIL-E (A GROUP MADE UP OF 2 DJS WHO INCIDENTALLY ARE BROTHERS)

DJs

⭐ we cut scratch transform with finesse

8. JURASSIC 5 (CUT CHEMIST & NU-MARK) 9. KURTIS BLOW (DAVY DMX & AJ SCRATCH) 10. LL COOL J (BOBCAT & CUT CREATOR) 11. MC LYTE (K-ROCK & MASTER T) 12. MAIN SOURCE (SIR SCRATCH & K-CUT) 13. N.W.A (DR. DRE & YELLA) 14. ORIGINAL CONCEPT (DOCTOR DRÉ & EASY G ROCKWELL) 15. SOUTH CENTRAL CARTEL (KAOS & GRIPP) 16. ULTRAMAGNETIC MC'S (MOE LOVE & T.R. LOVE)

Tape Kingz' Iain McNee Chooses The 10 Greatest Mix Tapes Of All-Time.

1. ***Best Of Biggie Smalls***—DJ Mister Cee, 1995
People who weren't in Brooklyn missed a lot of freestyles or songs that Biggie had done with lesser-named artists and they all appeared on this tape—the freestyles from the Budweiser Superfest in '94 that he did with 2Pac at Madison Square Garden, the freestyle he did over "Elie's Theme" from *Shaft*, etc. The full Biggie picture of that time.

2. ***'95 Live***—Doo Wop, 1995
Revolutionary at that time. People had had big name artists drop freestyles at the beginnings of their tapes before. But this was a whole bunch of them, like 20 minutes of freestyles by big name artists. It was one of those things that you could listen to from beginning to end and was just phenomenal.

3. ***Blends 1***—Ron G, 1992
When Kid Capri stopped making tapes, Ron G took the crown. He was the first person to blend hip hop beats to R&B which, of course, is what R&B is today. And he still gets no credit for that. He would even blend "Sittin' On The Dock Of They Bay" with "I Know You Got Soul"—a bugged combination.

4. ***10/9/89***—Kid Capri, 1989
The intro to this tape was massive: Stephanie Mills' "Something In The Way You Make Me Feel" with The Honey Drippers' "Impeach The President" underneath. If you walked down 125th Street at that time, all along the street people were outdoors selling tapes and that intro is all you would hear. People would just rewind it.

5. ***52 Beats***—Kid Capri, 1989
A tape of all breakbeats that is still relevant. Pure hip hop.

6. ***50 MC's***—Tony Touch, 1996
Took the Doo Wop *'95 Live* concept, but instead of 20 minutes

DJs.

⭐ you all fucked up like an offbeat blend.

he made it 90 minutes. Pioneering.

7. ***2/10/93*—DJ S&S, 1993**
S&S had Uptown locked at that time. He got his name by dropping exclusives and here you've got Naughty By Nature's "Hip Hop Hooray" months before it came out.

8. ***Spring '93, Part II*—Doo Wop, 1993**
Prior to *'95 Live*, Doo Wop had his own squad, the Bounce Squad, which was Snagglepuss, U-Neek, Lord Tariq, Chris G and Rampage (not The Last Boy Scout). Hearing these guys freestyle in the first 10 minutes was the highlight of Doo Wop's tapes because at that time there was nobody getting really hardcore like them in New York. And on this one particular tape, Chris G and Rampage were making death threats against Kid Capri. Whatever their beef was, it was obviously ridiculous and stupid and it's finished now.

9. ***Five Deadly Venoms Of Brooklyn*—Tony Touch, 1997**
Five key DJs handpicked by Tony Touch on one tape: himself, Premier, Mister Cee, P.F. Cuttin' and Evil Dee.

10. ***Bad Boy Volume 1*—DJ Clue, 1995**
For a big label like Bad Boy to put out a mix tape was a surprise. But they proved over the course of four volumes of tapes (later with Stretch Armstrong, S&S and Doo Wop) that it was a worthwhile experiment. There were so many exclusives, especially Bad Boy exclusives, that people would run to the stores. It got Bad Boy a street audience.

Mix tape impresario Iain McNee is not only the founder of Tape Kingz (www.tapekingz.com), but is also the author of the controversial sports novel, England's Number One: The Adventures Of A Serial Soccer Yob *(Pig Publishing).*

PRODU

CTION.

Hip Hop's Greatest Producers.

1. Marley Marl
2. Dr. Dre
3. DJ Premier
4. The Bomb Squad
5. RZA
6. Erick Sermon
7. Pete Rock
8. Prince Paul
9. Organized Noize
10. Large Professor
11. Rick Rubin
12. Mantronik
13. Hurby "Luv Bug" Azor
14. DJ Pooh
15. Larry Smith

Little Known Facts About The Creations Of 21 Famous Rap Songs.

1. **"Ain't No Fun (If The Homies Can't Have None)"—Snoop Doggy Dogg featuring Nate Dogg, Kurupt & Warren G (Death Row, 1993)**
On the insistence of Death Row Records' head and former Blood gang member Suge Knight, Warren G reputedly amended his cameo with the lyric, "In my Chevy 6-4—*red* to be exact," as a concession to the colors repped by his boss. It's all gang-related.

2. **"Beats To The Rhyme"—Run-D.M.C. (Profile, 1988)**
In an unprecedented experiment, the vocals to this song were recorded separately, pressed up on an a cappella test vinyl and scratched-in over the instrumental track for the final recording by Jam Master Jay—hence the *wikka-wikka* effect that precedes Run's first lyrics. Now that's a fuckin' blend!

3. **"Dangerous"—Busta Rhymes (Elektra, 1997)**
Bussa Bus' 1997 dance floor anthem culled its insistent hook from the jingle of a poison control public service announcement shown on local Long Island TV. Who says hip hop and drugs don't mix?

4. **"Eric B. Is President"—Eric B. & Rakim (Zakia, 1986)**
Rakim's historic debut might never have happened had Eric B.'s first choice, Freddie Foxxx, made it for the session. When Freddie failed to show, a teenaged Ra dropped the new rap language that revolutionized hip hop.
    In addition, the song was conceived as an answer record to Janet Jackson's "What Have You Done For Me Lately?" Rakim's third verse exposes the remains of this idea most explicitly: "But now it's out of hand because you told me you hate me/ And then you ask what have I done lately?" With answer records losing their popularity in hip hop, however, the concept was scrapped.

5. **"Ghetto Supastar (That Is What You Are)"—Pras featuring Ol' Dirty Bastard & Mya (Interscope, 1998)**
During the recording of this Top 40 favorite, Wu-Tang Clan drunken master Ol' Dirty Bastard accidentally bumrushed Pras' recording session when he stumbled into the wrong studio. After ODB was invited to contribute vocals, the formerly squeaky-clean *Bulworth* smash was given its now-famous Dirty treatment.

6. **"Hard Knock Life (Ghetto Anthem)"—Jay-Z (Roc-A-Fella, 1998)**
This 45 King-produced smash reworking of the song from the Broadway hit *Annie* might have languished in obscurity had Kid Capri not spun an early instrumental version (pressed up independently by 45 King) while DJing one night on Puff Daddy's "No Way Out" tour. Immediately taken by what he heard, fellow tour member Jay-Z accosted Capri for the track's origin and phoned 45 King from the venue to secure its availability.

7. **"I'm Bout It, Bout It"—TRU featuring Mia X (No Limit, 1995)**
The track for this No Limit anthem was stuck in creative limbo as a song for NL soldier Mr. Serv-On titled "Buckin' Like A Winchester." Fortunately, Beats By The Pound producer KLC's baby daughter, Crashan, was in her dad's home studio while he was hookin' up dope tracks. Her accidental tapping on the drum machine helped him coalesce the beat for this gangsta classic.

8. **"It's Yours"—T La Rock & Jazzy Jay (Partytime, 1984)**
Def Jam co-founder Rick Rubin's original choice of vocalist for his first foray into rap was the Treacherous Three's Kool Moe Dee. Under contract to Sugar Hill Records at the time, Moe Dee was unable to perform on the song but suggested as a replacement T La Rock, the brother of his T3 bandmate Special K.

PRODUCTION.

9. **"Jenifa (Taught Me)"—De La Soul (Tommy Boy, 1989)**
The tambourines on this track were not, in fact, tambourines, but fists of loose change shaken near the microphone.

10. **"Jingling Baby (Remixed And Still Jingling)"—LL Cool J (Def Jam, 1990)**
According to producer Marley Marl, the track for LL's biggest comeback single was originally slated for Biz Markie. But after Marley and Cold Chillin', Biz's label, began feuding (eventually resulting in Marley's disassociation with the label and the official demise of the Juice Crew), the superproducer elected to give it to his newest collaborator, LL.

11. **"Killing Me Softly With His Song"—Fugees (Ruffhouse, 1996)**
The Fugees' biggest hit was originally not a straight cover of the Roberta Flack number, but a battle cry of band unity which detailed the trio's struggles for respect and acceptance in the hip hop community. In this version, the introductory chorus goes, "Killing a sound boy with this sound/ Taking sound boy's lives with this dub/ Killing them softy with this song." Bo!

12. **"Nobody Beats The Biz"—Biz Markie (Prism, 1987)**
The hook for this song—as eloquently sung by resident Juice Crew crooner TJ Swan—was lifted from the TV commercial jingle to New York electronics franchise The Wiz, who sued Biz for copyright infringement. Parent label Cold Chillin' wound up coughing up an undisclosed sum in an out-of-court settlement—an experience they would unfortunately re-live during Biz's much publicized 1991 legal furor regarding an uncleared Gilbert O'Sullivan sample.

13. **"Planet Rock"—Afrika Bambaataa & The Soul Sonic Force (Tommy Boy, 1982)**
According to Tommy Boy Records founder Tom Silverman, emcee Pow Wow's now famous nonsensical lines from the start of the fifth verse ("zuh-zuh-zuh-zuh-zuh, zuh-zuh-zuh") were uttered when the Zulu Nation vocalist forgot the lyrics he'd written.

14. **"Player's Ball"—OutKast (LaFace, 1993)**
It's actually a Christmas song! Originally titled "Socks & Drawers," the ATL duo's debut single made its initial appearance on the holiday compilation, *A LaFace Family Christmas*. A closer listen to the song reveals lyrical references to chimneys and stockings, a chant of "ho, ho, ho" and sleigh bells in the mix of the track.

15. **"Raw"—Big Daddy Kane (Prism, 1987)**
During the scratching that follows Kane's final verse, DJ Mister Cee's copy of James Brown's "Papa Don't Take No Mess" skips, unintentionally releasing a perfectly timed bass hit. This musical stab was never removed from the final version of the song.

16. **"Rock The Bells"—LL Cool J (Def Jam, 1985)**
The pride of Farmers Blvd. was literally taking creative notes from his mentors, Run-D.M.C., in 1985. It was while recording his debut LP that LL was granted an advance listen to Run, Darryl & Jay's forthcoming "Peter Piper." Inspired by his heroes' latest creation, Uncle L duplicated the "Piper" track's liberal usage of Bob James' "Take Me To The Mardi Gras" for his original recording of "Rock The Bells." Incensed, a pre-Reverend Run screamed on the teenager and forced him to re-configure "Bells" into its now-classic Trouble Funk-sampled rendition.

17. **"The Show"—Doug E. Fresh & The Get Fresh Crew (Reality, 1985)**
The subtext of this biggest of party anthems is a classic good vs. evil struggle. MC Ricky D's (b/k/a Slick Rick) incessant "six minutes, six minutes, six minutes" chant is intended to represent 666, the mark of the Beast. Countering it are the frequent interjections of the phrases, "Oh my God!" (sampled, incidentally, off of the intro to the Cold Crush Brothers' "Punk Rock Rap") and "Is it real?" (which, if said in rapid repetition, becomes "Israel"). After Rick's departure from the group, Doug E. would indulge his religious message even more explicitly on the subsequent *Oh My God!* LP and its hit single, "All The Way To Heaven."

18. **"The Symphony"—Marley Marl featuring Masta Ace, Craig G, Kool G Rap & Big Daddy Kane (Cold Chillin', 1988)**
During the recording of the greatest of all posse cuts, the loquacious Kool G Rap reportedly rhymed for so long that the tape reel ran out and snapped. Eventually, his part was shortened to an acceptable length.

19. **"Ten Crack Commandments"—The Notorious B.I.G. (Bad Boy, 1997)**
Ironically, this unapologetic, DJ Premier-produced chronicle of drug dealer codes of conduct first appeared as a promotional track for New York radio station "Hot 97" featuring the staunchly righteous Jeru The Damaja.

20. **"Top Billin'"—Audio Two (First Priority, 1987)**
The stuttering beat to this minimalist masterpiece was accidentally created when the Two's Giz programmed the drum loop to The Honey Drippers' "Impeach The President" incorrectly. After consultation with producer Daddy-O, it was decided to keep the rhythm as it was.

21. **"2,3 Break"—B-Boys (Vintertainment, 1983)**
According to engineer Mark Mandelbaum, the chorus to this song was originally intended to only feature the group shouting, "Break!" Unable to come in on time after repeated takes, Donald D and company were advised to count, "two, three," to themselves as a lead in. Instead, they shouted, "two, three—break!" thus creating the title hook to one of the most memorable of early-'80s rap classics.

MAKE THE MUSIC WITH YOUR MOUTH:
20 Indispensible Human Beat Box Songs.

1. "A One Two"—Biz Markie (Prism, 1986)
2. "Bite It"—U.T.F.O. (Select, 1984)
3. "Breath Control"—Boogie Down Productions (Jive, 1989)
4. "Def Fresh Crew"—Roxanne Shanté featuring Biz Markie (Pop Art, 1986)
5. "Fat Girl"—Eazy-E (Ruthless, 1987)
6. "Faye"—Stetsasonic (Tommy Boy, 1986)
7. "Freestyle Live"—Roxanne Shanté featuring Biz Markie (Pop Art, 1987)
8. "Get Fresh Hev"—Heavy D (Universal, 1997)
9. "Human Beat Box"—Fat Boys (Sutra, 1984)
10. "Jockbox (America Loves The Skinny Boys)"—Skinny Boys (Warlock, 1986)
11. "La Di Da Di"—Doug E. Fresh & MC Ricky D (b/k/a Slick Rick) (Reality, 1985)
12. "Latoya"—Just-Ice (Fresh, 1986)
13. "The Lesson (Part 1)"—The Roots (Geffen, 1994)
14. "Nuthin'"—Doug E. Fresh & The Get Fresh Crew (Reality, 1986)
15. "The 'P' Is Free"—Boogie Down Productions (B-Boy, 1986)
16. "Son Of Byford"—Run-D.M.C. (Profile, 1986)
17. "Stick 'Em"—Fat Boys (Sutra, 1984)
18. "Three Minutes Of Beatboxing"—T La Rock featuring Greg Nice (Nice & Smooth) (Fresh, 1987)
19. "Uh Oh"—KRS-One (Jive, 1993)
20. "Veronica"—Bad Boys featuring K Love (Starlite, 1985)

R-O-C-K IN THE G-H-E-T-T-O:
Great Uses Of Rock Samples & Interpolations In '80s Hip Hop.

1. **"It's Magic"—Fearless Four (Enjoy, 1982)**
   ORIGIN: "Was Dog A Doughnut"—Cat Stevens (A&M, 1977)
2. **"Planet Rock"—Afrika Bambaataa & The Soul Sonic Force (Tommy Boy, 1982)**
   ORIGIN: "Trans-Europe Express"—Kraftwerk (Capitol, 1977) & "The Mexican"—Babe Ruth (Harvest, 1973)
3. **"Rockin' It"—Fearless Four (Enjoy, 1982)**
   ORIGIN: "The Man-Machine"—Kraftwerk (Capitol, 1978)
4. **"White Lines (Don't Do It)"—Grandmaster Melle Mel (Sugar Hill, 1983)**
   ORIGIN: "Cavern"—Liquid Liquid (99, 1983)
5. **"Roxanne, Roxanne"—U.T.F.O. (Select, 1984)**
   ORIGIN: "Big Beat"—Billy Squier (Capitol, 1980)
6. **"Rock The Bells"—LL Cool J (Def Jam, 1985)**
   ORIGIN: "Let's Get It Up"—AC/DC (Atlantic, 1981)
7. **"That's A Lie"—LL Cool J (Def Jam, 1985)**
   ORIGIN: "Owner Of A Lonely Heart"—Yes (Atco, 1983)
8. **"Dope Beat"—Boogie Down Productions (B-Boy, 1986)**
   ORIGIN: "Back In Black"—AC/DC (Atlantic, 1980)
9. **"It's Tricky"—Run-D.M.C. (Profile, 1986)**
   ORIGIN: "My Sharona"—The Knack (Capitol, 1979)
10. **"Rhymin' & Stealin'"—Beastie Boys (Def Jam, 1986)**
    ORIGIN: "When The Levee Breaks"—Led Zeppelin (Atlantic, 1971)
11. **"50 Ways"—Kool Moe Dee (Jive, 1987)**
    ORIGIN: "50 Ways To Leave Your Lover"—Paul Simon (Columbia, 1975)
12. **"Funky"—Ultramagnetic MC's (Next Plateau, 1987)**
    ORIGIN: "Woman To Woman"—Joe Cocker (A&M, 1972)
13. **"Nobody Beats The Biz"—Biz Markie (Prism, 1987)**
    ORIGIN: "Fly Like An Eagle"—Steve Miller Band (Capitol, 1976)

PRODUCTION.

14. **"Daddy's Home"—Chubb Rock (Select, 1988)**
ORIGIN: "Reignition"—Bad Brains (SST, 1986)

15. **"Doin' Damage"—J.V.C. Force (B-Boy, 1988)**
ORIGIN: "Louie, Louie"—The Kingsmen (Wand, 1963)

16. **"Survival Of The Fittest"—MC Lyte (First Priority, 1988)**
ORIGIN: "Magic Man"—Heart (Mushroom, 1976)

17. **"Total Confusion"—Original Concept (Def Jam, 1988)**
ORIGIN: "Kashmir"—Led Zeppelin (Swan Song, 1975)

18. **"Ya Slippin'"—Boogie Down Productions (Jive, 1988)**
ORIGIN: "Smoke On The Water"—Deep Purple (Warner Bros., 1972)

19. **"Eye Know"—De La Soul (Tommy Boy, 1989)**
ORIGIN: "Peg"—Steely Dan (ABC, 1977)

20. **"The Fuck Shop"—2 Live Crew (Luke, 1989)**
ORIGIN: "Ain't Talkin' 'Bout Love"—Van Halen (Warner Bros., 1978) & "Sweet Child O' Mine"—Guns & Roses (Geffen, 1987)

21. **"Funky Cold Medina"—Tone-Lōc (Delicious Vinyl, 1989)**
ORIGIN: "Honky Tonk Woman"—Rolling Stones (London, 1969) & "Hot Blooded"—Foreigner (Atlantic, 1978)

22. **"Let The Words Flow"—Chill Rob G (Wild Pitch, 1989)**
ORIGIN: "Voices Inside My Head"—The Police (A&M, 1980)

23. **"Music Man"—Masta Ace (Cold Chillin', 1989)**
ORIGIN: "Nothing Is The Same"—Grand Funk Railroad (Capitol, 1970)

24. **"Sounds Of Silence"—Beastie Boys (Capitol, 1989)**
ORIGIN: "When I'm Sixty-Four"—The Beatles (Capitol, 1967) & "Carry That Weight"—The Beatles (Apple, 1969)

25. **"Taxin'"—Special Ed (Profile, 1989)**
ORIGIN: "Sgt. Pepper's Lonely Heart's Club Band"—The Beatles (Capitol, 1967)

DJ Premier's Quarterpound Of Underacknowledged Hip Hop Cuts.

1. "Holy War (Live)"—Divine Force (Yamak-ka, 1987)
2. "My Mic Is On Fire"—Lord Shafiyq (NUWR, 1987)
3. "Any Day Can Be Your Last"—Half-A-Mil (Half-A-Mil, 1993)
4. "How About Some Hardcore"—M.O.P. (Select, 1994)
5. "Walk With A Limp"—Money Boss Players (Warning, 1996)
6. "Yes You May (Remix)"—Lord Finesse featuring Big L (Giant, 1992)
7. "Day One"—D.I.T.C. (D.I.T.C., 1997)
8. "Late Night Hype"—Compton's Most Wanted (Orpheus, 1990)
9. "They Call Me Puma"—Seeborn & Puma (Select, 1987)
10. "The Do Do"—Biz Markie (Cold Chillin', 1988)
11. "Essays On BDP-ism"—Boogie Down Productions (Jive, 1988)
12. "Sunnyside"—Finsta & Bundy (Big Willie, 1995)
13. "Extra Extra"—Paula Perry (Mad Sounds, 1998)
14. "That's How I'm Livin'"—Black Rock & Ron (Next Plateau, 1987)
15. "Bait"—Ultramagnetic MC's (Let's Go, 1987)
16. "You Know How To Reach Us"—Kings Of Pressure (Let's Go, 1987)
17. "Rhyme Time"—Kool G Rap & DJ Polo (Cold Chillin', 1987)
18. "Many Styles"—Audio Two (First Priority, 1988)
19. "Lock Shit Down"—Dark Skinned Assassins (4 Doe Loe, 1995)
20. "I'm Not Playing"—Ultimate Force (Strong City, 1989)
21. "It's The Beat"—Hollis Crew (Def Jam, 1985)
22. "Me, Not The Paper (Remix)"—Jeru The Damaja (Payday, 1997)
23. "Ready To Penetrate"—Sugar Bear (Coslit, 1988)
24. "Be Down"—Geto Boys (Rap-A-Lot, 1988)
25. "The Other Side"—Levi 167 (B-Boy, 1987)

Underground savior DJ Premier is hip hop's most respected boardsman. His long list of classic credits includes productions for The Notorious B.I.G., Rakim, and KRS-One amongst many others. With his partner Guru in Gang Starr, he is responsible for masterful albums such as 1998's Moment Of Truth.

Songs That Were Sabotaged By Sample Clearance Refusals.

1. **"The Dream Shatterer"—Big Punisher (Loud, 1998)**
   UNCLEARED SAMPLE: "Under The Influence Of Love"—Love Unlimited (20th Century, 1973)

2. **"In The World"—Akinyele (Stress, 1996)**
   UNCLEARED SAMPLE: "90% Of Me Is You"—Gwen McCrae (Cat, 1975)

3. **"J.D.'s Revenge"—Diamond D featuring Gina Thompson (Mercury, 1997)**
   UNCLEARED SAMPLE: "Tell Me"—Groove Theory (Epic, 1995)

4. **"Life Ain't Cool"—Mystikal featuring Master P & Silkk The Shocker (No Limit, 1998)**
   UNCLEARED SAMPLE: "All I Do"—Stevie Wonder (Tamla, 1980)

5. **"Me & My Bitch"—The Notorious B.I.G. (Bad Boy, 1994)**
   UNCLEARED SAMPLE: "Take A Little Trip"—Minnie Riperton (Epic, 1974)

6. **"Return Of The Boom Bap"—KRS-One (Jive, 1993)**
   UNCLEARED SAMPLE: "The Oscar Mayer Bologna Jingle"

7. **"Think Big"—Pudgee Tha Phat Bastard featuring Sadat X & Lord Tariq (Perspective, 1996)**
   UNCLEARED SAMPLE: "Vegetable Wagon"—Donny Hathaway (Atco, 1972)

8. **"Thugs R Us"—DJ Clue featuring Noreaga (Roc-A-Fella, 1998)**
   UNCLEARED SAMPLE: "Under The Influence Of Love"—Love Unlimited (20th Century, 1973)

9. **"You Do I Do"—Def Squad (Def Jam, 1998)**
   UNCLEARED SAMPLE: "Thank You For Talkin' To Me, Africa"—Sly & The Family Stone (Epic, 1971)

10. **"Your World Don't Stop"—AZ (EMI, 1995)**
    UNCLEARED SAMPLE: "You're Welcome, Stop On By"—Lou Donaldson (Blue Note, 1974)

| 183.750 | 183.760 | 183.770 | 183.780 | 183.790 |

27 dB Left Channel

12 dB Right Channel

PRODUCTION.

Rap Productions By Non-Rap Producers.

1. "Bad Times (I Can't Stand It)"—Captain Rapp (Magic Disc, 1983): Produced by Jimmy Jam, Terry Lewis & Rich Carson
2. "Beat Bop"—K-Rob vs. Rammelzee (Tartown, 1982): Produced by Jean-Michel Basquiat
3. "Escapades Of Futura 2000"—Futura 2000 (Celluloid, 1982): Produced by The Clash
4. "Magic's Wand"—Whodini (Jive, 1982): Produced by Thomas Dolby
5. "Play That Funky Music, White Boy"—B.M.O.C. (Rat, 1988): Produced by Nile Rodgers
6. "We Rap More Mellow"—The Younger Generation (Brass, 1979): Produced by Terry Lewis
7. "What's It All About"—Run-D.M.C. (Profile, 1990): Co-produced by Glen E. Friedman
8. *Wild Style* Soundtrack (Animal, 1983): Produced by Chris Stein (Blondie)
9. "World Famous"—Malcolm McLaren & The World Famous Supreme Team (Island, 1983): Produced by Trevor Horn

10 Songs Marley Marl Wishes He Had Produced.*

1. "DWYCK"—Gang Starr (Chrysalis, 1992)
2. "So Wat Cha Sayin'"—EPMD (Fresh, 1989)
3. "Genius Of Love"—Tom Tom Club (Sire, 1981)
4. "Warning"—The Notorious B.I.G. (Bad Boy, 1994)
5. "Mr. Big Stuff"—Jean Knight (Stax, 1971)
6. "Streets Is Watching"—Jay-Z (Roc-A-Fella, 1997)
7. "Impeach The President"—The Honey Drippers (Alaga, 1973)
8. "I Need A Beat"—LL Cool J (Def Jam, 1984)
9. "Funky Drummer"—James Brown (King, 1970)
10. "Theme From *S.W.A.T.*"—Rhythm Heritage (ABC, 1975)

*In no particular order.

Marley Marl simply changed the way hip hop was heard forever. His extensive list of epochal production credits—which include classics by Eric B. & Rakim, LL Cool J, and the entire Juice Crew—are literally too numerous to mention individually. On the real, all you crab producers know the deal.

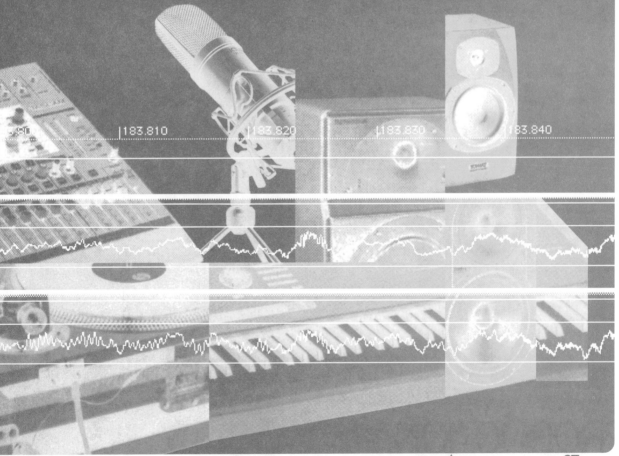

A-ALIKES:
20 Songs You'd Swear Were Done By Somebody Else.

1. "Beat 'Em In The Head"—Hostyle (Hydra, 1997): The Notorious B.I.G.
2. "Come Off Hard"—Mister Voodoo (Fortress, 1994): KRS-One
3. "Dope On Plastic"—Uptown (Tommy Boy, 1989): MC Shan
4. "Down To The Gristle"—Cool C (Hilltop Hustlers, 1988): MC Shan
5. "Find An Ugly Woman"—Cash Money & Marvelous (Fresh, 1988): DJ Jazzy Jeff & The Fresh Prince
6. "Hawaiian Sophie"—The Jaz (EMI, 1989): DJ Jazzy Jeff & The Fresh Prince
7. "I Got An Attitude"—Antoinette (Next Plateau, 1987): Rakim
8. "I Shed Tears For The World"—Crazy (Ruff Era, 1998): 2Pac
9. "Life Of An Entertainer"—MC Rell & The Houserockers (Mercury, 1989): Rakim
10. "Mix Tapes"—The Nonce (Wild West, 1995): Q-Tip
11. "My Posse"—C.I.A. (Kru'-Cut, 1987): Beastie Boys
12. "Nights Of Fear"—Ak Skills (Tru Criminal, 1996): Nas
13. "No Joke"—Harmony (Criminal, 1987): LL Cool J (play on vinyl at -5 speed for best effect)
14. "101 Things To Do While I'm With Your Girl"—Kwest The Madd Lad (American, 1996): Diamond Shell
15. "Ride The Crossfade"—Jewel T (Jewel, 1987): LL Cool J
16. "Season Of The Vic"—Justin Warfield (Qwest, 1992): Q-Tip
17. "Shit We Do"—Hard 2 Obtain (Atlantic, 1994): Grand Puba
18. "So Now You Know"—Diezzle Don & The Govener (Lockdown, 1995): Redman & The Notorious B.I.G.
19. "True Confessions"—Tragedy & Imam Thug (25 To Life, 1997): Raekwon & Ghostface Killah
20. "What People Do For Money"—Divine Sounds (Specific, 1984): Run-D.M.C.

20 Classic James Brown Productions...

1. "Funky President (People It's Bad)"—James Brown (Polydor, 1974)
2. "Funky Drummer"—James Brown (King, 1970)
3. "Get Up Offa That Thing"—James Brown (Polydor, 1976)
4. "Blues & Pants"—James Brown (Polydor, 1971)
5. "I Know You Got Soul"—Bobby Byrd (King, 1968)
6. "Pass The Peas"—The JBs (People, 1972)
7. "Don't Tell It"—James Brown (Polydor, 1976)
8. "Blow Your Head"—Fred Wesley & The JBs (People, 1974)
9. "Mama Feelgood"—Lyn Collins (People, 1973)
10. ""Cross The Track (We Better Go Back)"—Maceo & The Macks (People, 1974)
11. "You Can Have Watergate Just Gimme Some Bucks And I'll Be Straight"—The JBs (People, 1973)
12. "Think (About It)"—Lyn Collins (People, 1972)
13. "Damn Right I Am Somebody"—Fred Wesley & The JBs (People, 1974)
14. "Unwind Yourself"—Marva Whitney (King, 1968)
15. "Papa Don't Take No Mess"—James Brown (Polydor, 1974)
16. "Can I Get Some Help"—James Brown (King, 1969)
17. "Hot Pants Road"—The JBs (People, 1972)
18. "The Message From The Soul Sisters"—Myra Barnes (a/k/a Vicki Anderson) (King, 1970)
19. "Can Mind"—James Brown (King, 1971)
20. "In The Land Of Milk & Honey"—Vicki Anderson (Brownstone, 1972)

PRODUCTION.

ERIC B.
Featuring Rakim
1. ERIC B. IS PRESIDENT 5.00
(ERIC BARRIER, WM. GRIFFIN)
2. MY MELODY 6:15
(ERIC BARRIER, WM. GRIFFIN)
ZAKIA RECORDS 2030   NEW YORK, N.Y 10027

...& The Rap Songs That Made Them Famous Again.

1. "Eric B. Is President"—Eric B. & Rakim (Zakia, 1986)

2. "It's A Demo"—Kool G Rap & DJ Polo (Cold Chillin', 1986)

3. "South Bronx"—Boogie Down Productions (B-Boy, 1986)

4. "Do The James"—Super Lover Cee & Casanova Rud (Citi-Beat, 1987)

5. "I Know You Got Soul"—Eric B. & Rakim (4th & B'way, 1987)

6. "The Overweight Lover's In The House"—Heavy D & The Boyz (Uptown, 1987)

7. "Poetry"—Boogie Down Productions (B-Boy, 1987)

8. "Public Enemy No. 1"—Public Enemy (Def Jam, 1987)

9. "Raw"—Big Daddy Kane (Prism, 1987)

10. "Do This My Way"—Kid 'N Play (Select, 1988)

11. "Hype Time"—The Bizzie Boyz (Payroll, 1988)

12. "It Takes Two"—Rob Base & DJ E-Z Rock (Profile, 1988)

13. "Let The Rhythm Run"—Salt-N-Pepa (Next Plateau, 1988)

14. "The 900 Number"—45 King (Tuff City, 1988)

15. "Vapors"—Biz Markie (Cold Chillin', 1988)

16. "A Chorus Line"—Ultramagnetic MC's (Next Plateau, 1989)

17. "Fight The Power"—Public Enemy (Motown, 1989)

18. "In Control Of Things"—YZ & G Rock (Diversity, 1989)

19. "All For One"—Brand Nubian (Elektra, 1990)

20. "Live At The Barbeque"—Main Source featuring Nas, Joe Fatal & Akinyele (Wild Pitch, 1991)

Producers & The Groups They Were In Before They Made A Name For Themselves.

1. Alchemist: The Whooliganz
2. Deric "D-Dot" Angelettie & Ron "Amen-Ra" Lawrence (The Hitmen): Two Kings In A Cipher
3. Diamond D: Ultimate Force
4. Dr. Dre & Yella: The World Class Wrekin' Cru
5. KLC (Beats By The Pound): 3-9 Posse
6. Kutmasta Kurt: Red, Black And Green
7. DJ Muggs: 7A3
8. Nashiem Myrick (The Hitmen): Stix 'N Stonz
9. Ivan "Doc" Rodriguez: The Chosen Ones
10. Shawn J. Period: Down South
11. Ski: The Bizzie Boyz; Original Flavor
12. T-Ray: The White Boys

Artists Who Had Their Verses Removed From The Final Versions Of Songs.

1. **Akinyele**
REMOVED FROM: "Back To The Grill"—MC Serch featuring Red Hot Lover Tone, Nas & Chubb Rock (Def Jam, 1992); "Fast Life"—Kool G Rap featuring Nas (Epic, 1995) & "4 My Peeps"—Red Hot Lover Tone featuring The Notorious B.I.G., Prince Poetry (Organized Konfusion) & M.O.P. (Select, 1995)

2. **Black Sheep, De La Soul, Jarobi, Jungle Brothers & Chris Lighty**
REMOVED FROM: "Scenario"—A Tribe Called Quest featuring Leaders Of The New School (Jive, 1991)

3. **Busta Rhymes**
REMOVED FROM: "Driver's Seat"—Capone-N-Noreaga (Penalty, 1997)

4. **Cormega**
REMOVED FROM: "La Familia"—Foxy Brown featuring Nature, Nas & AZ (Def Jam, 1996)

5. **Crustified Dibbs (b/k/a R.A. The Rugged Man)**
REMOVED FROM: "4 My Peeps"—Red Hot Lover Tone featuring The Notorious B.I.G., Prince Poetry (Organized Konfusion) & M.O.P. (Select, 1995)

6. **Diamond D**
REMOVED FROM: "The Funkiest"—Sadat X (Loud, 1996)

7. **Tha Dogg Pound**
REMOVED FROM: "What We Go Through"—Warren G featuring Mr. Malik, Perfec & Bad Azz (Def Jam, 1997)

8. **Dr. Dre & Ice Cube**
REMOVED FROM: "Can't C Me"—2Pac featuring Gerorge Clinton (Death Row, 1996)

9. **Inspectah Deck**
REMOVED FROM: "Got My Mind Made Up"—2Pac featuring Tha Dogg Pound, Method Man & Redman (Death Row, 1996)

10. **Kool G Rap**
REMOVED FROM: "Raw"—Big Daddy Kane (Prism, 1987)

11. **Method Man**
REMOVED FROM: "Brick City Mashin'"—Redman (Def Jam, 1998)

12. **Nas**
REMOVED FROM: "No Love Lost"—Shaquille O'Neal featuring Lord Tariq & Jay-Z (Interscope, 1996); "I Love My Life"—Noreaga (Penalty, 1998)

13. **The Notorious B.I.G.**
REMOVED FROM: "Think Big"—Pudgee Tha Phat Bastard featuring Sadat X & Lord Tariq (Perspective, 1996)

14. **Sam Sneed**
REMOVED FROM: "Natural Born Killaz"—Dr. Dre & Ice Cube (Death Row, 1994)

15. **Erick Sermon**
REMOVED FROM: "All The Way Live"—Tha Alkaholiks featuring Q-Tip (Loud, 1995)*; "Brick City Mashin'"—Redman (Def Jam, 1998)

16. **Snoop Doggy Dogg**
REMOVED FROM: "Zoom"—Dr. Dre & LL Cool J (Interscope, 1998)

17. **3rd Bass**
REMOVED FROM: "Heal Yourself"—H.E.A.L. Project featuring Harmony, Kid Capri, Big Daddy Kane, Freddie Foxxx, LL Cool J, MC Lyte, Queen Latifah, KRS-One, Ms. Melodie, D.M.C. & Jam Master Jay (Edutainer, 1991)

*Q-Tip replaced the Green-Eyed Bandit when it was discovered that he had kicked the same lyrics on Keith Murray's "Straight Loonie" (Jive, 1994).

PRODUCTION.

Prince Paul's All-Time Favorite Hip Hop Skits.

1. **All skits—N.W.A, *Efil4zaggin* (Ruthless, 1991)**
The N.W.A skits took skit-making to some other level. Dre made them so life-like—especially the audio perspective of how a voice sounds outdoors or indoors, if it had echo or it didn't have echo, the sound of cars passin' by. This album just blew me away. I didn't even want to make skits after that. It was too intense.

2. **"Intro"—Ice Cube, *Lethal Injection* (Priority, 1993)**
The perfect use of the element of surprise. Obviously, when you hear it for the second time you know what's going to happen. But hearing it the first time when Cube pulled out the gun and shot the patient—that was so dope! I remember my girlfriend at the time was like, "Nah, I don't see it." I was like, "Awww! The *intensity*! I wasn't expectin' it!"

3. **"Diary Of A Madman"—Gravediggaz, *6 Feet Deep* (Gee Street, 1994)**
I worked hard on this one. It was my first real attempt at being competitive in skit-making. I'd heard the stuff that Dre was doin', I'd heard Ice Cube's stuff and I was like, "Yo, I'm gonna make my joint match the intensity of everything I ever heard." I had people read out their parts and I pieced them together line by line—nobody actually acted against one another.

4. **"Where My *Killer* Tape?"—Wu-Tang Clan, *Enter The Wu-Tang: 36 Chambers* (Loud, 1993)**
This one's just funny. Technically, it's not good. But what they say sticks in your head forever.

5. **"The Driveby"—Ice Cube, *AmeriKKKa's Most Wanted* (Priority, 1990)**
I think this one qualifies just for the fact that they're about to do a driveby and in the car they're playin' "Bust A Move"—the happiest song there is! It's a joke on everybody who says, 'Gangsta rap music is causing kids to go wild.' It's like doing a driveby to Will Smith's "Miami."

HONORABLE MENTION:
"Living For The City"—Stevie Wonder, *Innervisions* (Tamla, 1973)
To me, this is still the all-time greatest—the first and best one ever. Technically he didn't have computers to piece it all together and it still sounds like it's done live in the streets somewhere. I don't know how they did it.

Former Stetsasonic and Gravediggaz member Prince Paul (a/k/a "The Dew Doo Man") pioneered the art of rap album skits as the nutty professor producer of De La Soul's 3 Feet High And Rising. *The Strong Island dramalord can also be heard acting up on albums like* Psychoanalysis (What Is It?).

Q-Tip's Notable Non-A Tribe Called Quest Productions.

1. "Come On Everybody"—Run-D.M.C. (Profile, 1993)
2. "Crooklyn"—Crooklyn Dodgers (MCA, 1994)
3. "Drink Away The Pain (Situations)"—Mobb Deep featuring Q-Tip (Loud, 1995)
4. "Gangsta Bitch"—Apache (Tommy Boy, 1992)
5. "Get Down (Q-Tip Remix)"—Craig Mack featuring Q-Tip (Bad Boy, 1995)
6. "Give Up The Goods (Just Step)"—Mobb Deep featuring Big Noyd (Loud, 1995)
7. "Got 'Til It's Gone (Ummah's Uptown Saturday Night Mix)"—Janet Jackson featuring Q-Tip (Virgin promo, 1997)
8. "Honey (Bad Boy Remix)"—Mariah Carey featuring The Lox & Ma$e (Columbia, 1997)*
9. "Illusions (Q-Tip Remix)"—Cypress Hill (Columbia, 1996)
10. "K.I.S.S."—Diamond D (Chemistry, 1992)
11. "One Love"—Nas (Columbia, 1994)
12. "On The Road Again (Q-Tip Remix)"—Jungle Brothers (Warner Bros. promo, 1993)
13. "Sometimes (The Ummah Remix)"—Brand New Heavies featuring Q-Tip (Delicious Vinyl, 1997)
14. "Temperature's Rising"—Mobb Deep (Loud, 1995)
15. "Who Planned It"—Tiger featuring Q-Tip (CHAOS, 1993)
16. "The World Is Yours (Tip Mix)"—Nas (Columbia, 1994)

*Uncredited.

POTHOLES IN MY ALBUM:
17 Bumpy Songs On Otherwise Bumpin' L.P.s.

1. "The Bomb": *AmeriKKKa's Most Wanted*—Ice Cube (Priority, 1990)
2. "Chinese Arithmetic": *Paid In Full*—Eric B. & Rakim (4th & B'way, 1987)
3. "Closer": *The War Report*—Capone-N-Noreaga (Penalty, 1997)
4. "Club Scene": *Youngest In Charge*—Special Ed (Profile, 1989)
5. "Confused": *Stunts, Blunts & Hip Hop*—Diamond D (Chemistry, 1992)
6. "Every Ghetto, Every City": *The Miseducation Of Lauryn Hill*—Lauryn Hill (Columbia, 1998)
7. "Let's Get Crazy": *The Great Adventures Of Slick Rick*—Slick Rick (Def Jam, 1988)
8. "Mamacita": *Aquemini*—OutKast (LaFace, 1998)
9. "Officer": *The Bizarre Ride II The Pharcyde*—The Pharcyde (Delicious Vinyl, 1992)
10. "Powaful Impak!": *Enta Da Stage*—Black Moon (Nervous, 1993)
11. "Psychobetabuckdown": *Cypress Hill*—Cypress Hill (Ruffhouse, 1991)
12. "Respect": *Ready To Die*—The Notorious B.I.G. (Bad Boy, 1994)
13. "She Knowz What She Wantz": *Moment Of Truth*—Gang Starr (Noo Trybe, 1998)
14. "To Be Your Man": *It's A Big Daddy Thing*—Big Daddy Kane (Cold Chillin', 1989)
15. "Try To Do Me": *One For All*—Brand Nubian (Elektra, 1990)
16. "Who Am I (What's My Name)?": *Doggystyle*—Snoop Doggy Dogg (Death Row, 1993)
17. "You Had Too Much To Drink": *Unfinished Business*—EPMD (Fresh, 1989)

Hip Hop's Greatest Two-Sided Singles.

1. "Eric B. Is President" b/w "My Melody"—Eric B. & Rakim (Zakia, 1986)
2. "It's Like That" b/w "Sucker MC's"—Run-D.M.C. (Profile, 1983)
3. "The Show" b/w "La Di Da Di"—Doug E. Fresh & The Get Fresh Crew (Reality, 1985)
4. "P.S.K." b/w "Gucci Time"—Schoolly D (Schoolly D, 1985)
5. "My Adidas" b/w "Peter Piper"—Run-D.M.C. (Profile, 1986)
6. "It's My Thing" b/w "You're A Customer"—EPMD (Fresh, 1987)
7. "Public Enemy No. 1" b/w "Timebomb"—Public Enemy (Def Jam, 1987)
8. "New Rap Language" b/w "Love Rap"—Spoonie Gee & Treacherous Three (Enjoy, 1980)
9. "Friends" b/w "Five Minutes Of Funk"—Whodini (Jive, 1984)
10. "Run's House" b/w "Beats To The Rhyme"—Run-D.M.C. (Profile, 1988)
11. "Protect Ya Neck" b/w "Method Man"—Wu-Tang Clan (Loud, 1993)
12. "Jack Of Spades" b/w "I'm Still #1 (Numero Uno Re-Recording)"—Boogie Down Productions (Jive, 1988)
13. "Juicy" b/w "Unbelievable"—The Notorious B.I.G. (Bad Boy, 1994)
14. "Smooth Operator" b/w "Warm It Up, Kane"—Big Daddy Kane (Cold Chillin', 1989)
15. "Just To Get A Rep" b/w "Who's Gonna Take The Weight?"—Gang Starr (Chrysalis, 1990)
16. "Mic Checka (Remix)" b/w "Jussumen (Remix)"—Das EFX (EastWest, 1992)
17. "Big Poppa" b/w "Who Shot Ya?"—The Notorious B.I.G. (Bad Boy, 1995)
18. "Express Yourself" b/w "A Bitch Iz A Bitch"—N.W.A (Ruthless, 1989)
19. "Funky For You" b/w "No Bones In Ice Cream"—Nice & Smooth (Fresh, 1990)
20. "Tramp" b/w "Push It"—Salt-N-Pepa (Next Plateau, 1987)
21. "I Got Cha Opin (Remix)" b/w "Reality (Killing Every Nigga In Sight)"—Black Moon (Nervous, 1994)
22. "Straight Out The Jungle" b/w "The Promo"—Jungle Brothers (Idlers, 1988)
23. "Crossover" b/w "Brothers From Brentwood Long Island"—EPMD (Def Jam, 1992)
24. "8 Million Stories" b/w "AJ Scratch"—Kurtis Blow (Mercury, 1984)
25. "To The Max" b/w "It's My Turn"—Stezo (Fresh, 1989)

PRODUCTION.

I THINK WE NEED BACK-UP:
10 Important Studio Musicians & Bands.

1. **Priest "Soopafly" Brooks**
Although a producer and funky rhyme sayer himself, Brooks is best known for playing keyboards on Tha Dogg Pound's debut and Dr. Dre & Ice Cube's "Natural Born Killaz."

2. **Stevie Blass Griffin**
The microphone God Rakim's brother is the multi-instrumentalist whose skills are best displayed on Eric B. & Rakim's *Paid In Full* and *Follow The Leader* LPs.

3. **Harlem Underground Band**
Paul Winley Records' longtime in-house band (which in the early '70s included a pre-nose job George Benson) kept the grooves live for Afrika Bambaataa's "Zulu Nation Throwdown" records, Tanya Winley's "Vicious Rap" and Paulette & Tanya Winley's "Rapping And Rhyming."

4. **Orange Krush**
The musicians responsible for all of the music not provided by Jam Master Jay's turntable scratches on Run-D.M.C.'s first two albums. This Russell Simmons/Larry Smith nurtured outfit also recorded an influential break-beat record, "Action," featuring future Def Jam signee, vocalist Alyson Williams.

5. **Anton Puchansky**
Bass and guitar man as well as engineer on many classic Large Professor productions, including Main Source's *Breaking Atoms* and Kool G Rap's "Streets Of New York." Puchansky later led the group Sample This.

6. **Pumpkin (a/k/a "King Of The Beat")**
Drummer and bandleader on all the classic Enjoy Records

sessions as well as creator of several later hits on Profile.

7. **Stan The Guitar Man**
Utilized by Dr. Dre extensively during his Ruthless tenure on classic albums from N.W.A, Eazy-E and The D.O.C.

8. **Mike "Crazy Neck" Sims**
Not only does this studio rat's fretwork appear on several Ruthless productions, but his voice can be readily identified portraying crooked police officers and stiff, caucasian radio announcers on N.W.A's *100 Miles And Runnin'* EP and Above The Law's *Livin' Like Hustlers*.

9. **Underground Railroad**
These fixtures in the South Central Los Angeles jazz scene, led by bassist/percussionist JMD, performed as session players for Freestyle Fellowship's 1993 *Innercity Griots* LP and periodically collaborate with other members of the Heavyweights clique.

10. **Wood, Brass & Steel (b/k/a the Sugar Hill Records house band)**
The celebrated rhythm section of guitarist Skip MacDonald, bassist Doug Wimbish (later of Living Colour) and drummer Keith LeBlanc was supplemented by percussionist Ed "Duke Bootee" Fletcher and keyboardists Gary Henry, Duane Mitchell, Reggie Griffin and Jiggs Chase and the horn section Chops. Together, they formed the way 2 fonkay musical basis of all the Sugar Hill Records' old school sides.

MICROPHONE SCHEME: Mikah 9 rips with Underground Railroad, Los Angeles, 1992.

Long-Ass Old School Songs.

1. "Rhapazooty In Blue"—Sicle Cell & Rhapazooty (Showstoppers, 1980), **16:08**
2. "Rappin' And Rocking The House"—Funky 4 + 1 (Enjoy, 1979), **16:00**
3. "Adventures Of Super Rhyme (Rap)"—Jimmy Spicer (Dazz, 1980), **15:30**
4. "Rapper's Delight"—Sugarhill Gang (Sugar Hill, 1979), **15:00**
5. "The Rappin Spree"—The Jazzy Three (New City, 1980), **13:00**
6. "Rhythm Rap Rock"—Count Coolout (Boss, 1980), **12:43**
7. "Do You Like That Funky Beat (Ahh Beat, Beat)"—Kool Kyle The Starchild And The Disco Dolls (Enjoy, 1980), **12:32**
8. "Superappin'"—Grandmaster Flash & The Furious Five (Enjoy, 1979), **12:03**
9. "Philosophy Rappin' Spree"—Super 3 (Delmar International, 1980), **10:59**
10. "Beat Bop"—K-Rob vs. Rammelzee (Tartown, 1983), **10:10**

Long-Ass New School Songs.*

1. "Entropy"—DJ Shadow & The Groove Robbers (SoleSides, 1993), **17:48**
2. "The Session"—The Roots (Remedy, 1993), **12:43**
3. "B-Boy Bouillabaisse"—Beastie Boys (Capitol, 1989), **12:33**
4. "Puffin' On Blunts And Drankin' Tanqueray"—Dr. Dre featuring The Lady Of Rage & Tha Dogg Pound (Death Row, 1992), **12:00**
5. "Do You Hear The Bells"—RZA As Bobby Digital (Gee Street promo, 1998), **11:19**
6. "Bop Gun (One Nation)"—Ice Cube featuring George Clinton (Priority, 1993), **11:05**
7. "A Day Like Any Other"—Siah & Yeshua (Fondle 'Em, 1996), **11:00**
8. "Le Temps"—DJ Krush featuring DJ Cam (Mo' Wax, 1997), **9:36**
9. "A Thug's Love Story (Chapter 1, 2, 3)"—Kool G Rap (Illstreet, 1998), **9:29**
10. "Close The Crackhouse"—Professor X featuring Brother J, Wise Intelligent, Big Daddy Kane, Money B (Digital Underground; Raw Fusion), Shock G & Humpty Hump (Digital Underground), Ex-Girlfriend, Chuck D, Sister Souljah, Freedom Williams, YZ, College Boyz & Two Kings In A Cipher (Polygram, 1993), **9:14**

*Excludes the Too $hort catalog because a lotta his raps are crazy long.

Hip Hop's 25 Greatest Remixes.

1. "Shut 'Em Down (Pete Rock Mix)"—Public Enemy (Def Jam, 1991)
   REMIXED BY: Pete Rock
2. "Paid In Full (Seven Minutes Of Madness)"—Eric B. & Rakim (4th & B'way, 1987)
   REMIXED BY: Coldcut
3. "Play That Beat Mr. DJ (Lesson 1: The Payoff Mix)"—G.L.O.B.E. & Whiz Kid (Mastermix promo, 1983)
   REMIXED BY: Double Dee & Steinski*
4. "Jingling Baby (Remixed And Still Jingling)"—LL Cool J (Def Jam, 1990)
   REMIXED BY: Marley Marl
5. "The Choice Is Yours (Revisited)"—Black Sheep (Mercury, 1991)
   REMIXED BY: Black Sheep
6. "Scenario (Remix)"—A Tribe Called Quest featuring Kid Hood & Leaders Of The New School (Jive, 1992)
   REMIXED BY: A Tribe Called Quest
7. "Poppa Large (East Coast Mix)"—Ultramagnetic MC's (Mercury, 1992)
   REMIXED BY: Da Beatminerz (Ike Lee & Aaron Lyles)
8. "I'm Still #1 (Numero Uno Re-Recording)"—Boogie Down Productions (Jive, 1988)
   REMIXED BY: Ivan "Doc" Rodriguez
9. "Serious (Ceereeus BDP Remix)"—Steady B (Jive, 1988)
   REMIXED BY: KRS-One & Ivan "Doc" Rodriguez
10. "Buddy (Native Tongue Decision)"—De La Soul featuring Jungle Brothers, A Tribe Called Quest & Monie Love (Tommy Boy, 1989)

PRODUCTION.

REMIXED BY: The Mentor And His Three Sons (b/k/a Prince Paul & De La Soul)

11. **"Nappy Heads (Remix)"—Fugees (Ruffhouse, 1994)**
REMIXED BY: Salaam Remi

12. **"One More Chance (Stay With Me Remix)"—The Notorious B.I.G. (Bad Boy, 1995)**
REMIXED BY: Sean "Puffy" Combs & Rashad Smith

13. **"On The Run (Dirty Untouchable Remix)"—Kool G Rap & DJ Polo (Cold Chillin', 1992)**
REMIXED BY: Trackmasters

14. **"Mic Checka (Remix)"—Das EFX (EastWest, 1992)**
REMIXED BY: Chris Charity & Derek Lynch for Solid Scheme Productions

15. **"Caught Up (Remix)"—Chubb Rock featuring Hitman Howie Tee (Select, 1988)**
REMIXED BY: Hitman Howie Tee

16. **"I Got Cha Opin (Remix)"—Black Moon (Nervous, 1994)**
REMIXED BY: Da Beatminerz (Evil Dee & Mr. Walt)

17. **"At Your Own Risk (Old English Mix)"—King Tee (Capitol, 1990)**
REMIXED BY: Marley Marl

18. **"Tonight's Da Night (Remix)"—Redman (Def Jam, 1992)**
REMIXED BY: Reggie Noble

19. **"Yes You May (Remix)"—Lord Finesse featuring Big L (Giant, 1992)**
REMIXED BY: T-Ray

20. **"The Next Level (Nyte Time Mix)"—Show & AG (Payday, 1995)**
REMIXED BY: DJ Premier

21. **"It's A Boy (Remix)"—Slick Rick (Def Jam, 1991)**
REMIXED BY: Large Professor

22. **"Resurrection (Extra P Remix & Large Professor Remix)"—Common (Relativity, 1995)**
REMIXED BY: Large Professor

23. **"That's How It Is (Disseshowedo Mix)"—Casual (Jive, 1993)**
REMIXED BY: Casual

24. **"Soul On Ice (Remix)"—Ras Kass (Priority, 1996)**
REMIXED BY: Diamond D

25. **"Product Of The Environment (Project Remix)"—3rd Bass (Def Jam, 1990)**
REMIXED BY: Marley Marl

*Was originally the winning entry in a remix contest held by Tommy Boy Records.

Greatest Post-Old School Live Performers.

1. KRS-One
2. Run-D.M.C.
3. Doug E. Fresh
4. Public Enemy
5. LL Cool J
6. Fugees
7. The Roots
8. Luke
9. Biz Markie
10. DMX
11. Big Daddy Kane
12. Whodini
13. Beastie Boys
14. Method Man
15. Redman

POPPA WAS A ROLLING STONE:
Daddy-O's Top Tour Memories.

1. **LL's House.**
It was 1987 and Stetsasonic was on tour with Public Enemy, Eric B. & Rakim, Doug E. Fresh, Whodini and LL Cool J. The other tour going on at the time was with Run-D.M.C. and the Beastie Boys. What happened was we were in Atlanta and the two tours had to come together. When we was on the road we were very supportive of each other, so all of us used to watch and support our headliner, which was LL. On this particular night they wouldn't let LL bring his stage set because Run-D.M.C. was gonna headline. LL used to have the giant radio onstage and all of that stuff and he was heated that he couldn't use it. But that night, he busted Run's ass with his show! He didn't like performing on Run's set, so he hurt 'em! And it was the first night I seen him rip his shirt off. I always tell groups to this day that *that* was the epitome of a live performance. Here was an artist who went out on the road every night with mad special effects, but when it came down to it, it was just about him and that microphone.

2. **Ice Ice Baby.**
Another thing that stands out was Ice-T's intro every night when we was on the road with him, Luke, Public Enemy and Hammer. His stage show represented a ghetto block. He had big guys in the back pumpin' weights. Guys on cell phones. Guys shootin' dice. Then when he came out, he would have the mic with the headset—the kind that Janet Jackson uses to rock—and he'd be poppin' a bottle of champagne. In the midst of all this street activity going on on the stage, he'd come out with confetti falling down, doing "Colors." His intro was crazy.

3. **Def Jam In The Motherland.**
We was performing in Senegal for like 90,000 people. What was so ill is that we had to use a translator. At Stet shows, we liked to do a lot of crowd participation stuff. But when we did shows overseas, we couldn't correspond with the audience. This time we were performing with a brother named Robert Aaron who used to play instruments on some of our stuff. He spoke French, so we would tell Robert what we wanted to say and he'd tell the crowd and then the crowd would respond. But what was so ill was that it was such a delayed reaction. You'd say something, then you had to wait a few seconds for 90,000 people to respond.

4. **Miami Bass . . . In Your Face.**
One time we was in Miami for a show with 2 Live Crew. We was doing a sound check and I saw Luke and his boys carrying their 2 Live Crew sign with lights in it. I guess they were trying to get the soundman to display the sign. Now, I don't even remember hearing the man say no, but the next thing I know they was beatin' the shit out of that soundman. And to this day, I don't think that he said no. I still remember duke looking back squealing, "I didn't say anything! I didn't say anything!" I think they told him to put it up and he was just delayed in his action.

5. **Now I'm Gonna Show You How The West Coast Rocks.**
I remember the first time I ever saw N.W.A perform. The tour was us, N.W.A, EPMD and P.E. The first stop was at the Joe Louis Arena in Detroit. N.W.A's show was so dynamic. They all came out with these jail suits and they weren't doing dance steps, but they had syncopated moves that were right to the beat. Yella would start scratching and Cube would just run out there doing "Dope Man" and the whole arena went crazy. It was so dope

BLACK WATCH: Daddy's road warriors in Milwaukee, WI on the Nation Of Millions Tour, December, 8, 1988.

to see them get that support because prior to that me and Chuck D was like the only N.W.A fans. I remember when we was on that LL tour, we would play "Dope Man" on the tour bus and no one was feeling it. We loved that record. And after that night everyone else did too.

6. **International Bell Ringing.**
We did two shows in England to perform "A.F.R.I.C.A.," the song we did for Nelson Mandela, who at the time was still locked up. At the first show at the Brixton Academy in England, the Reverend Jesse Jackson performed the song with us and we brought Winnie Mandela out. That was so emotional and dope.

The next night was the show at Wembley, which held about 80,000 people. It was a huge benefit for Nelson and the artists on the bill were like Paul Young and Natalie Cole—we were the only rap act. We did a good show, but the thing I remember most was coming off stage and the first person to hug us was Denzel Washington. He was like, "That was incredible. You guys were great!" That was our first time meeting him and he was giving us mad props.

7. **Protect Yourself.**
Kedar Massenburg (currently Motown Records' President & CEO) used to manage Stet, but before that he worked for a pharmaceutical company. Now, on the road a lot of cats used to get burnt and catch gonorrhea. So we used to sell them this medicine that was like ampicillin but it was a quicker formula. We used to come off! Kedar gave us a crazy supply. It was a three-pill, three-day formula. It got to the point that cats would be knockin' on our hotel door all the time like, "What's up, you got the stuff?"

8. **Where's The Flavor?**
Back on the LL tour, Stet and P.E. would share a bus. One night we were down south somewhere and we stopped at a truck stop in the middle of the night to get something to eat. We finished eating and we got back on the bus to continue to head to the next town. We were just about to pull off and we looked around and we didn't see Flavor. So I looked at Professor Griff and his face got real crazy. The next thing I know Griff had Flavor in a headlock and was dragging him on the bus. It damn near looked like Flavor was foaming at the mouth and he was mumbling, "Get off me, Griff." Flav got on the bus and he went straight to the back to sit with us. Flav was real mad and he was saying, "Man, I'm quitting tomorrow. I'm quitting, Daddy-O. I'm going home." He ain't quit shit!

Daddy-O was the leader of the original hip hop band, Stetsasonic, who were responsible for such classics as "Go Stetsa I," "Sally" and "Talkin' All That Jazz." While rolling with Rush Productions in the late '80s, the "Odad" and company were on the road more than Willie Nelson, participating in nearly every major rap tour that came to your godforsaken town. Maximum respect.

18 Live-Ass Songs About Performing.

1. "Award Tour"—A Tribe Called Quest featuring Trugoy (De La Soul) (Jive, 1993)
2. "Burnin' Hot In Cali On A Saturday Night"—Latyrx (SoleSides, 1997)
3. "5 Minutes 2 Showtime"—Powerule (Poetic Groove, 1991)
4. "Get N' Paid"—Schoolly D (Schoolly D, 1987)
5. "Hush The Crowd"—J-Live (Raw Shack, 1996)

6. "J.Beez Comin' Through"—Jungle Brothers (Warner Bros., 1989)
7. "Live On Stage"—Roxanne Shanté (Cold Chillin', 1989)
8. "Move The Crowd"—Eric B. & Rakim (4th & B'way, 1987)
9. "No Sleep 'Til Brooklyn"—Beastie Boys (Def Jam, 1986)
10. "Oodles Of O's"—De La Soul (Tommy Boy, 1991)
11. "Raise The Roof"—Public Enemy (Def Jam, 1987)
12. "Rap Promoter"—A Tribe Called Quest (Jive, 1991)
13. "The Show"—Doug E. Fresh & The Get Fresh Crew (Reality, 1985)
14. "Showtime"—Stetsasonic (Tommy Boy, 1988)
15. "Soliloquy Of Chaos"—Gang Starr (Chrysalis, 1992)
16. "Think Not"—Al Tariq (Correct, 1996)
17. "Travel Jam"—Brand Nubian (Elektra, 1992)
18. "What's The Reaction"—Kwest Tha Madd Lad (American, 1996)

FUNKY FRESH IN THE FLESH: Rammellzee rocks the mic while Rock Steady's Kippy D (right) and a fellow b-boy make with the freak-freak at Studio 54, Manhattan, mid-'80s.

FRIDAY 81' HARLEM
OCT. 2
129 LENO

MC Serch's Favorite '80s Hip Hop Venues.*

1. **Hinchcliff Coliseum, NJ**
A real good quality high school football field out in New Jersey. I did three shows there from '85 to '88 and the guy who promoted them used to put on the dopest shows. It would be like BDP, Kid 'N Play, Eric B. & Rakim and Salt-N-Pepa. It was one of those venues you couldn't forget because it was so wack that it was dope. He would have security lined up around the track so that the crowd could only sit in the stands. The stage was at the 40-yard line so cats looked like ants to the audience. But the system was sick. You would get on the mic and it would echo, so it really gave you the sense of what a coliseum show felt like.

2. **Harlem World, Harlem, NY**
There were actually only maybe four spots in the early '80s that had real stages—The Roxy, Area, Devil's Nest and Harlem World. Everything else was like a club that had a makeshift place for you to perform. Harlem World was the most slept-on venue to see a show because of the location and because of the stage set-up. It was so deep in the back and it was also cramped. The shows I saw there were Crash Crew vs. Furious Four battles.

3. **Homebase, Manhattan, NY**
I got to be honest, with the exception of maybe three shows, I never really saw any good shows at The Roxy. There was a spot, though, around the corner from The Roxy. It became a lot of different things, but the last name I remember it being called was Homebase. At that venue in '85, I saw the Bad Boys, Roxanne Shanté, Dr. Jeckyll & Mr. Hyde and Dana Dane all in one night. Great system, small room. You had the stage and then you had the dancefloor and the bar was through an alcove. You got such a great vibe from the spot.

4. **After Midnight, Philadelphia, PA**
This was a roller rink, but after midnight it was a club. It lasted so long that there was a two-month period after the Latin Quarter shut down, that instead of hanging out in New York, we'd make the hour run down to Philly to go to the After Midnight. There were so many great shows going on down there. I remember Public Enemy got on stage one night and tore the building down.

5. **L'Amour's East, Queens, NY**
Another great place to see a show in the '80s, right on Queens Blvd. The Albino Twins used to DJ, Coke La Rock used to DJ. When Red Alert ran the spot from '85 to '88— whooooo! Mikey D, Spyder-D, Eric B. & Rakim, Kid 'N Play, Salt-N-Pepa would just come on stage. They wouldn't even be announced. And it was a great venue. It was literally, you walked in—boom—the bar, and then it felt like a football field where the dancefloor was.

6. **Union Square, Manhattan, NY**
I know a lot of people complain about it, but Union Square was a great place to see a show. The thing that made Union Square so great was that it was another place that actually had a stage, so you had monitors and good sound. The place was so long, that it felt like you were performing in front of 10,000 people. And then you had a balcony, so people were looking over and down. You got good crowd response because the place felt deep. The first time I met Will Smith was at Union Square. I remember watching Jazzy Jeff do his "Bluebird" routine; KRS tearing down the building.

7. **The Red Parrot, Manhattan, NY**
The Red Parrot was cool because it was one of the only spots where you could see the stage from all the way around the club. The dressing room was above it, so you'd go down the

stairs and onto the center of the stage. And I'll never forget Roxanne Shanté coming down those stairs in a long white mink with Biz Markie in a Dapper Dan suit to do "Def Fresh Crew." She was just blazing like you couldn't tell her nothing. The sound was banging there. And because the stage was almost like in the round, the sound would hit you from every angle. It was an egg-shaped venue, so you could literally sit and have a drink at a table and look at the stage because it was originally made to be a jazz venue.

8. **The Palladium, Manhattan, NY**
People really slept on The Palladium as a rap venue. Towards the late '80s, rap shows went on there during the week. I remember one night in particular, it was like transvestite night and Whodini was performing! But it was a great place to see a show. They did the laser backdrops where they had the names behind the groups on stage. The feeling you got when you looked back was like you were looking up to the heavens. The place went on forever with the dance floor being so big and that balcony with all the seats. I remember seeing Eric B. & Rakim do a show there in '87 and it literally felt like there were 20,000 people in there.

9. **Irving Plaza, Manhattan, NY**
'88 to '90 was when Beaver and Patrick Moxey were doing parties there. The DJ set-up was right on the stage and it was one of the few places where the booth was really apparent. With all the other venues, the DJ booth was always off to the side or up top. The Plaza had a real stage right up in front and you had a balcony over the top. That's when the Native Tongues were really blowing up. And you'd see shows with like Tribe and De La and Black Sheep together. Rob Base's first show doing "It

Takes Two" was on that stage. A great all-around venue.

10. **Latin Quarter, Manhattan, NY**
The best venue in the early '80s to see hip hop. Classy venue. You could sit at tables, you could watch from the dance floor, you could watch from the balcony. The sound was always great. There was a high stage, but you had the choice of rocking the high stage or the low stage, whichever way you wanted to go. And because the stage was so high, you truly got star presence. People had to look up to you. That's what really made it great—that pedestal appearance. The first and only time Doug E. Fresh and Biz Mark ever beat-boxed together was there. The KRS vs. Melle Mel battle was there too.

I don't think those things would have been that memorable in hip hop folklore if they didn't happen at the Quarter. If they had happened at the Devil's Nest, it would have been too tight of a venue. The Parrot wasn't the right place to have it because people wouldn't have appreciated it. But because it happened at the Quarter on that stage, it was like watching your idols. And I remember being this undergound emcee who wanted to be on that stage so badly because it made you feel like you were a better person than anyone in there. A bigger person. It was the number one spot to see a show in New York and there's never been another spot like it.

*In no particular order.

MC Serch made steppin' to the a.m. a nightly operation as a fixture of the '80s hip hop club scene. A member of 3rd Bass, he stomped into the '90s with smashes like "The Gas Face" and "Pop Goes The Weasel," cementing his rep as the self-proclaimed "baddest white boy to ever touch the mic."

MOVE THE CROWD PART I:
Official All-The-Way-Live Songs.

1. "The Anatomy Of An Ass Whippin' (Kwest Fucks L-Smooth's Shit Up At NYC MC Battle, 1990)"—Kwest Tha Madd Lad (Ill Labels, 1993)
2. "Back In The Dayz"—Doug E. Fresh & The New Get Fresh Crew (Bust It, 1992)
3. "Black Cop"; "The Bridge Is Over" & "South Bronx Medley"—KRS-One (from *Tibetan Feedom Concert*—Grand Royal, 1997)
4. "Blue Funk"; "Is It Good To You"; "The Overweight Lover's In The House" & "Yes Y'all"—Heavy D (from *Uptown Unplugged*—Uptown, 1993)
5. "Brand New Funk (Live At Nassau Coliseum)"—DJ Jazzy Jeff & The Fresh Prince (Jive, 1988)
6. "Cocaine (Live)"—MC Shan (Cold Chillin', 1986)
7. "Compton's In The House (Live)"—N.W.A (Ruthless, 1996)
8. "Flash To The Beat"—Grandmaster Flash & The Furious Five (Bozo Meko, 1982)
9. "Fu-Gee-La"—Fugees (from *Tibetan Freedom Concert*—Grand Royal, 1997)
10. "Here We Go (Live At The Funhouse)"—Run-D.M.C. (Profile, 1985)
11. "Killing Me Softly With His Song (Live At The Brixton Academy)"—Fugees (Ruffhouse, 1996)

12. "Let Me Clear My Throat (Old School Reunion Remix)"—DJ Kool featuring Biz Markie & Doug E. Fresh (American, 1996)
13. "Life Is Too Short (Live In Oakland, 1990)"—Too $hort (Jive, 1990)
14. "Live At Tramps (July 11, '97)"—Ultramagnetic MC's (Next Plateau, 1997)
15. "Live At Union Square (November, 1986)"—DJ Jazzy Jeff & The Fresh Prince (Jive, 1988)
16. "Me & My Bitch (Live From Philly)"—The Notorious B.I.G. (from *The Show* Soundtrack—Def Jam, 1995)
17. "Me, Myself And I"—De La Soul (from *Tibetan Freedom Concert*—Grand Royal, 1997)
18. "Nobody Beats The Biz" & "Star Spangled Banner"—Biz Markie (from *Tibetan Freedom Concert*—Grand Royal, 1997)
19. "Oh My God"—A Tribe Called Quest (from *Tibetan Freedom Concert*—Grand Royal, 1997)
20. "One Night Stand" & "Pimp Or Die"—Father MC (from *Uptown Unplugged*—Uptown, 1993)
21. "O.P.P. (Live)"—Naughty By Nature (Tommy Boy, 1991)
22. "Pharcyde Live At Dodger Stadium"—The Pharcyde

LIVE!

(Delicious Vinyl, 1993)*

23. "Proceed II (Live Version With Joe Sample & Phil Woods)"—The Roots featuring Roy Ayers (from *Stolen Moments: Red Hot & Cool*—GRP, 1994)
24. "Punk-Bitch Game"—Geto Boys (Rap-A-Lot, 1991)
25. "Put That Head Out (Live At Danceteria)"—Funk Master Wizard Wiz (Tuff City, 1984)
26. "Root Down"—Beastie Boys (from *Tibetan Freedom Concert*—Grand Royal, 1997)
27. "The Rubbers Song (Live Version With Members Of Groove Collective)"—The Pharcyde (GRP, 1994)
28. "2nd Quarter—Free Throws"—KRS-One (Jive, 1997)
29. "Wrath of Kane (Live)"—Big Daddy Kane (Cold Chillin', 1989)
30. "Yvette (Live At Danceteria)"—Cold Crush Brothers (Tuff City, 1989)

*Recorded live, but not really at Dodger Stadium.

Official All-The-Way-Live Albums.

1. *The Cold Crush Brothers Live In '82*—Cold Crush Brothers (Tuff City, 1994)
2. *Cold Crush Brothers vs. Fantastic Romantic 5*—DJ Charlie Chase (Slammin', 1998)
3. *Death Mix Live!*—Afrika Bambaataa (Paul Winley, 1983)
4. *Extremely Live*—Vanilla Ice (SBK, 1991)
5. *Illstyle Live*—Music From The Elektra Entertainment Group (EastWest, 1995)
6. *Live Convention '81*—Various Artists (Disco Wax, 1981)
7. *Live Convention '82*—Various Artists (Disco Wax, 1982)
8. *Live Hardcore Worldwide*—Boogie Down Productions (Jive, 1991)
9. *Live In Concert*—2 Live Crew (Effect, 1990)
10. *Rap Archives: Vol. 1*—Various Artists (Urban London, 1996)
11. *Root Down EP*—Beastie Boys (Grand Royal, 1995)*
12. *Survival Of The Illest*—Various Artists (Def Jam, 1998)
13. *Unplugged*—Arrested Development (Reprise, 1992)
14. *Wild Style* Soundtrack—Various Artists (Animal, 1983)

*Tracks 1 through 3 are studio remixes. tracks 4 through 10 were recorded live in Germany.

Jon Shecter's Live Show Rules.

1. **Keep Everything Live.**
   A live DJ is an essential part of any live show—he or she must control the flow of the set by making the transitions smooth and livening up the party with cutting skills and exciting drops. Rappers: if you don't have a talented live DJ, you will inherently suck when you get on stage. Bottom line: there is no room for a pre-recorded show in hip hop—it simply goes against the basis of the artform itself.

2. **Don't Blame The Sound Man.**
   For any rappers doing this, I have news for you—you look like assholes. We know the messed-up sound isn't your fault, so be constructive about it. If a mic isn't working, stop

   the show, point out the problem and fix it (this is another problem with using a DAT—you can't pause the performance if something goes wrong). If it still doesn't run right, work around it.

3. **Organize.**
   Look, we're usually paying money to see you perform, the least you can do is take some time and put together a nice little show. We're not looking for much—just a dope routine, your hits, maybe a couple of freestyles and then you're outta there. Keep the show exciting and consider adding elements to make the performance more lively. Dancers are okay, especially if they're female and sexy. Above all else, put in

LIVE!

some rehearsal time; this is your job as an artist.

4. **Give The People What They Want.**
The rap audience is notoriously short-sighted and unfaithful. Understand that hip hop crowds primarily want to hear things that they're familiar with. That means rappers should primarily stick to their hits when setting up a show. If you're a new artist you can still do a new single, but strongly consider using familiar instrumentals or breakbeats for any other rhyming that takes place. By no means should you launch into three or four completely new cuts—that's absolutely too much new material for the crowd to digest.

5. **Most Of All, Entertain!**
Surprise us, bring out a guest emcee—the wilder the combination the better. One way to make the crowd jump like mad is to perform a hot posse cut. Finally, don't forget the old show biz adage, "Leave them wanting more." Stopping your set at the height of the energy will leave the crowd mad charged.

Jon Shecter (a/k/a "J The Sultan") is the founding editor of The Source *magazine and currently the CEO of Game Records. A true hip hop connoisseur with a low tolerance for wackness, he is a white man who commands any crowd with his wisdom. New jack performers, study your lessons.*

Important Los Angeles Hip Hop Clubs.

1. **Uncle Jam's Army**
   This massive, mobile electro hip hop party commenced in 1980 as Unique Dreams under the helm of Rodger Clayton and some neighborhood friends, and remained one of Los Angeles' largest dance gatherings for years. It had the ability to attract big name acts such as Run-D.M.C. to perform all-ages shows at major venues like the L.A. Sports Arena and the Shrine Auditorium. Its name was inspired by Funkadelic's *Uncle Jam Wants You* LP.

2. **Eve's After Dark**
   Producer Lonzo Williams, founder of The World Class Wrekin' Cru (a group composed of Dr. Dre, DJ Yella, rappers Cli 'N Tel and others), ran this popular club which boasted the talents of the Cru's DJs and a largely teenaged audience. Williams later sold the club to get into the record game.

3. **World On Wheels**
   An extremely popular roller skating rink in midtown that doubled as a blue-collar, Crip-friendly club and featured frequent live performances by established acts.

4. **Skateland USA**
   This Compton equivalent to World On Wheels may have been home turf to the Bloods, but like WOW, served as a prime recruiting ground for KDAY's future Mixmaster DJs.

5. **Radio (a/k/a Radiotron, under different management)**
   Established circa 1982, this East Coast-flavored spot was based on New York's famed Roxy, which at the time was enjoying its own success. Pioneers such as Rhyme Syndicate members Afrika Islam and Hen-Gee & Evil-E as well as popular Zulu Nation DJ, Grandmixer

LIVE!

D.ST, helped introduce New York rap to The City Of Angels. Under such guidance, this was the perfect refuge for Los Angeles' burgeoning b-boy crews.

6. **United Nations At Mr. J's**
Early '90s New York-style hip hop party closely associated with Ice-T's Rhyme Syndicate organization and Delicious Vinyl Records. Later known as Water The Bush at former bank turned nightclub, Hollywood Live.

7. **Jamaica House**
Recognized as one of L.A.'s longest-running parties, this roving jam was hosted by Howard Lynch and David Fergurson, the fine folks who brought the world Paperboy. Among the upscale, downtown venues that housed Jamaica House were Vertigo (later known as the Prince-owned Glam

Slam) and the elegant, landmark theater, The Mayan.

8. **Good Life**
A health food store located on Crenshaw Boulevard by day, this setting was converted into curse-free open mic performances on Thursday evenings. It was not only the launching pad for self-proclaimed "True School" emcees such as Freestyle Fellowship, Urban Prop and Volume 10, but some of the key figures to emerge from here went back underground to start the similarly themed Project Blowed.

9. **Unity**
An enduring, roving showcase for big-name and local rap talent, Unity—commandeered by behind-the-scenes man of many hats, Bigga B—provided the chance for underground heads to catch their favorite acts in a gangsta-free atmosphere.

mackey travel ltd.

RAISING HELL WORLD TOUR 1986

Wednesday	August 6	Grand Rapids,MI	Welsh Auditorium	Amway Plaza Hotel
Thursday	August 7	Saginaw,MI	Civic Center	Florentine Inn
Friday	August 8	Detroit,MI	Joe Louis Arena	Hyatt Regency
Saturday	August 9	Toledo,OH	Toledo Sports Arena	Hyatt Regency
Sunday	August 10	Detroit,MI	Joe Louis Arena	Hyatt Regency
Monday	August 11	DAY OFF	NO SHOW	NO HOTEL
Tuesday	August 12	DAY OFF	NO SHOW	NO HOTEL
Wednesday	August 13	DAY OFF	NO SHOW	NO HOTEL
Thursday	August 14	San Bernadino,CA	Orange Pavillion	Franklin Plaza Suites
Friday	August 15	Fresno,CA	Selland Arena	Fresno Hilton
Saturday	August 16	Oakland,CA	Coliseum	Hyatt Regency
Sunday	August 17	Long Beach,CA	Arena	Franklin Plaza Suites
Monday	August 18	Los Angeles,CA	Palladium	Franklin Plaza Suites
Tuesday	August 19	Los Angeles,CA	NO SHOW	Franklin Plaza Suites
Wednesday	* August 20	West Palm Beach,FL	T.B.A.	Hyatt Palm Beaches
Thursday	August 21	Greenville,SC	Memorial Auditorium	Hyatt Regency
Friday	August 22	Columbia,SC	Carolina Coliseum	Radisson Hotel Columbia
Saturday	August 23	Charlotte,NC	Coliseum	Marriott Hotel
Sunday	August 24	Macon,GA	Coliseum	Hilton Hotel
Monday	August 25	DAY OFF	NO SHOW	NO HOTEL
Tuesday	August 26	DAY OFF	NO SHOW	NO HOTEL
Wednesday	August 27	DAY OFF	NO SHOW	NO HOTEL
Thursday	August 28	Providence,RI	Civic Center	Marriott Hotel
Friday	August 29	Nassau,NY	Nassau Coliseum	NO HOTEL
Saturday	August 30	Largo,MD	Captiol Center	Holiday Inn Greenbelt

TO BE CONTINUED.....

* Run DMC/Beastie Boys show only!

LIVE!

Chris Lighty's Road Manager Rules To Live By.

1. **Don't Drink Or Get High With The Group.**

2. **Get Your Group Out Of Town The Night Before You're Supposed To Leave.**
   If you're not in town for the after party to get in trouble, you won't get in trouble. This means your group's game has to be tight because you're leaving out at two or three in the morning. Especially if you're the tour's opening or middle act, don't break night at the hotel. Be the first act in the next town so you can headline next year.

3. **Get Your Group To Places On Time.**
   This means if the wake-up time is 7 a.m., you have to be up by 5 a.m. You'll quickly learn it takes at least an hour-and-a-half to two hours to get any group moving.

4. **You Gotta Have A Psychiatry Major.**

5. **You Must Lie.**
   Sometimes it's your only option.

6. **Find Out Who In The Group Is The Traveling Leader.**
   Remember, whoever is the leader on record may not be the traveling leader. Notice who's waking up quicker and use him to help keep the others in line.

7. **You Have To Watch *Star Wars*, *The Empire Strikes Back* And *Return Of The Jedi* And Learn Jedi Mind Tricks.**
   Nine out of ten artists don't wanna go to radio or retail, but you gotta get them there anyway. If you trick them right, the groups will eventually come to you and be like, "What are we doing tomorrow?" If you do your job well, then they'll begin to rely on you to make all their moves for them. They won't move unless you move.

8. **Develop An Immunity To Lack Of Sleep.**

9. **Be Careful About What You Eat On The Road.**
   When outside of America, learn to read and find the basics. When I was in Europe, I survived on bread and water. Don't be afraid to hire a chef on the road. Bite the bullet and pay the extra money. Fast food's too dangerous. The only mainstay that's probably a safe bet is Mickey D's.

10. **When Staying At Hotels, Don't Forget The Concierges.**
    It's their job to help you. They can help you find a restaurant *and* get your laundry clean.

11. **When Doing A Show, Don't Bring Your Group To The Venue Until You Have Your Money.**
    I wouldn't come down to the venue unless I got half upfront and half before I brought the group in the building.

12. **Get The Group To Focus On Money And Not Girls.**
    Every now and then you gotta say shit like, "Yeah, remember those rape charges L and them niggas caught?" and "This guy got arrested and they locked him up." You gotta bring up the foul shit every now and then. Be prepared to be the bad guy.

Before becoming big willie CEO of Violator Records and Violator Management, "Baby" Chris Lighty got his rep as the tough-nosed, ever-efficient R-M for the Jungle Brothers. A key figure at Red Alert Productions, he coordinated tours with the JB's, A Tribe Called Quest, Brand Nubian and De La Soul.

Is It Live?

1. Ant Live (Kool G Rap)
2. Channel Live
3. Cooly Live
4. J-Live
5. Live Squad
6. Mr. Live
7. Real Live
8. 2 Live Crew

Top 10 Things Most Commonly Banned From Hip Hop Clubs.

10. Guns.
9. Knives.
8. Razor blades.
7. Sneakers.
6. Timberlands.
5. Puffy coats.*
4. Baseball caps.
3. Puerto Ricans/Dominicans.
2. Baggy jeans.
1. Niggas.

*Not to be confused with Sean "Puffy" Combs, who always gets love up in the clubs.

NAM

MES.

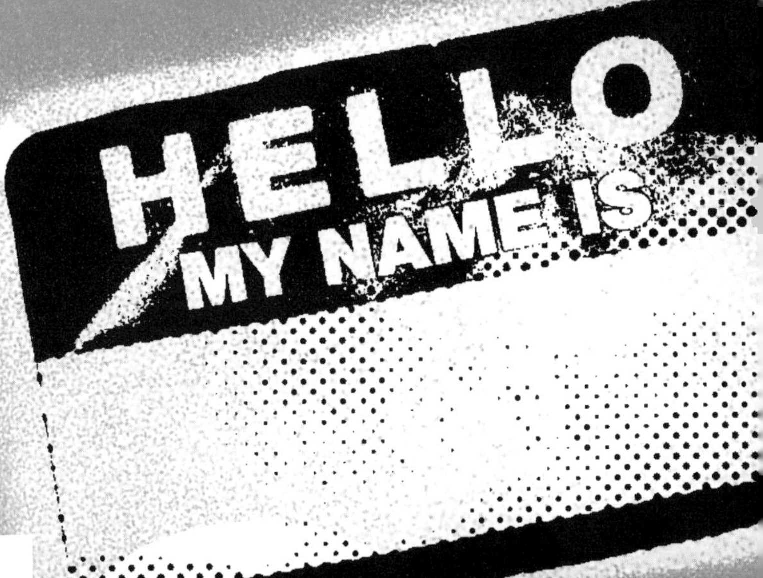

Countdown.

10. Mack 10; Ten Theives; Volume 10
9. K-9 Posse; Mikah 9 (Freestyle Fellowship); Nine
8. MC Eiht; Eightball; 8-Off
7. Mark 7 (Jurassic 5)
6. 06 Style; Three 6 Mafia
5. Fab 5 Freddy; Fantastic Five; Furious Five; The Jazzy 5; Jurassic 5; Rappermatical 5
4. Awesome Foursome; Disco Four; Fearless Four; Gifted 4; Just Four
3. Chapter Three; Disco 3; Fantasy Three; Fresh 3 MC's; The Jazzy Three; The Maximus Three; Nice & Nasty 3; Rockmaster Scott & The Dynamic Three; Super 3; Three Times Dope; 3XKrazy; Treacherous Three; Ultimate 3 MC's
2. Audio Two; Awesome Two; Classical Two; N2Deep; Spanish Fly & The Terrible Two; 2-Bigg MC; Two Kings In A Cipher; 2 Live Crew; 2 Much; 2Pac; II Tru
1. KRS-One; Main One; Spice 1; Tame One (Artifacts)

BONUS: 3rd Bass; 3-2; 4th Disciple; Funky 4 + 1; 5th 40 Thevz; 45 Ward Boyz; 6-7 (Hard 2 Obtain); 7A3; E-40; King; 60 Sec. Assassin; The 69 Boyz; Ninety-9; Cold 187um; Oaktown's 3.5.7.

Hi, My First Emcee Name Was . . .

1. Big Moon Dog—Big Punisher
2. Chill-O-Ski—Busta Rhymes
3. Kid Wizard—Rakim
4. MC Love Child—Q-Tip
5. MC New York—2Pac
6. Paul Juice—Large Professor

THE MEANING OF THE NAME:
How 10 Artists Received Their Rap Monikers.

1. **Busta Rhymes**
Chuck D dubbed his Long Island protégé after Oklahoma college football star Buster Rhymes.

2. **C-Bo**
Short for "Cowboy."

3. **DMX**
New York's top rap dawg originally built his rep on his Yonkers home turf as a human beat box, taking his name as a funky homosapien answer to the classic DMX beatmaking drum machine—much like Just-Ice's mid-'80s beat-box sidekick, "Cool" DMX. Wow, what a coincidence!

4. **E-40**
Named for his ability to drink four to five 40 oz. bottles of malt liquor a day.

5. **Grandmixer D.ST**
An abbreviation of the Lower East Side's Delancey Street, where it was joked he used to boost clothes from shops.

6. **Khujo (Goodie Mob)**
Named himself after an African slave who was granted his freedom after being illegally shipped to the United States.

7. **LL Cool J**
Stole his name from DJ Cut Creator (Jay Philpott), then known as "Cool Jay."

8. **Noreaga**
Named after Panamanian ruler General Manuel Noriega.

9. **DJ Quik**
Quik is the name. But the "C" (as in Crip) was allegedly left out due to this real Compton G's reputed one-time Blood gang affiliation.

10. **Ras Kass**
Inspired by a book about Menelik II, an Ethiopian king who battled a rival named Ras Kass for control of the kingdom of Shoa. That Ras Kass used the alias for his real name, John IV. Rapper Rass' government name is John and he is also the fourth John in his family.

NAMES.

A.A.A.:
Amazing Artist Acronyms.

1. Big Daddy Kane—King Asiatic Nobody's Equal
2. B.O.X.—Beyond Ordinary X-istence
3. DL (Hard 2 Obtain)—Down Low
4. D.M.C.—Darryl Mac; Devastating Mic Controller
5. DMX—Dark Man of the Unknown
6. DV Alias Christ—Deep Voice
7. MC Eiht—Experienced In Hardcore Thumpin'
8. Guru—Gifted Unlimited Rhymes Universal
9. Ja Rule—Jeff Atkins Represents Unconditional Love's Existence
10. J.D.L. (Cold Crush Brothers)—Jerry D. Lewis
11. Kool G Rap—Kool Genius of Rap
12. KRS-One—Knowledge Reigns Supreme Over Nearly Everyone
13. K-Solo—Kevin Self Organization Left Others
14. LL Cool J—Ladies Love Cool James
15. Memphis Bleek—Makin' Easy Money Pimpin' Hoes In Style
16. Mr. Serv On—Surviving Every Rugged Vendetta On Me
17. N.A.R.D. (Do Or Die)—Niggas Ain't Ready to Die
18. P.A. Mase (De La Soul)—Public Announcer Making A Soulful Effort
19. The PreC.I.S.E. M.C.—Pre-beginning Change of Interest in Sister Effectiveness
20. Tash—Tough Ass Son of Harold
21. MC Twist—Talking With Innovative Street Terminology

G.A.M.E.:
Group Acronyms Made Easy.

1. The Afros—A Funky Rhythmical Organization of Sound
2. Almighty RSO—Rock Shit On; Real Strong Organization
3. ALT & The Lost Civilization—Another Latin Timebomb
4. ATBAN Clan (b/k/a Black Eyed Peas)—A Tribe Beyond A Nation
5. Beastie Boys—Boys Entering Anarchistic States Towards Internal Excellence
6. Black Moon—Brothers Lyrically Acting Combined Kicking Music Out On Nations
7. BWP—Bytches (Beautiful Young Talented College Honeys) With Problems
8. Ed O.G & Da BULLDOGS—Every Day Other Girls & Da Black United Leaders Living Directly Off Grooving Sounds
9. Goodie Mob—The Good Die Mostly Over Bullshit
10. J.J. Fad—Just Jammin' Fresh And Def
11. Junior M.A.F.I.A.—Masters At Finding Intelligent Attitudes
12. J.V.C. Force—Justified by Virtue of Creating For Obvious Reasons Concerning Entertainment
13. K.M.D.—Kausin' Much Damage; a positive Kause in a Much Damaged society
14. The Lox—Living Off X-perience
15. P.A.—Parental Advisory
16. TRU—The Real Untouchables
17. U.N.L.V.—Uptown Niggas Living Violent
18. U.T.F.O.—Untouchable Force Organization
19. WC And The MAAD Circle—Minority Alliance of Anti-Discrimination; Muthafuckas Armed And Down
20. Wu-Tang Clan—We Usually Take All Niggas' Garments; Witty Unpredictable Talent And Natural Game
21. Yaggfu Front—You Are Gonna Get Fucked Up If You Front

Original Names Of 15 Rap Groups.

1. Band Aid Boys—Bone Thugs-N-Harmony
2. Disco Construction—The World Class Wrekin' Cru
3. DVX—Cypress Hill
4. Easy Street—De La Soul
5. High Tech—Black Moon
6. The Houserockers Crew—Fearless Four
7. The KA's—Sugarhill Gang
8. The LD's; Force MC's—Force MD's
9. New Crew—Main Source
10. Poetical Prophets—Mobb Deep
11. Simply Too Positive (S.T.P.)—Organized Konfusion
12. Square Roots—The Roots
13. 3 The Hard Way—3rd Bass
14. 2 Shades Deep; Misfits Of The Outback—OutKast
15. The Warlocks—The Lox

20 Wack Album Titles.

1. *Album With No Name*—Redhead Kingpin & The F.B.I. (Virgin, 1991)
2. *Attitude: A Hip Hop Rapsody*—Shazzy (Elektra, 1990)
3. *Dearest Christian, I'm So Very Sorry For Bringing You Here. Love, Dad*—PM Dawn (Gee Street, 1998)
4. *Dropping Soulful H2O On The Fiber*—Gumbo (Chrysalis, 1993)
5. *Endtroducing . . .*—DJ Shadow (Mo' Wax, 1996)
6. *From Where???*—Mad Skillz (Big Beat, 1996)
7. *Hello Nasty*—Beastie Boys (Grand Royal, 1998)
8. *Illegal Drugs Really Hurt*—FaceDown (Big Beat, 1991)
9. *Life In 1472*—Jermaine Dupri (So So Def, 1998)
10. *Look Ma Duke, No Hands*—Madkap (Loud, 1993)
11. *Naaah, Dis Kid Can't Be From Canada?!!*—Maestro Fresh Wes (LMR, 1994)
12. *People's Instinctive Travels And The Paths Of Rhythm*—A Tribe Called Quest (Jive, 1990)
13. *Reachin' (A New Refutation Of Time And Space)*—Digable Planets (Pendulum, 1993)
14. *Scout's Honor . . . By Way Of Blood*—Rampage (Elektra, 1997)
15. *Spiral Walls Containing Autumns Of Life*—Divine Styler (Giant, 1992)
16. *Suburban Etiquette*—Anttex (Tuff City, 1991)
17. *Take A Look Over Your Shoulder (Reality)*—Warren G (Def Jam, 1997)
18. *Theme + Echo = Krill*—The Legion (Mercury, 1994)
19. *Where's My Receipt?*—Dazzie Dee (Capitol, 1996)
20. *Zingalamaduni*—Arrested Development (Chrysalis, 1994)

ORIGINAL CONCEPTS:
Rejected Titles Of 20 Rap Albums.

1. **America's Most Blunted—Cypress Hill**
   RELEASED AS: *Cypress Hill* (Ruffhouse, 1991)

2. **And The Band Played On—Stetsasonic**
   RELEASED AS: *Blood, Sweat & No Tears* (Tommy Boy, 1991)

3. **Black Little Bastards—Illegal**
   RELEASED AS: *The Untold Truth* (Rowdy, 1993)

4. **Black Rage—Intelligent Hoodlum**
   RELEASED AS: *Tragedy—Saga Of A Hoodlum* (Tuff Break, 1993)

5. **Don't Be A Faggot—Beastie Boys**
   RELEASED AS: *Licensed To Ill* (Def Jam, 1986)

6. **Eargasms—The Lady Of Rage**
   RELEASED AS: *Necessary Roughness* (Death Row, 1997)

7. **Flavortism—The Sophomoric Effort—Diamond D**
   RELEASED AS: *Hatred, Passions And Infidelity* (Mercury, 1997)

8. **Hell Up In Harlem—Puff Daddy & The Family**
   RELEASED AS: *No Way Out* (Bad Boy, 1997)

9. **I'm Coming Agg—Scarface**
   RELEASED AS: *The World Is Yours* (Rap-A-Lot, 1993)

10. **Just When You Thought It Was Over—Nice & Smooth**
    RELEASED AS: *Jewel Of The Nile* (RAL, 1994)

11. **The Last Original Nigga—Coolio**
    RELEASED AS: *It Takes A Thief* (Tommy Boy, 1994)

12. **Niggamortis—Gravediggaz***
    RELEASED AS: *6 Feet Deep* (Gee Street, 1994)

13. **Pin The Tail On The Honky—Da Lench Mob**
    RELEASED AS: *Guerillas In Tha Mist* (Street Knowledge, 1992)

14. **Revelations—The Pharcyde**
    RELEASED AS: *Labcabincalifornia* (Delicious Vinyl, 1995)

NAMES.

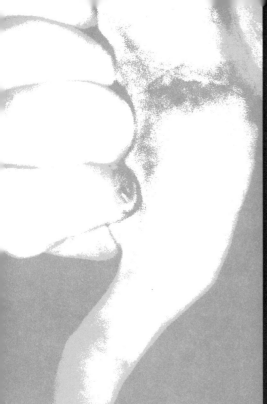

20 Great Album Titles

1. *AmeriKKKa's Most Wanted*—Ice Cube (Priority, 1990)
2. *ATLiens*—OutKast (LaFace, 1996)
3. *De La Soul Is Dead*—De La Soul (Tommy Boy, 1991)
4. *Doggystyle*—Snoop Doggy Dogg (Death Row, 1993)
5. *Fear Of A Black Planet*—Public Enemy (Def Jam, 1990)
6. *Fuck New York*—Rodney O & Joe Cooley (Psychotic, 1992)
7. *Genocide & Juice*—The Coup (Wild Pitch, 1994)
8. *The Ghetto's Tryin' To Kill Me*—Master P (No Limit, 1993)
9. *KKKill The Fetus*—Esham (Reel Life, 1993)
10. *Music To Driveby*—Compton's Most Wanted (Orpheus, 1992)
11. *My Balls And My Word*—Young Bleed (No Limit, 1998)
12. *Operation Stackola*—Luniz (Noo Trybe, 1995)
13. *Rhyme Pays*—Ice-T (Sire, 1987)
14. *Runaway Slave*—Show & AG (Payday, 1992)
15. *Sellin' Cocaine As Usual*—Young "D" Boyz (River T, 1994)
16. *Smile Now, Die Later*—Kid Frost (Ruthless, 1995)
17. *Stunts, Blunts & Hip Hop*—Diamond D (Chemistry, 1992)
18. *Vagina Diner*—Akinyele (Interscope, 1993)
19. *www.thug.com*—Trick Daddy (Slip N Slide, 1998)
20. *Your Entertainment, My Reality*—Poppa LQ (Rap-A-Lot, 1995)

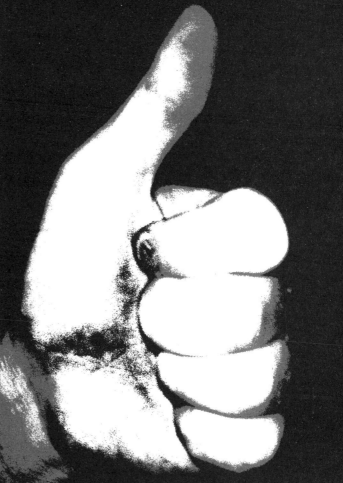

15. **Save The Children**—Eric B. & Rakim
RELEASED AS: *Don't Sweat The Technique* (MCA, 1992)

16. **Smithsonian**—LL Cool J
RELEASED AS: *Mr. Smith* (Def Jam, 1995)

17. **Starved Bandit**—DJ Quik
RELEASED AS: *Safe + Sound* (Profile, 1995)

18. **Still Standing**—Run-D.M.C.
RELEASED AS: *Down With The King* (Profile, 1993)

19. **Three The Hard Way**—Onyx
RELEASED AS: *All We Got Iz Us* (Def Jam, 1995)

20. **We Fell Into A Bottle Of Plastic Shwingalokate, So We Opened A Radio Station**—De La Soul
RELEASED AS: *De La Soul Is Dead* (Tommy Boy, 1991)

*Released with original title in Europe—land of progressive fucks.

1. CAPPADONNA:
CAPPACHINO THE GREAT;
CAPPA DONNA GOINES; CAPPA-RAY;
DONNA JAY BIRD;
POPPI WARDROBE KING

2. THE GENIUS:
GZA; MAXIMILLION

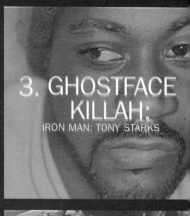

3. GHOSTFACE KILLAH:
IRON MAN; TONY STARKS

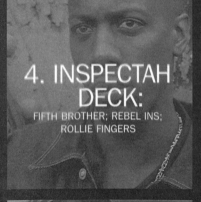

4. INSPECTAH DECK:
FIFTH BROTHER; REBEL INS;
ROLLIE FINGERS

5. MASTA KILLA:
HIGH CHIEF; NOODLES

6. METHOD MAN:
HOTT NIKKELS; IRON LUNG;
JOHN JOHN McCLANE; JOHNNY BLAZE;
JOHNNY DANGEROUS; METHICAL;
THE PANTY RAIDER; SHA-KWON; TICAL;
TICALLION STALLION

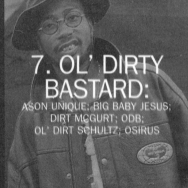

7. OL' DIRTY BASTARD:
ASON UNIQUE; BIG BABY JESUS;
DIRT McGURT; ODB;
OL' DIRT SCHULTZ; OSIRUS

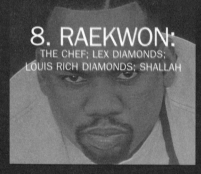

8. RAEKWON:
THE CHEF; LEX DIAMONDS;
LOUIS RICH DIAMONDS; SHALLAH

9. RZA:
THE ABBOTT; BOBBY DIGITAL;
BOBBY STEELS; PRINCE RAKEEM;
RZARECTA

Wu-Tang Killer Aliases.

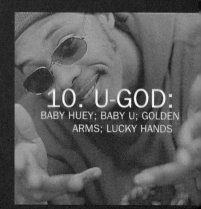

10. U-GOD:
BABY HUEY; BABY U; GOLDEN
ARMS; LUCKY HANDS

HELLO MY NAME IS

NAMES.

98 ego trip's book of rap lists. ⭐ upon a plateau no mortal can go...

Names Inspired By Characters From Comic Strips, Comic Books & Cartoons.

1. Big Punisher
2. Chali 2na (Jurassic 5)
3. Charlie Brown (Leaders Of The New School)
4. DJ Clark Kent
5. Crazy Toones (The MAAD Circle)
6. Dr. Octagon
7. Dr. Seuss (Madkap)
8. Fresh Gordon
9. Grandmaster Flash
10. Grand Puba
11. Johnny Blaze (Method Man)
12. Kurious [Jorge]
13. Magoo
14. McGruff
15. Pebblee-Poo
16. Plastic Man
17. Pop The Brown Hornet (G.P. Wu)
18. Professor X
19. Q-Bert (Invisibl Skratch Piklz)
20. Richie Rich
21. Scoob Lover
22. Scrap Lover
23. DJ Smurf
24. Snagglepuss
25. Snoop Doggy Dogg
26. Sugar Bear
27. Tony Starks (Ghostface Killah)
28. The X-Men
29. Yogi (Cru)
30. Yukmouth

Rap Artists With The Same Names.

1. Afrika Bambaataa—Afrika Baby Bam (Jungle Brothers)
2. A-Plus (Hieroglyphics)—A Plus (Wreckx-N-Effect)—A+
3. AZ—AZ (Mob Style)
4. MC Breeze—Breeze The Singing MC—Breez Evahflowin'
5. Cam'Ron—Kamron (Young Black Teenagers)
6. DJ Clark Kent (Producer)—Clark Kent (Herculords)
7. Def Jef—DJ Deff Jeff (Almighty RSO)
8. DMX—DMX (Just-Ice's beat box)
9. Donald D (The B-Boys; Rhyme Syndicate)—Donald D ("Don's Groove")
10. Dr. Dre—Doctor Dré (Original Concept)
11. Grand Puba—Grand Pubah (Krown Rulers)
12. Harmony (BDP)—Harmony (LL soundalike)
13. Havoc & Prodigy (Mobb Deep)—Havoc & Prode'Je (South Central Cartel)
14. Hell Razor (Long Island rapper a/k/a Robert S.)—Hell Razah (Sunz Of Man)
15. Kam—Kam (Dismasters)
16. Kool DJ EQ (Invisibl Skratch Piklz)—DJ EQ (The Poetess, Tam-Rock)
17. L.A. Posse—Mikey D & The L.A. Posse
18. Mack 10—Mack 10 (Brokin English Klik)
19. Mike G (Jungle Brothers)—Mike G (Extra Prolific)
20. DJ Jazzy Jeff—Jazzy Jeff (Funky Four + 1)
21. Jay-Z—Jay-Z (DJ/producer Hobo Junction)
22. Ma$e—P.A. Mase (De La Soul)
23. DJ Mister Cee (Big Daddy Kane)—Mr. Cee (RBL Posse)
24. O.C.—Master O.C. (Fearless Four)
25. Onyx—Onyx (K.M.D.)
26. DJ Pooh—MC Pooh (b/k/a Pooh-Man)
27. Richie Rich—DJ Richie Rich (b/k/a Daddy Rich)
28. Royal Flush (Blunt Records)—Royal Flush (Yo! Records)
29. Sonny Cheeba (Camp Lo)—Sunny Cheeba (Punk Barbarians)
30. Sugar Bear—Shooga Bear (Redman's cousin)
31. Sweet Tee—Sweet Tee (b/k/a Tanya Winley)
32. T.J. Swann (old school rapper)—TJ Swan (Juice Crew)
33. Willie D (Geto Boys)—Willie D (Boogie Down Productions)

ORDINARY PEOPLE/EXTRAORDINARY PERFORMERS:
14 Rap Artists Who Revel In Using Their Government Names.

1. Devin "The Dude" Copeland
2. Jermaine Dupri
3. Melissa "Missy" Elliott
4. John Forté
5. Lauryn Hill
6. Nasir "Nas" Jones
7. Tracey Lee
8. Craig Mack
9. Keith Murray
10. Kenny Parker
11. Erick Sermon
12. Tupac "2Pac" Shakur
13. Justin Warfield
14. Wyclef Jean

Sons Of The Father.

1. Busta Rhymes—Trevor Smith Jr.
2. Coolio—Artis Ivey Jr.
3. Funkmaster Flex—Aston Taylor Jr.
4. Just-Ice—Joseph Williams Jr.
5. Kid Frost—Arturo Molina Jr.
6. Master O.C. (Fearless Four)—Oscar Rodriguez Jr.
7. Noreaga—Vincent Santiago Jr.
8. P.A. Mase—Vincent L. Mason Jr.
9. Paris—Oscar Jackson Jr.
10. Q-Tip—John Davis Jr.
11. Rakim—William Griffin Jr.
12. Schoolly D—Jesse B. Weaver Jr.
13. Spice 1—Robert Green Jr.
14. Yukmouth—Jerold Ellis Jr.

Longest Rap Alias Ever.

Dr. Wolfgang Von Bushwickin The Barbarian

—(b/k/a Bushwick Bill)

NAMES.

Mother-Funky Stay High Dollar Billster

BROADC

ASTING.

Hip Hop Broadcast Personalities & The Groups They Were In Before Their Acclaimed On-Air Careers.

1. Cocoa Channelle: Kings Of Swing
2. Doctor Dré: Original Concept
3. Funkmaster Flex: Deuces Wild
4. Miss Jones: Doug E. Fresh & The New Get Fresh Crew
5. Sista Dee: Body & Soul
6. DJ Skribble: Young Black Teenagers

HONORABLE MENTION: MTV's funny cracker Tom Green once busted moves with monsters of Canadian rap, Organized Rhyme.

Chuck D's 5 Reasons Why Radio Sucks More Than Ever.

1. **The Formation Of White-Owned Black Radio Stations.**
"Radio—suckers never play me" is a line I'm known for from one of my records, "Rebel Without A Pause," from 1987. This lyric depicted Black radio's rap blackout at that time. Actually, I was speaking for the whole genre of hip hop/rap, which was then being stereotyped by many as this "jail music outta New York."

Large amounts of rap were being released from major and independent companies (mostly from New York) at the time. Black-owned station WBLS—which broke the first rap joint, "Rapper's Delight," via program director Frankie Crocker in 1979—had a chance to establish a lock on maintaining hip hop within its playlists. It didn't happen because WBLS claimed it didn't want to scare off its older audience or sponsors. So as Black music became more popular to other demographics, thus came the formation of the "urban station"—in other words, white-owned Black radio.

2. **Restricted Formats.**
In 1999, rap music has infiltrated the realm of pop radio and this creates a problem for traditional Top 40 situations. The more young, white kids are exposed to Black culture, the more they'll seek the "more authentic" stuff. The downside is that white-owned Black radio has co-opted only those elements of rap music digestible for listeners comfortable with the R&B format, thus closing the door on the diversity of the genre. These radio-ized versions have created an illusionary vault of financial reward that focuses artists' attention on the green brick road of riches. White-owned Black radio has masqueraded these versions as being the rule of the game while other aspects from the artform remain the exception.

3. **Payola, Playola & Crayola (Colored Radio Pay).**
White-owned Black radio makes its selections based on the money it receives, creating the puppet strings that control the audience. Black folk are religious to their radio stations, almost never moving the dial to any place other than where

BROADCASTING.

Black music is aired. Thus anyone can get behind the boards and dictate the flow of an entire regional population. Reflect a little, dictate a lot, and thus direct the flow of thought, style, spending and action of a community.

4. **Wack On-Air Personalities.**
White-owned Black radio sucks in '99 because the masters that own it endorse the policy of more music, less talk. This policy further limits the information delivered to the people via the creation of the transparent DJ—colorless individuals unable to interpret the sounds they're playing for their audience. Mix and college hip hop jocks are the closest thing we have today to the Black personality jocks of the 1950s and '60s—DJs who the people relied on for everything in the 'hood, from local business support to various community activities. But corporations consider air time that could be devoted to such services to be sponsor time and not DJ time. That way it doesn't take much talent to be a radio jock these days. (Who wants to hear a damn weather report 30 times a damn day?!)

5. **No Sense Of History.**
The selection of music is so limited on these stations that instead of supporting the legacy of past Black music and how it sows a path to today's sound, a station would rather play the current, paid-for music until its support funds run out. White-owned Black radio is the major cause in keeping the Black community behind and dumb. Isn't it strange that while more and more folk are into rap music more than ever, there's just as many people clueless of its origins, legacy, individual contributions, etc.? Why, then, should we wonder when current styles tend to evaporate into the air like steam? Don't get me wrong, today's music is great. It's just that the jocks and the stations are wack.

This has been a Public (Enemy) Service Announcement from Chuck D, esteemed lyricist, writer, and former college radio hip hop show host.

...what they need is arbitron on the funky, funky jeep. ⭐ ego trip's book of rap lists. **105**

Doctor Dré's Greatest Comedic Influences.

1. Richard Pryor
2. Bill Cosby
3. Abbott & Costello
4. Martin & Lewis
5. David Letterman
6. Johnny Carson
7. Don Rickles----a very funny man
8. The Dean Martin Celebrity Roasts
9. Danny Kaye

Doctor Dré, a self-described "television baby," dominated the airwaves for seven years as the whimsical co-host of the groundbreaking Yo! MTV Raps.

The History Of Super Rockin' Mr. Magic.

1. The Genesis.

I was in junior high school when I got my first taste of radio. My class went to a career day fair at the New York Coliseum. We visited WCBS in New York, which was a caucasian station. We went in there and they let everyone get a chance to be an honorary DJ. That was my first real taste of radio and I kinda liked the feeling.

2. First Man On The Radio.

After high school, I was working at this electronic store uptown and I'd heard about this new station, WHBI, where you could buy your own air time. At the time, I was hanging out in the Bronx at a club called Disco Fever. While working at the electronic store, I met the guys from the Fever like Kurtis Blow and Flash. They used to come by and buy their equipment from me. I started thinking I could go buy some air time and get these guys to come on my show. At WHBI, air time was $75 an hour. I bought two hours worth before anybody else in rap. My show was on Saturday night/Sunday morning from 2-4 a.m. I got a couple of stores to sponsor me and I was on the air from about '79-'81. It was an underground thing. There wasn't no real record pools back in those days or nuthin'. If you had a record, I'd just hook up with you. I'd tell Kurtis to come down after he left the Fever and he'd just come through and be rockin' on the mic!

3. Welcome To The Next Level.

We were making noise at WHBI and Frankie Crocker, the top jock at WBLS, called me. His music director had a young daughter who always used to sneak and listen to me late at night. So Crocker plugged me in with the right people and eventually I went to go work at WBLS.

Back then at 'BLS, Crocker wouldn't allow anyone in his studio. But me and my producer, Fly Ty Williams, used to house it cuz he wasn't there. WBLS didn't even know that we had a DJ [Marley Marl] for our show. I had met Marley outside of 'BLS one night and he was poppin' shit about how nice he was. He was "Marlon The Magician." So I told him to come by the show cuz Junebug, my first DJ, had died. Me and Marley had a non-verbal communication. I never really had to say nothing because Marley always knew how to do shit right.

But back then at the station, the rule was you weren't allowed to have a DJ. One day, Crocker called us in and said, "The only person allowed in the studio is the engineer. Every on-air personality has to run his own board." And I told him that you need a crew cuz one guy couldn't do everything and the DJ was vital to hip hop. Crocker looked at me and said, "I don't give a fuck. If I tell you to jump, you stay up there until I say come down." He didn't know who he was dealing with. I said, "What motherfucker? Suck my dick!" And I told him he was just jealous of me cuz I was better than him.

Later, me and Crocker made peace. He even came around and told the executives at 'BLS that I had heart.

4. Operation: Shut 'Em Down.

WBLS was really anti-rap, but I got the ratings numbers for them. They gave me the nickname Sir Juice and that's how the whole Juice Crew thing originally got started. (I'd gotten the saying "juice" from hanging out at the Fever—that was just the slang.)

In 1984, our show, *Mr. Magic's Rap Attack*, had the highest numbers ever in New York City so we wanted to renegotiate our contract. Charles Warfield, who was the station's general manager, hated hip hop. We had a meeting and he said, "The major labels are giving me a lot of hassles. They don't have any

BROADCASTING.

rap artists. They aren't making any money on rap. Magic, all the kids are listening to you. We got a new format we call the Quiet Storm, and we want you to do that."

I said, "Quiet Storm?! I don't even like slow music! That sounds like something more for Vaughn Harper" [the WBLS disc jockey who eventually took the position] "not for me." He said, "We want to kill rap and if you tell the kids that it ain't happenin' no more, they'll think it ain't happenin' and it will be dead." I said, "I can't do that shit. What about Kurtis Blow? What about Run? How they gonna eat? You're talking about taking away peoples' livelihoods!" Then he said, "Quiet Storm or nothing." We chose nothing. We broke out and went back to 'HBI—back to paying to be on the radio. About a year later though, 'BLS brought us back cuz Red Alert [from rival station 98.7 KISS FM] was killing them in the ratings.

5. Roxanne, Roxanne.
At around the time when we went back to WHBI, U.T.F.O. had made "Roxanne, Roxanne," which we liked. Their manager, Steve Salem, was trying to get us to play the A-side, "Hangin' Out," cuz it had singing on it. But we kept playing "Roxanne, Roxanne" and it came off. So Steve Salem promised us a show at Broadway International [a popular NYC night club] so we could raise some money. But two weeks before the show, Ty called Steve and Steve said to him, "We don't have to do the show now cuz KISS just added our record."

This was Christmas time and we were broke. Our girls were looking at us like we're complete idiots cuz we'd quit 'BLS, the #1 station in the world, to go save rap. We were mad and hanging out at Marley's house one night. This was when the Juice Crew had started to come together. Marley had a little studio in his house in the projects and he used to have people come over. That night Shanté was there and she said, "Why don't you let me make a tape dissing them?" We was like, "Go away, little girl, you're buggin'." But that next night, Marley came to us and was like, "Yo, remember Shanté? She made a tape dissing U.T.F.O. and them." We put the shit on the air and it took off right away.

6. BDP Beef.
I was in Power Play Studios in Queens and Boogie Down Productions had a meeting with Ty that I didn't know about. I thought they was just somebody trying to get their record played, so I threw them out. I'll admit, I was a little souped-up back then. I ain't even gonna front. I was like, "What the fuck you coming in here for?" After the initial beef, though, Ty was close to getting Scott La Rock signed with Cold Chillin'. A lot of people don't know this, but BDP and the Juice Crew was gonna be down. We went on tour together and was milking it for all it was worth. Kris and Shan was always cool. They'd already figured the shit out. We was like, "People think we hate each other, so let's go on tour—Juice Crew vs. BDP—and make this money."

The tour was fun and our crew was good for ranking people out. They used to dog poor Kris out. They'd talk about his nose, his fat girl, alladat. And back then, he wasn't quick-witted enough to come back. But that made him better. We used to play the rhyming game with him. Everybody in the Juice Crew would freestyle in the limo and if you couldn't hang you got roasted. That's why Kris, Ty, Shan and me are so close now. Cuz we went through a lot together.

7. No More Music By The Suckers.
Def Jam sent me this record called "Miuzi Weighs A Ton" by Public Enemy and we thought they was garbage. So I took it and broke it on the air. That was just the spontaneity of the show. We'd start to play a record and if we didn't like it, we'd snatch it off the turntable and break it. It was never a plot against anyone. I always knew Chuck had skills. It's just that I wouldn't be easy on muthafuckas who I thought was talented but who didn't give me their best effort. I felt like I saved hip hop and I didn't do it for anyone else to fuck it up. Can't nobody dispute that fact. Think about how many muthafuckas would have quit if they were given the same scenario as me: take the Quiet Storm job and forget hip hop or leave the #1 station in the world and get nothing.

8. The Mouth That Roared Takes L.A.
I may have caught some heat over the years for the things I said, but I don't really give a fuck. I felt like as long as I could be true to myself and my conscience, that's all that mattered. If I said it, I'd stand behind it—like the time I cursed muthafuckas out in L.A. over some bullshit. Me and Ty had gone out there for a convention in '88 to see what the gang shit was about. This is when that gang shit was big, but I didn't believe it. I did not believe that muthafuckas were actually fighting and shooting and killing each other over a fuckin' color! I couldn't comprehend it. We brought Kool G Rap to perform out there and in those days you had to do a show for the Crips *and* another show for the Bloods. So I went to each gang's roller skating rink shows and told 'em how I felt. And I think they understood what I was saying.

9. The Secret To Success.
I feel that all my shows are good. Today, if a computer goes down or something, it seems like a lot of the jocks at Hot 97 panic. I'm not gonna panic because I've been doing this for 20 years and if I have one bad show—big deal. I always look at it as competition: can I sound better than the next guy? On every show, I give a full effort.

When I left 'BLS, I moved to Baltimore and did a little radio, but I mostly chilled out. I tried to get into the sneaker and clothing businesses with my brother-in-law, but I missed hip hop. To this day, I still love to hear niggas that got skills kick the flavor. To hear some new fat shit and want to press rewind—that's hip hop.

Don't get it twisted, Mr. Magic was the first DJ to ever host a rap radio program anywhere. Celebrating his 20th year in broadcasting (and still teamed with Fly Ty), the self-dubbed "Official Voice Of Hip Hop" now hosts the Sunday night Classic Showcase on WQHT, 97.1 FM, in New York City.

Greg Mack's Top KDAY Memories.

1. **Eazy-E Cleans Up His Act.**
   Dr. Dre, who was the DJ for my radio show, introduced me to Eazy-E at a place called La Casa Camino Real in downtown L.A. I remember Eazy was a real quiet guy. At the time, he was sellin' tapes out of his car and he was sellin' a bunch of 'em because everywhere I went they were playing "Boyz-N-The Hood." Eazy came up to me and asked, "What do I need to do to make what I'm doin' radio air-playable?" And I said, "Well, you just need to clean up the lyrics." The very next day he handed me the record with clean lyrics. Not only that, he customized it and put a rap in there about the station.

2. **Kings Of Rock Conquer California.**
   We used to do live broadcasts from some of our different events and we brought Run-D.M.C. out once. God, I wish I had a tape of that because they just turned it out. And they even cussed on the air. They said, "This is for all y'all muthafuckas listenin' at home!" So I'm sittin' there like, "Oh, shit! No they didn't!" But because of that performance they solidified their status in L.A.

3. **Mack Puts Hammer In The Mix.**
   MC Hammer used to beg me to death, "Greg, c'mon, man. I got some good stuff. Play my records. Blah blah blah." He even used to follow me around to events and stuff. I was like, "Who is this guy following me around, annoying me?" The next thing I know, we're playing his music and before you know it, he's a major star.

4. **"Batterram": The Underground Phenomenon.**
   The kids at every school that KDAY did events at were all asking me, "How come y'all don't play that Toddy Tee?" I was like, "Who the hell is Toddy Tee?" Almost every kid in L.A. already had a tape of "Batterram." So I tracked Toddy Tee down and told

him, "Man, do you have a version that I can play on the air?" He gave me a reel because he didn't even have the song pressed up. I started playing the song and it became so big that he had to press it up and put it out himself. And he sold a ton of records.

5. **Rolling With Rush.**
   One of the most memorable moments of all was when a guy named Russell Simmons came up to me and said, "Greg, I'm Run's brother and I'm starting this record company. I got this lil' artist named LL Cool J. He's about 16. I wish you would give his single a shot and play it." The next thing you know, LL just blew up. And with every group that Russell brought me it was the same thing.

6. **The Infamous Long Beach Arena Concert Debacle.**
   A bad memory was when we hosted the Raising Hell Tour in 1986, at the Long Beach Arena. Run-D.M.C. was headlining and right in the middle of Whodini's performance, a body comes flying over the rail and onto the stage. Some of the gangs had thrown somebody over the rail. All of a sudden, everybody's fighting. While all hell was breaking loose, I was backstage talking with Vanessa Williams and she was like, "I'm not gonna let it ruin my evening. I'm just gonna sit here and talk." I was like, "Hey, I got people out there!"—cuz the Mixmasters, a group that I was working with at the time, was out in the audience. So I told the security guys, "Help me get out there and get 'em!" And one guy was like, "Look dude, they pay me minimum wage. I ain't riskin' my ass for you or nobody to go out there in that audience." See, the gangs were signaling out the security first. So if you had a security uniform on, you automatically had an ass-whipping coming. So the security guys actually were pullin' off their security shirts just so they wouldn't be identified.
   So I ran out there, pushin' and shovin'. I found the Mixmasters, ran through backstage and out to the car. And there's a gangbanger parked next to me in a big ol' Cadillac

BROADCASTING.

whippin' out his shotgun, sayin' "Let's go get 'em, Cuz!" Man, we jumped in the car and I lowered down so low, I could barely see over the steering wheel, just in case those guys shot. I was just hauling. And, unfortunately, the people that were inside couldn't get out as quickly as I did because they had to go through the regular doors. As you can imagine, there was mass hysteria. It was the last rap concert Long Beach ever had. It was a real sad time for rap, period.

7. **Ain't No Party Like A World On Wheels Party.**
I remember we did a show at a popular club called World On Wheels. They had good air-conditioning, but there would be so many people in there and it would get so hot that at the end of the night you'd see jheri curl juice all on the floor. People's jheri curls would literally melt.

Anyway, one night, we brought in LL Cool J and the Force MD's. This was when LL had just come out with "Rock The Bells" and the Force MD's were just as big as him with "Tender Love." It was pouring rain and the streets were flooded. I was so worried that the rain was gonna kill our event. But, man, we had to turn away over a 1,000 people for that show. They were standing out there with umbrellas and everything. We were charging three times what you normally pay to get into World On Wheels and we packed it in there with about 2,000 people. Legally, the place held about 1,500 people. But we never stayed legal. That night we just had a ball. Plus, there was no fights. There was nothing but love in that audience.

From 1983 to 1991, Greg Mack was the music director/assistant program director at Los Angeles' KDAY 1580 AM—the first 24 hour rap-oriented station in the universe. Currently the operations manager/program director for Power 94 FM The Party in Fresno, California, Mack's silky smooth voice was immortalized on Eazy-E's 1988 love letter to the airwaves, "Radio."

1. **"Brooklyn Zoo"—Ol' Dirty Bastard (Elektra, 1995)**
Gun-cock sound effects obscure the naughty words and Dirty adds great new lyrics that climax with him screaming, "Get outta here!!!"

2. **"Dead Presidents"—Jay-Z (Roc-A-Fella, 1996)**
A fine curseless performance by Jay-hova.

3. **"Love's Gonna Get'cha (Material Love)"—Boogie Down Productions (Jive, 1990)**
KRS-One brings the ruckus sans profanity with his pioneering use of gunshots, whistles and piano stabs.

4. **"Nuthin' But A 'G' Thang"—Dr. Dre featuring Snoop Doggy Dogg (Death Row, 1992)**
Seamlessly performed curse-free rendition that still has the G in it.

5. **"Shame On A Nuh"—Wu-Tang Clan (Loud, 1993)**
Highly inventive way to say the "n" word makes this version as good as the original.

6. **"The S—t Is Real (Remix)"—Fat Joe (Relativity, 1993)**
Preemo's use of scratching to eliminate curses is revolutionary.

7. **"Skin Care"—Kwest Tha Madd Lad (American, 1996)**
In an impressive display of verbal gymnastics, Kwest hilariously bleeps out his own curses.

8. **"T.O.N.Y."—Capone-N-Noreaga featuring Tragedy (Penalty, 1997)**
Dramatic whirling sound effects blot out the bad words and match the intensity of the lyrics and performances.

Bobbito Recounts
11 Artists That Were Broken By
The Stretch Armstrong Radio Show.

1. **The Notorious B.I.G.**

   Biggie Smalls came up to our show in late '91 through Matty C, who had the Unsigned Hype column in *The Source*. Matty C had given a copy of the demo—which was Big rhymin' over the "Blind Alley" beat—to both me and Stretch. Back then, we used to do demo battles and I put Biggie's demo against this demo from a group called the Bronx Zoo. We used to let the callers decide who would win and the Bronx Zoo won. So when Biggie came up to our show, he was kinda pissed off that he had lost. He was on the air sayin', "Yo, I wanna battle those kids," which is funny now cuz no one remembers who the Bronx Zoo were and Biggie went on to become one of the biggest rap artists in the history of music.

2. **DMX**

   DMX The Great was also up at the station in 1991. Lyrically, he used to be into the spelling shit, but when he came up he was just kicking a regular rhyme—a pretty rough one at that. Conceptually, he never changed, but his voice sounds a little more gravely now. The first time anyone heard DMX was on our show and that was fucking eight years ago!

3. **Organized Konfusion**

   No one knew about Organized Konfusion when they came up for the first time in 1991. I had gotten their demo from working at Def Jam and I fucking loved them.

   When Organized came back to the show they were kicking some of the rhymes that would later be heard on their first album and some rhymes that they never had on any record. And then in the middle of one rhyme, the power in the station went out, so there was dead air for like 10 seconds. We were like, "Yo, they overpowered our station!"

4. **Nas**

   Nas came up there on Valentine's Day, 1991. It was him, Akinyele and Lord Finesse. "Live At The Barbeque" wasn't out yet when they came up. Nas kicked his rhyme from "Live At The Barbeque" and this other one that never came out officially.

5. **Cypress Hill**

   I remember Cypress Hill came up and after they left all these kids called up and were like, "Yo, those kids were fucking wack. How could you have 'em up in there?!" Three months later, everybody in all the New York clubs were singing all their songs.

6. **The Beatnuts**

   The Beatnuts used to come up to the show back in '91 just to say, "What's up," and shit. They weren't even rhymin' yet. When I first heard the *Intoxicated Demons* EP, I was bugging because I had thought Les and Ju Ju were kinda shy. And on the record they were talking about " . . . pop the trunk, hit the deck!"

BROADCASTING.

7. **Wu-Tang Clan**
The first time Wu-Tang came up to the show it was just Prince Rakeem and Ason Unique—which is RZA and Ol' Dirty Bastard—and they rhymed. Later, in the summer of '92, we got the test pressing of "Protect Ya Neck." Stretch was out of town that day and I was up there DJing. I remember putting it on and being like, "What the fuck is this karate shit?!"

8. **Hieroglyphics**
Starting in '92, Souls Of Mischief and the whole Hiero crew including Casual started coming up and they would all rhyme off the top of their heads. Sometimes we would let them rap for like 25-30 minutes straight because we didn't have to play commercials.

9. **Cam'Ron & Ma$e**
December of 1993 was the first time that Cam'Ron and Ma$e came up to our show. They were down with Big L. McGruff was in that clique as well. Ma$e used to be Murder Mase. Cam'Ron used to be Killa Kam.

10. **Fugees**
We were the first radio show that the Fugees ever went up to. This was before Salaam Remi's "Nappy Heads" remix blew them up. Lauryn Hill never came up, it was just Pras and Wyclef. They brought out candles and lighted them while we were on the air. Me and Stretch was like, "What the fuck are they doin'?" But they were completely cool.

11. **Big Punisher**
Big Pun came up to our show on August 31, 1995 with Fat Joe, Armageddon and this kid named Keith Nut. Pun used to call himself Big Dog The Punisher. He was fat, he had long hair and he was nasty. He fucking ripped it. He's another cat who is huge right now that people heard on our show before he even had a record out.

Although no longer affiliated with the Stretch Armstrong Show, you can still hear Bobbito "The Barber" Garcia supporting new hip hop talent on WKCR 89.9 FM's "The CM Fam-A-Lam Show," along with Lord Sear, from 1 to 5 a.m. on the first, third and fifth Thursday nights of each month. Got it? The rest of his time is spent overseeing his cool NYC hip hop shop, Bobbito's Footwork, and his record label, Fondle 'Em.

PLUG TUNIN':
18 Notable Rappers Who've Made TV Or Radio Commercials.*

1. Chuck D: Nike
2. Coolio: Reebok
3. Daddy-O: Dark & Lovely hair conditioner; Polly-O cheese
4. Foxy Brown: Mystic fruit drink
5. Funkmaster Flex: Starter
6. Guru: Fila
7. MC Hammer: British Knights; KFC; Pepsi; Taco Bell
8. DJ Jazzy Jeff: Starter
9. Jeru The Damaja: Squeez'r Juice
10. KRS-One: Nike
11. LL Cool J: Fubu; Gap
12. Method Man: Coca-Cola; Reebok
13. Peace (Freestyle Fellowship): Nike
14. PM Dawn: Nike
15. Queen Latifah: Cheerios
16. Redman: Reebok
17. Run-D.M.C.: Gap; Coca-Cola
18. Young MC: Pepsi; Taco Bell

*Does not include advertisements for St. Ides malt liquor. Stop drinking that poison, people.

THEY GOT BIZ-ZY:
Rappers Who Appeared On The Penultimate Episode Of The *Arsenio Hall Show* (May 26, 1994).*

1. Yo Yo
2. MC Lyte
3. Naughty By Nature
4. A Tribe Called Quest
5. Fu-Schnickens
6. CL Smooth
7. Guru
8. Das EFX
9. Wu-Tang Clan
10. KRS-One
11. Mad Lion
12. Pete Rock

*In order of appearance.

During Arsenio Hall's late night television reign, he brought more thugs to America's living rooms than Cops. Despite having a soft spot for the College Boyz (who were on the show a record twelve times! Just kidding), Chunky A provided a broadcasting outlet for rap talent that has yet to be properly filled since his departure.

BUT I AM STILL THIRSTY:
Rap Personalities Who've Appeared In Sprite Commercials.

1. "News Rap"—Kurtis Blow, 1986
2. "I Like The Sprite In You"—Heavy D, 1990
3. "I Like The Sprite In You"—Kid 'N Play, 1991
4. "I Like The Sprite In You"—Kris Kross, 1993
5. "Obey Your Thirst" / "Underground"—A Tribe Called Quest, 1994
6. "Obey Your Thirst" / "Freestylin'"—Grand Puba, Large Professor & Pete Rock & CL Smooth, 1995
7. "Obey Your Thirst" / "Rhyme For Rhyme"—Kid Capri, Kool DJ Red Alert, KRS-One, Mr. Magic & MC Shan, 1996
8. "Obey Your Thirst" / "Wild Style"—Crazy Legs, Grandmaster Flash & Lost Boyz, 1997
9. "Obey Your Thirst" / "Wild Style: Double Trouble"—AZ & Nas, 1998
10. "Obey Your Thirst" / "Wild Style: Court Rap"—Missy Elliott & Grandmaster Caz, 1998
11. "Obey Your Thirst" / "Voltron"—Afrika Bambaataa, Common, Fat Joe, Goodie Mob, Jazzy Jay & Mack 10, 1998

BROADCASTING.

HEY VJ! Uncle Ralph McDaniels inspects his deck.

10 Morsels Of Mildly Interesting Rap Video Trivia.

1. Samuel L. Jackson appears as a concerned family member of Flavor Flav in Public Enemy's "911 Is A Joke" video (Def Jam, 1990).

2. Future Fugee superwoman Lauryn Hill is a dancer in the video for MC Lyte's "Cappucino" (First Priority, 1990).

3. Members of The Pharcyde appear as a band of dancing Egyptians in Michael Jackson's "Remember The Time" video (Epic, 1991).

4. Adult film star (and former Latin Quarter coat check girl) Heather Hunter can be seen hugging up on Big Daddy Kane in his "Cause I Can Do It Right" video (Cold Chillin', 1990).

5. Ice-T is one of the students dancing around the classroom in Joeski Love's "Pee-Wee's Dance" video (Vintertainment, 1986).

6. Heavy D gives the camera the finger at the end of his video for "Don't Curse" (Uptown, 1991).

7. Henry Rollins portrays Vanilla Ice in 3rd Bass' "Pop Goes The Weasel" video (Def Jam, 1991).

8. Before directing videos for everybody in the rap game, Hype Williams got his start as an intern for *Video Music Box*. And his government name is Harold.

9. In the clip for "Killing Me Softly With His Song" (Ruffhouse, 1996), the Fugees are sitting in a movie theater watching the original version of the song's video—which the group had rejected.

10. In Masta Ace's "Me And The Biz" video (Cold Chillin', 1990), the Biz Markie puppet was created as a last-minute replacement when the real Biz Markie was unable to attend the shoot.

    BONUS: In the infamous Pamela Anderson/Tommy Lee home sex video, the couple groove to the sounds of MC Hammer's "It's All Good" in between swinging episodes.

KNOCK 'EM OUT THE IDIOT BOX:
Rap Songs That Flipped TV Show Themes Lovely.

1. **"Bad Boys"—Bad Boys featuring K Love (Starlite, 1985)**
   UTILIZES: *Inspector Gadget*

2. **"Bust This Rhyme"—MC Chill (Fever, 1986)**
   UTILIZES: *Gilligan's Island*

3. **"Cabfare"—Souls Of Mischief (Hieroglyphics, 1997)***
   UTILIZES: *Taxi*

4. **"Count Basey"—Grandmaster Caz (Tuff City, 1985)**
   UTILIZES: *The Tonight Show*

5. **"Early To Rise"—Nice & Smooth (Fresh, 1989)**
   UTILIZES: *Fat Albert*

6. **"Fire It Up"—Busta Rhymes (Elektra, 1998)**
   UTILIZES: *Knight Rider*

7. **"Force MD's Meet The Fat Boys"—Force MD's & The Fat Boys (Tommy Boy, 1985)**
   UTILIZES: *Gilligan's Island*

8. **"Girls Ain't Nothing But Trouble"—DJ Jazzy Jeff & The Fresh Prince (Word Up, 1986)**
   UTILIZES: *I Dream Of Jeannie*

9. **"Gordy's Groove"—Choice MC's (Tommy Boy, 1986)**
   UTILIZES: *The Andy Griffith Show*

10. **"Here We Come"—Timbaland featuring Magoo & Missy Elliott (Blackground, 1998)**
    UTILIZES: *'60s Spider Man*

11. **"Hey"—M.F. Doom (Fondle 'Em, 1996)**
    UTILIZES: *Scooby Doo*

12. **"Horse & Carriage (Remix)"—Cam'Ron featuring Charli Baltimore, Silkk The Shocker, Big Punisher & Wyclef Jean (Untertainment, 1998)**
    UTILIZES: *Night Court*

13. **"I'm Bad"—LL Cool J (Def Jam, 1987)**
    UTILIZES: *S.W.A.T.*

14. **"It's The Beat"—Heartbeat Bros. (Public, 1986)**
    UTILIZES: *The Odd Couple*

15. **"My Flows Is Tight"—Lord Digga (Game, 1998)**
    UTILIZES: *The Price Is Right*

16. **"Murder Rap"—Above The Law (Ruthless, 1990)**
    UTILIZES: *Ironside*

17. **"Nightmares"—Dana Dane (Profile, 1986)**
    UTILIZES: *The Munsters*

18. **"(Nothing Serious) Just Buggin'"—Whistle (Select, 1985)**
    UTILIZES: *Green Acres*

19. **"Princess Of The Posse (45 King Remix)"—Queen Latifah (Tommy Boy, 1989)**
    UTILIZES: *Barney Miller*

20. **"The Show"—Doug E. Fresh & The Get Fresh Crew (Reality, 1985)**
    UTILIZES: *Inspector Gadget*

21. **"Skew It On The Bar-B"—OutKast (LaFace, 1998)**
    UTILIZES: *Police Woman*

22. **"Step By Step"—Nice & Smooth (RAL, 1991)**
    UTILIZES: *Sanford & Son*

23. **"Step Up Front"—Positive K (First Priority, 1988)**
    UTILIZES: *Ironside*

24. **"Style (Peter Gunn Theme)"—Grandmaster Flash (Elektra, 1986)**
    UTILIZES: *Peter Gunn*

25. **"Success Is The Word"—12:41 (Sleeping Bag, 1985)**
    UTILIZES: *Gilligan's Island*

26. **"357"—Cam'Ron (Untertainment, 1998)**
    UTILIZES: *Magnum P.I.*

27. **"Trivial Pursuit"—J.V.C. Force (Idlers, 1990)**
    UTILIZES: *Electric Company*

28. **"Untouchable"—Above The Law (Ruthless, 1990)**
    UTILIZES: *Ironside*

29. **"Word To The Jaz"—The Jaz (EMI, 1989)**
    UTILIZES: *Baretta*

30. **"Wu-Tang Clan Ain't Nuthing Ta Fuck Wit"—Wu-Tang Clan (Loud, 1993)**
    UTILIZES: *Underdog*

31. **"You Know What I'm About"—Lord Finesse (Sire, 1992)**
    UTILIZES: *Scooby Doo*

*Recorded earlier, but officially released in 1997.

BROADCASTING.

CARTOON CREW:
Rappers Who've Appeared In Animation.

1. Cypress Hill—*The Simpsons*, "Homerpalooza" episode (FOX, 1996)
2. Hammer—*Hammerman* cartoon (ABC, 1991)
3. Kid 'N Play—*Kid 'N Play's Funhouse* cartoon (NBC, 1990)
4. K-Solo—"Letterman" video (Atlantic, 1992)
5. Master P—"Kenny's Dead" video (American, 1998)
6. Public Enemy—"Give It Up" video (Def Jam, 1994)
7. Schoolly D—"Mr. Big Dick" video (Jive, 1988)
8. Slick Rick—"Behind Bars" video (Def Jam, 1994)
9. 2Pac—"Do For Love" video (Jive, 1997)

RIDE OR DIE: Master P goes cruisin' with Chef.

The *ego trip* Emmys.

1. **Greatest Reason To Watch Public Television Back In The Day Emmy:**
   Style Wars
   Henry Chalfant's and Tony Silver's aerosol art documentary originally aired on January 18, 1984. The first and still the best look at the revolution that wasn't yet fully televised.

2. **The Self-Hate Emmy:**
   Big Daddy Kane On The *Arsenio Hall Show*
   Appearing to promote one of his anemic early '90s long-players, Kane refused to perform with a backdrop mural done by Hawaii's well-respected futuristic graf technician, Slick. The Big Popi (a/k/a Sexual Chocolate)—then busy cultivating his love-man image—claimed that the artwork was offensive and stereotypical of hip hop followers.

3. **The Murphy Brown-Skinded Woman Emmy:**
   Queen Latifah On *Living Single*
   For the boob tube, Latifah honed her acting chops as the Editor-In-Chief of the fictitious urban lifestyle Bible, *The Flavor*. Ironically, in real life, two white girls were already making hip hop history in the shadow of Seattle's way-cool grunge scene with their own hip hop magazine of the same name. Yet another case of art imitating life. Go figure.

4. **In The Long Run Emmy:**
   Fresh Prince Of Bel-Air
   Before conquering Hollywood, jigmasta Will Smith blazed trails for rappers on television with his '80s Beverly hip hop hillbillies sitcom in a role originally created with MC Shan in mind. The big pay-off? Today, you can now see cheap knock-offs of *FPOB* on corporate monolith-sponsored plantations like UPN (Unpaid Nigga Network) and the WB (We Black!) Network.

5. **Watched Channel Zero Emmy:**
   New York Undercover
   This Dr. Jeckyll-produced program played like *Cop Rock* (yeah, Steven Bochco up in this bitch) on the wick-wick-wack hip hop tip. Starring Malik *"Cool Runnings"* Yoba and the Latin dude, Michael DeLorenzo, producers filled the show with rappers every chance they could. The result was like one bad, long-ass music video. Fuck tha fake police.

BROADCASTING.

6. **Love Is Love Emmy:**
   Onyx's Fredro Starr On *Moesha*
   Fredro penetrated the tight-knit wholesomeness of goodie-two-shoe Brandy's show when his thuggy character got the opportunity to lock lips with the R&B princess. But true to cool Mo's virgin image, she deaded the rapper's advances and Fredro backed-dafucup and left the show before he could hit it.

7. **Sweet Love Emmy:**
   LL Cool J On *Saturday Night Live*
   On a mid-'80s episode of *SNL*, first-time musical guest LL raised the roof with his stirring performance of "Go Cut Creator Go." However, it was a young Mr. Smith's unexpected cameo in a skit as host Sean Penn's gay lover that really had the studio audience wide open.

8. **Quiet Brotha Doin' His Thang Emmy:**
   Daryl "Chill" Mitchell
   Ever since his auspicious debut in *House Party* as the fella who kept bumping into the turntables, "Chill" (formerly of Groove B Chill) has been steadfastly holding it down on network television programs like *The John Laroquette Show*. He was most recently cast alongside Sam Malone's ex-squeeze, Kirstie Alley, on NBC's *Veronica's Closet*. It ain't nuthin' like, it ain't nuthin' like, it ain't nuthin' like TV sitcoms.

9. **Sista To Sista Emmy:**
   BWP, Harmony, MC Lyte & Yo Yo On *Donahue*
   The June 5, 1991 episode of the popular daytime chat show was so volatile it was reportedly blacked-out by some local affiliate stations. Highlights included BDP's Harmony dissing BWP's Lyndah and the Alice In Chains promotional garb worn by one of the Bytches, which bore the slogan, "Who the fuck is Alice?" Where the fuck was the love? Ladies, *please*!

10. **The Mos Forgotten Black Star Emmy:**
    You Take The Kids
    This short-lived wannabe *Cosby* series starred Nell *"Gimme A Break"* Carter and Roger *"Magnum, P.E."* Mosley and featured a 16-year-old Danté Beze (better known today as acclaimed rapper Mos Def) sporting some menacing O-Dog-styled braids. Hey, brothers and sisters—didn't that take the cake?

UNFINISHED SHOW BUSINESS: Erick and Parrish in a full clip from 1989's "The Big Payback" video.

BODY

MOVIN'.

Dance, Dance, Dance!

1. "Belly Dancin' Dina"—Jungle Brothers (Warner Bros., 1989)
2. "Dance For Me"—Queen Latifah (Tommy Boy, 1989)
3. "Dance To My Ministry"—Brand Nubian (Elektra, 1990)
4. "Dance With The Devil"—Big Daddy Kane (Cold Chillin', 1989)
5. "Freaky Dance"—Kinsu (Blunt, 1997)
6. "Get On The Dance Floor"—Rob Base & DJ E-Z Rock (Profile, 1988)
7. "Got To Dance"—Kurtis Blow (Mercury, 1983)
8. "Let's Dance"—King Tee (Capitol, 1988)
9. "Life Is Like A Dance"—Whodini (Jive, 1988)
10. "Now Dance"—Kool T With Technolo G (Wild Pitch, 1988)
11. "187 Dance"—C-Bo (Awol, 1995)
12. "Something 2 Dance 2"—N.W.A (Ruthless, 1988)
13. "They Don't Dance No Mo'"—Goodie Mob (LaFace, 1998)
14. "Trapped On The Dance Floor"—DJ Jazzy Jeff & The Fresh Prince (Jive, 1991)
15. "Who's Makin' Ya Dance"—Steady B (Jive, 1988)
16. "You Can't Dance"—LL Cool J (Def Jam, 1985)

10 MC Hammer Songs You Can't Dance To.

1. "It's Gone" (Capitol, 1988)
2. "Son Of The King" (Capitol, 1988)
3. "Help The Children" (Capitol, 1990)
4. "Good To Go" (Capitol, 1991)
5. "Street Soldiers" (Capitol, 1991)
6. "Tell Me (Why Can't We Live Together)" (Capitol, 1991)
7. "Sleepin' On A Master Plan" (Giant, 1994)
8. "Somethin' 'Bout The Goldie In Me" (Giant, 1994)
9. "I Hope Things Change" (Giant, 1995)
10. "Nothing But Love (A Song For Eazy)" (Giant, 1995)

THEY DON'T NO MO':
Rap Artists Who Began Their Careers As Dancers.

1. Black Eyed Peas 2. Boo-Yaa T.R.I.B.E. 3. Buckshot & 5Ft. Excellerator (Black Moon) 4. Bushwick Bill 5. Defari 6. Devin 7. Doctor Ice & Kangol (U.T.F.O.) 8. Jermaine Dupri 9. Freestyle Fellowship 10. Ice-T 11. Jemini

BODY MOVIN'.

The Gifted One 12. Onyx 13. Peter Paul (Ten Thievz) 14. The Pharcyde 15. Puff Daddy 16. Ras Kass 17. Saafir 18. Stezo 19. Super Lover Cee 20. T.R. Love (Ultramagnetic MC's) 21. 2Pac 22. The W.I.S.E. Guyz 23. Zhigge

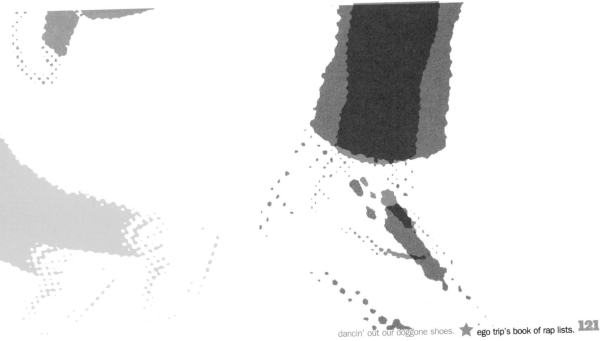

16 Songs That, Contrary To Their Titles, Are Not About Dancing.

1. "Ain't No Half Steppin'"—Big Daddy Kane (Cold Chillin', 1988)
2. "Can't Knock The Hustle"—Jay-Z featuring Mary J. Blige (Roc-A-Fella, 1995)
3. "Get Down"—LL Cool J (Def Jam, 1987)
4. "Give Up The Goods (Just Step)"—Mobb Deep featuring Big Noyd (Loud, 1995)
5. "The Hustle"—The Pharcyde (Delicious Vinyl, 1995)
6. "I'm Housin'"—EPMD (Fresh, 1988)
7. "Jungle Music"—Jeru The Damaja (Payday, 1994)
8. "Move!"—Public Enemy (Def Jam, 1991)
9. "Move Somthin'"—2 Live Crew (Luke Skywalker, 1988)
10. "Pony Ride"—De La Soul (Tommy Boy, 1996)
11. "Shakin'"—Positive K (Island, 1992)
12. "Shimmy Shimmy Ya"—Ol' Dirty Bastard (Elektra, 1995)
13. "Spirit Of The Boogie"—Finsta Bundy (Big Willie, 1995)
14. "Step To The Rear"—Brand Nubian (Elektra, 1990)
15. "Track The Movement"—Lord Finesse & DJ Mike Smooth (Wild Pitch, 1990)
16. "We Can Get Down"—A Tribe Called Quest (Jive, 1993)

The Electric Boogaloos' Top 10 Poppin' Songs.

1. "(Not Just) Knee Deep"—Funkadelic (Warner Bros., 1979)
2. "More Bounce To The Ounce"—Zapp (Warner Bros., 1980)
3. "So Ruff, So Tuff"—Roger Troutman (Warner Bros., 1981)
4. "Rigamortis"—Cameo (Chocolate City, 1975)
5. "Cutie Pie"—One Way (MCA, 1982)
6. "Peanut Butter"—Lenny White & The 29 (Elektra, 1979)
7. "Sun Is Here"—Sun (Capitol, 1978)
8. "O-H-I-O"—Ohio Players (Mercury, 1978)
9. "Get Up"—Brass Construction (UA, 1978)
10. "Those Who Like To Groove"—Ray Parker Jr. & Raydio (Arista, 1980)

Fresno, CA's Electric Boogaloos are the West Coast's pre-eminent poppin' and boogalooin' dance dynasty. They consist of Boogaloo Sam, Pop'in Pete, Skeeter Rabbit, Pop 'N' Taco, Sugar Pop, and the ever-flexible Mr. Wiggles, who is also a member of the world famous Rock Steady Crew.

21 Rap Songs Dedicated To Dances.

1. "Bankhead Bounce"—Diamond featuring D-Roc (EastWest, 1995)
2. "Bart Dance"—Busy Bee (Pandisc, 1992)
3. "The Biz Dance"—Biz Markie (Prism, 1986)
4. "Da' Dip"—Freak Nasty (Hard Hood, 1996)
5. "Do The Bart"—Luke (Luke, 1990)
6. "Do The Fila And The Pee-Wee's Dance"—MC Boob (b/k/a Steady B) (Three Way, 1986)
7. "Do The James"—Super Lover Cee & Casanova Rud (Citi-Beat, 1987)
8. "Do The Kid 'N Play Kick Step"—Kid 'N Play (Select, 1988)
9. "Do The Whop"—Disco Twins & Starchild (Profile, 1986)
10. "Dumb Dancin'"—DJ Jazzy Jeff & The Fresh Prince (Jive, 1991)
11. "Fat Boys Dance"—Fat Boys (Tin Pan Apple, 1987)
12. "The Gator (Dance)"—Biz Markie (Cold Chillin', 1993)
13. "The Humpty Dance"—Digital Underground (Tommy Boy, 1990)
14. "K.G. Dance (Wop)"—Sean Baby & Ninja D (B-Boy, 1987)
15. "Larry's Dance Theme"—Grandmaster Flash (Elektra, 1985)
16. "Let's Whop"—Vandy C & Bill Blast (Whop Records, 1986)
17. "Mudd Foot"—Biz Markie (Cold Chillin', 1989)
18. "Pee-Wee's Dance"—Joeski Love (Vintertainment, 1986)
19. "Return Of The Biz Dance"—Biz Markie (Cold Chillin', 1988)
20. "Steve Martin"—EPMD (Fresh, 1988)
21. "Woppit"—B Fats (Posse, 1986)

BODY MOVIN'.

Ben Higa Revisits 10 Early '80s Pop & R&B Videos Featuring B-Boying & Popping.

1. **"All Night Long"—Lionel Richie (Motown, 1983)**
Before he started dancing on the ceiling, the ex-Commodore leader was backed by numerous street-style dancers from Los Angeles in this popular video.

2. **"Crosseyed And Painless"—Talking Heads (Sire, 1980)**
Directed by choreographer Toni "Hey Mickey" Basil, this video boasts selected Electric Boogaloos and Ana Marie "Lollipop" Sanchez. Look for Pop'in Pete backsliding and a pre-"Beat It" knife fight under an East L.A. bridge.

3. **"I Feel For You"—Chaka Khan featuring Grandmaster Melle Mel (Warner Bros., 1984)**
True poppers were feeling this re-edited version of a Norma Kamali fashion video, which recreated the original Radio club in a studio and featured Shabadoo, Boogalo Shrimp, Lollipop, Pop 'N' Taco, the Unique Dominos and a DJing Chris "The Glove" Taylor.

4. **"I.O.U."—Freeze (Streetwise, 1982)**
The clip for this enormous electro smash features a group of Black European dancers robottin' in the streets.

5. **"Meeting In The Ladies Room"—Klymaxx (MCA, 1984)**
Showcases the hard-hitting popping moves of the afore-mentioned Pop 'N' Taco as he sits in a chair while the soul sistas serenade him.

6. **"Party Train"—Gap Band (Total Experience, 1983)**
Filmed at the famous boardwalk on Venice Beach, CA, this musical freakshow comes complete with flamboyant roller-skaters, bikini-clad biddies, iron-pumpin' muscleheads and poppers goin' for theirs inside a makeshift boxing ring.

7. **"Save The Overtime (For Me)"—Gladys Knight And The Pips (Columbia, 1983)**
As Ms. Knight and her Pips belt out this tune on an immaculate brownstone stoop (á la some Sesame Street shiznit), the New York City Breakers bust footworks and power moves on linoleum in front of them.

8. **"Street Dance"—Break Machine (Sire, 1983)**
In addition to performing their huge international hit, the singing trio is seen poppin' and b-boyin' around the grimy streets of New York.

9. **"Why You Wanna Break My Heart"—Dwight Twilley (EMI, 1984)**
This entry from the soundtrack to the Lorenzo "You Look Marvelous" Lamas rapstravaganza, *Body Rock*—smattered with clips from the cinematic dud—is boosted by the inclusion of a beret-wearin' popper.

10. **"Young Turks"—Rod Stewart (Warner Bros., 1981)**
Cool Pockets of Chain Reaction pops in the famous alley scene and is also seen atop an open train car. Rod merely sings his soccer-lovin' ass off.

Photojournalist Ben Higa was the West Coast contributing editor on Rap Pages' *acclaimed 1996 graffiti and breakdance special issues. He lives and works in Los Angeles, CA.*

ROCKIN' STEADY: Crazy Legs kicks it live, circa early '80s.

10 Songs Dedicated To The Pleasures Of Lap Dances.

1. "Bitch Betta Have My Money"—Ja Rule (Def Jam, 1998)
2. "Lap Dance"—Ras Kass (Priority, 1998)
3. "Shake Something"—Mia X & Mystikal (No Limit, 1998)
4. "Shake Whatcha Mama Gave Ya (But Make Sho Your Niggas Pay Ya)"—Mia X (Heavyweight, 1998)
5. "Strip Club"—Luke (Luke, 1990)
6. "Strokes"—The Beatnuts (Relativity, 1997)
7. "Table Dance"—Hi-C (Skanless, 1993)
8. "Table Dance"—Tela (Rap-A-Lot, 1998)
9. "Table Dance (Skit)"—Above The Law (Tommy Boy, 1996)
10. "We Be Clubbin'"—Ice Cube (Heavyweight, 1998)

25 Mighty Healthy Rap Cameos On R&B Tracks.

1. AZ: "Lady (Remix)"—D'Angelo (EMI, 1996)
2. Big Daddy Kane & Roxanne Shanté: "Loosey's Rap"—Rick James (Reprise, 1988)
3. Da Brat & Jermaine Dupri: "In My Bed (Remix)"—Dru Hill (Island, 1997)
4. Dr. Dre & Queen Pen: "No Diggity"—Blackstreet (Interscope, 1996)
5. Foxy Brown: "Touch Me, Tease Me"—Case (Def Jam, 1996)
6. Ghostface Killah: "This Is For The Lover In You (Puffy's Extended Face To Face Remix)"—Babyface (Epic promo, 1996)
7. Grandmaster Melle Mel: "I Feel For You"—Chaka Khan (Warner Bros., 1984)
8. Grand Puba: "What's The 411?"—Mary J. Blige (Uptown, 1992)
9. Heavy D: "Alright"—Janet Jackson (A&M, 1990)
10. Jay-Z: "I Don't Wanna Be Alone"—Shai (Gasoline Alley, 1995)
11. MC Lyte, Yo Yo & Queen Latifah: "I Wanna Be Down (Human Rhythm Hip Hop Remix)"—Brandy (Atlantic, 1995)
12. Master P & Silkk The Shocker: "Let's Ride"—Montell Jordan (Def Jam, 1998)
13. The Notorious B.I.G.: "Be Happy"—R. Kelly (Jive, 1995)
14. The Notorious B.I.G.: "Can't You See"—Total (Tommy Boy, 1995)
15. The Notorious B.I.G. & Ma$e: "Only You (Remix)"—112 (Bad Boy, 1996)
16. Ol' Dirty Bastard: "Fantasy"—Mariah Carey (Columbia, 1995)
17. Q-Tip: "Got 'Til It's Gone"—Janet Jackson (Virgin, 1997)
18. Q-Tip: "Groove Is In The Heart"—Dee-Lite (Elektra, 1990)
19. DJ Quik: "Let's Get Down"—Tony Toni Toné (Mercury, 1996)
20. Raekwon & Ghostface Killah: "Freek'n You (Mr. Dalvin's Freek Mix)"—Jodeci (Uptown, 1995)
21. Rakim: "Friends"—Jody Watley (MCA, 1989)
22. Redman: "Curiosity (Remix)"—Aaron Hall (MCA, 1995)
23. Redman: "Me And Those Dreamin' Eyes of Mine (Def Squad Remix)"—D'Angelo (EMI, 1995)
24. Smif-N-Wessun: "I Love You (Remix)"—Mary J. Blige (Uptown promo, 1995)
25. Wu-Tang Clan: "Anything (Remix)"—SWV (RCA, 1994)

BODY MOVIN'.

Beats By The Pound's History Of Bounce Music.

Part I:
The Pre-Bounce Hip Hop Classics.

1. "The Adventures Of Grandmaster Flash On The Wheels Of Steel"—Grandmaster Flash (Sugar Hill, 1981)
2. "Funky Soul Makossa"—Nairobi featuring The Awesome Foursome (Streetwise, 1982)
3. "Looking For The Perfect Beat"—Afrika Bambaataa & The Soul Sonic Force (Tommy Boy, 1982)
4. "Planet Rock"—Afrika Bambaataa & The Soul Sonic Force (Tommy Boy, 1982)
5. "Drop The Bomb (Live)"—Trouble Funk (D.E.T.T., 1983)
6. "Get Tough"—CD III (Prelude, 1983)
7. "Hobo (Scratch)"—Malcolm McLaren & The World Famous Supreme Team (Island, 1983)
8. "It's In The Mix"—Slim (D.E.T.T., 1983)
9. "Jam On Revenge"—Newcleus (Sunnyview, 1983)
10. "Renegades Of Funk"—Afrika Bambaataa & The Soul Sonic Force (Tommy Boy, 1983)
11. "Sucker MC's"—Run-D.M.C. (Profile, 1983)
12. "It's Yours"—T La Rock & Jazzy Jay (Partytime, 1984)
13. "What Are We Gonna Do?"—Ultimate 3 MC's (Partytime, 1984)
14. "Fresh Is The Word"—Mantronix (Fresh, 1985)
15. "Here We Go (Live At The Funhouse)"—Run-D.M.C. (Profile, 1985)
16. "Marley Marl Scratch"—Marley Marl featuring MC Shan (Nia, 1985)
17. "P.S.K." b/w "Gucci Time"—Schoolly D (Schoolly D, 1985)
18. "Rock The Bells"—LL Cool J (Def Jam, 1985)
19. "Cold Gettin' Dumb"—Just-Ice (Fresh, 1986)
20. "Drap Rap"—The Showboys (Profile, 1986)
21. "It's My Beat"—Sweet Tee (Profile, 1986)
22. "Peter Piper"—Run-D.M.C. (Profile, 1986)
23. "6 'N The Mornin'"—Ice-T (Techno-Hop, 1986)
24. "Throw The 'D'"—2 Live Crew (Luke Skyywalker, 1986)
25. "The Bridge Is Over"—Boogie Down Productions (B-Boy, 1987)
26. "Dope Man"—N.W.A (Ruthless, 1987)
27. "Got To Be Tough"—MC Shy-D (Luke Skyywalker, 1987)
28. "Rock The Beat"—Derek B (Profile, 1987)
29. "I'm Gettin' Ready (Remix)"—Doug E. Fresh & The Get Fresh Crew featuring Rare Essence (Reality, 1988)
30. "Scarface"—Geto Boys (Rap-A-Lot, 1989)

Part II:
More Bounce To The Ounce New Orleans Style.

1. "We Destroy"—Ninja Crew (4-Sight, 1986)
2. "Buck Jump Time"—Gregory D (Uzi, 1987)
3. "Get It Girl"—Warren Mayes (Atlantic, 1989)
4. "Where They At?"—DJ Jimmy (Soulin', 1990)*
5. "Where They At?"—MC T.T. Tucker & DJ Irv (Siuol, 1990)*
6. "I Don't Give A Damn About Your Boyfriend"—Tim Smooth (J.G., 1991)
7. "Marrero"—MC Thick (Alliv, 1991)
8. "Nasty Bitch"—Bust Down (Disotell, 1991)
9. "Pass The Snake" b/w "Ask Dem Hoes"—3-9 Posse (Parkway Pumpin', 1991)
10. "Bounce Baby Bounce"—Everlasting Hitman (Mr. T, 1992)
11. "Get The Gat"—Lil' Elt (Parkway Pumpin', 1992)
12. "It's All About Yo' Lips"—Poppa Doc (Pac, 1992)
13. "Sista Sista"—Silky Slim (Muggs, 1992)
14. "Goin' Off"—Black Menace (Prime Suspect, 1993)
15. "Gotta Be Real"—Pimp Daddy (Pack, 1993)
16. "It Ain't Where Ya From"—Joe Blakk (Mercenary, 1993)
17. "Not Yo Trick Daddy"—Daddy Yo (Express, 1993)
18. "The Payback"—Mia X (Lamina, 1993)
19. "Where's Dat Nigga?"—Females In Charge (Express, 1993)
20. "Slide Giddy Up"—Full Pack (Pack, 1994)

*These two records mark the beginning of the Bounce Music Era.

New Orleans natives and longtime DJs Craig B and KLC are two members of the five-man hit squad known as Beats By The Pound—No Limit Records' tireless in-house production staff. Worshippers of the slow roll 808-kick, their boombastic work may be heard on jams like TRU's "I'm Bout It, Bout It," Master P's "Make 'Em Say Unngh!" and Silkk The Shocker's "It Ain't My Fault," amongst many others.

CUZ WE'RE HOUSIN':
10 Hip House Songs That Don't Suck. . .

1. "Adding On"—Lakim Shabazz (Tuff City, 1988)
2. "Come Into My House"—Queen Latifah (Tommy Boy, 1989)
3. "Do It To The Crowd"—Twin Hype (Profile, 1989)
4. "The House That Cee Built"—Big Daddy Kane (Cold Chillin', 1989)
5. "I'll House You"—Jungle Brothers (Idlers, 1988)
6. "Kicked Out The House"—De La Soul (Tommy Boy, 1991)
7. "Lyte As A Rock (House Mix)"—MC Lyte (First Priority, 1988)
8. "Planet E"—KC Flight (Popular, 1989)
9. "Rhythm Is The Master"—DJ Chuck Chillout & Kool Chip (Mercury, 1989)
10. "We Got Our Own Thang"—Heavy D (Uptown, 1989)

. . .& 10 More That Really, Really Do.

11. "Dance All Nite (House Mix)"—Poison Clan (Luke, 1991)
12. "Get Wild Go Crazy"—K-9 Posse (Arista, 1991)
13. "Hip House Attack Positively Black Style"—Positively Black (Select, 1989)
14. "It Ain't A Hip Hop Record"—MC Shan (Cold Chillin', 1990)
15. "It's Time To Party"—EPMD (Fresh, 1989)
16. "Slick Rick-The Ruler"—Slick Rick (Def Jam, 1991)
17. "Soul Man"—Kid 'N Play (Select, 1988)
18. "Traveling At The Speed Of Thought (Hip House Remix)"—Ultramagnetic MC's (Next Plateau, 1988)
19. "Turn This House Into A Home"—Craig G (Atlantic, 1989)
20. "We In The House"—J.J. Fad (Ruthless, 1990)

Hot Steppin' Hip Hop Back-Up Dancers & The Artists They Hit The Floor For.

1. The Boyz (G-Wiz & Trouble T-Roy): Heavy D
2. Cliff Love: Whodini
3. Fendi: EPMD
4. Hot Dog (A-Teem): Chubb Rock
5. Kool Breeze Kenny & Suave Shawn (TCF Crew): Kool G Rap
6. Leg 1 & Leg 2: MC Lyte
7. Peek-A-Boo & A-Sharp: Kwamé
8. Safari Sisters (007 & 99): Queen Latifah
9. Scoob & Scrap Lover: Big Daddy Kane
10. Soul Brothers (Kraig E, Legend & V-Love): Def Jef

Top 10 Reasons Hip Hop Dancers Are No More.

10. No scrubs.
9. Funny haircuts are played out.
8. Guns and cell phones continually fall out of waistlines while bustin' a move.
7. Too blunted on reality, not choreography.
6. MC Hammer.
5. Niggas are too busy bouncin'.
4. Gangstas don't dance, they boogie.
3. Ju Ju of The Beatnuts eliminated them.
2. Dancers all rap now.
1. No more dancin' for whitey, family. Jigaboo time is over!

BODY MOVIN'.

WALLFLOWERS:
10 Anti-Dance Rappers.

1. **Breeze**
   EVIDENCE: "Ain't with the dancin'/ But still I get more cheers than Ted Danson" from "Free Style Ghetto"—King Tee also featuring Tha Alkaholiks & Xzibit (MCA, 1994)

2. **Del The Funkeé Homosapien**
   EVIDENCE: "Brothers don't shake your rumps/ Wearing biker shorts is like choking on your nuts" from "Pissin' On Your Steps" (Elektra, 1991)

3. **MC Eiht**
   EVIDENCE: "I ain't with breakin' my back/ Tryin' to impress a girl who ain't givin' up jack" from "I Don't Dance"—Compton's Most Wanted (Orpheus, 1991)

4. **Grand Puba**
   EVIDENCE: "I can shake a leg if I want to/ But I don't want to cuz that's what my dancers do" from "Lickshot" (Elektra, 1992)

5. **Guru**
   EVIDENCE: "Not the type to really dance too much although I used to/ Rather bust a fresh line and get loose to . . ." from "Mostly Tha Voice"—Gang Starr (Chrysalis, 1994)

6. **Ice Cube**
   EVIDENCE: "I don't party and shake my nuts/ I leave that to the brothers with the funny hair cuts" from "Jackin' For Beats" (Priority, 1990)

7. **Ja Rule**
   EVIDENCE: "We don't dance no more, all we do is cock and spit/ Dedicated to giving you nuthin' but thug shit" from "Murdergram"—Murder Inc. (Roc-A-Fella, 1998)

8. **Kool Moe Dee**
   EVIDENCE: "If you're up and dancing then you won't really hear/ The smokin' rhyme that I designed for you all to compare" from "Don't Dance" (Jive, 1987)

9. **Lord Finesse**
   EVIDENCE: "I'm quick to send a nigga home in stitches/ Don't sing and dance, but I still get the bitches" from "Fat For The '90s" (Giant, 1992)

10. **Too $hort**
    EVIDENCE: "I'm not a tongue-twisting rapper with a funny style/ Don't dress hip hop and dance real wild" from "In The Trunk" (Jive, 1992)

    HONORABLE MENTION: Props to P.E.'s Chuck D for his lyrics from "Rightstarter (Message To A Black Man)" (Def Jam, 1987): "Many have forgotten what we came here for, never knew or had a clue so you're on the floor/ Just growin', not knowin' about your past, now you're lookin' pretty stupid while you're shakin' your ass."

CLANS, POSS
CREWS & CL

ES,
QUES.

Greatest Groups Of All-Time.

1. Run-D.M.C.
2. Public Enemy
3. N.W.A
4. Wu-Tang Clan
5. Treacherous Three
6. Cold Crush Brothers
7. Grandmaster Flash & The Furious Five
8. EPMD
9. De La Soul
10. Beastie Boys
11. A Tribe Called Quest
12. OutKast
13. 2 Live Crew
14. Salt-N-Pepa
15. Ultramagnetic MC's

Too Much Posse Cuts: The Good ...

1. "Ain't No Fun (If The Homies Can't Have None)"—Snoop Doggy Dogg featuring Nate Dogg, Kurupt & Warren G (Death Row, 1993)
2. "Assassination Squad"—45 King featuring Apache, Lakim Shabazz, Queen Latifah, Double J & Lord Alibaski (Tuff City, 1990)
3. "Buddy"—De La Soul featuring Jungle Brothers & Q-Tip (Tommy Boy, 1989)
4. "Diggin' In The Crates"—Show & AG featuring Diamond D & Lord Finesse (Showbiz, 1991)
5. "Don't Curse"—Heavy D featuring Kool G Rap, Grand Puba, CL Smooth, Big Daddy Kane, Pete Rock & Q-Tip (MCA, 1991)
6. "Flava In Ya Ear (Remix)"—Craig Mack featuring The Notorious B.I.G., Rampage, LL Cool J & Busta Rhymes (Bad Boy, 1994)
7. "Head Banger"—EPMD featuring K-Solo & Redman (Def Jam, 1992)
8. "I Got 5 On It (Bay Ballas Remix)"—Luniz featuring Dru Down, Richie Rich, E-40, Shock G, Humpty Hump, Spice 1 & Captain Save 'Em (Noo Trybe promo, 1995)
9. "I'm The Man"—Gang Starr featuring Lil' Dap & Jeru The Damaja (Payday, 1992)
10. "I Shot Ya (Remix)"—LL Cool J featuring Keith Murray, Prodigy (Mobb Deep), Fat Joe & Foxy Brown (Def Jam, 1995)
11. "Live At The Barbeque"—Main Source featuring Nas, Joe Fatal & Akinyele (Wild Pitch, 1991)
12. "Make 'Em Say Unngh!"—Master P featuring Fiend, Silkk The Shocker, Mia X & Mystikal (No Limit, 1998)
13. "Played Like A Piano"—King Tee featuring Ice Cube & Breeze (Capitol, 1990)
14. "Scenario"—A Tribe Called Quest featuring Leaders Of The New School (Jive, 1991)
15. "The Symphony"—Marley Marl featuring Masta Ace, Craig G, Kool G Rap & Big Daddy Kane (Cold Chillin', 1988)

... The Bad ...

1. "Back From Hell (Remix)"—Run-D.M.C. featuring Ice Cube & Chuck D (Profile, 1991)
2. "Beef"—Chubb Rock featuring Das EFX & PMD (Select, 1997)
3. "Down The Line"—Nice & Smooth featuring Preacher Earl, Melo T., Bãs Blasta, Asu & Guru (RAL, 1991)
4. "5 Deadly Venomz"—2Pac featuring Treach (Naughty By Nature), Live Squad & Apache (Interscope, 1993)
5. "Game Over"—Scarface featuring Too $hort, Ice Cube & Dr. Dre (Rap-A-Lot, 1997)
6. "Got The Flava"—Show & AG featuring D Flow, Wali World, Party Arty & Method Man (Payday, 1995)
7. "The Ill Shit"—Erick Sermon featuring Kam & Ice Cube (Def Jam, 1993)
8. "The Ladies In Da House"—Big Kap featuring Bahamadia, Precise, Treep, U-Neek & Lauryn Hill (Tommy Boy, 1994)
9. "No Hook"—Shaquille O'Neal featuring RZA & Method Man (Jive, 1994)
10. "No Shorts And No Sleep"—PMD featuring Zone 7, 3rd Eye & Top Quality (PMD, 1994)

CLANS, POSSES, CREWS & CLIQUES.

11. "Protect Ya Neck II The Zoo"—Ol' Dirty Bastard featuring Buddha Monk, Prodigal Sun, Zoo Keeper, Murdoc, Killah Priest, 12 O' Clock, Shorty Shit Stain & 60 Sec. Assassin (Elektra, 1995)
12. "Real Live Shit (Remix)"—Real Live featuring Ghostface Killah, Cappadonna, Lord Tariq & Killa Sin (Big Beat, 1996)
13. "Show & Prove"—Big Daddy Kane featuring Big Scoob, Sauce Money, Shyheim, Jay-Z & Ol' Dirty Bastard (MCA, 1994)
14. "The Symphony, Pt. II"—Marley Marl featuring Masta Ace, Craig G, Big Daddy Kane, Little Daddy Shane & Kool G Rap (Cold Chillin', 1991)
15. "Two To The Head"—Kool G Rap featuring Scarface, Bushwick Bill & Ice Cube (Cold Chillin', 1992)

... The Slept-On ...

1. "Actual Facts"—Lord Finesse featuring Sadat X, Large Professor & Grand Puba (Penalty, 1995)
2. "Bring It On"—Geto Boys featuring 2Low, Seagram, Too Much Trouble, 5th Ward Boyz, Odd Squad, Ganksta Nip, DMG, 3-2 & Big Mello (Rap-A-Lot, 1993)
3. "Collaboration Of Mics"—Artifacts featuring Lord Jamar (Brand Nubian) & Lord Finesse (Big Beat, 1997)
4. "Color Blind"—Ice Cube featuring Threat, Kam, WC, Coolio, King Tee & J-Dee (Da Lench Mob) (Priority, 1991)
5. "Firewater"—Fat Joe featuring Raekwon, Armageddon & Big Punisher (Relativity, 1996)
6. "Free Style Ghetto"—King Tee featuring Xzibit, Breeze & Tha Alkaholiks (MCA, 1994)
7. "Da Graveyard"—Big L featuring Lord Finesse, Microphone Nut, Jay-Z, Party Arty & Grand Daddy I.U. (Columbia, 1995)
8. "Mansion And A Yacht"—Kurious featuring Sadat X & Mike G (Columbia, 1994)
9. "Metal Thangz"—Street Smartz featuring O.C. & Pharoahe Monch (Organized Konfusion) (Tru Criminal, 1997)
10. "Money In The Bank"—Kool G Rap featuring Large Professor, Freddie Foxxx & Ant Live (Cold Chillin', 1990)
11. "Spontaneous (13 MC's Deep)"—Leaders Of The New School featuring Blitz, Cool Whip Brittle Lo, Kollie Weed, Pudge God, Rampage & Rumpletilskinz (Elektra, 1993)
12. "Super Nigga"—King Tee featuring DJ Pooh & Rashad

(MCA, 1994)
13. "Wishful Thinking"—Big Punisher featuring B-Real, Fat Joe & Kool G Rap (Loud, 1997)
14. "You Can't Front (Shit Is Real)"—Diamond D featuring Sadat X & Lord Finesse (Chemistry, 1993)
15. "You Don't Work, U Don't Eat"—WC And The MAAD Circle featuring Ice Cube, J-Dee (Da Lench Mob) & MC Eiht (Priority, 1991)

... & The Weird.

1. "A Buncha Niggas"—Heavy D featuring 3rd Eye, Guru, The Notorious B.I.G., Rob-O & Busta Rhymes (Uptown, 1992)
2. "Can You Handle It"—Heavy D featuring Tha Dogg Pound, McGruff & DJ Rogers, Jr. (Universal, 1997)
3. "Come On Down"—Big Daddy Kane featuring Q-Tip & Busta Rhymes (Cold Chillin', 1991)
4. "Feel The Vibe"—Frankie Cutlass featuring Rampage, Doo Wop & Heltah Skeltah (Relativity, 1997)
5. "Hit 'Em High"—B-Real, Coolio, Method Man, LL Cool J & Busta Rhymes (Atlantic, 1996)
6. "Let's Get It On"—Eddie F featuring The Notorious B.I.G., 2Pac, Heavy D & Grand Puba (Atlantic, 1994)
7. "Live Wires Connect"—U.G.K. featuring Lord Jamar (Brand Nubian) & Keith Murray (Island, 1996)
8. "Massive Heat"—Lord Tariq & Peter Gunz featuring Sticky Fingaz (Onyx) & Kurupt (Columbia, 1998)
9. "No Doubt"—Das EFX featuring M.O.P. & Teflon (EastWest, 1998)
10. "Nuttin' But Flavor"—Funkmaster Flex & The Ghetto Celebs featuring Charlie Brown (Leaders Of The New School), Ol' Dirty Bastard & Biz Markie (Nervous, 1994)
11. "Nuthin' But The Gangsta"—MC Eiht featuring Spice 1 & Redman (Epic, 1994)
12. "Penile Reunion"—MC Shan featuring Neek The Exotic, Diezel, Kool G Rap & Snow (Livin' Large, 1993)
13. "The Rhythm"—Bas Blasta featuring Godfather Don, Ju Ju, Lord Finesse & Fat Joe (RCA, 1994)
14. "Strange Fruit"—Pete Rock featuring Tragedy, Cappadonna & Sticky Fingaz (Onyx) (Loud, 1998)
15. "You Must Be Out Your Fuckin' Mind"—Fat Joe featuring Apache & Kool G Rap (Relativity, 1993)

"_____ IS DOWN WITH US!"
One-Time Members Of Boogie Down Productions.

1. Channel Live
2. D-Nice
3. D-Square
4. Harmony
5. Jamal-Ski
6. DJ Jazzy Jay Kramer
7. Kool DJ Red Alert
8. KRS-One
9. Mad Lion
10. McBoo
11. Sidney Mills
12. Scottie Morris
13. Ms. Melodie
14. Kenny Parker
15. Rebekah
16. Robocop
17. Scott La Rock
18. Simone
19. Willie D

Ice Cube Spin-Offs.

1. Del The Funkeé Homosapien
2. Don Jagwarr
3. Kam
4. Kausion
5. K-Dee
6. Da Lench Mob
7. Mack 10
8. Short Khop
9. Westside Connection
10. Yo Yo

Run-D.M.C. Spin-Offs.

1. The Afros
2. FU2
3. Jayo Felony
4. My Name's Divine
5. Onyx
6. Serious Lee Fine
7. Sin Assassinz
8. Smooth Ice
9. Soul Tempo
10. Zoe Brothers

Hip Hop Supergroups.

1. C.E.B.: Cool C, DJ Eaze & MC Boob (b/k/a Steady B)
2. The Click: B-Legit, D-Shot, E-40 & Suga T
3. Concentration Camp: Boo The Boss Playa, C-Loc, Growl Nitty, J-Von, Lay-Lo, Leetyme, Lucky Knuckles, Maxmanelli & Young Bleed
4. Deadly Venoms: Champ MC, Finesse, J-Boo & N-Tyce
5. Def Squad: Keith Murray, Redman & Erick Sermon
6. D.I.T.C.: AG, Big L, Buckwild, Diamond D, Fat Joe, Lord Finesse, O.C. & Show
7. Fab 5: Rock & Ruck (Heltah Skeltah); Louieville Sluggah, Starang Wondah & Top Dog (Originoo Gunn Clappaz)
8. Da 504 Boyz: Master P, Mystikal & Silkk The Shocker
9. Flipmode Squad: Baby Sham, Busta Rhymes, Lord Have Mercy, Rah Digga, Rampage & Spliff Star
10. The Firm: AZ, Foxy Brown, Nas & Nature
11. Geto Boys: (multiple lineups)
12. Golden State Project: Ras Kass, Saafir & Xzibit
13. Gravediggaz: Fruitkwan, Too Poetic, Prince Paul & RZA
14. Hot Boys: B.G., Juvenile, Lil' Wayne & Turk
15. Indelible MC's: Big Juss, Breeze, El-P & J-Treds
16. Missin' Linx: Al Tariq, Black Attack & Problemz
17. Murder Inc.: DMX, Ja Rule & Jay-Z
18. Natural Elements: A-Butta, L-Swift & Mr. Voodoo
19. N.W.A: Dr. Dre, Eazy-E, Ice Cube, MC Ren & Yella
20. Polyrhythm Addicts: Apani B. Fly Emcee, Mr. Complex, Shabaam Sahdeeq & DJ Spinna
21. Screwball: Hostyle, Poet; KL & Solo (Kamakazee)
22. TRU: C-Murder, Master P & Silkk The Shocker
23. TWDY: Ant Banks, Captain Save 'Em & Rappin' 4-Tay
24. Westside Connection: Ice Cube, Mack 10 & WC
25. Wu-Tang Clan: The Genius, Ghostface Killah, Inspectah Deck, Masta Killa, Method Man, Ol' Dirty Bastard, Raekwon, RZA & U-God

BONUS: RUMORED SUPERGROUPS

1. The Commission: Charli Baltimore, Jay-Z & The Notorious B.I.G.
2. Four Horsemen: Canibus, Killah Priest, Kurupt & Ras Kass
3. The Good, The Bad & The Ugly: Dan The Automator, Dust Brothers, Prince Paul & DJ Shadow
4. Nasal Tongues: Adrock (Beastie Boys), B-Real (Cypress Hill), Busy Bee & Q-Tip
5. Psychic Friends: Black Thought (The Roots), Common, Jeru The Damaja & Pharoahe Monch (Organized Konfusion)

CLANS, POSSES, CREWS & CLIQUES.

GETO BOYS:
A Gangsta Rap Franchise.

Ten years in existence, the name Geto Boys has become synonymous with the best in gangsta rap. Conceived by Rap-A-Lot founder James "Lil' J" Smith (neé Prince) to represent the gritty street life of Houston, Texas, the group's line-up has gone through many phases. Below is a comprehensive guide to the ever-changing faces of the Geto Boys.

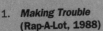

1. **Making Trouble (Rap-A-Lot, 1988)**
Spelled G-H-E-T-T-O, the original B-O-Y-S line-up consists of two young rappers, Sire Juke Box and Prince Johnny C, and one DJ Ready Red. Never really gaining an identity as a group, the trio are often overshadowed at shows by their charismatic dancer, Lil' Billy.

2. **Grip It! On That Other Level (Rap-A-Lot, 1989)**
After dismissing Juke Box and Johnny C, Lil' J holds a Houston-wide search and finds two solo artists named Akshen (b/k/a Scarface) and Willie D as replacements. Promising the duo that they can later record solo records as long as they give 100% towards the success of the group, Lil' J pairs them up with remaining member Ready Red and dancer-turned-rapper Lil' Billy (b/k/a Bushwick Bill). Grip It! becomes an independent smash, moving 450,000 units and catching the attention of all major labels.

3. **Geto Boys (Rap-A-Lot, 1990)**
Now a major player in the rap game, Lil' J meets Rick Rubin and with his encouragement decides to re-release Grip It! with two new songs for Geffen Records. Unfortunately, Geffen gets cold feet due to the album's adult content and backs out of the deal at the last minute because of the intensely negative mainstream media coverage (the album is later distributed by Irving Azoff's Giant Records).

4. **We Can't Be Stopped (Rap-A-Lot, 1991)**
A distribution deal with Priority records secured, the GB's fourth album is released with its controversial cover photo of Bushwick Bill being carted off by his bandmates in a hospital shortly after shooting himself in the eye in a botched suicide attempt. The LP is also marked by the absence of DJ Ready Red and the GB's first breakthrough single, "Mind Playing Tricks On Me."

5. **Uncut Dope (Rap-A-Lot, 1992)**
Aiming to keep the GB's a house hold name, Lil' J releases a greatest hits collection highlighted by the previously unavailable "Damn It Feels Good To Be A Gangsta."

6. **Till Death Do Us Part (Rap-A-Lot, 1993)**
Thirsty for more solo recognition, Willie D decides to leave the group and is replaced by the Convicts' Big Mike. Despite the high profile personnel change, the album garners yet another gold plaque for H-Town's finest.

7. **The Resurrection (Rap-A-Lot, 1996)**
Everyone loves a reunion, so Willie D returns home to the place where everyone knows his name. But don't cry for Big Mike. He moves on to a successful solo career.

8. **Da Good, Da Bad & Da Ugly (Rap-A-Lot, 1998)**
Good things don't last forever. After a serious falling-out with the Rap-A-Lot family, Bushwick Bill bolts, leaving the crew down to two. Lil' J contemplates adding Facemob member DMG as the new official third member, but he scraps the idea at the last minute. Still, the influx of guests on this release (The Outlawz, Devin, Tela, Yukmouth, etc.) leaves fans wondering: who are the real Geto Boys?

Rappers United For The Cause.

1. **"Evolution"—Juice Crew All-Stars featuring Debbie D as Harriet Tubman, Kool G Rap as Malcolm X, Glamorous as Maya Angelou, MC Shan as Martin Luther King Jr. & TJ Swan as himself (Cold Chillin', 1987)**
CAUSE: Schooling the masses on Black History Month and allowing the Juice Crew to test its thespian skills.

2. **"Self Destruction"—Stop The Violence Movement featuring KRS-One, Delite (Stetsasonic), Kool Moe Dee, MC Lyte, Daddy-O (Stetsasonic), Wise (Stetsasonic), D-Nice, Ms. Melodie, Doug E. Fresh, Just-Ice, Heavy D, Fruitkwan (Stetsasonic), Chuck D & Flavor Flav (Jive, 1988)**
CAUSE: Condemning Black-on-Black crime.

3. **"We're All In The Same Gang"—The West Coast Rap All-Stars featuring King Tee, Body & Soul, Def Jef, Michel'le, Tone-Lōc, Above The Law, Ice-T, MC Ren, Dr. Dre, J.J. Fad, Young MC, Shock G & Humpty Hump (Digital Underground), Oaktown's 3.5.7., MC Hammer & Eazy-E (Warner Bros., 1990)**
CAUSE: Condemning gang violence.

4. **"Ndodemnyama (Free South Africa)"—Hip Hop Artists Against Apartheid featuring X Clan, Lakim Shabazz, Jungle Brothers, U.T.F.O., Ultimate Force, Grand Puba, Kings Of Swing, Queen Latifah, Revolucion, Solo, Linque & Arthur X (Warlock, 1990)**
CAUSE: The title says it all.

5. **"Heal Yourself"—H.E.A.L. Project featuring Harmony, Kid Capri, Big Daddy Kane, Freddie Foxxx, LL Cool J, MC Lyte, Queen Latifah, KRS-One, Ms. Melodie, D.M.C. & Jam Master Jay (Edutainer, 1991)**
CAUSE: Human Education Against Lies.

6. **"Bring 'Em Home Safely"—Chubb Rock featuring 3rd Bass & a bunch of M.I.A. no-names (Select, 1991)**
CAUSE: Prayers for the troops serving in Desert Storm.

7. **"Keep Control"—Marley Marl featuring Tragedy, King Tee, Grand Puba, Def Jef & Chubb Rock (Cold Chillin', 1991)**
CAUSE: Rap Industry For Social Evolution.

8. **"Rap Declares War"—A Lighter Shade Of Brown, Hispanic MC's, Proper Dos, Hi-C & Kid Frost (Avenue, 1992)**
CAUSE: Eradicating the really bad stuff from the Latin community. *Oralé.*

9. **"Get The Fist"—Get The Fist Movement featuring King Tee, Yo Yo, MC Eiht, B-Real, J-Dee (Da Lench Mob), Kam, Threat & Ice Cube (Mercury, 1992)**
CAUSE: Los Angeles Brotherhood Crusade Black United Fund.

10. **"Love Hurts"—The Poetess featuring Def Jef, Almigh-T & Kool G Rap (Interscope, 1992)**
CAUSE: Condemning domestic violence.

11. **"Close The Crackhouse"—Professor X featuring Brother J, Wise Intelligent, Big Daddy Kane, Money B (Digital Underground; Raw Fusion), Shock G & Humpty Hump (Digital Underground), Ex-Girlfriend, Chuck D, Sister Souljah, Freedom Williams, YZ, College Boyz & Two Kings In A Cipher (Polygram, 1993)**
CAUSE: Give a hoot, don't pollute—the neighborhood—with drugs.

12. **"The Points"—The Notorious B.I.G., Coolio, Redman, Ill Al Skratch, Big Mike, Busta Rhymes, Buckshot (Black Moon) & Bone Thugs-N-Harmony (Mercury, 1995)**
CAUSE: Bigging up the Black Panthers legacy.

13. **"Where Ya At?"—Ice Cube, Mobb Deep, Ice-T, Chuck D, Smooth B (Nice & Smooth), RZA, Killah Priest, Shorty (Da Lench Mob), DA Smart & Kam (Mergela, 1995)***
CAUSE: Supporting the Million Man March.

14. **"East Coast/West Coast Killas"—Group Therapy featuring Dr. Dre, RBX, KRS-One, B-Real (Cypress Hill) & Nas (Aftermath, 1996)**
CAUSE: Promoting bi-coastal unity.

*A second version replaces Ice Cube, Ice-T, Smooth B, Shorty (Da Lench Mob) & Kam with Merchant, E-Rule, Sunz Of Man & Brooklyn Zoo.

HONORABLE MENTION: Run-D.M.C. are the Kings of Rock *and* charity. On "Sun City" (Manhattan, 1985), they rap against apartheid alongside Grandmaster Melle Mel, Scorpio, Duke Bootee, Fat Boys & Afrika Bambaataa. And on "King Holiday" (Polygram, 1985), they appear with Kurtis Blow, Fat Boys, Grandmaster Melle Mel & Whodini for the national observance of Martin Luther King Jr.'s birthday. *And* they stood on-stage at Live Aid (where the people played and the poor got paid).

CLANS, POSSES, CREWS & CLIQUES.

Who Is The "Fourth" Beastie Boy?

1. CEY ADAMS   2. BIZ MARKIE   3. MARIO CALDATO JR.
4. LYOR COHEN   5. THE DALI LAMA   6. DOCTOR DRÉ
7. DJ DOUBLE R (B/K/A RICK RUBIN)   8. HURRICANE
9. MIXMASTER MIKE   10. MONEY MARK   11.
RICKY POWELL   12. MOLLY RINGWALD

LEFT THEM LONELY:
People Who Left Or Were Kicked Out
Of Major Hip Hop Groups Before They Blew Up.

1. Arabian Prince: N.W.A
2. John Barry & Kate Schellenbach: Beastie Boys
3. Big Shug, Damo D-Ski, DJ 1-2 B Down: Gang Starr
4. Bo-Dee & Mike Ski: Fearless Four
5. The Chill MC: Compton's Most Wanted
6. Cormega: The Firm
7. Finsta: Black Moon
8. Keith K.C. Hams: Wreckx-N-Effect

9. Jarobi: A Tribe Called Quest
10. DJ K La Boss: EPMD
11. Kurtis Blow: Grandmaster Flash & The Furious Five
12. The Original Spinderella: Salt-N-Pepa
13. Playa Fly: Three 6 Mafia
14. Spoonie Gee: Treacherous Three
15. Scott Storch: The Roots

FIRST FAMILY FOR LIFE:
Rappers Who Have Recorded A Song With A Parent On Wax.

1. **Cam'Ron & his mother**
"Me, My Moms & Jimmy" (Untertainment, 1998)

2. **Common & his father**
"Pop's Rap" (Relativity, 1994);
"Pop's Rap Part 2/ Fatherhood" (Relativity, 1997)

3. **Nas & his father**
"Life's A Bitch" (Columbia, 1994);
"Jungle Jay"—Olu Dara (Atlantic, 1998)

4. **O.C. & his mother**
"Ma Dukes" (Wild Pitch, 1994)

5. **Xzibit & his father**
"Outro" (Loud, 1998)

Great Songs About Parents.

1. "All That I Got Is You"—Ghostface Killah featuring Mary J. Blige (Razor Sharp, 1996)
2. "Dear Mama"—2Pac (Interscope, 1995)
3. "Everything's Gonna Be Alright (Ghetto Bastard)" —Naughty By Nature (Tommy Boy, 1991)
4. "Family Problems"—Royal Flush (Blunt, 1997)
5. "Fuck My Daddy"—WC And The MAAD Circle (Priority, 1991)
6. "Grand Groove"—Tragedy (Tuff Break, 1993)
7. "Guess Who"—Goodie Mob (LaFace, 1995)
8. "Millie Pulled A Pistol On Santa"—De La Soul (Tommy Boy, 1991)
9. "Parents Just Don't Understand"—DJ Jazzy Jeff & The Fresh Prince (Jive, 1988)
10. "Your Mom's In My Business"—K-Solo (Atlantic, 1990)

RHYME RELATED—IT'S A FAMILY AFFAIR
Part I: Brothers Gonna Work It Out (& Sisters Too).

1. Apache & Latee
2. Baby Girl & Jazzy (H.W.A.)
3. Big Daddy Kane & Little Daddy Shane
4. Biz Markie & Diamond Shell
5. Boo-Yaa T.R.I.B.E.
6. MC Breed & Al Breed (DFC)
7. Dr. Dre & Warren G*
8. E-40, D-Shot & Suga T
9. DJ Evil Dee & Mr. Walt (Da Beatminerz)
10. Foxy Brown & Pretty Boy
11. Freequon & Ikeim (Lil' Soldiers)
12. Grandmaster Melle Mel & Kidd Creole (Furious Five)
13. Grand Wizard Theodore, Claudio & Mean Gene (L Brothers)
14. Hen-Gee & Evil-E
15. Jacken & Mr. Duke (Psycho Realm)
16. Jalil (Whodini) & Doctor Ice (U.T.F.O.)
17. Juicy J (Three 6 Mafia) & Project Pat
18. Kangol (U.T.F.O.) & Jazz (Whistle)
19. KRS-One & Kenny Parker
20. MC Lyte, Milk Dee & Giz (Audio Two)
21. Ma$e & Blinky Blink (Harlem World)
22. Master P, Silkk The Shocker & C-Murder
23. Mr. Cheeks & Freaky Tah (Lost Boyz)
24. Ms. Melodie & Harmony
25. Nard & AK-47 (Do Or Die)
26. Nas & Jungle (Bravehearts)
27. Ol' Dirty Bastard & 12 O'Clock
28. DJ Paul & Lord Infamous (Three 6 Mafia)
29. Redman & Roz
30. Ruck (Heltah Skeltah) & Illa Noyz
31. Run & Russell Simmons
32. Saafir & King Saan (The WhoRidas)
33. Sean B & Brett B (7A3)
34. Sen Dog & Mellow Man Ace
35. Hank & Keith Shocklee (The Bomb Squad)
36. Sir Scratch & K-Cut (Main Source)
37. Smoothe Da Hustler & Trigger Tha Gambler
38. Sticky Fingaz (Onyx) & X-1
39. TCD & Stevie D (Force MD's)
40. T La Rock & Special K (Treacherous Three)
41. T La Rock & Tony Tone (Style)
42. Nick & Erik Vidal (Baka Boyz)
43. WC & Crazy Toones
44. Tanya & Paulette Winley
45. Zev Love X & Subroc (K.M.D.)

*Brothers by marriage.

CLANS, POSSES, CREWS & CLIQUES.

★ back in the days parents used to take care of us…

Part II: What's Up, Cousin?

1. Baby Girl & Diva (H.W.A.)
2. Biz Markie & Cool V
3. Busta Rhymes & Cut Monitor Milo (Leaders Of The New School)
4. Busta Rhymes & Rampage
5. Capone & Royal Flush
6. Ced Gee & Moe Love (Ultramagnetic MC's)
7. Cold 187um & Kokane
8. Dr. Dre & Sir Jinx
9. E-40 & B-Legit
10. E-40 & Mac Mall
11. Grand Puba & CL Smooth
12. Grand Puba & Dr. Who (Masters Of Ceremony)
13. Heavy D & Pete Rock
14. Ice Cube & Del The Funkeé Homosapien
15. Kool DJ Red Alert & Afrika Baby Bam & Mike G (Jungle Brothers)
16. Kool DJ Red Alert & Jazzy Jay
17. Larry-O (Real Live) & Wonder Mike (Sugarhill Gang)
18. Layzie Bone & Wish Bone
19. Master P & Mo B. Dick
20. Ol' Dirty Bastard & 60 Sec. Assassin (Sunz of Man)
21. Poet & KL (Screwball)
22. Q-Tip & Consequence
23. R&B & Fred Fonk (Me & My Cousin)
24. Redman & Shooga Bear
25. Redman & Tame One (Artifacts)
26. RZA, The Genius & Ol' Dirty Bastard
27. Slick Rick & Vance Wright
28. Snoop Doggy Dogg, Daz Dillinger & RBX
29. Sticky Fingaz & Fredro Starr (Onyx)
30. Wyclef Jean & Pras

RAP IS FOR THE CHILDREN:
16 Songs About Kids.

1. "The Baby Doesn't Look Like Me"—K-Solo (Atlantic, 1992)
2. "Be A Father To Your Child"—Ed O.G & Da BULLDOGS (PWL, 1991)
3. "A Better Tomorrow"—Wu-Tang Clan (Loud, 1997)
4. "Biggest Part Of Me"—Bahamadia (Chrysalis, 1996)
5. "Children R The Future"—Big Daddy Kane (Cold Chillin', 1989)
6. "The Foundation"—Xzibit (Loud, 1996)
7. "4 Da Children"—Monie Love (Warner Bros., 1993)
8. "Help The Children"—MC Hammer (Capitol, 1990)
9. "It's A Boy"—Slick Rick (Def Jam, 1991)
10. "Just The Two of Us"—Eminem (WEB, 1998)
11. "Just The Two of Us"—Will Smith (Columbia, 1997)
12. "Mommie's Angels"—Mia X (No Limit, 1997)
13. "Teach My Kids"—MC Breed (Ichiban, 1994)
14. "Teach The Children"—Eric B. & Rakim (MCA, 1992)
15. "Thank God 4 The Children"—40 Thevz (Mercury, 1997)
16. "To Zion"—Lauryn Hill (Ruffhouse, 1998)

Twins 4 Life.

1. Albino Twins
2. Disco Twins & Starchild
3. Ecstacy (Whodini) & Dynasty (Dynasty & Mimi)
4. Fat Joe & Big Pun*
5. Ghetto Twiinz
6. Kane & Abel
7. Ma$e & Baby Stase (Harlem World)
8. Nigger Twins (Herculords)
9. Twin Hype
10. Twinz

*Not really twins but included out of respect.

Mother's Finest.

1. "Baby Mama Drama"—Daz Dillinger (Death Row, 1998)
2. "Early Mother's Day Card"—Whodini (Jive, 1987)
3. "Get Your Mother Off The Crack"—Audio Two (First Priority, 1990)
4. "I Wanna Fuck Your Mama"—Willie D (Ichiban, 1994)
5. "Mama Alwayz Told Me"—B.O.X. (PWL, 1991)
6. "Mama Don't"—Yomo & Maulkie (Ruthless, 1991)
7. "Mama Feel Good"—Schoolly D (Jive, 1989)
8. "Mama, I'm In Love With A Gangsta"—Coolio featuring LeShaun (Tommy Boy, 1994)
9. "Mama Raised Me"—Master P (No Limit, 1998)
10. "Mama Said Knock You Out"—LL Cool J (Def Jam, 1990)
11. "Mama's Always On Stage"—Arrested Development (Chrysalis, 1992)
12. "Mama Told Me"—Dana Dane (Maverick, 1995)
13. "Mama Used To Say"—Pooh-Man (In-A-Minute, 1997)
14. "Mom Dukes"—Private Investigators (Virgin, 1993)
15. "Momma Was A Rolling Stone"—Chubb Rock featuring Hitman Howie Tee (Select, 1988)
16. "My Baby Mamma"—Luniz (Noo Trybe, 1997)
17. "My Baby'z Mama"—Eazy-E (Ruthless, 1996)
18. "My Mother"—Divine Sounds (Reality, 1986)
19. "My Mother (Yes I Love Her)"—Jazzy Jeff (Jive, 1985)
20. "Play Witcha Mama"—Willie D featuring Ice Cube (Ichiban, 1994)
21. "Ya Mama"—The Pharcyde (Delicious Vinyl, 1992)
22. "Ya Mama"—Wuf Ticket (Prelude, 1982)
23. "Yo Momma Told Me . . ."—AMG (Select, 1991)
24. "Yo Mutha"—Steady B (Pop Art, 1986)
25. "Your Mother Has Green Teeth"—Stetsasonic (Tommy Boy, 1991)

FAMILY GOT TO GET BUSY:
Hip Hop Offspring Of Famous People.

1. **Adrock (Beastie Boys)**
   The son of playwright Israel Horovitz.

2. **May May Ali**
   The daughter of boxing great Muhammad Ali. Released own punchless solo album, *The Introduction* (Scotti Bros., 1992).

3. **Eric Bobo**
   A part-time member of Cypress Hill and the Beastie Boys and the son of Latin percussion giant Willie Bobo.

4. **Chilly Tee**
   The son of Nike founder/CEO Phil Knight. Released The Bomb Squad-produced flop, *Get Off Mine* (MCA, 1993).

5. **Damon Elliott**
   Producer of Flesh-N-Bone's *T.H.U.G.S.* (Def Jam, 1996) and the son of Dionne Warwick.

6. **Qur'an "Q-Ball" Goodman (Da Youngstas)**
   The son of Pop Art Records CEO Lawrence Goodman.

7. **Mad Skill (The Whooliganz)**
   The son of actor James Caan. The group released a 1993 single "Put Your Handz Up" on Tommy Boy Records and submitted an album that was never commercially released.

8. **Professor X**
   X Clan's founder is the son of Black nationalist/political activist Sonny Carson.

9. **QDIII**
   The son of Quincy Jones is an established producer who has worked with Too $hort, LL Cool J and Ice Cube.

10. **Rahshawnna (Infamous Syndicate)**
    The daughter of blues legend Buddy Guy.

11. **Tim Reid II (06 Style)**
    The son of actor/producer Tim "Venus Flytrap/*WKRP In Cincinnati*" Reid.

12. **Salaam Remi**
    Acclaimed producer of the Fugees, Ini Kamoze and Mega Banton and the son of producer/musician Van Gibbs.

13. **Joey Robinson Jr.**
    The son of Sugar Hill Records' president Joey Robinson Sr., Joey Jr. is a former member of the West Street Mob and is currently the replacement for Guy "Master Gee" O'Brien in the Sugarhill Gang.

14. **Gamilah Shabazz**
    The daughter of Malcolm X made her debut on "Who Am I" from Big Daddy Kane's *Taste Of Chocolate* (Cold Chillin', 1990). Two years later, she released a single, "America's Living In A War Zone" (BMG, 1992). The song featured Ice Cube and Grand Puba amongst other rap heavyweights.

15. **2Pac**
    Rap's original "thug" and the son of Black Panther Afeni Shakur.

HONORABLE MENTION: Cold 187um of Above The Law is the nephew of soul singer Willie Hutch.

CLANS, POSSES, CREWS & CLIQUES.

THE SECOND HARDEST WORKING MEN IN SHOW BIZNESS:
Hip Hop's #1 Sidemen.

1. C & H (DRU DOWN) 2. DANNY BOY (HOUSE OF PAIN) 3. E LOVE (LL COOL J) 4. FLAVOR FLAV (PUBLIC ENEMY) 5. FREAKY TAH (LOST BOYZ) 6. LIL' CEASE (THE NOTORIOUS B.I.G.) 7. SEN DOG (CYPRESS HILL) 8. SPLIFF STAR (BUSTA RHYMES) 9. 2-BIGG MC (MC HAMMER) 10. VINNIE (NAUGHTY BY NATURE) 11. WILLIE D (KRS-ONE)

IT WAS V

WRITTEN.

16 Songs That Assassinate The Media.

1. **"Ain't U The Masta?"—Masta Ace (Delicious Vinyl, 1993)**
Ace's *Slaughtahouse* LP went so against the grain of hip hop conformity, that the Masta didn't flinch at the chance to spew these anti-critique sentiments: "I'm a stab a fuckin' critic with his pen/ So write that, put that in your magazine and stick it."

2. **"A Letter To The New York Post"—Public Enemy (Def Jam, 1991)**
From *Apocalypse '91... The Enemy Strikes Black*, this ditty was an angry response to the coverage of Flavor Flav's arrest for a domestic dispute with his girlfriend. Not only does *The Post* literally get ripped (the sound of newsprint being torn can be heard on the track in the background), but *Jet* magazine also gets slammed for failing to research the story properly.

3. **"All The Critics In New York"—Westside Connection (Priority, 1996)**
Addressing the East Coast bias of many hip hop scribes, the Cali power trio rhymed, "Fuck all the critics in the NYC/ And your articles trying to rate my LP."

4. **"Back From Hell (Remix)"—Run-D.M.C. featuring Ice Cube & Chuck D (Profile, 1991)**
D.M.C.'s verse displayed the first sign of defensiveness emanating from Hollis' finest—then on the mend from charges of having fallen off. But his memorable quip, "Lyrics that I kick might get me into bigger shit that I'm not with/ And critics get the di-dick," couldn't save this disap-

pointing remix from going nowhere.

5. **"Bulworth (They Talk About It While We Live It)"—Method Man, KRS-One, Prodigy & Kam (Interscope, 1998)**
KRS-One chastised mainstream publications like *Rolling Stone*, *Spin* and *Details* for a lack of Black editors on his verse from the soundtrack to Warren Beatty's poor political farce. The Teacher ripped into rap rags too when he announced, "KRS is the source/ Fuck these magazines leading hip hop off course."

6. **"Check It Out"—Del The Funkeé Homosapien (Elektra, 1993)**
"You can't write and you're not bright/ You fail to notice the dopeness cuz you have no insight" is the mildest dis in an otherwise scathing diatribe directed at then-freelance Bay Area writer Danyel Smith. Her review of a Hieroglyphics' live show, apparently, did not sit well with the clique's spiritual leader.

7. **"Don't Believe The Hype"—Public Enemy (Def Jam, 1988)**
One of P.E.'s greatest singles was composed in sardonic dedication to longtime *Village Voice* rock scribe Robert Christgau and *Spin*'s then-hip hop columnist, John Leland, for their misrepresentation of Chuck D's lyrical bent. "Suckers, liars get me a shovel/ Some writers I know are damn devils," an incensed Mistachuck fumed.

8. **"Fuck The Media"—The Terrorists featuring Bushwick Bill (Rap-A-Lot, 1991)**
This slow and low dismissal of writers and reporters receives a personal touch when little Geto Boy Bill—the

IT WAS WRITTEN.

subject of media probes after his attempted suicide—starts venting at the song's conclusion. "Yeah, I tried to kill myself and I got shot in the eye," he growls, "and now the media wanna ask me why. What if I was to put you under the same pressures you put me under? How would you like the microscope to be on your ass?"

9. **"How High"—Redman & Method Man (Def Jam, 1995)**
Hip hop's answer to Jake and Elwood Blues found a moment between hydro puffs to take a stiff jab at the rap press *vis-á-vis* Meth's line, "Fuck a rap critic/ He talk about it while I live it."

10. **"Let It Rain"—Cypress Hill (Ruffhouse, 1995)**
"Fuck all y'all comin' off the wall/ I got a nigga from *The Source* swingin' from my balls," goaded B-Real at former *Source* editors James Bernard and Reginald C. Dennis, two outspoken critics of the group's later output.

11. **"Luchini (Remix)"—Camp Lo (Profile, 1997)**
Angered by their record review by our own light-skinded journalist, Elliott Wilson, the uptown duo rhymed, "To the cat that gave us three mics in *The Source*/ He sips ammonia."

12. **"Parole Violators"—Capone-N-Noreaga featuring Havoc (Mobb Deep) (Penalty, 1997)**
Nore's call-out of writer Greg Tate ("Greg Tate/ Leave his mouth taped—eliminate") came in response to a few derogatory remarks the journalist aired in *The Village Voice* regarding the thugged-out Queens rap phenomenon.

13. **"The Predator"—Ice Cube (Priority, 1992)**
After *Billboard* editor Timothy White made his unfavorable views on the gangsta rap genre known, Cube responded with the cut-throat couplet, "Fuck *Billboard* and the editor/ Here comes The Predator."

14. **"Ride"—Master P (No Limit, 1998)**
"Niggas don't kill niggas, the media kills niggas," an agitated P states at the song's outset in reference to the media-hyped East-West conflicts, before compassionately adding, "I feel your pain, Suge Knight, nigga."

15. **"Yeah You Get Props"—The Beatnuts (Relativity, 1994)**
Psycho Les' venomous line, "Ask you a question, three seconds to answer/ Kill a photographer shooting as a freelancer," was a shot directed at respected veteran photojournalist B+, whom Les felt was being nosy about his beat-digging secrets during an *Urb* magazine profile.

16. **"Zealots"—Fugees (Ruffhouse, 1996)**
Wyclef's defensive lyric ("You can try but you can't divide the tribe/ 'These cats can't rap'—Mr. Author I feel no vibe/ The magazine says the girl shoulda went solo, the guys should stop rappin'/ Vanish like Menudo") was written in response to a *Vibe* magazine profile of the group by journalist Cheo H. Coker.

DON'T BELIEVE THE HYPE:
Bill Adler's Top 5 Mainstream Media Rap Coverage Travesties.

1.   The Together Forever Tour With Run-D.M.C. & Beastie Boys.

Even though this 1987 summer tour's theme of racial harmony was built right into its name, police groups put together a nationally concerted campaign to defame it through the press. (In all fairness, I'll note that Run-D.M.C.'s Raising Hell Tour during the summer of '86 had been disrupted by violence on several occasions and that the Beasties' Licensed To Ill Tour during the spring of '87 had been designed to outrage respectable citizens.) In Cincinnati, the chief of police told the *Cincinnati Enquirer*, "We have information from 20 other cities indicating that this act [the Beasties] is garbage." The newspaper dutifully ran the story several days before the show under a frankly inflammatory banner front-page headline announcing, "It's The Neo-Nasty Era." In Seattle, local venue operators cancelled the show after the police chief expressed "fear that the concert would become 'a forum for confrontations' for local youths of different races." The headline in the *Seattle Times* read, "Rock Concert Cancelled: Fear Of Violence Cited." In Portland, the *Oregonian* had a police spokesman cite "'intelligence' reports, which he declined to describe," to justify his concerns about "possible gang fights." In Jacksonville, the *Florida Times-Union* reported, "Beastie Boys Tickets Carry Warning Notices," after local officials ordained that tickets to the show had to carry warnings about the Beasties' sexism "in all newspaper, radio and TV ads and on all tickets"—an initiative overturned after the Beasties' lawyer threatened to sue the city.

These efforts by the police predate the F.B.I.'s 1989 campaign to derail N.W.A in the wake of "Fuck Tha Police," as well as . . .

2.   The "Cop Killer" Controversy.

In 1992, Body Count, the speed-metal band conceived and fronted by rapper Ice-T, released an album containing a song called "Cop Killer." National police organizations and the religious right-wing—looking for a political football during an election year and fronted by NRA flack Charlton Heston and hysterical former Civil Rights activist C. DeLores Tucker—decided that "Cop Killer" was it. Their strategy was to attack not Ice-T nor Warner Bros. Records, but to complain at a meeting of the shareholders of Time-Warner, Warner Bros.' parent company, that the song incited violence against the police. Under the guise of standing up for the police, the right-wing intended to raise the specter of wantonly murderous Black youth and drive white voters to the polls with the pressing need for "law and order."

Sure enough, some of the mainstream press dutifully followed the script laid out by Heston and Tucker—that America would suffer a plague of cop killing if this evil song wasn't taken out of circulation. "Vice President Calls Corporation Wrong Selling Rap Song," read a *New York Times* headline. "Cop Killer Is Iced," stated the *New York Daily News*. And even *Jet* magazine reported, "Ice-T's Controversial Record Triggers Boycott." No matter that Ice maintained that the problem wasn't cop killers, it was killer cops—ones like the L.A.P.D. gang who had been videotaped beating the piss out of Rodney King half a year earlier. No one backed Ice up. Warner—who cared nothing about these issues, but cared a lot about negative publicity depressing the value of its stock—were more than glad to let Ice go.

Sister Souljah:
Clinton gave
me a bad rap   Thousands
flee riot at

3. **Sister Souljah vs. Bill Clinton.**
At just about the same time Ice-T was under attack by the right-wing, Sister Souljah was singled out for condemnation by then-Democratic Presidential candidate Bill Clinton. In an interview with the *Washington Post,* Souljah (ostensibly inhabiting the mindset of an L.A. rioter) had wondered, "If Black people kill Black people every day, why not have a week and kill white people?" A week later, Clinton, as a guest at a meeting of Jesse Jackson's Rainbow Coalition, attacked Souljah for sowing "racial divisiveness." His remarks made national news for a week.

But as Marshall Frady's excellent biography of Jesse Jackson reveals, Clinton could have cared less about Souljah and rap. He cynically attacked her as a way of taking a big public whack at Jackson, his host that day. The charismatic Reverend, always a big player in Democratic politics, was looking to leverage his standing in the African-American community for some clout in the would-be Clinton administration. Clinton's advisors had convinced the candidate that it was important for him to "stand up" to Jackson to demonstrate that Clinton didn't need Jackson to win the African-American vote. And they were right—Bill won anyway, without Jesse's support. Although Souljah herself understood it well enough (she claimed that Clinton was trying to make her into that year's Willie Horton), very few in the mainstream press understood at that time that Souljah was just a pawn in the game.

OST, FRIDAY, JANUARY 29, 1993

4. *Newsweek,* **March 19, 1990.**
This issue's cover story featuring a photo of *Tone-Lōc* (!) was headlined, "Rap Rage." Written by a guy named Jerry Adler, it was a hatchet job that described rap music as "sullen," "furtive," "ugly," "macho," "savage," "violent," "anti-Semitic," "obscene," "bombastic," "self-aggrandizing," "appalling," "vile," "revolting," "brutal," "repulsive," "empty," "nihilistic," and "as scary as sudden footsteps in the dark." It was so off-base that 49 music writers, led by *Entertainment Weekly's* Greg Sandow (and representing publications including *Time, USA Today, The Los Angeles Times, The Washington Post, Rolling Stone* and *The Village Voice*) wrote a letter to the editors of *Newsweek* insisting that Adler had "invented a nightmarish and racist fantasy about ignorant Black men who scream obscene threats. This is more than an artistic misjudgement. Adler has slandered a major strain of contemporary Black culture."

5. **Busta Rhymes'** *New York Post* **Headline.**
On Sunday night, December 29, 1998, a car driven by Busta Rhymes was stopped by New York City police for changing lanes without signaling. The cops found an unlicensed gun in the car, which Busta claimed he was carrying after having been robbed twice. Although the rapper had no previous criminal record, was described by one of the arresting officers as "a total gentleman," and was released without bail, the *New York Post* ran the story on its front page two days later under the headline, "BUSTA CRIMES!" with the subhead, "Top Rap Star Nabbed On Gun Charge." The story on page three was accompanied by a sidebar headlined, "It's The Same Old Song Of Violence And Crime," accompanied by photos of Ol' Dirty Bastard, Snoop Doggy Dogg, 2Pac and Vinnie of Naughty By Nature. In other words, it was business as usual for *The Post,* an institution which practices racial divisiveness with a dedication that Mayor Rudolph Giuliani might admire.

Bill Adler (a/k/a "Ill Badler") was the Director Of Publicity for Def Jam Records and Rush Productions from 1984 to 1990 where he was instrumental in garnering mainstream press exposure for some of hip hop's greatest artists. He is currently president of Mouth Almighty Records and Mouth Almighty Books.

9 ARRESTED IN FAT
RAP SHOW RAMPA

his 2-year-old daughter.

6 Seminal Hip Hop Albums That Were Panned By *Rolling Stone.*

1. *AmeriKKKa's Most Wanted*—Ice Cube (Priority, 1990)
"The relentless profanity grows wearisome, the Bomb Squad beats lose steam and Cube's attitudes toward women are simply despicable . . . Ice Cube ultimately sounds like the Andrew Dice Clay of rap."
(July 12, 1990)

2. *Back In Black*—Whodini (Jive, 1986)
"Unfortunately, the raps by Jalil and Ecstacy, who are virtually indistinguishable from one another, aren't so funky fresh. This record features boast rap, cliché rap and, worst of all, sexist rap. . . . *Back In Black* is day-old rap; it sounds just a little bit stale."
(September 11, 1986)

3. *Efil4zaggin*—N.W.A (Ruthless, 1991)
". . . listening to [*Efil4zaggin*] is like hearing the loudest guys at a neighborhood barbecue strut, brag, wolf-whistle and lie about sex. . . . The loosest stuff on the record, when the band members sloppily rant, is also the most difficult to follow; the rest is so hateful toward women, and in such a pathetic and sleazy manner, that it's simply tiresome."
(July 7, 1991)

4. *The Great Adventures Of Slick Rick*—Slick Rick (Def Jam, 1988)
". . . this is a truly hateful record. . . . There's certainly nothing wrong with rapping frankly about sex and relationships, but the degree and prevalence of the woman-hating raps on this record undermine its ample strengths. Worse, the raps also reinforce stereotypes that should have been broken down long ago."
(June 1, 1989)

5. *People's Instinctive Travels And The Paths Of Rhythm*—A Tribe Called Quest (Jive, 1990)
". . . the rappers of A Tribe Called Quest tend to mumble in understated monotones that feel self-satisfied, even bored . . . this is one of the least *danceable* rap albums ever—there's no forward motion. Sound effects or no, the backing tracks frequently add up to the sort of funkified quiet-storm pseudo-jazz you might expect young Afrocentric upwardly mobiles to indulge in when they crack open that bottle of Ameretto and cuddle up in front of the gas fireplace . . . Maybe A Tribe Called Quest has hit upon the perfect middlebrow college-radio format for the early 1990s: Nutritiously Eclectic Adult-Contemporary Comedy Rap."
(April 19, 1990)

6. *We Can't Be Stopped*—Geto Boys (Rap-A-Lot, 1991)
". . . when [the Geto Boys'] emotions range only from spite to malice, their claim of holding a mirror to a young, Black generation is revealed as a lie—the hatred is their own, and it pervades the entire album."
(September 5, 1991)

HONORABLE MENTION: *3 Feet High And Rising*—De La Soul (Tommy Boy, 1989)
"One of the most original rap records to come down the pike." RATING: A paltry three stars out of possible five.
(March 23, 1989)

IT WAS WRITTEN.

RAP SCHOLARS:
Artists Whose Writings Have Been Published.

1. Apani B. Fly Emcee
2. Capital D (All Natural)
3. Chuck D
4. Doctor Dré & Ed Lover
5. Fab 5 Freddy
6. Dorsey Fuller (O6 Style)
7. Ice-T
8. Kool Kim (UMC's)
9. KRS-One
10. Large Professor
11. LL Cool J
12. Masta Ace
13. Pharoahe Monch (Organized Konfusion)
14. Phife Dawg (A Tribe Called Quest)
15. The Poetess
16. Queen Latifah
17. ?uest Love (The Roots)
18. Sister Souljah
19. Speech
20. T-Love
21. AJ Woodson (J.V.C. Force)

HONORABLE MENTION: Posdnuos and Trugoy of De La Soul wrote their group's publicity bios for its first two albums.

IT WAS A GOOD DAY:
Artists Who Appeared On The Cover Of *The Village Voice*'s Hip Hop Nation Issue (January 19, 1988).*

(back row, from left)
1. D.M.C.
2. Jam Master Jay
3. PaPa Jam
4. Cowboy
5. Don Barron
6. Kool DJ Red Alert
7. Daddy-O
8. D.B.C.
9. Grandmaster Flash

(middle row, from left)
10. MC Shan
11. Barry B
12. Chill Will
13. Busy Bee**
14. Fruitkwan
15. Delite (in front of Fruitkwan)
16. Rahiem
17. Kidd Creole

(front row, from left)
18. Grandmaster Melle Mel
19. Mr. Magic & his baby daughter
20. Roxanne Shanté
21. Doug E. Fresh
22. Wise
23. Run
24. Scorpio (in front of Run)

*Photo shown here is an alternate shot from the same session.
**The Chief Rocker did not appear in the original cover shot.

RAPPIN' IS FUNDAMENTAL:
Songs & Albums Based On Literature.

1. **The Art Of War—Bone Thugs-N-Harmony (Ruthless, 1997)**
Sun Tzu's ancient Chinese tome gets a thumbs up from the Bone brothas.

2. **Autobiography Of Mistachuck—Chuck D (Mercury, 1996)**
A play off of *The Autobiography Of Malcolm X.*

3. **"Behold The Pale Horse"—Boogiemonsters (EMI, 1997)**
Based on Ralph Cooper's new world order primer.

4. **"Cinderfella Dana Dane"—Dana Dane (Profile, 1987)**
Based on the classic children's story, *Cinderella.*

5. **"Goines' Tale"—Cru (Def Jam, 1997)**
A collection of references to characters from realist author Donald Goines' novels.

6. **The Miseducation Of Lauryn Hill—Lauryn Hill (Columbia, 1998)**
Based on *The Miseducation Of The Negro* by Carter G. Woodson and activist Sonny

Carson's *The Education Of Sonny Carson.*

7. **"Portrait Of The Artist As A Hood"—3rd Bass (Def Jam, 1991)**
Educated white rappers based this *Derelicts Of Dialect* single on James Joyce's *Portrait Of The Artist As A Young Man.*

8. **"Romeo"—Super Lover Cee & Casanova Rud (Epic, 1991)**
Shakespeare in Queens.

9. **"Romeo & Juliet"—Biz Markie (Cold Chillin', 1991)**
The Diabolical meets The Bard.

10. **"Shadrach"—Beastie Boys (Capitol, 1989)**
From the original book, The Bible. Find it in there somewhere.

11. **Soul On Ice—Ras Kass (Priority, 1996)**
From former Black Panther Eldridge Cleaver's novel of the same name.

12. **"Waiting To Excel"—Chino XL (American, 1996)**
Based on Terry McMillan's *Waiting To Exhale.*

13. **War & Peace—Ice Cube (Priority, 1998)**
Based on Tolstoy's epic novel and nearly as long.

IT WAS WRITTEN.

14 Rap Songs Based On Nursery Rhymes.

1. **"Adventures Of Super Rhyme (Rap)"—Jimmy Spicer (Dazz, 1980)**
Based on the children's nursery rhyme, "This Old Man."

2. **"Cradle Rock"—Method Man (Def Jam, 1998)**
Based on the nursery rhyme, "Rock A Bye, Baby."

3. **"Dirty Nursery Rhymes"—2 Live Crew (Luke, 1989)**
The title says it all.

4. **"Gangsta's Fairytale"—Ice Cube (Priority, 1990)**
A series of fairytale adaptations from a young G's perspective.

5. **"Have U.N.E. Pull"—Black Sheep (Mercury, 1991)**
Arrogant jingle bases its chorus on "Baa, Baa, Black Sheep."

6. **"Jack B. Nimble"—Masta Ace (Delicious Vinyl, 1993)**
A cautionary tale inspired by "Jack Be Nimble."

7. **"Jimi Crack Korn"—Down South (Big Beat, 1994)**
Former Bobbito associates based this ditty on the nursery rhyme of the same name.

8. **"Knick Knack Patty Wack"—EPMD (Fresh, 1989)**
Also based on the nursery rhyme, "This Old Man."

9. **"Nigga Bridges"—Onyx (Def Jam, 1993)**
Based on the ghetto anthem, "London Bridge Is Falling Down."

10. **"Perhaps She'll Die"—KRS-One (Jive, 1997)**
Anti-drug rant based on "There Was An Old Lady."

11. **"Peter Piper"—Run-D.M.C. (Profile, 1986)**
Based on the tongue-twisting children's riddle of the same name.

12. **"Pigs"—Cypress Hill (Ruffhouse, 1991)**
A "Fuck Tha Police" twist on "This Little Piggy."

13. **"10 Lil' Sucka Emceez"—Three Times Dope (Arista, 1990)**
An adaptation of the nursery rhyme, "Ten Little Indians."

14. **"Three Little Indians"—Run-D.M.C. (Profile, 1993)**
Also based on "Ten Little Indians." (What'd you think?)

13 Special Moments In Rap Liner Notes History.

1. **As Nasty As They Wanna Be—2 Live Crew (Luke, 1989)**
   The world's most crucified rap group reveals its TLC side by individually thanking every member of its fan club on the album's inner sleeve. Hello, *Nasty*!

2. **Baller's Lady—Passion (MCA, 1996)**
   The Oakland pimpstress ends her thank you's with a personal message to her producer, Kirv: "Exxtra special thanks—Kirv my mentor & best friend. Nigga I'm hearing rumors that you wanna be with me. Is it true?" We guess Lady Ballers get lonely too.

3. **De La Soul Is Dead—De La Soul (Tommy Boy, 1991)**
   P.A. Mase writes, "To the Amityville community: you are the people who say when people like us get successful we never come back and contribute to our community. Well, we came to you on so many occasions and, in so many words, you said, 'Fuck De La Soul' and now I'm saying, 'FUCK YOU.'" Damn, damn, damn!

4. **The Four Horsemen—Ultramagnetic MC's (Wild Pitch, 1993)**
   Finest group member bios of any album in history. Highlights include Moe Love's description as "The Wildabeast," Ced Gee as a flunk-out from the "William Schatner (sic) School for wannabe space guys," T.R. Love as a former "Grimace at local McDonald's openings" and Kool Keith as "winner of the coveted *Magic Dick Award*." Undeniably Ultra.

5. **The Great Adventures Of Slick Rick—Slick Rick (Def Jam, 1988)**
   Most succinct shout-out ever: "Slick Rick would like to thank Columbia Records and all other rappers."

6. **Heaven's Movie—Bizzy Bone (Ruthless, 1998)**
   Bizzy's "Fuck you's" include one to "Seals And Crofts for despising hip hop" and another to "Paul McCartney for making me take that shit off my album just because [Bone] broke the Beatles' record [for the fastest rising #1 song]." He hates you, yeah, yeah, yeah.

7. **Naughty By Nature—Naughty By Nature (Tommy Boy, 1991)**
   Vinnie writes: "Special thanks to all of my friends who think I'm making a big mistake by pursuing a career in the entertainment industry!!! I told you all that I was rollin' wit Queen Latifah and I would be alright." Naughty By Nature is no longer affiliated with Queen Latifah's Flavor Unit Management, but the trio's career continues to flourish.

8. **N.O.R.E.—Noreaga (Penalty, 1998)**
   Nore provides tasty food for thought when he drops "To my real thugs on da run eating—avoid court, da C.O.'s, da P.O.'s, county and state police. When in and out of state remember your name or attribute change with da town, so as u travel remain eatin'. All authorities are crazy for trying to take on our destiny in their hands." Proof positive that real niggas give *real good* advice.

9. **Now, That's More Like It—Craig G (Atlantic, 1991)**
   Rather than thank everybody who helped out on his second effort, QB's freestyle fanatic got positively word stingy when he simply left six blank slots on the album's inside artwork. "If you feel you should be thanked," Craig wrote, "sign your name here."

10. **On The Strength—Grandmaster Flash & The Furious Five (Elektra, 1988)**
    Amongst the shout-outs to friends and colleagues is the group's special thanks "to Martin Luther King for being Black." J. Edgar Hoover, hold your head.

11. **Stupid Doo Doo Dumb—Mac Dre (Romp, 1997)**
    While Mac finds room to include a glossary of his Bay Area "Romp Vocab," he does Craig G one better in the laconism department by sending out "one love to nobody."

12. **Three The Hard Way —Rodney O & Joe Cooley (Atlantic, 1990)**
    Memorable for sidekick General Jeff's wisdom: "This album is based on the Manny, Moe & Jack theory. Because Manny of our songs will Moe-tivate all Nu-Jacks. Think about it!!!!!!!!!" Okay, got it!!!!!!!!!

13. **Walking With A Panther—LL Cool J (Def Jam, 1989)**
    "Special thanks are unnecessary," LL wrote in typically humble fashion. "I sweat, cried and bled for this album." We simply waited for the "Jingling Baby" remix.

IT WAS WRITTEN.

LEARN THE WORDS, YOU WON'T SING THIS:

10 Rap LPs It Was Unnecessary To Print The Lyrics To In The Liner Notes But They Did Anyway.

1. *Be Aware*—Wee Papa Girls (Jive, 1990)
2. *Brainstorm*—Young MC (Capitol, 1991)
3. *Cat Got Ya Tongue*—Bobcat (Arista, 1989)
4. *Fully Loaded*—Oaktown's 3.5.7. (Capitol, 1991)
5. *Icy Blu*—Icy Blu (Giant, 1991)
6. *Mind Blowin*—Vanilla Ice (SBK, 1994)
7. *More Than Just A Pretty Face*—MC Peaches (EastWest, 1991)
8. *Nothing Can Stop Us*—Serious Lee Fine (Arista, 1989)
9. *Speech*—Speech (Chrysalis, 1996)
10. *Too Legit To Quit*—MC Hammer (Capitol, 1991)

Public Enemy's "Disciples For The Future 17" —From The Liner Notes To *Fear Of A Black Planet* (Def Jam, 1990).

1. Digital Underground
2. Divine Styler
3. Freshco
4. The Jaz
5. Lakim Shabazz
6. Last Asiatic Disciples
7. Leaders Of The New School
8. No Face
9. Positively Black
10. Prince Akeem
11. Red, Black And Green
12. Too Nice
13. Total Look And The Style
14. Twin Hype
15. The W.I.S.E. Guyz
16. X Clan
17. YZ

KRS-One's Greatest Quotes.*

1. "No [other rappers are on my level], none of them. Here, let me put it like this . . . In the sky, there are a million stars, but when the sun appears, you see none of them. I am the sun." (*The Source*, July 1989)

2. "I want to be remembered as the first ghetto kid to jump up for world peace, because the stereotype is that all ghetto kids want to do is sell drugs and rob each other, which isn't fact. I came from the heart of the ghetto—there ain't no suburbia in me." (*Stop The Violence: Overcoming Self-Destruction*, Pantheon, 1990)

3. "I am rap music. Where I go, rap goes. Rap is like my dog, it's like my little pet. And where I go, I lead my little pet with me." (*The Source*, April 1992)

4. "America sat back and watched Hitler kill as many Jews as he wanted to until Hitler said, 'I'm coming for the world.' Then America got together the rest of the continents and they went and took Hitler out. I still think he's alive actually. It's only history. If you look at it from that point of view, does anything I say sound irrational?" (*Break It On Down*, Citadel Press, 1992)

5. "The only real reality is the fact that we're all gonna die." (*Spin*, May 1992)

IT WAS WRITTEN.

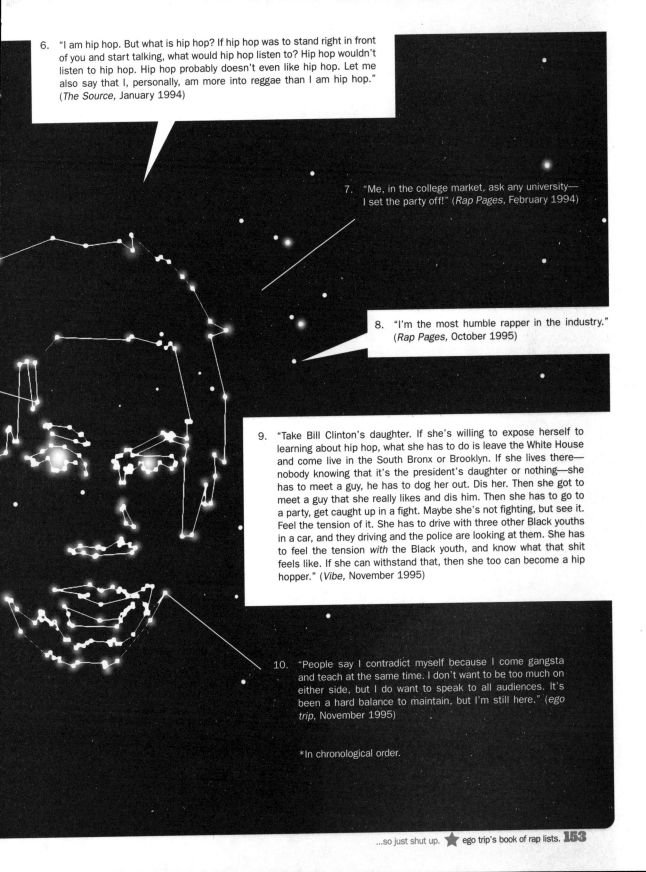

6. "I am hip hop. But what is hip hop? If hip hop was to stand right in front of you and start talking, what would hip hop listen to? Hip hop wouldn't listen to hip hop. Hip hop probably doesn't even like hip hop. Let me also say that I, personally, am more into reggae than I am hip hop." (*The Source*, January 1994)

7. "Me, in the college market, ask any university—I set the party off!" (*Rap Pages*, February 1994)

8. "I'm the most humble rapper in the industry." (*Rap Pages*, October 1995)

9. "Take Bill Clinton's daughter. If she's willing to expose herself to learning about hip hop, what she has to do is leave the White House and come live in the South Bronx or Brooklyn. If she lives there—nobody knowing that it's the president's daughter or nothing—she has to meet a guy, he has to dog her out. Dis her. Then she got to meet a guy that she really likes and dis him. Then she has to go to a party, get caught up in a fight. Maybe she's not fighting, but see it. Feel the tension of it. She has to drive with three other Black youths in a car, and they driving and the police are looking at them. She has to feel the tension *with* the Black youth, and know what that shit feels like. If she can withstand that, then she too can become a hip hopper." (*Vibe*, November 1995)

10. "People say I contradict myself because I come gangsta and teach at the same time. I don't want to be too much on either side, but I do want to speak to all audiences. It's been a hard balance to maintain, but I'm still here." (*ego trip*, November 1995)

*In chronological order.

RECORD L

ABELS.

Artists Who Were At One Time Rumored To Have Signed To Death Row Records.

1. Big Daddy Kane
2. Convicts
3. Craig Mack
4. Grandmaster Melle Mel
5. MC Hammer
6. Kool G Rap
7. K-Solo
8. PeAce (Freestyle Fellowship)
9. Rakim
10. Run-D.M.C.
11. Various members of Wu-Tang Clan

6 REASONS TO HATE RECORD LABELS:
Notable Rap Albums That Were Never Released.

1. **Black Bastards—K.M.D. (Elektra, 1994)**
This Five Percent trio had reduced itself to a duo—leader Zev Love X and his brother Subroc—by the time of its second LP, and with the change in personnel came a more pronounced musical and lyrical aggressiveness. *Bastard*'s sonic landscape—formatted around sound bites from original Last Poet Gylan Kain's album, *The Blue Guerilla* (Juggernaut, 1970)—provided a bewitching structure for songs like "Sweet Premium," "Black Bastards & Bitches" and the dizzying introductory collage, "Garbage Day." However, what should have been a celebration of K.M.D.'s *Low End Theory*-like maturation was never realized. Elektra Records' disapproval of the LP's cover art and eventual dropping of the group supplied the first huge setback. Subroc's sudden death in a car accident represented a final, tragic post-script.

2. **It Takes A Nation Of Suckers To Let Us In—Resident Alien (Dew Doo Man, 1991)**
Hot off of his success with De La Soul and 3rd Bass, producer Prince Paul conceived this off-the-wall concept LP (about the lives and times of three green card-carrying West Indian emcees on Strong Island) as the inaugural release for his Def Jam-distributed Dew Doo Man Records. One vividly entertaining single was issued—1991's "Mr. Boops" b/w "Shakey Grounds" & "Ooh The Dew Doo Man"—and hinted at the possibilities of Paul's demented take on the immigrant experience. But label head Russell Simmons decided he didn't like the album and Dew Doo Man was swiftly scrapped.

3. **The LP—Large Professor (Geffen, 1996)**
"Buy the album when I drop it," Large Pro teased on Tribe's *Midnight Marauders* in 1993. Three years and two unsuccessful singles ("The Mad Scientist" and "I Just Wanna Chill") later, Extra P himself was dropped from Geffen Records with this solo album left in limbo. Though it's no *Breaking Atoms,* the aborted *The LP* contains a number of vintage LP moments. The agitated "Get Off That Bullshit," the ominous "The Mouth That Swindles" and the magnificently ethereal title track are all testaments to P's eccentric and defiantly purist hip hop sensibility. Having little to do with rap music's changing, commercially-conscious orientation, its fate was predictably doomed.

4. **Night Of The Bloody Apes—Crustified Dibbs (b/k/a R.A. The Rugged Man) (Jive, 1994)**
Named after a Mexican horror movie, R.A. The Rugged Man's first LP (as Crustified Dibbs) featured such shock anthems as the underage love story "Staggie (Toolin' It)," the Biggie Smalls duet "Cunt Renaissance" and the self-explanatory "Every Record Label Sucks Dick." Sadly, the last title would be the one most applicable to *Bloody Apes'* destiny. After R.A. was accused of behavioral misconduct by female employees at his label, Jive Records, he and Jive became entangled in a legal stalemate that obliterated any chance of the LP ever seeing daylight.

5. **Scars & Pains EP—Jemini The Gifted One (Mercury, 1995)**
Scars' fusion of state-of-the-art beats (from the likes of Buckwild and Organized Konfusion) and Jemini's old school-informed lyricism yielded a minor hit in its first single, "Funk-Soul Sensation" b/w "Brooklyn Kids." But like Large Pro's *The LP,* this was another case of an underground record falling through major label cracks. The six-song effort was completed down to the artwork and vinyl promos when Mercury Records suddenly tightened its purse strings and gave up on the project.

6. **Testament—Cormega (Def Jam, 1998)**
Former Firm exec Cormega's impassioned debut was indefinitely shelved by hip hop powerhouse Def Jam Records—most likely due to the buzz-killing gap between Mega's final appearances with ex-Firmsters Nas, Foxy & AZ and *Testament*'s much-delayed release. It's a crying shame, as *Testament* is a fine primer of the Queensbridge illegal life—from the Mobb Deep-guested " '98 Live (Killa Theme)" to the sweeping title track to the charmingly unpolished love ballad, "Coco Butter."

RECORD LABELS.

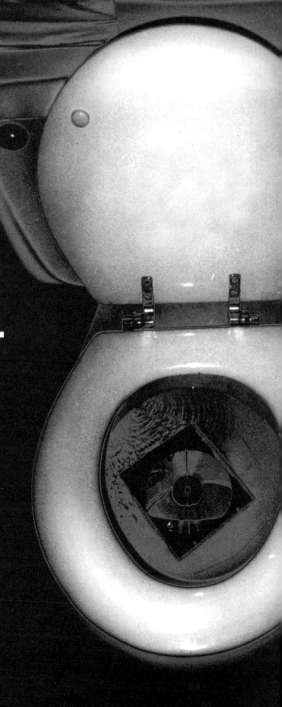

Dante Ross Lists The Top 10 Things Rappers Do To Ruin Their Careers.

1. Pull guns on A&R men.
2. Threaten record company employees with acts of violence.
3. Say, "My man is doing my beats."
4. Say, "My cousin is my manager."
5. Get caught up in the bitches/baby mama drama.
6. Get incarcerated.
7. Have too much money, not enough brains.
8. Try to act like they're from another state that they're not from. Y'know, like when cats from out here try to act like they're all Cali'ed-out. They start wearing Dickies, Converse lo-tops and hoo-ridin' in New York—and their shit flops.
9. Get too jiggy with it.
10. Think they're all that.

Whether you call him a scrub or a Stimulated Dummy, producer/A&R Dante Ross (who has worked with De La Soul, 3rd Bass, Grand Puba, House Of Pain, etc.) is one smart dude who remains on top of this music game.

LET'S BREAK A DEAL:
10 Anti-Record Company Songs.

1. "Del's Nightmare"—Del The Funkeé Homosapien (Hieroglyphics, 1997)
2. "Gunn Clapp"—Originoo Gunn Clappaz (Priority, 1996)
3. "How Not To Get Jerked"—Boogie Down Productions (Jive, 1992)
4. "Labels"—The Genius (Geffen, 1995)
5. "The Music Of Business"—Ras Kass (Priority, 1998)
6. "My Soul"—The Pharcyde (Mad Sounds, 1994)
7. "Negro Baseball League"—Natural Resource (Makin', 1996)
8. "Record Deal"—Menace Clan (Rap-A-Lot, 1995)
9. "Record Label Murder"—Paris (Unleashed, 1998)
10. "Show Business"—A Tribe Called Quest featuring Brand Nubian & Diamond D (Jive, 1991)

Best Rap Advertising Copy.

1. **"Dis. Respect."**
   Penicillin On Wax—Tim Dog (Ruffhouse, 1991)

2. a) **"Doubt Me. Tell Me I Can't Make Powerful Beats. Tell Me I Can't Rap. Disrespect Me. Ignore Me. Tell Me I'm Wack. Go Ahead. I Want You To. IMG FOR LIFE!!!!!"**

   b) **"Right Now, There's A Player Hater Looking At This And Saying, 'The Hell With E-A-Ski!' But Look Here, Through All That Hating I See The Fear And With Fear Comes Reality. I'm Unstoppable, Unfadable, Unpredictable, Under-estimated. I'M AN EARTHQUAKE!"**

   c) **"Right Now You're Saying To Yourself, 'Damn, E-A-Ski Gotta Double Page Ad. But Will This Ad Program Me To Buy The Album?' Many Ads Do, But Then The Album Sucks. Not Mr. Ski. So I'll Be Damn If I Don't Shake Ya'll Up."**
   Earthquake—E-A-Ski (Relativity, 1997)*

3. **"Drink In The Flavor From The New Jim Jones."**
   I Hate You With A Passion—Dre Dog (In-A-Minute, 1995)

4. **"Guerillas In The Mist. Can't Catch 'Em. Can't Cage 'Em."**
   Guerillas In Tha Mist—Da Lench Mob (Street Knowledge, 1992)

5. **"In '91, We Let Our Nuts Hang. In '92, We're Taking The Industry By The Balls. None Of That 'Me-Me' Rappin'."**
   Rap-A-Lot Records Label Slogan, 1992

6. **"It Doesn't Take A Genius To Know Just How Stupid This Album Is. It Just Took A Genius To Record It."**
   Kwamé The Boy Genius Featuring A New Beginning—Kwamé (Atlantic, 1989)

7. a) **"Jesus Was A Black Jew."**

   b) **"Send The Redneck Right Over. Ka-blammm. . ."**
   Future Prophets—Blood Of Abraham (Ruthless, 1993)

8. **"Play Pussy, Get Fucked."**
   Geto Boys—Geto Boys (Rap-A-Lot, 1990)

9. **"Real African Lyrics From Real Africans!"**
   Zimbabwe Legit EP—Zimbabwe Legit (Hollywood BASIC, 1992)

10. **"Sentenced To A Lifetime Of Hit-Making."**
    Death Row Records Label Slogan, 1993

*At the time of this writing, this album had yet to be released.

RECORD LABELS.

Worst Rap Advertising Copy.

1. **"A Boy From The Hood Who Gives A Funk. (Yeah, He Ain't Packin'—You Got A Problem With That?)"**
   Ahmad—Ahmad (Giant, 1994)

2. **"Get Ready To Be Clawed To Def!"**
   Cat Got Ya Tongue—Bobcat (Arista, 1989)

3. **"The Gimmick Is There Is No Gimmick. Bump Ya Head."**
   From The Ground Up—Mad Flava (Priority, 1994)

4. **"He's The East Coast Rapper Who Offers Novel Insights Into Teenage Romance And All The Latest Developments On The Neighborhood Street Corner."**
   "Planet E"—KC Flight (Popular, 1989)

5. **"Jeep Music For The '90s. A Cornucopia Of Soul Sounds."**
   The Valley Of The Jeep Beats—Terminator X (Def Jam, 1991)

6. **"Sam Sever And Bosco Money Make A Naughty Pair!"**
   Downtown Science—Downtown Science (Def Jam, 1991)

7. **"Say It Loud, She's White And She's Proud."**
   The Power Of A Woman—Tairrie B (MCA, 1990)

8. **"Supercalifragilisticespiala-Joeski!"**
   Joe Cool—Joeski (Columbia, 1990)

9. **"This Mother Wears Combat Boots!"**
   In A Word Or 2—Monie Love (Warner Bros., 1993)

10. **"Two New Acts That'll Smack The Wax Off Your Eardrums."**
    Ghetto Street Funk—P.A. (MCA, 1993) & *The Swoll Package*—Capital Tax (MCA, 1993)

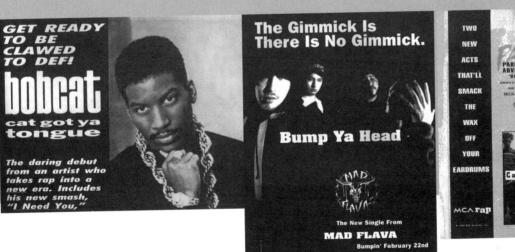

. . . AND ALL WE GOT WAS THIS STUPID T-SHIRT:

Unforgettable Record Company Promo Items.

1. Tha Alkaholiks barf bag containing a toothbrush, toothpaste, aspirin and Alka-Seltzer—Tha Alkaholiks (Loud, 1993)
2. Brooklyn Lager Brew—3rd Bass (Def Jam, 1989)
3. "Chocolate City" chocolate bar—Da Lench Mob (Priority, 1995)
4. "Come Clean" bar of soap—Jeru The Damaja (Payday, 1993)
5. Dew Doo Man Records toilet tissue labeled, "We Got The Fly Shit"—Prince Paul (Dew Doo Man, 1991)
6. "Kill The White People" T-shirt—Apache (Tommy Boy, 1993)
7. *Lethal Injection* ballpoint pen—Ice Cube (Priority, 1993)
8. *On Fire* matchbook—Stetsasonic (Tommy Boy, 1986)
9. *The Recipe* cooking pot—Mack 10 (Hoo Bangin', 1998)
10. "Second Round K.O." boxing gloves—Canibus (Universal, 1997)

RECORD LABELS.

10 Things That Lyor Cohen Says To Motivate His Artists.

1. "It's not about you, it's about your family."
2. "If you can't think about yourself, think about your kids."
3. "Never step away from the poker table, someone will take your place. If you have to go to the bathroom, ask them to bring you a pail."
4. "When you perform, if the ticket price is $25, make you sure you give a $60 performance."
5. "Don't be wack, motherfucker."
6. "Please come out of your dressing room. You've got 25,000 people waiting and the union costs are too expensive."
7. "When you're hot, crouch at the bar. When you're cold, stand up straight."
8. "You're gonna have to toss me out of a fuckin' window and the answer will still be fuckin' no!"
9. "If you're a baker, you make your living off of baking. If you're a construction worker, you make your living doing construction. If you're a rapper, RAP, motherfucker."
10. "Ditto #9."

Lyor "The Check Writer" Cohen is the CEO of Def Jam Records. A notoriously boisterous live motivator, he has indefatigably led hip hop's greatest record label to unprecedented levels of chart-topping, cheddar-clocking success.

Cash Money Records' Rules (As Posted At The Cash Money Offices By CEO Bryan "Baby" Williams).

1. U Can't Be Baby!!
2. U Must Know When 2 Go Home.
3. Your Problem Is Your Problem.
4. Rappers Take Drug Tests: "No Heroin Or Coke."
5. No Benz On 1st Album (Only The CEOs & Producer—6 Years Of Experience).
6. Promotional Shows Are A Must.
7. Royalty Paid When Royalty Due.
8. No Advances From M.F. (Mannie Fresh, label producer)
9. U Artists Are An Investment.
10. No Friends In Studio Sessions.
11. Baby Has Favoritism With Certain Rappers.
12. Your Reputation Is More Valuable Than "Hoes."
13. Keep Hoes Out Of Your Business.
14. U Don't Work, U Don't Eat.
15. Cash Money Records "Rap Hussle:" U Better Ask Somebody. If U Laggin', Catch Tha Sideline And Lay Off!!!!

RUNAWAY SLAVE:
R.A. The Rugged Man Reveals His Top 10 Ways To Get Dropped From A Record Label.

10. Bootleg every song on your album that has a special guest appearance on it and collect mad money behind your label's back.
9. Tell your A&R man your true feelings about him.
8. Make sure your label understands that you're used to being poor and you don't care what happens to you or them.
7. Go on the radio and dis anybody who's important to your project.
6. Walk around the office with a mannequin finger sticking out the zipper of your pants.
5. Refuse to hand in two commercial singles for the label to work at radio.
4. Run through your record label with a few of your friends and wave guns at everybody.
3. Sexually harass every female recording artist with a platinum record on your label.
2. Make songs like "Cunt Renaissance" and "Every Record Label Sucks Dick."
1. Glorify violence, keep your label in fear at all times and make them believe that making mistakes on your project will contribute to the end of their lives.

R.A. The Rugged Man is New York hip hop's Andre The Giant. Despite experiencing his share of record company difficulties, his career has continued to flourish through much-loved underground singles like "'Till My Heart Stops" and "Smithhaven Mall."

10 Milestones In Rap Artist-Record Label Relations.

HELLA TIGHT: Ruthless Records honchos Jerry Heller and Eazy-E hard at work in 1994.

1. **Bittersweet Nothings.**
Fresh off of the success of the Sugarhill Gang's "Rapper's Delight," Sylvia Robinson's Sugar Hill Records begins signing the cream of Bronx hip hop pioneers. Though the Englewood, NJ-based label soon boasts an all-star roster that includes Grandmaster Flash & The Furious Five, the Treacherous Three and Funky 4 + 1, several of these artists will grow unhappy with Sugar Hill. "I signed with Sugar Hill because I figured, 'Well, if I'm going to get jerked, I'll get jerked by a Black lady. It can't be that bad,'" former T3 leader Kool Moe Dee tells *Spin* magazine in 1989. "No, [I didn't make a cent out of that label]." The now familiar industry scenario of rapper-hates-his-label is born.

2. **Label Hell.**
After raising rap's commercial upside to new heights with 1986's triple-platinum *Raising Hell*, Run-D.M.C. attempts to break its deal with Profile Records and jump to hip hop powerhouse Def Jam. The plan doesn't work. Extensive haggling winds up delaying the release of *Hell*'s crucial follow-up, *Tougher Than Leather*, for a full year, initiating a career tailspin the group never fully overcomes. In addition, their newly "re-negotiated" contract commits them to a shocking 10 *more* albums for Profile. It's tricky, indeed.

3. **Bad Boys.**
KRS-One of Boogie Down Productions becomes the first major rap artist to bring his label woes to wax in the midst of modern hip hop's Golden Age. On "Nervous" (Jive, 1988) the Blastmaster explains: "Me and my crew, we made hit records all over the place. But we left B-Boy Records. And you know what happened after that point? They just got Nerrrrrrvous!" Later that summer on "I'm Still #1 (Numero Uno Re-Recording)" Kris states even more directly, "B-Boy Records you just can't trust."

Three years later De La Soul puts its own unique twist on the routine when the Strong Island trio disses its own label on "Pass The Plugs" (Tommy Boy, 1991): "Radio wants it, public consumes it/ Tommy Boy wants another 'Say No'— huh!"

4. **From Ashy To Classy.**
Ex-Compton, CA street hustler Eazy-E forms Ruthless Records in 1986, playing the dual roles of CEO and artist. He quickly discovers that his old occupation of dealing with fiends, lowlifes and crooks has provided him with the ideal preparation for running a record company. Ruthless will subsequently become one of the most successful independent labels of all-time through the suc-

RECORD LABELS.

cess of N.W.A, J.J. Fad, The D.O.C. and Bone Thugs-N-Harmony.

5. **Knight Of Fear.**
In April of 1991, former bodyguard Marion "Suge" Knight somehow persuades Eazy-E to release Ruthless' prized signee, N.W.A producer Dr. Dre, from his contract and forms Death Row Records. Eazy charges that Knight, accompanied by a group of lead pipe-wielding cohorts, arrived at the Ruthless offices threatening to engage him in some human fungo if Eazy refused to sign over Dre's release. Regardless of how close to the truth Eazy's account actually is, the rumor quickly reaches mythic status and seals Knight's reputation as the most intimidating figure in the music industry.

6. **Of Mice & Men.**
Artist-label relations hit another low in late 1992 when a disgruntled Treach of Naughty By Nature visits Tommy Boy Records' offices with a group of friends holding what appears to be harmless McDonald's Happy Meals. Dissatisfied with a discussion with the label's president concerning the state of Naughty's forthcoming album, Treach and his entourage open their Happy Meal cardboard lunch boxes and unleash an unhappy battalion of mice and garden snakes. Unsuspecting TB personnel frantically begin grabbing poster tubes in order to stomp out the creatures in self-defense. Ironically, less than a year later everything's rated AG as Naughty enjoy one of the biggest hits of its career with the feel good anthem "Hip Hop Hooray."

7. **It's A Wu World After All.**
Staten Island, NY's nine-member Wu-Tang Clan sign to Loud Records after the late 1992 success of its independently-released single, "Protect Ya Neck." Exhibiting remarkably seasoned business savvy for a "new" group, the Wu bucks industry convention by structuring its contract to enable each Clan member to sign a solo deal of his own volition in the open market. Releases from Method Man, Ol' Dirty Bastard, Raekwon, The

Genius and Ghostface Killah all go either gold or platinum between 1994 and 1997, thus proving that the Gods are most definitely not crazy.

8. **Throw Ya Chairz In The Air.**
In a meeting with bigwigs at Mercury Records in 1995, members of Onyx do not react well to the news that their Brooklyn protégés, All City, have been dropped from the baldheads' Armee Records imprint. A *melee* ensues in a conference room in which office furniture takes flight. Predictably, Armee Records is soon thereafter dishonorably discharged from the Mercury corporate compound.

9. **$hort Changed.**
Too $hort becomes the first rap artist to prematurely "retire" from the rap game in 1996 after his label, Jive Records, refuses to re-negotiate his contract. In doing so, the perennial gold-selling $hort is able to force Jive's hand into putting a better deal on the table. A year's vacation later, $horty The Pimp promptly unretires and continues on with his career screaming "beeyotch" on his own imprint, $hort Records. You see pimpin's big business. And it's been goin' on since the beginning of time. And it's gonna continue straight ahead 'til somebody up there turns out the lights on this small planet.

10. **Enemy Strikes Back.**
A decade after uttering the immortal lyrics, "Tables turn, suckers burn to learn, they can't disable the power of my label/Def Jam—tells you who I am" on "Rebel Without A Pause" (Def Jam, 1987), an exasperated Chuck D of Public Enemy decides that the honeymoon is over. He embarks on an internet campaign designed to get P.E. off of its longtime label by releasing songs from the group's as-yet-unreleased *There's A Poison Goin' On* LP free of charge over the net. Chuck also begins referring to the label in public as "Def Scam," co-founder Russell Simmons as "Hustle Scrimmons" and CEO Lyor Cohen as "Liar Conman." It's announced in the fall of '98 that P.E. and Def Jam will officially divorce in early 1999.

Defunct Label Imprints Of 15 Notable Artists.

1. Armee (Onyx)
2. Bust It (MC Hammer)
3. Dangerous (Too $hort)
4. Dew Doo Man (Prince Paul)
5. Edutainer (KRS-One)
6. Flavor Unit (Queen Latifah)
7. Hoppoh (Prime Minister Pete Nice)
8. JDK (Run-D.M.C.)
9. JMJ (Jam Master Jay)
10. One Love (Black Sheep)
11. PMD (PMD)
12. Slam Jamz (Chuck D)
13. Soul Brother (Pete Rock)
14. Street Knowledge (Ice Cube)
15. Strong City (Jazzy Jay)

25 Great EP, 12" & CD Single Covers.

1. "Beat Bop—K-Rob vs. Rammelzee (Tartown, 1983)
2. "Biz Is Goin' Off"—Biz Markie (Cold Chillin', 1988)
3. "The Body Rock"—Mos Def, Tash & Q-Tip (Rawkus, 1997)
4. "Burnt Pride"—Lyrics Born (SoleSides, 1996)
5. "Droppin' Science"—Marley Marl featuring Craig G (Cold Chillin', 1988)
6. "Ego Trippin' (Part Two)"—De La Soul (Tommy Boy, 1993)
7. "End To End Burners"—Company Flow (Rawkus, 1998)
8. "Gangsta, Gangsta"—N.W.A (Ruthless, 1988)
9. "Insane In The Brain"—Cypress Hill (Ruffhouse, 1993)
10. "Jane, Stop This Crazy Thing"—MC Shan (Cold Chillin', 1986)
11. *Kill At Will* EP—Ice Cube (Priority, 1990)
12. *Love American Style* EP—Beastie Boys (Capitol, 1989)
13. "Needle To The Groove"—Mantronix (Sleeping Bag, 1985)
14. "Product Of The Environment"—3rd Bass (Def Jam, 1990)
15. *The Real Deal* EP—Lifers Group (Hollywood BASIC, 1991)
16. *Return Of The B-Girl* EP—T-Love (Pickininny, 1998)
17. "A Roller Skating Jam Named 'Saturdays'"—De La Soul featuring Q-Tip (Tommy Boy, 1991)
18. "Saturday Nite Fever"—Lordz Of Brooklyn (Ventrue, 1995)
19. "Shadrach"—Beastie Boys (Capitol, 1989)
20. "Sleepin' On My Couch"—Del The Funkeé Homosapien (Elektra, 1991)
21. *The Spot* EP—The Beatnuts (Relativity, 1998)
22. "Teenage Love"—Slick Rick (Def Jam, 1988)
23. "That's When Ya Lost"—Souls Of Mischief (Jive, 1993)
24. " 'Till My Heart Stops"—R.A. The Rugged Man featuring 8-Off (Rawkus, 1997)
25. "Wrong Side Of Da Tracks"—Artifacts (Big Beat, 1994)

ART.

50 Great Album Covers.

1. *Act A Fool*—King Tee (Capitol, 1988)
2. *AmeriKKKa's Most Wanted*—Ice Cube (Priority, 1990)
3. *Bizarre Ride II The Pharcyde*—The Pharcyde (Delicious Vinyl, 1992)
4. *The Biz Never Sleeps*—Biz Markie (Cold Chillin', 1989)
5. *Blacks' Magic*—Salt-N-Pepa (Next Plateau, 1990)
6. *Black Sunday*—Cypress Hill (Ruffhouse, 1993)
7. *Bobby Digital In Stereo*—RZA As Bobby Digital (Gee Street, 1998)
8. *Business As Usual*—EPMD (Def Jam, 1992)
9. *By All Means Necessary*—Boogie Down Productions (Jive, 1988)
10. *City Life*—Boogie Boys (Capitol, 1985)
11. *Daily Operation*—Gang Starr (Chrysalis, 1992)
12. *Dare Iz A Darkside*—Redman (Def Jam, 1994)
13. *Death Certificate*—Ice Cube (Priority, 1991)
14. *Death Mix Live!*—Afrika Bambaataa (Paul Winley, 1983)
15. *Da Dirty 30*—Cru (Def Jam, 1997)
16. *Efil4zaggin*—N.W.A (Ruthless, 1991)
17. *Endtroducing . . .*—DJ Shadow (Mo' Wax, 1996)
18. *Follow The Leader*—Eric B. & Rakim (Uni, 1988)
19. *Da Game Is To Be Sold, Not To Be Told*—Snoop Doggy Dogg (No Limit, 1998)
20. *Geto Boys*—Geto Boys (Rap-A-Lot, 1990)
21. *Illmatic*—Nas (Columbia, 1994)
22. *King Of Rock*—Run-D.M.C. (Profile, 1985)
23. *Kool & Deadly (Justicizms)*—Just-Ice (Fresh, 1987)
24. *Licensed To Ill*—Beastie Boys (Def Jam, 1986)
25. *Life After Death*—The Notorious B.I.G. (Bad Boy, 1997)
26. *The Low End Theory*—A Tribe Called Quest (Jive, 1991)

27. *Mama Said Knock You Out*—LL Cool J (Def Jam, 1990)
28. *Meiso*—DJ Krush (Mo' Wax UK, 1995)*
29. *Midnight Marauders*—A Tribe Called Quest (Jive, 1993)
30. *Mos Def And Talib Kweli Are Black Star*—Black Star (Rawkus, 1998)
31. *Mr. Hood*—K.M.D. (Elektra, 1991)
32. *Muddy Waters*—Redman (Def Jam, 1996)
33. *Never Dated*—Milk (American, 1994)
34. *No Way Out*—Puff Daddy & The Family (Bad Boy, 1997)
35. *Ocean Of Funk*—ESG (Perrion, 1995)
36. *Paul's Boutique*—Beastie Boys (Capitol, 1989)
37. *Power*—Ice-T (Sire, 1988)
38. *Pre-Life Crisis*—Count Bass-D (Hoppoh, 1995)
39. *Psychoanalysis (What Is It?)*—Prince Paul (Tommy Boy, 1997)**
40. *Radio*—LL Cool J (Def Jam, 1985)
41. *Raising Hell*—Run-D.M.C. (Profile, 1986)
42. *Ready To Die*—The Notorious B.I.G. (Bad Boy, 1994)
43. *Return To The 36 Chambers: The Dirty Version*—Ol' Dirty Bastard (Elektra, 1995)
44. *Romeo-Knight*—Boogie Boys (Select, 1988)
45. *6 Feet Deep*—Gravediggaz (Gee Street, 1994)
46. *Stakes Is High*—De La Soul (Tommy Boy, 1996)
47. *Stress: The Extinction Agenda*—Organized Konfusion (Hollywood BASIC, 1994)
48. *Strictly Business*—EPMD (Fresh, 1988)
49. *III (Temples of Boom)*—Cypress Hill (Ruffhouse, 1995)
50. *Yo! Bum Rush The Show*—Public Enemy (Def Jam, 1987)

*Vinyl import only.
**Different artwork from the WordSound release.

Butter Albums, Butt Covers.

1. *Capital Punishment*—Big Punisher (Loud, 1998)
2. *The Chronic*—Dr. Dre (Death Row, 1992)
3. *Cypress Hill*—Cypress Hill (Ruffhouse, 1991)
4. *Doggystyle*—Snoop Doggy Dogg (Death Row, 1993)
5. *El Niño*—Def Squad (Def Jam, 1998)
6. *Enta Da Stage*—Black Moon (Nervous, 1993)
7. *Hell On Earth*—Mobb Deep (Loud, 1996)
8. *I Wish My Brother George Was Here*—Del The Funkeé Homosapien (Elektra, 1991)
9. *The One*—Chubb Rock (Select, 1991)
10. *Slaughtahouse*—Masta Ace (Delicious Vinyl, 1993)
11. *Something Serious*—Big Mike (Rap-A-Lot, 1994)
12. *Soul Food*—Goodie Mob (LaFace, 1995)
13. *2 Hype*—Kid 'N Play (Select, 1988)

Butter Covers, Butt Albums.

1. *All Balls Don't Bounce*—Aceyalone (Capitol, 1995)
2. *Forever Everlasting*—Everlast (Warner Bros., 1990)
3. *Future Profits*—Blood Of Abraham (Ruthless, 1993)
4. *Generation EFX*—Das EFX (EastWest, 1998)
5. *Order In The Court*—Queen Latifah (Motown, 1998)

Butter Butt Covers.

1. *Doin' It!*—U.T.F.O. (Select, 1989)
2. *Holla At Me, I'll Put It On Ya*—Babygirl (Popular, 1997)
3. *Living Up To My Rep*—Mack Lew (AHR, 1993)
4. *Move Somthin'*—2 Live Crew (Luke Skyywalker, 1988)
5. *"Pushem' Up"*—Armand Van Helden's Sampleslaya (Ruffhouse, 1998)
6. *The 7 Sins*—Kane & Abel (No Limit, 1996)
7. *"Shake Whatcha Mama Gave Ya"*—Stik-E & The Hoods (Phat Wax, 1995)

Cey Adams' Top 10 Things You Should Never Do On A Photo Shoot Or When Designing An Album Package.

1. Never tell an artist there's no room for their thank you's in the liner notes. (If you do, be ready to catch a bad one.)
2. Never tell a rapper to bring anyone else to the photo shoot because you'll have all of the rapper's homies who skipped work or cut school up in your face all day.
3. Never ever order from the gourmet deli. Stick to pizza or fried chicken—it tastes better and goes a long way.
4. Never let an artist know you're afraid to shoot in their 'hood. (Thugs can smell fear.)
5. Don't ever let a rapper leave to buy weed. (If you do... shoot over.)
6. Don't give a rapper your corporate card. (They might buy a platinum Lexus.)
7. Don't ever use pink in a design. (Even female rappers ain't havin' it.)
8. Remember: big name, bold letters, big photo and plenty of ice, cars and hoes *always* go on the front cover of any album.
9. Liner Notes Wisdom: thank God first, then the baby's mother. Bitches go last.
10. Never tint a photo in baby blue, pink or lime green. Keep it raw.

The colorful Cey Adams is co-founder of Def Jam Records' longtime design arm, The Drawing Board. His art direction credits include LL Cool J's Mama Said Knock You Out, The Notorious B.I.G.'s Ready To Die *and the Beastie Boys'* Hello Nasty. *Plus he used to bomb mad trains back in the day.*

Infamous
Rap Art Controversies.

1. **Black Bastards—K.M.D. (Elektra, 1994)**
    The irony of Zev Love X's hanging sambo character cover illustration went over the head of *Billboard* R&B columnist Terri Rossi who publicly condemned it, scaring Elektra (and its parent, Time-Warner) from releasing the critically acclaimed record. Adding insult to injury, those bastards at Elektra then dropped the duo from their roster.

2. **Da Bomb—Kris Kross (Ruffhouse, 1993)**
    Nearly 50 years after the atomic bombing of Hiroshima, Ruffhouse Records (making an appropriate nod to corporate parent, Sony) changed the Japanese edition of the diminutive duo's cover art which depicted a mushroom cloud, thus diffusing a potentially explosive situation.

3. **Don't Blame It On Da Music—Trinity Garden Cartel (Rap-A-Lot, 1994)**
    Blame it on the boys in blue. Rap-A-Lot Records was faced with an impending lawsuit by Houston police officers claiming their likenesses were used on this album cover without their consent. Although subsequently revised and re-released, original copies of the LP had already made it to retailers.

4. **Hell On Earth—Mobb Deep (Loud, 1996)**
    The "Official Queensbridge Murderers" got props for their third joint's early stickers and ads featuring a stylized dragon icon. Unfortunately, the same logo was also identified with New York's hardcore punk mainstays, Sick Of It All, who'd claimed it as theirs since 1986. Consequently, the Mobb's dragon was slayed.

5. **Home Invasion—Ice-T (Rhyme Syndicate, 1993)**
    Eager to get his first post-"Cop Killer" effort on the market, Ice-T couldn't catch a break when this LP's cover—depicting an African medallion-wearing white teen surrounded by books authored by Malcolm X and Iceberg Slim and listening to Ice-T records—made execs at his label, Warner Bros., nervous. Ice was released from his contract upon request and after signing with Priority Records issued the package intact. But retailers would still have the last say. Several banned the LP from their shelves for its threatening forecast of white youth's fascination with militant Black culture.

6. **"Night Of The Living Baseheads"—Public Enemy (Def Jam, 1988)**
    P.E.—defiantly standing on Old Glory—raised the ire of conservative groups who disapproved of its dramatic political statement. It would be the symbolic first brick that laid the group's foundation as hip hop's rebels to America.

7. **Sleeping With The Enemy—Paris (Scarface, 1992)**
    The hip hop Huey Newton parted ways with label Tommy Boy in part due to *Enemy*'s original Victor Hall photo-illustration cover image: Paris hiding behind a tree in front of the Capitol building about to snipe President George Bush. Curiously, even when Paris self-released the LP after parting ways with Tommy Boy, this art was relegated to the *interior* of the album and not the cover as was originally intended.

8. **"Soul Food"—Goodie Mob (LaFace, 1996)**
    This tasty single was recalled from retailers due to the cover art's appropriation of the Tabasco brand hot sauce label. The McIlhenny company's disapproval (and subsequent recall of the artwork) deprived a potentially hot single from ever reaching a boiling point.

5 Things
Pen & Pixel
Will Not Put
On An Album
Cover.*

1. A pregnant woman holding a shotgun.
2. Putting anybody on a crucifix. (We've done Christ-like figures, but no one's actually been crucified.)
3. Anything racist (specifically Blacks killing whites, whites killing Blacks . . . stuff like that).
4. Jeeps driving out of, ahem, women's "coochies."
5. We wouldn't *knowingly* illustrate blowing up somebody's car that belonged to a client's competitor. (But it's happened. Twice.)

*These are actual ideas suggested by clients.

From pit bulls with human heads to Cristal-sipping grizzly bears, Houston's Pen & Pixel Graphics, Inc. has been cranking out controversial and wildly ghettoutrageous computer graphics for the many independent record labels of the dirty south since 1992. Check out Eightball's Lost *or Lil' Sin's* Frustrated By Death, *if you don't believe us, playa.*

BROTHER FROM ANOTHER COVER:
Rap Album Artwork Based On Other LP Covers.

1.

2.

5.

6.

9.

10.

13.

1. ***Bazerk, Bazerk, Bazerk*—Son Of Bazerk (SOUL, 1991)**
   BASED ON: *Please, Please, Please*—James Brown (King, 1959)

2. ***Dare Iz A Darkside*—Redman (Def Jam, 1994)**
   BASED ON: *Maggot Brain*—Funkadelic (Westbound, 1971)

3. ***Delinquent Habits*—Delinquent Habits (PMP, 1996)**
   BASED ON: *The Warriors* Soundtrack (A&M, 1979)

4. ***Intoxicated Demons* The EP—The Beatnuts (Relativity, 1993)**
   BASED ON: *The Turnaround*—Hank Mobley (Blue Note, 1965)

5. ***Jurassic 5* EP—Jurassic 5 (Rumble, 1997)**
   BASED ON: Prism Records' generic jacket. (Prism, circa 1986)

ART.
170 ego trip's book of rap lists. ⭐ you have to have style or learn to be original...

3. 4.

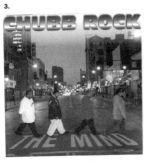   

7. 8.

11. 12.

6. *Lōc-ed After Dark*—**Tone-Lōc (Delicious Vinyl, 1989)**
BASED ON: *A New Perspective*—Donald Byrd (Blue Note, 1963)

7. *The Mind*—**Chubb Rock (Select, 1997)**
BASED ON: *Abbey Road*—The Beatles (Apple, 1969)

8. *Retaliation, Revenge And Get Back*—**Daz Dillinger (Death Row, 1998)**
BASED ON: *In Our Lifetime*—Marvin Gaye (Tamla, 1981)

9. *Riders Of The Storm: The Underwater Album*—**Boogiemonsters (Pendulum, 1994)**
BASED ON: *Soul Sauce*—Cal Tjader (Verve, 1965)

10. *Rock The House*—**DJ Jazzy Jeff & The Fresh Prince (Word Up, 1987)***
BASED ON: *King Of Rock*—Run-D.M.C. (Profile, 1985)

11. *Dah Shinin'*—**Smif-N-Wessun (Nervous, 1995)**
BASED ON: *He's Coming*—Roy Ayers Ubiquity (Polydor, 1972)

12. *Uptown Saturday Night*—**Camp Lo (Profile, 1997)**
BASED ON: *I Want You*—Marvin Gaye (Tamla, 1976)

13. *Young Black Teenagers*—**Young Black Teenagers (SOUL, 1991)**
BASED ON: *Meet The Beatles*—The Beatles (Capitol, 1964)

*Pre-Jive Records release cover art.

WHAT'S MY NAME?

Graf Writers Who Rapped & Rappers Who Wrote Graf.

1. "Ase": Masta Ace
2. "Blas": Freshco
3. "Crack": Fat Joe
4. "Crane": K-Rob
5. "Futura 2000"
6. "Iris 1": Iriscience (Dilated Peoples)
7. "Kaves" (Lordz Of Brooklyn)
8. "Kool Herc"
9. "Koor": El The Sensai (Artifacts)
10. "KRS-One"
11. "Lune": Big Juss (Company Flow)
12. "Nal": Havoc (Mobb Deep)
13. "Peso" (Fearless Four)
14. "Phase 2"*
15. "Rammelzee"
16. "Spade": Bushwick Bill
17. "Spin": Fab 5 Freddy
18. "Tame 1" (Artifacts)

*Phase 2 is an aerosol *artist*.

10 Logos Haze Wishes He Had Created.

1. **Warner Bros.**
Timeless, classic—love the staff jackets with Bugs jumping out, too.

2. **Sex Pistols**
Graphic design was never the same.

3. **Grandmaster Flash & The Furious Five**
They never really did have a logo, did they?

4. **(Original) NY Knicks**
. . . And the team was dressing mad fly in '71 too.

5. **Rolling Stones tongue**
Sexy, classic and looks great on the back of that denim vest.

6. *Shaft*
One bad mutha'. Defined that whole genre of design.

7. **Air Jordan silhouette logo**
Now that's what you call high-powered merchandising!

8. **MTV**
Big league name recognition . . . would look kinda fly in my book.

9. **Playstation**
Way original and will not look dated anytime soon.

10. **007**
Whew, almost forgot that one. Last but definitely not least—way smooth.

Aerosol art O.G., graphic designer and streetwear mogul Haze has created some of hip hop's most enduring iconography. Amongst his credits are identities for record labels like Delicious Vinyl, Tommy Boy and Cold Chillin', LP covers for Public Enemy, LL Cool J and the Beastie Boys, not to mention the everlasting EPMD logo. In other words, Haze is the phrase that pays.

HA, HA, HA . . . STICK 'EM:
10 Cool Stickers.

1. **"Big Pun"—Big Punisher (Loud, 1997)**
Big, bold and damned near ugly. But it got the point across—so much so that its oversaturation contributed to New York City's ban on public posting of promo stickers.

2. **"Ego Trippin' (Part Two)"—De La Soul (Tommy Boy, 1993)**
In the immortal words of Slick Rick, "Mirror, mirror, on the wall/ Who is the top choice of them all?" You or anyone else vain enough to get down with this clever, star-shaped reflective sticker.

3. **Floating Heads Series—Leaders Of The New School (Elektra, 1993)**
The ready-to-stick stunned faces of Dinco, Milo, Charlie and Busta that accompanied the release of their sophomore *T.I.M.E.* album had nothing to do with the LP's lackluster sales. Or maybe they did.

4. **"Hey Ladies"—Beastie Boys (Capitol, 1989)**
Über-cool sticker resembling a men's restroom sign signaled the return of the über-hip Beasties from their three-year hiatus after *Licensed To Ill.*

5. **Hiero/Souls Of Mischief (Jive, 1993)**
An unforgettable logo that came in different metallic colors.

6. **"I ⊗ NY"—Onyx (Def Jam, 1995)**
Back in the 1970's, a financially devastated New York City looked to designer Milton Glaser's acclaimed "I (heart) NY" campaign to change its downtrodden image, uplift the citizenry and lead its denizens towards a brighter future. In 1995, the "Afficial Nastee Niggas" took pleasure in pissing on the whole concept. Fuck love.

7. **"Jealous One's Envy"—Fat Joe (Relativity, 1995)**
Our money's on Joe and Joe's on the money, literally. Joe's mug on a Benjie is priceless.

8. **"Shut Your Punk Ass Up"—Threat (Da Bomb, 1993)**
Simple, clever, and best of all, offensive.

9. *Stone Crazy*—**The Beatnuts (Relativity, 1997)**
Sex sells. So while this LP's first single may have been "Do You Believe?" its B-side, "Give Me Tha Ass," provided a much more interesting subject matter to, ahem, assess.

10. **"You Down Wit O.P.P.?"—Naughty By Nature (Tommy Boy, 1991)**
In the summer of '91, these stickers—like the hit song they promoted—were everywhere . . . including the rear-end of an unsuspecting female in the video.

Rappers Who Attended Manhattan's High School Of Art & Design.

1. Havoc (Mobb Deep)
2. Kwamé
3. Mr. Complex
4. Percee P
5. Pharoahe Monch (Organized Konfusion)
6. Prince Poetry (Organized Konfusion)
7. Prodigy (Mobb Deep)

THE OUTSIDAZ:
Artsy Types Who've Made Contributions To Hip Hop.

1. **Kyle Baker**
   The popular indie comic-book illustrator collaborated with KRS-One on his H.E.A.L. Project single as well as 1995's KRS/Marvel comic and companion cassette, *Break The Chain.*

2. **Glenn L. Barr**
   Them cool-ass covers of Funkdoobiest's "Bow Wow Wow" and *Which Doobie U B?*, as well as the '70s western-meets-*The Evil Dead* soundtrack flavor of DJ Muggs' *The Soul Assassins Chapter 1*, were done by the Motor City's cool-ass underground comic artist and painter.

3. **Jean-Michel Basquiat**
   '80s art world superstar found time between excessive partying and painting to get his productive ass all over the K-Rob vs. Rammelzee single, "Beat Bop." And not only did he design the jacket and label, but he also produced the psychedelic old school classic.

4. **Glen E. Friedman**
   Underground subculture lensman also known for his '70s skate and punk rock flicks is responsible for numerous memorable cover photos, including choice images for Run-D.M.C., Ice-T, King Tee and Public Enemy.

5. **Annie Leibovitz**
   Celebrity photographer can claim MC Hammer (for his *Too Legit To Quit* LP) among her famous subjects.

6. **Pushead**
   This skate-punk Picasso has laced the pages of *Thrasher* magazine and Zorlac skateboards consistently for over a decade. He delved into the rap world by supplying the ill, dangerous *Dr. Octagon* cover in 1996.

7. **Bill Sienkiewicz**
   Celebrated comic illustrator has hooked-up RZA's *Bobby Digital In Stereo* and EPMD's *Business As Usual* cover art. Dope as usual.

8. **Albert Watson**
   Megabucks fashion photographer made even mo' money making PM Dawn all pretty for its *Jesus Wept* joint.

9. **Robert Williams**
   The brilliant lowbrow artist's painting, "The Riddle Of Delphi," was used as the cover for Boogie Down Productions' *Sex And Violence* after KRS-One admired it in a Los Angeles art gallery.

ART.

13 Comic Book-Inspired Jacket Designs.

1. *ATLiens*—OutKast (LaFace, 1996)
2. *Back Up Off Me*—Doctor Dré & Ed Lover (Relativity, 1994)
3. *"Bang, Zoom, Let's Go-Go!"*—The Real Roxanne featuring Hitman Howie Tee (Select, 1986)
4. *Chubb Rock Featuring Hitman Howie Tee*—Chubb Rock featuring Hitman Howie Tee (Select, 1988)
5. *Don't Try This At Home*—Dangerous Crew (Jive, 1995)
6. *Jam On Revenge*—Newcleus (Sunnyview, 1984)
7. *Liquid Swords*—The Genius (Geffen, 1995)
8. *Masters Of The Rhythm*—DJ Chuck Chillout & Kool Chip (Mercury, 1989)
9. *No Goats, No Glory*—The Goats (Ruffhouse, 1994)
10. *No Need For Alarm*—Del The Funkeé Homosapien (Elektra, 1993)
11. *"Renegades Of Funk"*—Afrika Bambaataa & The Soul Sonic Force (Tommy Boy, 1983)
12. *Return Of The 1 Hit Wonder*—Young MC (Overall, 1997)
13. *"You Want Bass!"*—DJ Magic Mike & MC Madness (Cheetah, 1991)

THE ART OF FACTS:
Little Known Design Trivia.

1. **Will The Real Bad Boy Please Stand Up?**
Contrary to rumor and remarkable resemblance, the adorable baby with the blowout 'fro on the cover of The Notorious B.I.G.'s *Ready To Die* album is neither a baby photo of Biggie nor any of his kin.

2. **P.E. Love.**
According to Stepsun Records president and former Def Jam Records vice president Bill Stephney, the silhouetted "b-boy in crosshairs" of Public Enemy's famed logo is actually LL's former sideman, E Love, taken from a photo originally published in a rap teenzine.

3. **Def Jam Tells You Who I Am . . .**
Def Jam Records co-founder, Rick Rubin, designed the label's classic turntable tone-arm logo.

4. **The *Paul's Boutique* Conspiracy.**
A snippet from a New York radio program used on the Beastie Boys' second album states that Brooklyn is the home of "Paul's Boutique . . . the best in men's clothing." But a close inspection of the cover reveals that the actual location of the famous panoramic photo is the corner of Ludlow and Rivington Streets on Manhattan's Lower East Side.

5. **The '95 To Infinity Award Goes To . . .**
The only rap CD booklet designed as one continuous looping piece of art (when both ends are joined together)—PM Dawn's "rave-y" cover for *Jesus Wept.*

6. **Intoxicated Demon.**
Skate luminary Natas Kaupas art directed the covers of Tha Alkaholiks' *Coast II Coast* and *Likwidation* LPs.

7. **The Tony Touch.**
When not being touted as "the next Slick Rick" due to his considerable mic skills and notable British accent, underground rapper Tony Bones (neé Anthony Harrison) spends his time as an art director at Arista Records. Brand Nubian's *Foundation* and DJ Quik's *rhythm-al-ism* are among his design credits.

8. **Ashhole.**
The peculiar circle at the center of rapper Ras Kass' self-designed logo is actually a cigarette burn and not a bullet hole as commonly thought.

9. **Mr. Incognito, Part 1.**
SoleSides Records homies Chief Xcel (of Blackalicious) and Lyrics Born (wearing a wig) are the beatheads browsing the racks of wax on the cover of DJ Shadow's *Endtroducing . . .* Appearing

---

BACK TO THE LAB:
Art Ideas That Didn't Make The Cut.

1. **Fade To Black.**
The original tone for The Notorious B.I.G.'s *Life After Death* cover was intended to present a much brighter motif, reflecting Biggie's rebirth after the grim ending of *Ready To Die*. However, the art direction was switched at the last minute to reflect a darker atmosphere. This creative choice became eerily ironic in light of Biggie's murder shortly thereafter.

2. **Not As *Nasty* As They Wanna Be.**
The Beastie's kooky *Hello Nasty* cover featuring the cosmic sardine can had been planned to be even *more* way out than it was. Capitol Records gave designers at The Drawing Board a rare monetary thumbs-up in these days of skimpy budgets. Instead of just the Boys laying down inside the fishy coffin, there was to be a die-cut window which would reveal numerous different items therein (such as sardines, rice and beans, the band, etc.) via a rotating "wonder-wheel" similar to that utilized on the classic LP jacket of *Led Zeppelin III*. Difficult production logistics and a rapidly-approaching release date, however, deaded what could've been hip hop's most elaborate album package.

3. **Cold Killin' Labels.**
In an embryonic sketch for The Genius' Geffen Records–released LP, *Liquid Swords*, the opponent falling victim to GZA's blade wore a sweatshirt emblazoned with the logo of his former label, Cold Chillin'. Meanwhile, the fallen body in the background of the completed version initially appeared as a sole decapitated head, which was said to belong to some sucka-ass A&R schmuck..

ART.

on the back cover is Bay Area hip hop icon Beni B.

10. **Mr. Incognito, Part 2.**
In the photograph located on the inner booklet of Capone-N-Noreaga's *The War Report,* there appears a cut-out silhouette standing at the far right among a crowd that is labeled "TRAITOR." Reputedly, this individual dropped dime on Capone before the album's release, sending him to prison for two years on a possession of firearms charge that violated his parole.

11. **All That Scratchin' . . .**
Eazy-E's posthumous *Str8 Off Tha Streetz Of Muthafukkin' Compton* LP holds the distinction of being the only rap CD cover to feature a lottery style scratch-off coating. But there's no big payoff; the cover-up merely censors the offending "Muthafukkin'" in the title for retail purposes.

12. **Noble Past.**
The 3-D computer-rendered illustrations inside Redman's *Doc's Da Name 2000* LP actually reference the Funk Doctor's previous album covers: a bucket of spilled paint, an empty ditch and a muddy baby buggy recall *Whut? Thee Album, Dare Iz A Darkside* and *Muddy Waters,* respectively.

13. **Scils To Pay The Bills.**
The Beastie Boys' *Licensed To Ill* Tour "trim co-ordinator," the late Dave Scilken, went on to become an Assistant Art Director at Jive Records. *The Source*'s current logo and the original stick-figured logo for A Tribe Called Quest are among his best recognizable credits.

14. **Finding Their Religion.**
The cryptic middle eastern script encircling Cypress Hill's famed logo on the front of *III (Temples Of Boom)* makes reference to a religious temple—a spooky coincidence considering that this fact wasn't actually discovered until shortly before the art was sent to be printed.

15. **The Ice Cream Man Cometh.**
Pen & Pixel's super-strong relationship with Master P began because they "pissed him off." The flamboyantly-steezed design outfit was commissioned by one of P's rivals to produce cover art that depicted an exploding ice cream truck (a dis that obviously didn't sit well in the mind of the brotha known for his hit, "Mr. Ice Cream Man"). When the grand Master himself came to their Texas compound to pitch a gangstafied bitch, the folks at P&P threw their hands up, claiming that they had no idea about the beef. P&P did, however, have some mighty fine ideas on how P could improve his packaging. The rest, as they say, is history.

4. *Edutainment* **Tonight.**
The Blastmaster's first idea for the cover of *Edutainment* would have truly been entertaining. Had he gotten his way, BDP's fourth installment would have depicted the cherry tree-choppin', hemp-growin' father of our country, George "You Bet I Inhaled" Washington, getting stabbed by Malcolm X. Kris' head was also to be chiseled onto Mount Rushmore in the distance. Fresh for 1990!

5. *Midnight* **In An Imperfect World.**
Following up group leader Q-Tip's winning cover concept for A Tribe Called Quest's *The Low End Theory,* Tip imagined at least two other ideas for 1993's *Midnight Marauders* that didn't fly before settling on Jive Records designer Jean Kelly's final printed piece.
Had Tip stuck with his gut instincts, *Midnight*'s face would have bore a blue-toned photo shot inside a huge loft with windows revealing money-makin' Manhattan's skyline. On a satin bed illuminated by moonlight would have sat a naked hottie sporting headphones—one hand on her ear, the other on her crotch—engrossed in the ATCQ's lyrical rapture. Scrapping that idea, a second plan was proposed surrounding Tribe's "Striped Lady" character. In this scenario, several of the group's peeps would be seen wearing headphones jacked into the dome-piece of the hip hop heroine, who was to be strolling pied piper-style in front of NYC's landmark Flatiron building. This ill-fated concept—featuring a female model rocking only a painted bodysuit—was actually photographed in the dead of a snowy winter. Eventually, Tip's instinctive tendencies gave *Midnight* a whole different scenario.

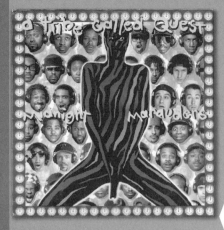

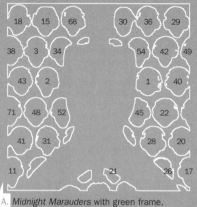

A. *Midnight Marauders* with green frame.

Personalities Pictured On The Cover Of A Tribe Called Quest's *Midnight Marauders* (Jive, 1993).

The cover of ATCQ's third LP was issued in three different versions with three different color schemes (with the "black" version being the rarest), each featuring a rotating line-up of hip hop luminaries and radio DJs. And like The Beatles' *Sgt. Pepper's Lonely Hearts Club Band*, it serves as a time capsule of the era; a who's who of hip hop circa 1993.

1. Adrock (Beastie Boys)
2. Afrika Baby Bam (Jungle Brothers)
3. Afrika Bambaataa
4. Almighty KG (Cold Crush Brothers)
5. AMG
6. Skeff Anselm
7. Ant Banks
8. A-Plus (Souls Of Mischief)
9. Dallas Austin
10. Buckshot (Black Moon)
11. Busta Rhymes
12. Casual
13. Charlie Chase (Cold Crush Brothers)
14. Chi Ali
15. Chuck D
16. Sean "Puffy" Combs
17. Crazy Legs (Rock Steady Crew)
18. Daddy-O
19. Del The Funkeé Homosapien
20. Diamond D
21. Doitall (Lords Of The Underground)
22. Doug E. Fresh
23. Easy AD (Cold Crush Brothers)
24. DJ Evil Dee (Black Moon)
25. Fat Lip (The Pharcyde)
26. 5Ft. Excellerator (Black Moon)
27. Grandmaster Caz (Cold Crush Brothers)
28. Grandmaster Dee (Whodini)
29. Grandmaster Flash
30. Heavy D
31. Ice-T
32. Imani (The Pharcyde)
33. Jazzy Jay
34. DJ Jazzy Joyce
35. DJ Kid Capri
36. Kool Moe Dee

ART.

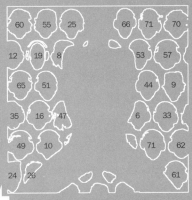

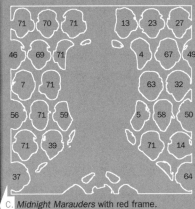

B. *Midnight Marauders* with black frame.

C. *Midnight Marauders* with red frame.

37. Kool DJ Red Alert
38. Large Professor
39. DJ Lord Jazz (Lords Of The Underground)
40. MCA (Beastie Boys)
41. MC Lyte
42. Mike D (Beastie Boys)
43. Mike G (Jungle Brothers)
44. Mr. Funkyman (Lords Of The Underground)
45. Mr. Wiggles (Rock Steady Crew)
46. Neek The Exotic
47. Opio (Souls Of Mischief)
48. P.A. Mase (De La Soul)
49. Pee Wee Dance (Rock Steady Crew)
50. Pharoahe Monch (Organized Konfusion)
51. Phesto (Souls Of Mischief)
52. Posdnuos (De La Soul)
53. Prime Minister Pete Nice
54. Prince Poetry (Organized Konfusion)
55. Romye (The Pharcyde)
56. DJ Ron G
57. Ruel (Rock Steady Crew)
58. MC Serch
59. DJ Silver D
60. Slim Kid Tré (The Pharcyde)
61. Rashad Smith
62. Special Ed
63. Special K (Awesome Two)
64. Sweet Tee
65. Tajai (Souls Of Mischief)
66. Teddy Ted (Awesome Two)
67. DJ Tony Tone (Cold Crush Brothers)
68. Too $hort
69. Zulu King Muhammad (Zulu Nation Supreme Council)
70. Unknown (Zulu Nation Supreme Council)
71. Unknown

Noreaga's Favorite Cinematic Love Stories.

1. *Candyman*
2. *Armageddon*
3. *Carlito's Way*
4. *Gone With The Wind*
5. *There's Something About Mary*
6. *City Of Angels*
7. *Titanic*

Nore (a/k/a Melvin Flynt) is a hard-rockin', half-Black/half-Puerto Rock with a soft spot for tales of camaraderie that spill out into violence, bloodshed and disaster. For further insight into the mind of this superthug, check out recordings like "I Love My Life," "Live On Live Long" (with his rhyme partner Capone) and "Hed."

ACT LIKE YA KNOW:
Hollywood Types On Rap's Bozack.

1. **Warren Beatty**
Lifetime Hollywood swinger Beatty caught the hip hop bug when he conceived his 1998 cinematic vehicle, *Bulworth*. In this offensively unfunny political satire, Mr. Annette Bening plays a corrupt politician on the brink of suicide who miraculously regains his moral fortitude and lust for life through the magic of drugs and rap music. Judging from how Beatty mangles his rhymes throughout the film, we should thank our lucky movie stars that "Warren B's" DJ Muggs-produced contribution to the soundtrack was mercifully left on the cutting room floor. *Bullshit*.

2. **Gary Coleman**
With his post-*Diff'rent Strokes* career hitting the skids, the once-immensely popular television tyke turned to rap music, getting busy with his main man, Dion, on the sweet novelty tune, "The Outlaw & The Indian." The song finds Gary "The Outlaw" and Dion "The Indian" squashing cultural differences and becoming buddy-buddy, buddy.

3. **Omar Epps**
Perennial "rising" star Epps has been busting rhymes with his crew, Wolf Pack, since he began sipping *Juice* as a teen. Isn't it time O.E. took a break from making blockbusters like *Mod Squad* and hit us with some musical eps?

4. **The Fat Kid From *Juice* & *Lean On Me***
Although the liner notes from his CD, *Chunky But Funky* (Ichiban, 1993), don't reveal his government name, the entertainer identified simply as Huggy has a face that is instantly recognizable as the actor who portrayed one of the homies in *Juice*. He may be best known, however, as the kid in *Lean On Me* who breaks down and cries like a baby girl when Morgan "Joe Clark" Freeman steps to him about straightening out his life. Huggy takes no shorts when it comes to this rap shit either. Peep track #5, "Gusto," to hear the chubbster trading verses with U.T.F.O.'s Doctor Ice. 'Nuff respect due.

5. **David Faustino**
Perhaps forever typecast as the horny, scheming runt Bud Bundy on the long-running, raw-humored *Married With Children*, Dave indulged in rapping both on the show (as "Grandmaster B") and behind the scenes. He also hosted a hip hop party in Los Angeles called Ballistics and probably still couldn't get laid. Christina Applegate, you shoulda put him on.

6. **Gerardo**
Rico Suavé himself was actually a struggling actor in Hollywood (check him out in *Colors*, homes) until "rap" saved his career. Thankfully, his reign at the top of the hip hop dance charts was shorter than KRS-One's

FILM.

⭐ we get more props and stunts than bruce willis.

part in *Who's The Man?*

7. Balthazar Getty
The great grandson of J. Paul Getty has appeared in art films like *Lord Of The Flies* and *Lost Highway,* but beatmaking was Brat Packer Balthazar's big jones. He produced tracks for the critically-panned group Mannish for the now-defunct Correct Records. No relation to Geddy Lee. And he wasn't rolling with Rush either.

8. Brian Austin Green
One minute, the *Beverly Hills 90210* heartthrob was mingling with The Pharcyde on your TV screen. The next thing anybody knew he'd tricked the group into helping him make a rap album, *One Stop Carnival* (Yab Yum, 1996). Next stop, cut-out bin.

9. Arsenio Hall
Reinventing himself as the Heavy D-inspired Chunky A—the fictional, corpulent, rhymin' sibling of himself—Hall revealed his eternal love for this rap shit. You ask us if we like Arsenio? Hell, yeah. Fuck Chris Spencer.

10. Corin Nemic
Back in 1992, the star of Fox's *Parker Lewis Can't Lose* reputedly wielded white hot rhyme skills as one time evidenced at an Ed Lover birthday bash. But the actor's winning streak came to an abrupt end when Nemic's anemic teeny-bopping *Parker* program was canned and the public lost sight of the young Corin. And now the microphone is his only friend.

11. Tyrin Turner
Embraced by the Houston rhyme cartel Rap-A-Lot Records, Turner is poised to translate his movie persona into a rap career. Maintaining the name Caine (his character from the Hughes Brothers' magnetic *Menace II Society*), TT Dynamite got his 16 bars off on the Geto Boys' "Dawn 2 Dusk" (Rap-A-Lot, 1997) and prepared to drop an album dubbed *Menace World* as the millennium approached. Hold ya head, Ma$e.

BONUS: Cop the *Rappin'* Soundtrack (Atlantic, 1985) and peep "Snack Attack," a song in which big-time movie types Mario Van Peebles, Eriq La Salle and Kadeem Hardison drop science on the M-I-C.

TWO MINUTE BROTHAS (& SISTAS):
26 Feature Film Cameos By Rappers.

1. AZ—*Belly* (Artisan Entertainment, 1998)
2. Bushwick Bill—*Original Gangstas* (Orion, 1996)
3. Digital Underground featuring 2Pac—*Nothing But Trouble* (Warner Bros., 1991)
4. MC Eiht—*Boyz N The Hood* (Columbia, 1991)
5. Everybody in the rap game—*Who's The Man?* (New Line, 1993)
6. Flavor Flav—*Private Parts* (Paramount Pictures, 1997)
7. Heather B.—*Dead Presidents* (Hollywood Pictures, 1995)
8. Ice-T—*Breakin'* (Cannon, 1984)
9. Kid Frost—*Mi Vida Loca* (Cineville Inc., 1993)
10. KRS-One—*I'm Gonna Git You Sucka* (United Artists, 1988)
11. LL Cool J—*Caught Up* (Live Entertainment, 1998) & *Wildcats* (Warner Bros., 1986)
12. Luniz—*Original Gangstas* (Orion, 1996)
13. Method Man—*Cop Land* (Miramax, 1997); *Great White Hype* (20th Century Fox, 1996) & *187* (Icon, 1997)
14. Mista Grimm—*Poetic Justice* (Columbia, 1993)
15. Nikki D—*Let's Get Bizzee* (Spectrum Clay Productions, 1992)
16. Q-Tip—*Poetic Justice* (Columbia, 1993)
17. Queen Latifah—*Juice* (Paramount, 1992) & *Jungle Fever* (Universal, 1991)
18. Saafir—*Menace II Society* (New Line, 1993)
19. MC Shan—*L.A. Story* (TriStar, 1991)*
20. Snoop Doggy Dogg—*Caught Up* (Live Entertainment, 1998); *Half Baked* (Universal, 1998) & *Ride* (Dimension Films, 1998)
21. Sticky Fingaz (Onyx)—*Dead Presidents* (Hollywood Pictures, 1995)
22. T-Bone (Da Lench Mob)—*Boyz N The Hood* (Columbia, 1991)
23. Too $hort—*Menace II Society* (New Line, 1993)
24. Treach (Naughty By Nature)—*Juice* (Paramount, 1992)
25. WC—*Friday* (New Line, 1995), *Set It Off* (New Line, 1997)
26. Yo Yo—*Boyz N The Hood* (Columbia, 1991)

*Billed in the film's credits as "Rap Waiter at L'idiot."

34 Rap Song Titles Based On Movie Titles.

1. "The Assignment"—Noreaga (Penalty, 1998)
2. "Black Sunday"—Organized Konfusion (Hollywood BASIC, 1994)
3. "Black To The Future"—Def Jef (Delicious Vinyl, 1989)
4. "Black Trek IV: The Voyage Home"—Chubb Rock (Select, 1992)
5. "Body Snatchers"—Scarface (Rap-A-Lot, 1991)
6. "Crocodile Dundee"—YZ (Tuff City, 1991)
7. "Desperado"—Gambino Family (No Limit, 1998)
8. "A Doggz Day Afternoon"—Tha Dogg Pound (Death Row, 1995)
9. "Driveby Miss Daisy"—Compton's Most Wanted (Orpheus, 1991)
10. "East Side Story"—Kid Frost (Virgin, 1992)
11. "Enter The Dragon"—Kool G Rap (Cold Chillin', 1996)
12. "E.T. (Extraterrestrial)"—OutKast (LaFace, 1996)
13. "5 Fingas Of Death"—Diamond D featuring Big L, Lord Finesse, AG & Fat Joe (Mercury, 1997)
14. "The Godfather"—Spoonie Gee (Tuff City, 1987)
15. "Killin' Fields"—Method Man (Def Jam, 1998)
16. "Lethal Weapon"—Ice-T (Sire, 1989)
17. "Long Kiss Goodnight"—The Notorious B.I.G. (Bad Boy, 1997)
18. "Mahogany"—Eric B. & Rakim (MCA, 1990)
19. "The Mask"—Fugees (Ruffhouse, 1996)
20. "Mr. Goodbar"—LL Cool J (Def Jam, 1990)
21. "Natural Born Killaz"—Dr. Dre & Ice Cube (Death Row, 1994)
22. "New Jack City"—M.O.P. (Relativity, 1996)
23. "Night Of The Living Baseheads"—Public Enemy (Def Jam, 1988)
24. "Public Enemy No. 1"—Public Enemy (Def Jam, 1987)
25. "Rebel Without A Pause"—Public Enemy (Def Jam, 1988)
26. "Saturday Nite Fever"—Lordz Of Brooklyn (American, 1995)
27. "Shaft's Big Score"—X Clan (4th & B'way, 1990)
28. "Silence Of The Lambs"—Show & AG (Payday, 1995)
29. "A Soldier's Story"—WC And The MAAD Circle (Priority, 1991)
30. "Steel Magnolia"—Cypress Hill (Ruffhouse, 1998)
31. "Tequila Sunrise"—Cypress Hill (Ruffhouse, 1998)
32. "Terminator"—Kid Frost (Electrobeat, 1985)
33. "To Live & Die In L.A."—Makaveli (Death Row, 1996)
34. "West Side Story"—Bobcat (Arista, 1989)

29 Rap Album Titles Based On Movie Titles.

1. *Apocalypse '91...The Enemy Strikes Black*—Public Enemy (Def Jam, 1991)
2. *The Badlands*—Papa Chuk (Pendulum, 1994)
3. *Black Sunday*—Cypress Hill (Ruffhouse, 1993)
4. *Cool Hand Lōc*—Tone-Lōc (Delicious Vinyl, 1991)
5. *Tha Doggfather*—Snoop Doggy Dogg (Death Row, 1996)
6. *Game Of Death*—Mob Style (Win Time, 1992)
7. *Goodfellas*—Show & AG (Payday, 1995)
8. *The Good, The Bad, The Ugly*—Mob Style (Grove St., 1990)
9. *Guerillas In Tha Mist*—Da Lench Mob (Street Knowledge, 1992)
10. *A Hero Ain't Nuttin' But A Sandwich*—The A.T.E.E.M. (Select, 1992)
11. *King Of New York*—Pudgee Tha Fat Bastard (Perspective, 1996)
12. *Little Big Man*—Bushwick Bill (Rap-A-Lot, 1992)
13. *Live And Let Die*—Kool G Rap & DJ Polo (Cold Chillin', 1992)
14. *Magnum Force*—Heltah Skeltah (Duck Down, 1998)
15. *The Natural*—Mic Geronimo (Blunt, 1995)
16. *No Way Out*—Puff Daddy & The Family (Bad Boy, 1997)
17. *Once Upon A Time In America*—Smoothe Da Hustler (Profile, 1996)
18. *Phantom Of The Rapra*—Bushwick Bill (Rap-A-Lot, 1995)
19. *Phenomenon*—LL Cool J (Def Jam, 1997)
20. *Planet Of Da Apes*—Da Lench Mob (Priority, 1994)
21. *Predator*—Ice Cube (Priority, 1992)
22. *The Professional*—DJ Clue (Roc-A-Fella, 1998)
23. *Reservoir Dog*—Schoolly D (PSK, 1995)
24. *Dah Shinin'*—Smif-N-Wessun (Nervous, 1995)
25. *Technics Chainsaw Massacre*—Jeep Beat Collective (Bomb, 1998)
26. *Tical 2000: Judgement Day*—Method Man (Def Jam, 1998)
27. *2Pacalypse Now*—2Pac (Interscope, 1991)
28. *Uptown Saturday Night*—Camp Lo (Profile, 1997)
29. *Usual Suspects*—5th Ward Boyz (Rap-A-Lot, 1997)

FILM.

O'SHEA CAN YOU SEE THE CONNECTION?

Rap-Related Career Highlights Of Hollywood Hot Boy, Ice Cube.

1. O'Shea Jackson first got his SAG on (as in "Screen Actors Guild," not gangbanging, fool) in John Singleton's heralded *Boyz N The Hood* (Columbia, 1991) co-starring as Doughboy, a 40-guzzling, philosophizing gangsta. In one scene, a dope fiend snatches a gold chain off of one of Cube's cronies. The crew chases his ass down and stomps the chump, who incidentally is wearing a "We Want Eazy" T-shirt.

2. In *The Glass Shield* (Miramax, 1994), a subdued but effective Cube plays Theodore Woods, a young Black male at the wrong place at the wrong time who becomes the scapegoat for racist white cops. Being administered the third degree by some dirty detectives, Cube blurts out, "Like the song says, 'My Skin Is My Sin.'" It so happens that this is also the title of one of his B-sides.

3. Cube isn't afraid to play a herb who tries herb for the first time in *Friday* (New Line, 1995), an entertaining weed comedy (penned by Jackson and DJ Pooh) about the perils of getting high on your own supply. While faded in his parent's living room, Cube and co-star Chris Tucker catch a video by Cube's Lench Mob Records artist K-Dee on the tube.

4. *Dangerous Ground* (New Line, 1997) tells the tale of an exiled South African student activist named Vusi Madlazi (Cube) who returns home 14 years later when his father dies. Model Elizabeth Hurley plays a hipless stripper/crackhead who helps our rapping hero find his lost brother. During their search, the duo enter a ramshackled apartment where you can spot an N.W.A poster hanging on a wall.

5. *Anaconda* (Columbia, 1997), the campy Amazon adventure about slippery, super-sized snakes, not only has the mesmerizing Butter Pecan Rican Jennifer Lopez in a wet tank top but features Ice Cube bumping his buddy Mack 10's "Foe Life" on his boombox in between serpent attacks. Cube portrays Danny Rich, a director of photography with a serious fetish for bandanas, Chuck Taylors and L.A. Dodger hats. His opening line, "Yeah, well today is a good day," immediately brings to mind his 1992 hit, "It Was A Good Day."

Film-Inspired Rap Names.

1. Hurby "Luv Bug" Azor:
   The *Herbie The Love Bug* Walt Disney series
2. Biggie Smalls (b/k/a The Notorious B.I.G.):
   Let's Do It Again
3. Charli Baltimore: *Long Kiss Goodnight*
4. Foxy Brown: *Foxy Brown*
5. Hansoul: *Star Wars*
6. Last Emperor: *The Last Emperor*
7. Lil' 1/2 Dead: *Penitentiary*
8. Luke Skyywalker: *Star Wars*
9. Phantasm (Cella Dwellas): *Phantasm*
10. Rampage (a/k/a The Last Boy Scout):
    The Last Boy Scout
11. Robocop (Boogie Down Productions):
    Robocop
12. Scarface: *Scarface*
13. Hank & Keith Shocklee (The Bomb Squad):
    The Gauntlet
14. The Wascals (Buckweed, A.L.Phie, Spit-anky,
    St. Imey): The *Our Gang* series
15. Wu-Tang Clan: Various kung-fu films, includ-
    ing *Shaolin vs. Wu-Tang*
16. Yoda Red (Boogiemonsters):
    The Empire Strikes Back

JACKIN' FOR TREATMENTS:
Music Videos Based On Movies.

1. **"Another Sign"—Schoolly D (Ruffhouse, 1994)**
   BASED ON: *Taxi Driver*
2. **"The City Is Mine"—Jay-Z featuring Blackstreet (Roc-A-Fella, 1997)**
   BASED ON: *Usual Suspects*
3. **"Fu-Gee-La"—Fugees (Ruffhouse, 1996)**
   BASED ON: *The Harder They Come*
4. **"Full Cooperation"—Def Squad (Def Jam, 1998)**
   BASED ON: *48 Hours; Trading Places & The Nutty Professor*
5. **"Hard Knock Life (Ghetto Anthem)"—Jay-Z (Roc-A-Fella, 1998)**
   BASED ON: *Fallen*
6. **"How High"—Redman & Method Man (Def Jam, 1995)**
   BASED ON: *Cheech & Chong's Nice Dreams*
7. **"Hypnotize"—The Notorious B.I.G. (Bad Boy, 1997)**
   BASED ON: *The Rock*
8. **"Incredible"—Keith Murray featuring LL Cool J (Jive, 1998)**
   BASED ON: *Batman*
9. **"N.O.R.E."—Noreaga (Penalty, 1998)**
   BASED ON: *Con Air & The Fugitive*
10. **"Put Your Hands Where My Eyes Can See"—Busta Rhymes (Elektra, 1997)**
    BASED ON: *Coming To America*
11. **"Rat Bastard"—Prime Minister Pete Nice & Daddy Rich (Def Jam, 1993)**
    BASED ON: *The Untouchables*
12. **"Street Dreams"—Nas (Columbia, 1996)**
    BASED ON: *Casino*
13. **"Watch For The Hook"—Cool Breeze featuring OutKast, Witchdoctor & Goodie Mob (LaFace, 1998)**
    BASED ON: *Reservoir Dogs*
14. **"Whateva Man"—Redman featuring Erick Sermon (Def Jam, 1996)***
    BASED ON: *The Blues Brothers*
15. **"Won Time"—Smif-N-Wessun (Nervous, 1995)**
    BASED ON: *The Shining*
16. **"You Know My Steez"—Gang Starr (Noo Trybe, 1998)**
    BASED ON: *THX 1138*

*Features Method Man—not Erick Sermon—in the part of Elwood.

FILM.

QUIET ON THE SET, NOT SO QUIET ON THE SOUNDTRACK:
20 Rap Theme Songs To Non-Rap Films.

1. **"Addams Groove"—MC Hammer (Capitol, 1991)**
   FROM: *Addams Family*

2. **"Are You Ready For Freddy"—Fat Boys (Tin Pan Apple, 1988)**
   FROM: *A Nightmare On Elm Street 2: Freddy's Revenge*

3. **"Crooklyn"—Crooklyn Dodgers (MCA, 1994)**
   FROM: *Crooklyn*

4. **"Deep Cover"—Dr. Dre featuring Snoop Doggy Dogg (Epic, 1992)**
   FROM: *Deep Cover*

5. **"Dick Tracy"—Ice-T (Warner Bros., 1990)**
   FROM: *Dick Tracy*

6. **"Gangsta's Paradise"—Coolio (MCA, 1995)**
   FROM: *Dangerous Minds*

7. **"Ghostbusters"—Run-D.M.C. (Profile, 1989)**
   FROM: *Ghostbusters II*

8. **"Gladiator"—3rd Bass (Def Jam, 1992)**
   FROM: *Gladiator*

9. **"Glory"—D-Nice (Jive, 1990)**
   FROM: *Glory*

10. **"Gravesend (Lake Of Fire)"—Lordz Of Brooklyn (Island, 1997)**
    FROM: *Gravesend*

11. **"Hangin' With The Homeboys And Dr. Feelgood"—2 Live Crew featuring Triple XXX (b/k/a Mötley Crüe) (Luke, 1991)**
    FROM: *Hangin' With The Homeboys*

12. **"Hoodlum"—Mobb Deep featuring Big Noyd & Rakim (Loud, 1997)**
    FROM: *Hoodlum*

13. **"Made In America"—Del The Funkeé Homosapien (Elektra, 1993)**
    FROM: *Made In America*

14. **"Ninja Rap"—Vanilla Ice (SBK, 1991)**
    FROM: *Teenage Mutant Ninja Turtles II: The Secret Of The Ooze*

15. **"Rap Summary (Lean On Me)"—Big Daddy Kane (Warner Bros., 1989)**
    FROM: *Lean On Me*

16. **"Revolution"—Arrested Development (Qwest, 1992)**
    FROM: *Malcolm X*

17. **"Ricochet"—Ice-T (Sire, 1991)**
    FROM: *Ricochet*

18. **"Rumble In The Jungle"—Fugees featuring John Forté, A Tribe Called Quest & Busta Rhymes (Mercury, 1997)**
    FROM: *When We Were Kings*

19. **"Tales From The Hood"—Domino featuring Chill (40 Acres And A Mule Musicworks, 1995)**
    FROM: *Tales From The Hood*

20. **"What's The Matter With Your World?"—Grandmaster Melle Mel & Van Silk (Posse, 1989)**
    FROM: *Police Academy 6: City Under Siege*

13 & GOOD:
Rap Movie Soundtracks That Don't Suck.

1. *Above The Rim* (Death Row, 1994)
2. *Colors* (Warner Bros., 1988)
3. *Fresh* (Loud, 1994)
4. *Friday* (Priority, 1995)
5. *Gang Related* (Death Row, 1997)
6. *Juice* (MCA, 1992)*
7. *Menace II Society* (Jive, 1993)*
8. *New Jersey Drive* (Tommy Boy, 1995)
9. *The Nutty Professor* (Def Jam, 1995)
10. *Soul In The Hole* (Loud, 1997)
11. *Trespass* (Sire, 1992)
12. *Who's The Man?* (Uptown, 1993)
13. *Wild Style* (Animal, 1983)

*In addition to their slammin' soundtracks, *Juice* and *Menace II Society* were the first rap films to feature original hip hop scores—composed by The Bomb Squad and QDIII, respectively.

Sampled Movie Dialogue Quiz.

1. "Crime Pays"—Al Tariq (Correct, 1996)
2. "Intro"—Big Punisher (Loud, 1998)
3. "Just Another Killer"—Schoolly D (Capitol, 1991)
4. "Heavyweights"—DJ Muggs featuring MC Eiht (Columbia, 1997)
5. "Urban Sound Surgeon"—4-Ever Fresh (Tommy Boy, 1988)
6. "Streets Is Watching"—Jay-Z (Roc-A-Fella, 1997)
7. "Ain't Got No Class"—Da Lench Mob (Street Knowledge, 1992)
8. "Love Letters Intro"—Psycho Realm (Ruffhouse, 1997)
9. "Mr. Scarface"—Scarface (Rap-A-Lot, 1991)
10. "Daddy Rich In The Land Of 1210"—3rd Bass (Def Jam, 1991)
11. "Me So Horny"—2 Live Crew (Luke, 1989)
12. "At The Speed Of Life"—Xzibit (Loud, 1996)
13. "Black On Black Crime"—Brand Nubian (Arista, 1998)
14. "First Day Of School"—Ice Cube (Priority, 1992)
15. "Wild Flower"—Ghostface Killah (Razor Sharp, 1996)
16. "MC Is My Ambition"—Diamond D (Mercury, 1997)
17. "Make A Move"—Cypress Hill (Ruffhouse, 1995)
18. "Farmers Blvd. (Our Anthem)"—LL Cool J (Def Jam, 1990)
19. "Runnin Yo' Mouth"—Original Concept (Def Jam, 1988)
20. "Patti Dooke"—De La Soul (Tommy Boy, 1993)

A. *Taxi Driver*
B. *Car Wash*
C. *Don't Be A Menace . . .*
D. *Fast Times At Ridgemont High*
E. *Foxy Brown*
F. *The Mack*
G. *Full Metal Jacket*
H. *JD's Revenge*
I. *American Me*
J. *A Rage In Harlem*
K. *The Five Heartbeats*
L. *King Of New York*
M. *Short Eyes*
N. *Fresh*
O. *Blue Velvet*
P. *Sleepers*
Q. *Petrified Forest*
R. *The Warriors*
S. *Pulp Fiction*
T. *Scarface*

ANSWERS: 1.L 2.N 3.M 4.O 5.R 6.P 7.J 8.O 9.T 10.B 11.G 12.A 13.C 14.I 15.H 16.E 17.S 18.F 19.D 20.K

FILM.
188 ego trip's book of rap lists. ★ you couldn't capture our potential on some film from Kodak.

Debi Mazar Recounts
6 Close Encounters With Hip Hop In The '80s.

1. Up In The Bronx Where The People Are Fresh.

When the '80s came around, me and a girlfriend of mine used to go up to the Bronx River House cuz we heard about this guy, DJ Kool Herc, and somebody called Bambaataa, who were spinnin' music. I had pretty much come out of a disco scene, but my friends and I really liked the music comin' from the Bronx. It was interesting cuz it was like hip hop and new wave kinda collided. You had The Sex Pistols, Debbie Harry, the Talking Heads, Devo, Kraftwerk and Kurtis Blow. People like Run-D.M.C. were doin' their own hardcore style rap. Stylistically, people started gettin' a lil' bit freaky—streakin' their hair and wearin' 25 earrings. It was a really fun time. And it was the first time I felt that color didn't divide. Everybody came together and nobody was judgin' anybody.

2. A Roller Skating Jam Called The Roxy.

I used to work the door at Danceteria and the Mudd Club when I was like 16. Believe it or not, I used to do security at the Roxy like in '83, '84. The Roxy at the time was a roller rink so they didn't want the floor to get damaged. It was kinda funny cuz my job was to walk around and tell people that they couldn't smoke. People would look at me and go, "Get the fuck out of here." So basically, I didn't really do my job. I was hangin' out and sneakin' my cigarettes and dancin' to the music. My job didn't last that long cuz I guess they realized that they were payin' me to do nuthin'.

3. D Rugs.

There were a lot of drugs back in the day, like dust was a really big thing. People were going away because they flipped out on dust. It was a shame—fabulous artists were getting totally wasted. You could always tell when someone was using because you could smell that mint smell. Crack hadn't even hit yet.

It was interesting too because it was a time when people from the ghetto could all of a sudden go to Europe. People were buying art, so artists were making money. Rock Steady blew up and they were traveling the world. That was very exciting because they were like role models for a lot of us.

4. Where My Dogs At?

I knew Run-D.M.C. At the time, nobody was large and everybody knew each other. I was doin' make-up then. Matter of fact, I even did their make-up on their "Christmas In Hollis" video where they had a pit bull play the reindeer. They had these cardboard antlers on him and the dog got really pissed off at me and snapped, almost biting me.

5. Sisters Gonna Work It Out.

At one point, me and my girls tried to have our own lil' crew. We called ourselves the Midtown Angels. We had our own little beads. It wasn't like a fighting thing or to signify like, "Yo, this is my territory." We just wanted to have our own lil' thing too. It was like, "All because we're white we're not down? Fuck that shit."

6. The Revolution Will Be Televised.

A bunch of friends of mine were involved with the hip hop television show *Graffiti Rock*—people like the show's creator Michael Holman, Rock Steady, Vincent Gallo, who went on to become a director, and my boyfriend at the time, Kel 139.

I knew Michael years before the show even ever happened. Michael was a filmmaker and he was also mulatto. He got very in touch with his Blackness and feelin' like very street. He was one of the first people that tried to infiltrate TV and try to spread the word about hip hop. I remember hearin' him talkin' about doing *Graffiti Rock*. We were all like, "Yeah, whatever, you're doin' a TV show." But then it got very real. And everybody was down with it. Like D.ST wanted to do it. People that were hot at the moment like Shannon were performing.

We taped *Graffiti Rock* in East Harlem. I remember it was up by about 114th Street in a big studio. We all knew each other from like hangin' out in the clubs and we were all really excited to be there. All I remember is having a lot of fun and it taking a long time to tape. Then I got bored after a while dancing to the same songs.

It was my first time on TV. My mother, all my friends watched it. It was kind of big news in the hip hop community at the time that that sort of stuff was getting on TV. But I guess the ratings weren't all that. We all watched it, but the rest of America didn't.

It didn't seem like we were doing anything that was so monumental in hip hop. It was just kids from the street and from our scene that were makin' something that was gonna be on TV and that was exciting enough. I didn't really appreciate it all until later.

After chilling with hip hop's seminal figures as a young b-girl, Debi Mazar moved on to become an acclaimed actress whose work has appeared in such films as Goodfellas, Jungle Fever and Malcolm X. Throughout her travels, this native New Yorker is always representing, putting Queens on the map.

1. **Crime Boss**

2. **Tha Doggfather**

3. **The Firm** THE ALBUM

The *ego trip* Oscars.

1. **The Fuck "Thriller" Video Oscar:**
   Game Of Survival: The Movie—Live Squad
   This fast-paced, ultra-violent 1993 long-form music video chronicles the life and times of a troubled orphan turned heartless murderahh. The most disturbing scene involves a toddler being tossed out of a window while his parents are tortured (and later torched). The final twist: in a climactic *Harlem Nights*-inspired bedroom *rendezvous*, our anti-hero gets blasted between the sheets. Famed director Michael Schultz (*Car Wash, Krush Groove* and *Sgt. Pepper's Lonely Hearts Club Band*) does his thing-thing on the editing tip.

2. **The Lady Is A Tramp Oscar: Lisa Nicole Carson**
   Years before Ally McBeal's buxom Black buddy got hot 'n heavy with Naughty By Nature's muscle-bound Treach in the otherwise forgettable *Jason's Lyric*, a young Lisa Carson could be seen tonguing-down Doug E. Fresh in the horrific *Let's Get Bizzee*. Carmen Electra, eat your heart out.

3. **Who's The Mack? Oscar: Ghostface Killah In *The Show***
   While the scene of Method Man vehemently jawing with his Wu cohorts on a Japanese monorail remains unforgettable, the film's real scene-snatcher is Tony Starks. Donning a kimono as he enters a Tokyo massage parlor, Ghost exudes more playboy charisma than James "Wrath Of . . ." Caan.

4. **Best Non-Hip Hop Hip Hop Film Oscar: The Warriors**
   Its epic gang speech scene is drama on par with Chuck Heston schooling the masses with his biblical tablets in *The*

Ten Commandments. And its impact continues to be felt through the works of such artists as N.W.A, Fat Joe, Schoolly D and Def Squad. Too many key scenes to name individually, but ultimately, this white man's voyeuristic look at '70s New York gangs sums up hip hop's genesis: it begins in the South Bronx, the story is forwarded by a DJ's patter and it contains a lot of gratuitous violence. Can you dig it?

5. **Best *Faux* Graffiti Flick Oscar: *Turk 182***
   Timothy *"Taps"* Hutton stars as the younger working class artist brother of Robert "Dan Tanna" Urich. Urich, a big-hearted fireman with a sweet tooth for strong liquor, gets injured saving a family while off-duty and fully lit. The City of New York, however, refuses to pay for his medical expenses and disability. In response, Hutton says fuck tha police, tha mayor and everyone else that stands in his way by painting his brother's nickname and badge number ("Turk 182") on subways and even scrawling it in lights across the Queensboro Bridge. We wonder if graffiti legend Taki 183 ever received a check from the studio. We doubt it, doubt it.

6. **Fear Of A Black Scientist Oscar: *T2: Judgement Day***
   Only in America could Austrian steroid superman, Arnold "I'm That Type Of . . ." Schwarzenegger, defend Old Glory's future against the laboratory fuck-ups of a bamboozled bourgeois Black scientist (played by distinguished thespian from another planet, Joe Morton). But even while brothas were being systematically and cinematically attacked, then-

FILM.

3. *The Firm The Album*—Nas, AZ, Foxy Brown & Nature (Aftermath, 1997) 4. "G.O.D. Pt. III"—Mobb Deep (Loud, 1996)
5. *Roots Of Evil*—Kool G Rap (Ill Street Records, 1998) 6. *The Score*—Fugees (Ruffhouse, 1996)

4.

5.

6.

adolescent star Edward Furlong knew which mother-fuckin' side he was on. His black Public Enemy T-shirt is proudly worn throughout this box office smash.

7. **Wack Spike Lee Ending™ Oscar:** *Juice*
Former Lee cinematographer Ernest "Goes To Hollywood" Dickerson's directorial debut was an authentic success for a solid hour-and-a-half. Unfortunately, Tupac Shakur's riveting performance as the hot-headed Bishop wasn't enough to save the film from its dismal final five minutes of fake funk. After 'Pac falls from a rooftop, a decidedly shook Omar Epps is told by a random brother, "You got the juice now." This hollow and contrived utterance was the lamest dialogue to cap a film since your man "Dap" yelped, "Wake Up!" at the conclusion of *School Daze*. Sho' 'nuff.

8. **The Original *I'm Bout It* Oscar:** *Tougher Than Leather*
Who would have thunk that 10 years after first (and last)-time feature film director Rick Rubin killed the career of hip hop's greatest group, Run-D.M.C., that his cinematic opus would be regarded as a genuine cult classic? While the film's payback plot is trite at best, the thugged-out Hollis trio are still engaging as they go out blasting, leaving a steady stream of brains on the sidewalk. Incredibly amateurish "live" appearances by the Beastie Boys, Slick Rick and the Junkyard Band, an interracial *ménage à trois*, Sheila E. looking all fine (oh shit, that was *Krush Groove*—our bad) and a don't-blink-or-

you'll-miss-it shot of Adam Yauch as a Hasidic Jew comprise this under-acknowledged precursor to direct-to-video rap epics as we know them today.

9. **Jacking For Storylines Oscar:** *Beat Street*
EXHIBIT A: *Style Wars* (documentary)—Renegade white dawg graffiti bomber Cap talks tough (at one point in the film he claims, "Niggas know") and crosses-out the comp with the precision of Captain Caveman.
Beat Street (Hollywood production)—Renegade no-talent-having, olived-skinned cracker by the name of Spit goes berserk like Red Alert and crosses-out the competition.

EXHIBIT B: *Wild Style* (low-budget feature)—Mystery writer Zorro (Lee Quinones) is courted by big bucks and the "legit" artworld.
Beat Street—Beatmaker Kenny is given the opportunity to work with his girlfriend (Rae Dawn Chong)'s father (Harry Belafonté) scoring a production in the world of Alvin Ailey-isms.

VERDICT: *Beat Street* is the Sugarhill Gang of rap flicks. Get off the dick.

10. **Enduring Rap Movie Trend Oscar:**
A Big Throwdown At The End Of The Movie
Check *Wild Style*; *Beat Street*; *Breakin'*; *Krush Groove*; *Rappin'*; *Body Rock*; *I'm Gonna Git You Sucka* and *Beneath The Planet Of The Apes*. The party don't stop.

CHE

ODAR.

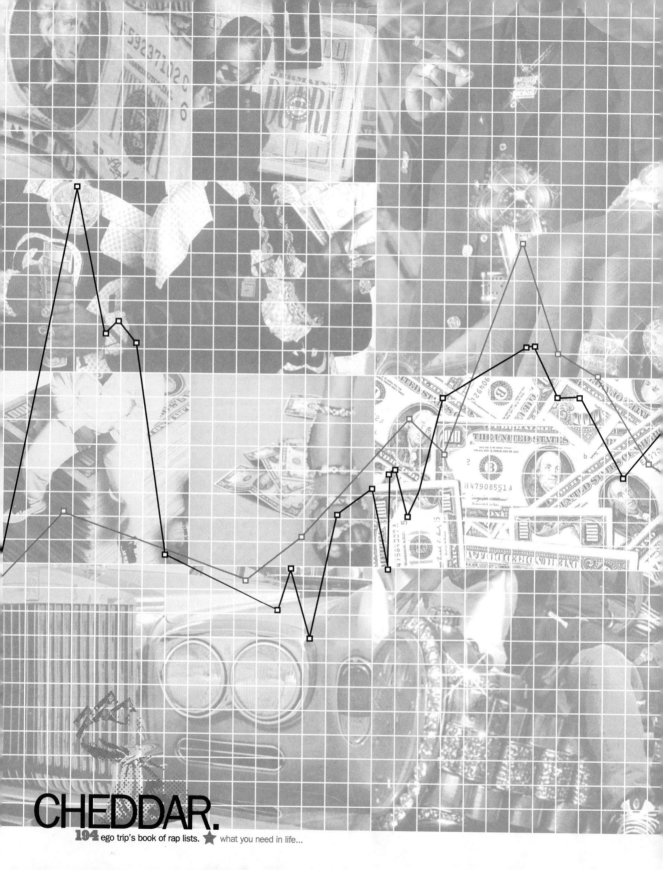

CHEDDAR.

Money Ain't A Thang.

1. $125 million: Estimated earnings of Death Row Records between 1992 and 1996.
2. $80 million: Amount Suge Knight alleges C. DeLores Tucker offered him to leave his post as CEO of Death Row Records in 1995 and work for her at a new Time Warner-distributed non-gangsta rap-affiliated record label.
3. $30 million: Estimated value of New Orleans' Cash Money Records' 1998 distribution deal with Universal Records.
4. $21 million: Average annual revenue generated by Miami-based pay-per-view video request network The Box during the mid-'90s.
5. $12 million: "Wild Wild" Will Smith's asking price per cinematic effort.
6. $3.5 million: Gross revenue for the 1984 Fresh Fest Tour featuring Run-D.M.C., Kurtis Blow, Whodini, Fat Boys, Newcleus and the Dynamic Breakers.
7. $3 million: Production cost for MC Hammer's too-expensive-to-believe "Too Legit To Quit" music video.
8. $1.7 million: Amount that De La Soul was sued for by has-been hippies Flo and Eddie of The Turtles for De La's unauthorized sample of "You Showed Me" on 3 Feet High And Rising.
9. $1.6 million: Amount awarded New York-born, Atlanta-based bass artist MC Shy-D for unpaid back royalties from his recordings for Luke Records.
10. $800,000: Amount of the bail posted by Russell Simmons to have Slick Rick released from jail in 1991.
11. $40,000: Value of the jewelry and gold chains 2Pac was robbed for when he was shot by assailants in the lobby of New York's Quad Recording studios in November of 1994. (It was not "60 G's worth of gun-clapping" as Mobb Deep erroneously described on their song, "Drop A Gem On 'Em.")
12. $25,000: Amount of reward put up by the City of Los Angeles for information leading to the arrest of a suspect in the murder of The Notorious B.I.G. The amount was later matched by B.I.G.'s mother, Voletta Wallace.
13. $15,000: Amount donated by Scarface and Rap-A-Lot Records to the victims of October 1994 floods in the greater Houston area.
14. $11,000: Estimated amount of damage done to a Gainesville, FL concert venue in a riot at a July 1995 Method Man concert. The fracas allegedly ensued after Johnny Blaze shouted, "Kill the sound man!" and stormed offstage, bringing his show to an abrupt close after a five-minute performance.
15. "A watch and a gold chain": What the D.O.C. reputedly received from Ruthless Records in exchange for his publishing rights on all material he composed and performed for the label.
16. $2,490: Cost of Eazy-E's seat at a 1991 Republican Senators Inner Circle luncheon.
17. $950: Estimated value of an ostrich on Public Enemy DJ Terminator X's ostrich farm in North Carolina.
18. $700: Recording cost for LL Cool J's 1984 debut single, "I Need A Beat."
19. $250: First prize for the winning group in the MC Throwdown Showdown held November 1980 at the Bronx's Ecstacy Garage Disco featuring the Fantastic Five, Funky 4 + 1, Cold Crush Brothers, Fearless Four, Treacherous Three, Force Of The 5 MC's (b/k/a Crash Crew), The Soul Sonic Force, The Cosmic Force and the Dynamic Duo (b/k/a Dr. Jeckyll & Mr. Hyde).
20. $30: Ticket price of a mezzanine seat at the Apollo Theatre for the February 1989 Get Busy Rap Concert featuring Public Enemy, Doug E. Fresh, Jungle Brothers, Biz Markie, Ultramagnetic MC's and Queen Latifah.
21. $25: Hourly rate at New York recording studio In The Red for the 1981 recording of Afrika Bambaataa & The Jazzy 5's "Jazzy Sensation."
22. $1.98: Per minute cost to dial saucy Vallejo, CA mack-stress Suga T's 1996 phone service line. Keep their heads ringin', ma.

PAID IN FULL:
Rappers Who've Made *Forbes* Magazine's Annual Highest-Paid Entertainers List.*

1. Master P: $56.5 million, 1998
2. Sean "Puffy" Combs: $53.5 million, 1998
3. Will Smith: $34 million, 1998
4. MC Hammer: $33 million, 1990–'91
5. MC Hammer: $28 million, 1991–'92

*Figures based on annual gross incomes.

PO', BROKE & LONELY:
Rappers Who Have Declared Bankruptcy

1. MC Hammer, 1994
2. Luke, 1995
3. Play (Kid 'N Play), 1997
4. Will Smith, 1989

CHEDDAR.

GIVE UP THE GOODS:
7 Costly-Ass Artists To Sample.

NOTE: Sample clearance fees are composed of two quotes—the master fee (the payment for use of the actual sampled original recording) and the publishing fee (the portion of the songwriting credit relinquished for use of the original composition).

1. **Barry White**
   The portly, *basso profundo* music maestro is consistently the most expensive artist to sample. Clearance quotes begin at $10,000 (even for minor musical usage) and can go as high as $30,000. In addition, Big Barry includes a clause in his publishing agreement that requires that all artists wishing to sample his music may do so *only* from his masters—no replayed versions to bring the cost down. He's gonna tax you, tax you, tax you just a lil' mo', baby.

2. **Zapp**
   A loop from the late, great funk lord Roger Troutman's repertoire can be yours, but you'll need as much as $15,000. This price quote includes a special, non-recoupable $5,000 fee paid directly to Troutman Productions for signing-off on the approval.

3. **Sting**
   Thanks to Puffy's full-scale hijacking of "Every Breath You Take" for "I'll Be Missing You," the cost of sampling any miniscule piece of music from Sting's catalogue means sacrificing at least 50%—in some cases even 100%—of the publishing on your new song.

4. **Anyone With EMI-Avant-Garde Publishing**
   Includes S.O.S. Band and anyone else produced by Jimmy Jam and Terry Lewis. EMI was one of the first entities to require the payment of advances in addition to the regular publishing percentage they claim. It's a minimum of $10,000 to $12,000 for use of their masters.

5. **Isaac Hayes**
   Quotes begin at $7,000 for pillaging the original baldhead slick's grooves. Expect to pay similar fees on Chef's Stax/Volt/Enterprise cohorts (i.e., the Bar-Kays, Mar-Keys, Rufus Thomas, etc.) and parent company Fantasy's library of jazz-funk sounds (i.e., the Blackbyrds, Pleasure, etc.).

6. **The Crusaders**
   Despite his Bobby Digital-esque moniker, Joe Sample and his merry band of instrumentalists are some costly-ass sample sources. Average master fees are in the $3,500 range. The Crusaders run about $8,000.

7. **Phil Collins**
   Another high master fee—around $8,000—with personal approval from the balding skins-beater required for your usage. He can feel it (the cash) comin' in the air tonight.

It All Comes Down To Money.

1. Ant Banks
2. Big Bank Hank (Sugarhill Gang)
3. DJ Cash Money
4. Ca$h Money Click
5. DJ Cheese
6. DJ Code Money
7. Dead Prez
8. EPMD
9. E-vette Money
10. 50 Grand (L.O.D.)
11. Gold Money
12. Half-A-Mil
13. JT Money
14. JT The Bigga Figga
15. Lootpack
16. Ma$e
17. Mo Money & Genovese
18. Money B (Digital Underground; Raw Fusion)
19. Money Boss Players
20. Money Mark
21. Paperboy
22. Peso (Fearless Four)
23. DJ Tat Money
24. T Money (Original Concept)
25. Too $hort

BUSINESS AS USUAL:
Rap Artists Who've Owned Their Own.

1. Big Boi (OutKast): Pitfall Kennels—Atlanta, GA
2. Big Punisher: Arcade Barbershop—Bronx, NY
3. B-Real (Cypress Hill): partner in *Industry Insider* magazine—Los Angeles, CA
4. Sean "Puffy" Combs: Justin's (restaurant)—New York, NY; *Notorious* magazine—New York, NY
5. Fat Joe: Fat Joe's Half Time Phat Hip Hop Gear—Bronx, NY; Fat Joe's Hip Hop Barber Shop—Bronx, NY
6. Heather B.: Nubian Nails And Hair—Jersey City, NJ
7. Kid Capri: Eboneese Hair Salon—Bronx, NY
8. Lordz Of Brooklyn: BMT Lines (clothing & graf memorabilia store)—Brooklyn, NY
9. MC Lyte: Harlem Café—New York, NY
10. Mack 10: Westside Graphics (T-shirt company)—Los Angeles, CA
11. Mike D (Beastie Boys): partner in Xtra Large (clothing retail store)—Los Angeles, CA; New York, NY; Tokyo, Japan
12. Mobb Deep: Infamous Store (clothing retail store)—New York, NY
13. Naughty By Nature: Naughty Gear—Newark, NJ
14. Pepa (Salt-N-Pepa): Hollyhood (retail clothing store)—Atlanta, GA
15. Play (Kid 'N Play) & Dana Dane: IV Plai (retail clothing store)—Elmhurst, NY
16. Prime Minister Pete Nice: American Baseball Experience (baseball memorabilia museum)—Cooperstown, NY
17. Queen Latifah: Videos To Go (video store)—Jersey City, NJ
18. Erick Sermon: Peachtree Motoring Accessories—Atlanta, GA
19. Spinderella: She Things beauty salon—Queens, NY
20. Talib Kweli (Black Star): Nkiru Books—Brooklyn, NY
21. Wu-Tang Clan: Wu Wear (clothing retail store)—Staten Island, NY; Atlanta, GA

CAN I BORROW A DOLLAR?
Most Expensive Hip Hop Records.*

1. "Beat Bop"—K-Rob vs. Rammelzee (Tartown, 1983)** $1,000
2. "Rappin' All Over"—The Younger Generation & The Marvelous Three (Brass, 1980) $300
3. "Lesson 4"—DJ Shadow (Hollywood BASIC promo, 1991) $250
4. *Live Convention '82*—Various Artists (Disco Wax, 1982) $250
5. *Live Convention '81*—Various Artists (Disco Wax, 1981) $200
6. "Think" b/w "Atom"—Main Source (Actual, 1989) $200
7. "Zulu Nation Throwdown Volume 2"—Afrika Bambaataa & The Soul Sonic Force (Winley, 1980) $175
8. *Death Mix Live!*—Afrika Bambaataa (Winley, 1983) $150
9. "High Powered Rap"—Disco Dave & The Force Of The 5 MC's (b/k/a Crash Crew) (Mike & Dave, 1980) $150
10. "Play That Beat Mr. DJ (Lesson 1: The Payoff Mix)" b/w "Lesson 2: The James Brown Mix"—Double Dee & Steinski (Mastermix promo, 1983) $150

*Prices are based on mint-conditioned copies at estimated 1998 international market rates.
**With Jean-Michel Basquiat's original cover artwork.

CHEDDAR.

20 Invaluable Songs About Money.

1. "All For The Money"—MC Eiht (Epic, 1994)
2. "C.R.E.A.M."—Wu-Tang Clan (Loud, 1993)
3. "Dead Presidents"—Jay-Z (Roc-A-Fella, 1996)
4. "Fat Pockets"—Show & AG (Payday, 1992)
5. "Foe Tha Love Of $"—Bone Thugs-N-Harmony (Ruthless, 1994)
6. "Funky Dividends"—Three Times Dope (Arista, 1989)
7. "Get Money"—Junior M.A.F.I.A. featuring The Notorious B.I.G. (Big Beat, 1995)
8. "Gold Digger"—EPMD (Def Jam, 1992)
9. "High Rollers"—Ice-T (Sire, 1988)
10. "It All Comes Down To The Money"—Terminator X featuring Whodini (RAL, 1994)
11. "It's All About The Benjamins"—Puff Daddy & The Family (Bad Boy, 1997)
12. "Love's Gonna Get 'Cha (Material Love)"—Boogie Down Productions (Jive, 1990)
13. "Making Cash Money"—Busy Bee (Sugarhill, 1982)
14. "Mo Money Mo Problems"—The Notorious B.I.G. featuring Ma$e & Puff Daddy (Bad Boy, 1997)
15. "Money Ain't A Thang"—Jermaine Dupri featuring Jay-Z (So So Def, 1998)
16. "Money (Dollar Bill Y'all)"—Jimmy Spicer (Spring, 1983)
17. "Money, Power & Respect"—The Lox featuring Lil' Kim & DMX (Bad Boy, 1998)
18. "Paid In Full"—Eric B. & Rakim (4th & B'way, 1987)
19. "What People Do For Money"—Divine Sounds (Specific, 1984)
20. "Where Dem Dollas At"—Gangsta Boo featuring DJ Paul & Juicy J (Relativity, 1998)

CAN'T KNOCK THE HUSTLE:
Rap Personalities Who Admit To Having Worked At Food Chains.

1. AG (Show & AG): McDonald's
2. Big Mike: Olive Garden
3. Tony Draper (CEO, Suave House Records): Olive Garden
4. E-40: McDonald's
5. Grandmixer D.ST: McDonald's
6. The Lady Of Rage: McDonald's
7. Posdnuos & Trugoy (De La Soul): Burger King
8. Queen Latifah: Burger King
9. Redman: Sizzler
10. Richie Rich: McDonald's
11. Romye (The Pharcyde): Taco Bell
12. Wyclef Jean: Burger King

BILLS, BILLS, BILLS? NEVER THAT!
Things Rappers Spend Their Money On.

1. Whips.
2. Jesus pieces.
3. Pieces.
4. Exorbitant allowances for straight outta wedlock children.
5. Cheeba, cheeba y'all!
6. Champagne rooms.
7. Acting lessons.
8. Johnny Cochran.
9. Millions of thugs on salary.
10. What money? Ha ha ha!

SPOF

D.M.C.'s All-NFL Dream Team.

COACH
1. John Madden

OFFENSE
2. Quarterback: Joe Montana
3. Running Back: Eric Dickerson
4. Running Back: John Riggins
5. Wide Receiver: Lynn Swann
6. Wide Receiver: Jerry Rice
7. Tight End: Shannon Sharpe
8. Offensive Tackle: Anthony Muñoz
9. Offensive Tackle: Art Shell
10. Guard: Larry Little
11. Guard: Jackie Slater
12. Center: Mike Webster

DEFENSE
13. Defensive Tackle: "Mean" Joe Greene
14. Defensive End: Bruce Smith
15. Defensive End: Ed "Too Tall" Jones
16. Inside Linebacker: Jack Lambert
17. Inside Linebacker: Mike Singletary
18. Outside Linebacker: Pepper Johnson
19. Outside Linebacker: Lawrence Taylor
20. Cornerback: Deion Sanders
21. Cornerback: Mel Blount
22. Safety: Rod Woodson
23. Safety: Ronnie Lott

SPECIAL TEAMS
24. Kicker: Morten Anderson
25. Punter: Ray Guy
26. Punt/Kick Returner: Billy "White Shoes" Johnson

D.M.C. is one third of hip hop's greatest group, Run-D.M.C., and one hell of a sportsman.

FOR THE SPORT OF IT:
14 Great Lyrical References For The Real Players.

1. "Can't Knock The Hustle"—Jay-Z featuring Mary J. Blige (Roc-A-Fella, 1996)
"Straight bananas—can a nigga see me?/ Got the U.S. Open—advantage Jigga/ Serve like Sampras, play fake rappers like a campus Lé Tigre, son you're too eager."

2. "Check One, Two"—Diamond D (Chemistry, 1992)
"Sing a simple song like Sylvester Stone/ And I catch you out there like Rick Cerrone."

3. "Exercise"—Akinyele (Interscope, 1993)
"Don't throw your soccer balls this way/ The name is Akinyele, not no motherfuckin' Pelé."

4. "F.A.L.A."—Gang Starr featuring Big Shug (Chrysalis, 1994)
Big Shug: "Word to Joe Frazier got to do what pays ya/ Give a nigga pain like dysplasia."

5. "Get Funky"—The Beatnuts (Relativity, 1994)
Ju Ju: "Dirty and low, I never do what the Pope says/ I'm tryin' to get money like Felipé Lopez."

6. "Have A Nice Day"—Roxanne Shanté (Cold Chillin', 1987)
"Cuz I'm an all-star like Julius Erving/ And Roxanne Shanté is only good for steady serving."

7. "I Love The Dough"—The Notorious B.I.G. featuring Jay-Z (Bad Boy, 1997)
B.I.G.: "Lost chips on Lakers—gassed off Shaq."

8. "Lyrics To Go"—A Tribe Called Quest (Jive, 1993)
Phife Dawg: "Always wanted this cuz it surely beats a scramble/ I'm Jordan with the mic, huh, wanna gamble?"

9. "A Name I Call Myself"—Souls Of Mischief (Jive, 1993)
A-Plus: "Yes, I knocked the boots like I was Riddick Bowe/ Get wid it ho, I get wit' no *Boomerang* broads wit' nasty toes."

10. "Rebel Without A Pause"—Public Enemy (Def Jam, 1987)
Chuck D: "Simple and plain give me the lane/ I'll throw it down your throat like Barkley."

11. "Silence Of The Lambs"—Show & AG (Payday, 1992)
Show: "I'm undisputed even when I'm buddha-ed/ So act like Bo Jackson after surgery and don't do it!"

12. "Da Story"—Noreaga featuring Maze (Penalty, 1998)
Nore: "Top of the league like Bulls and y'all cats is Lakers/ Trash since Magic left, but he was the greatest."

13. "Timebomb"—Public Enemy (Def Jam, 1987)
Chuck D: "You go 'ooh' and 'ahh' when I jump in my car/ People treat me like Kareem Abdul-Jabbar."

14. "The Wrong Nigga To Fuck Wit"—Ice Cube (Priority, 1991)
"Stop givin' juice to the Raiders/ Cuz Al Davis never paid us."

SPORTS.

JUST RHYMIN' WITH SHAQ:
Rappers Who've Assisted The World's Tallest Emcee.

1. B-Real
2. Deadly Venoms
3. Def Jef
4. Fu-Schnickens
5. General Sha
6. Ice Cube
7. Ill Al Skratch
8. Jay-Z
9. K-Raw
10. KRS-One
11. Loon (Harlem World)
12. Lord Tariq
13. Method Man
14. Mobb Deep
15. Mr. Ruffneck
16. Keith Murray
17. The Notorious B.I.G.
18. Peter Gunz
19. Phife Dawg
20. DJ Quik
21. Rakim
22. Redman
23. RZA
24. Sauce Money
25. Erick Sermon
26. Sonja Blade
27. Trigga*
28. Warren G

*Not Tha Gambler.

PLAYER'S BALL:
Rappers Who Ball (Well).

1. Al Tariq
2. Black Rob
3. Cam'Ron
4. C-Murder
5. Lord Have Mercy (Flipmode Squad)
6. Ma$e
7. Master P
8. Prime Minister Pete Nice
9. Sadat X
10. Silkk The Shocker
11. Snoop Doggy Dogg

BALLIN' OUTTA CONTROL:
15 Pro Hoopsters Who Rap (Badly).

1. Dana Barros
2. Kobe Bryant
3. Cedric Ceballos
4. Allen Iverson
5. Eddie Jones
6. Jason Kidd
7. Chris Mills
8. Shaquille O'Neal
9. Gary Payton
10. J.R. Rider
11. David Robinson
12. Dennis Scott
13. Malik Sealy
14. Brian Shaw
15. Chris Webber

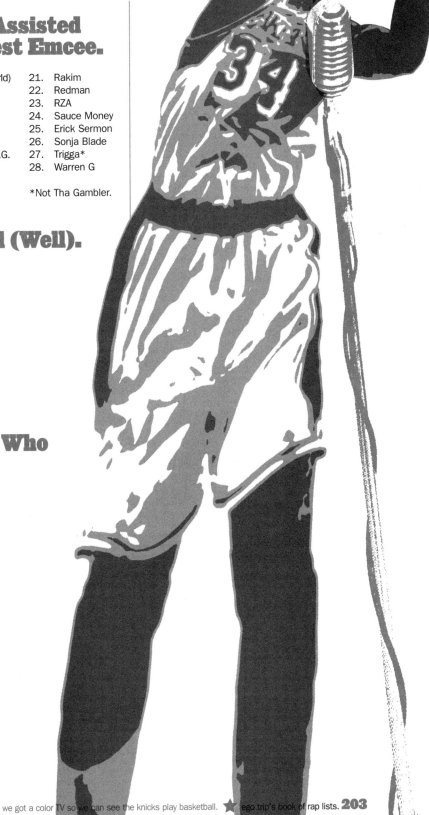

BASKETBALL RAP PART I:

Legendary Ballers Mentioned On Hurt 'Em Bad's "NBA Rap" (Groove Time, 1982).*

Contrary to popular belief, Kurtis Blow's "Basketball" was not the first rap song to pay homage to NBA greats. While Kurtis may have enjoyed a considerably more successful recording career, Las Vegas hoops fanatic Hurt 'Em Bad deserves credit for first dropping b-ball science on wax.

1. Julius "Dr. J" Erving
2. Kareem Abdul-Jabbar
3. Jack Sikma
4. David Thompson
5. George "Ice Man" Gervin
6. Larry Bird
7. Robert Parish
8. Earvin "Magic" Johnson
9. "Pistol" Pete Maravich
10. Bob McAdoo
11. Artis Gilmore
12. Bill Walton
13. Caldwell Jones
14. Bill Russell
15. Jerry West
16. Wilt "The Stilt" Chamberlain
17. Norm Nixon
18. Darryl Dawkins

*In the order they're mentioned.

BASKETBALL RAP PART II:

Legendary Ballers Mentioned On Kurtis Blow's "Basketball" (Mercury, 1984).*

Still, Kurtis' joint is classic.

1. Julius "Dr. J" Erving
2. Moses Malone
3. Nate "Tiny" Archibald
4. Earl "The Pearl" Monroe
5. Wilt "The Stilt" Chamberlain
6. "The Big O" Oscar Robertson
7. Jerry West
8. Earvin "Magic" Johnson
9. Larry Bird
10. Bernard King
11. Kareem Abdul-Jabbar
12. Clyde Drexler
13. Rick Barry
14. "Pistol" Pete Maravich
15. Isiah Thomas
16. George "Ice Man" Gervin
17. Adrian Dantley
18. Dominique Wilkins
19. Ralph Sampson
20. Bill Russell
21. Darryl Dawkins
22. Willis Reed
23. Dwayne "Pearl" Washington
24. Michael Jordan
25. Cazzie Russell

*Also in the order they're mentioned.

SPORTS.

THE RUSH PRODUCTIONS BASKETBALL ALL-STARS: (standing) Andrew "Dice" Rhamdanny, Mr. Hyde, DJ Galaxy, André Harrell, Earl "E Love" Matthias, Bill Adler, LL Cool J, Run; (kneeling) Ecstacy (Whodini), Jam Master Jay, Jay "Cut Creator" Philpot, Dynasty (Dynasty & Mimi); (crouched to the left of Harrell) Drew "Grandmaster Dee" Carter (Whodini) at Madison Square Garden, February 17, 1986.

DIAMOND DAWGS PART I:
'70s Baseball Players Who Get Shouted Out On "Two Brothers With Checks (San Francisco, Harvey)"—Ultramagnetic MC's (Wild Pitch, 1993).*

1. Don Hahn
2. Thurman Munson
3. Bucky Dent
4. Sparky Lyle
5. Jerry Grote
6. Joe Morgan
7. Ray Fosse
8. Charlie Hough

*In the order they're mentioned.

DIAMOND DAWGS PART II:
Negro League Baseball Players, Teams & Personalities Mentioned In "Saga Of Dandy, The Devil & Day"—Ultramagnetic MC's (Wild Pitch, 1993).*

1. Josh Gibson
2. Ray "Dandy" Dandridge
3. Satchel Paige
4. Buck Leonard
5. Willie "The Devil" Wells
6. Bacharach Giants
7. Homestead Grays
8. Brooklyn Eagles
9. Birmingham Black Barons
10. Newark Eagles
11. "Chi-Town" American Giants/Columbia Giants/Leland Giants/Union Giants
12. Leon Day
13. Bullet Joe Rogan
14. Smokey Joe Williams
15. Dick "King Richard" Lundy
16. Sammy T. Hughes
17. David "Impo" Barnhill
18. "Thunder Twins" (a/k/a Josh Gibson & Buck Leonard a/k/a "The Dynamite Twins" a/k/a "The Black Babe Ruth & Lou Gehrig")
19. Cool Papa Bell
20. Alec Radcliff
21. Ted "Double Duty" Radcliffe
22. Judy Johnson
23. Pittsburgh Crawfords
24. Dick "Cannonball" Redding
25. Abe Manley
26. Rufus Lewis

*In the order they're mentioned.

HE'LL THROW YOUR BRAIN IN THE COBRA CLUTCH:
Inspectah Deck Picks His Favorite Professional Wrestlers Of All-Time.

5. "Superfly" Jimmy Snuka
4. George "The Animal" Steele
3. Junkyard Dog
2. Iron Mike Sharpe
1. The Ultimate Warrior

Wu-Tang Clan's Inspectah Deck not only knows his wrestling, but he smokes on the mic like Smokin' Joe Frazier. His lyrical skills have been prominently featured on such modern rap standards as the Wu-Tang Clan's "C.R.E.A.M." and "Triumph."

SPORTS.

206 ego trip's book of rap lists. ⭐ time to drop these 'bows like dusty rhodes, then we yell, "ho!"

PROPS TO THE IRON MIKE:
Nuthin' But The Very Best Tyson Lyrical References.

1. "Fat Pockets"—Show & AG (Payday, 1992)
   AG: "But the sex I never take/ Cuz if that bitch screams rape like Mike Tyson, I'm upstate."

2. "Holocaust (Silkworm)"—RZA As Bobby Digital featuring Holocaust, Dr. Doom, Ghostface Killah & Ms. Roxy (Gee Street, 1998)
   Ghostface: "Unfaithfully married to rap, we been engaged for 12 years/ Tyson bit Holyfield ear, we love the sport."

3. "I'm Bad"—LL Cool J (Def Jam, 1987)
   "I'm like Tyson, icin', I'm a soldier at war/ Makin' sure you don't try to battle me no more."

4. "Poison"—Kool G Rap & DJ Polo (Cold Chillin', 1988)
   "With Polo and while he's slicin'/ I'll turn the mic's last name into Tyson."

5. "Public Enemy No. 1"—Public Enemy (Def Jam, 1987)*
   Chuck D: "Cuz I can go solo/ Like a Tyson bolo."

6. "Put Your Weight On It"—Big Daddy Kane (Cold Chillin', 1990)
   "My sharp tongue is like a license/ I strike like Mike Tyson, I be icin'."

7. "Rollin' Wit Umdada"—Masta Ace (Delicious Vinyl, 1993)
   "Four score and, um, seven years in the lab and/ I know rap like Mike Tyson knows booty grabbin'."

8. "The World Is Yours"—Nas (Columbia, 1994)
   "They locked the champ up leavin' my brains in handcuffs/ Headed for Indiana, stabbin' women like the Phantom."

9. "Wreck Your Ears (Can Do)"—The B.U.M.S. (Priority, 1995)
   E-Vocalist: "Awaking crews in a rude fashion/ On they ass like Mike Tyson at a beauty pageant."

10. "Zoom"—Dr. Dre & LL Cool J (Interscope, 1998)
    Dre: "'Nuff to burn, 10 mill sales confirmed/ The most anticipated since Tyson's return."

BONUS ROUNDS:

11. **"Mighty Mike Tyson"—Spoonie Gee (Tuff City, 1987)**
    "He don't float like a butterfly or sting like a bee/ But he's the hardest damn puncher you'll ever see," boasted the old school legend on the undisputed first tribute to hip hop's heavyweight champion.

12. **"I Think I Can Beat Mike Tyson"—DJ Jazzy Jeff & The Fresh Prince (Jive, 1989)**
    At the height of Tyson's dominance over the heavyweight division, the always witty Fresh Prince decided to compose a song where he would go toe-to-toe with the self-proclaimed baddest man on the planet. Taking a bow to Tyson's then invincible persona, "The Lightning Rod" Fresh Prince gets KO'd in the first round with one shot to the ribs. And his bowels release.

13. **"T.Y.S.O.N. (The Young Son Of No One)"—Breeze (Atlantic, 1989)**
    This bizarre tribute features verbal jabs like, "Ain't nobody hittin' like Tyson, I'm going the length." However, the track's reliance on vocal samples from a young Cassius Clay may leave you coming away thinking Ali was the greatest. Oh yeah, he was.

14. **"Bells Of War"—Wu-Tang Clan (Loud, 1997)**
    On the bridge to this *Wu-Tang Forever* track, Raekwon and Ghostface Killah engage in a deep discussion of boxing upsets, in particular, Holyfield's first victory over Tyson—of which the Chef says, "Mike got touched." They then discuss the initial postponement of the Holyfield vs. Tyson II bout, which would later be infamous for the ear-biting incident.

15. **"Second Round K.O."—Canibus (Universal, 1998)**
    A long-time avid rap fan, Tyson finally makes his first vocal apppearance on—surprise, the debut single of his former friend LL Cool J's arch nemesis, Canibus. Chew on that shit.

*Incidentally, in the LP's inner sleeve, the lyric is mistakenly printed as a "Sugar Ray bolo."

When Rap & Sports Collide.

1. Ice Cube's government name (O'Shea Jackson) was inspired by gridiron hero/acquitted murder suspect O.J. Simpson.

2. Patchwerk Records—home to Ras Kass, Meen Green and Vooodu—was founded by the Atlanta Falcons' Bob Whitfield.

3. *NFL Jams* (Castle, 1996) was a collection of horrendous collaborations between rappers and football players. "This is just the beginning of what we are certain will be sensational music from our talented players," wrote an impassioned Gene Upshaw, president of the NFL Players Association, on the CD's inner booklet. Slow-witted tailgaters across the nation patiently await the sequel.

4. The rappin' Mailman, E-40, is neighbors with Seattle SuperSonics' All-Star guard Gary Payton in Vallejo, CA.

5. In a move that displayed the diversity of their predilection for sports,

Run-D.M.C. performed at Wrestlemania 5 in Atlantic City in 1990.

6. In 1991, the NBA's most exciting team, the Golden State Warriors, were led by the three-guard tandem of Tim Hardaway, Mitch Richmond and Chris Mullin and were affectionately nicknamed Run-T.M.C. in homage to the legendary Hollis, Queens trio, Run-D.M.C. The team's ownership even went so far as to fly in Run, Darryl and Jay for a playoff game that year against the Los Angeles Lakers. Unfortunately, the inspirational presence of the Kings of Queens couldn't help the Warriors, who got outrun and gunned that night by Magic and company.

7. Also in 1991—the same year N.W.A's *Efil4zaggin* debuted at #2 on the pop charts—former

12 Sports Lyrics That Lose.

1. "Ah Yeah"—KRS-One (Avatar, 1995)
"You'll hear so many, 'Bo, bo, bo, bo's'/ You'll think I'm Riddick."

2. "B-Boy Bouillabaisse (Get On The Mic)"—Beastie Boys (Capitol, 1989)
Adrock: "You say, 'Fuck that', yo, homes, fuck this/ I'm the King Ad Wham and you're Dick Butkus."

3. "Executive Decision"—Nas, Foxy Brown, AZ & Nature (Aftermath, 1997)
Nas: "Jeeps Tahoe, shoes be Salvatore Ferragamo/ Catch a homo(cide), guns long like Mutumbo."

4. "Ghetto Fabulous"—Ras Kass featuring Mack 10 & Dr. Dre (Priority, 1998)
Ras Kass: "We say L.A. niggas got crazy game/ Like John Elway got a Super Bowl ring."

5. "The Infamous Date Rape"—A Tribe Called Quest (Jive, 1991)

Phife Dawg: "You know the science, you get buckwild/ Running mad game as if your name was Scott Skiles."

6. "Intro-Hand It Down"—Jay-Z featuring Memphis Bleek (Roc-A-Fella, 1998)
Memphis Bleek: "Niggas tryin' to kill me, dog—who wouldn't?/ Screw Gooden—I'll pitch in the PJs!"

7. "It's All About The Benjamins (Remix)"—Puff Daddy featuring The Lox, Lil' Kim & The Notorious B.I.G. (Bad Boy, 1997)
Puff: "Tryin' to get my hands on some Grants like Horace."

8. "Pass Dat Shit"—Diamond D featuring Whiz One, Maestro, Mike G.Q. & Fat Joe (Chemistry, 1992)
Fat Joe: "I must be a hit like my man Dave Magadan, who plays for the Mets/ But I love the Jets—see when you're a Jet, you're a Jet to your last cigarette."

SPORTS.

Philadelphia Eagles' All-Pro tight end Keith Jackson released a full-length rap LP, *K-Jack-N-America* (City Block), marked by R&B-flavored production and squeaky clean messages encouraging youngstas to remain abstinent and drug-free. It was Jackson's only album.

8. After his participation in the landmark rap-meets-sports single, the 1985 Chicago Bears' "Super Bowl Shuffle" (Red Label), overweight defensive end William Perry made headlines a year later via his collaboration with the Fat Boys, "Chillin' With The Refrigerator" (Sutra, 1986). It wasn't fat.

9. "I can get loose so don't you try/ I graduated from Crenshaw High," rhymed former New York Mets home run slugger Darryl Strawberry on his rap debut, "Chocolate Strawberry" (Strawesome, 1987). While the flavorless boast also featured the rhyming skills of Brooklyn's finest, U.T.F.O. and Whistle, it's true distinction was the furor it caused with the Mets organization, which felt Straw was more interested in rapping than playing ball.

10. Seattle Mariner All-Star center fielder Ken Griffey Jr. collaborated with local rap talent Kid Sensation on "The Way I Swing" (Nastymix, 1992). The bouncy groove featured Griffey The Pimp spitting game like a muhfuh: "If I see a fire, then I pull the fire alarm/ But if I see a girl I like, then I pull her by the arm." As you can see, MC Ken likes swingin'.

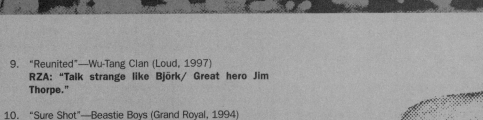

9. "Reunited"—Wu-Tang Clan (Loud, 1997)
   RZA: "Talk strange like Björk/ Great hero Jim Thorpe."

10. "Sure Shot"—Beastie Boys (Grand Royal, 1994)
    Mike D: "I've got more action than my man John Woo/ And I've got mad hits like I was Rod Carew."

11. "Triumph"—Wu-Tang Clan featuring Cappadonna (Loud, 1997)
    Raekwon: "Max mostly undivided then slide it—sickening/ Guaranteed made 'em jump like Rod Strickland"

12. "The Way We Live"—Noreaga featuring Chico DeBarge (Penalty, 1998)
    "Sometimes we hurt y'all, not understanding what we doin'/ Sweatin' at the foul line like Pat Ewing."

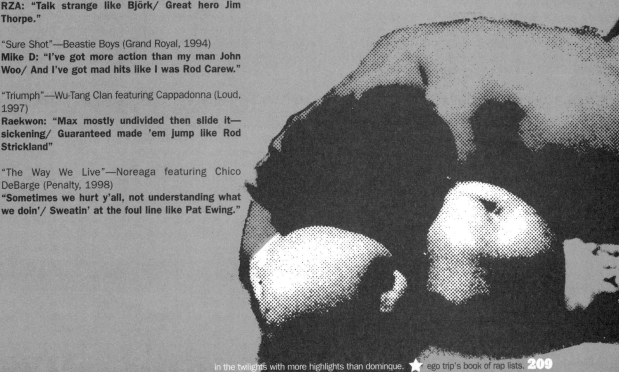

in the twilights with more highlights than dominique. ⭐

IN FUL

Models On Rap's Bozack.

1. **Naomi Campbell**
Sang back-up for Vanilla Ice on "Cool As Ice (Everybody Get Loose)" the lead (and only) single from the 1991 cinematic master-piece, *Cool As Ice*. In 1998, Nay-Nay appeared as the thugged-out hype lady on Wyclef's LL-bashing "What's Clef Got To Do With It?"

2. **Tyra Banks**
Sports Illustrated swimsuit cover girl and Victoria's Secret Angel appeared in a fashion spread for *The Source* maga-zine early in her career. No rela-tion to Ant.

3. **Mark Ronson**
Former part-time *ego trip* scribe blew like a really, really big explo-sion upon joining the Flip Squad DJ All-Stars and falling into Tommy Hilfiger's handsome boy heavy rotation.

Hip Hop's Greatest Sweater References Of All-Time.

1. "It's My Thing"—EPMD (Fresh, 1987)
Erick Sermon: "Now let's move on to something better/ And if it gets warm take off the hot sweater."

2. "Keep Risin' To The Top"—Doug E. Fresh & The Get Fresh Crew (Reality, 1988)
"Etcetera, etcetera in a cashmere sweater/ I'm in a Cherokee, Chill was in a Audi."

3. "C.R.E.A.M."—Wu-Tang Clan (Loud, 1993)
Raekwon: "My life got no better—same damn 'Lo sweater/ Times is rough and tough like leather."

4. "Big Poppa"—The Notorious B.I.G. (Bad Boy, 1994)
"Now I'm livin' better now/ Coogi sweater now."

5. "I'm That Type Of Guy"—LL Cool J (Def Jam, 1989)
"You're the type of guy to give her money to shop/ She gave me a sweater . . . Thank you, sweetheart!"

NOTE: Digital Underground's "Bran Nu Swetta" (Tommy Boy, 1993) sucks.

Items De La Soul Dismisses On "Take It Off" (Tommy Boy, 1989).*

1. Suede front.
2. Contacts.
3. Horse weave.
4. Shell toes.
5. Striped Lees.
6. Doo rag.
7. Mock neck.
8. Fat laces.
9. Bomber.
10. BVD.
11. Converse.
12. Cazals.
13. Kangol.
14. Jordache.
15. Afro.
16. Jheri Curl.
17. Lé Tigre.
18. Those acid wash, bell bottomed, designed-by-ya-mama jeans.

*In the order they're mentioned

IN FULL GEAR.

4. Tyson Beckford
Discovered by *The Source*. Later validated his hip hop status by carousing ice-grilled down a runway to the strains of Mobb Deep's "Shook Ones Pt. II" in a Sprite commercial.

5. Veronica Webb
Interviewed Heavy D in 1991 for—surprise!—*The Source*, appeared as a gyrating extra in Queen Latifah's "Dance For Me," turned up on LL Cool J's *Walking With A Panther* album cover as a champagne bottle-coddling hottie and, most importantly, is the long-time pal of Russell Simmons.

NEVER LEAVE THE PAD WITHOUT PACKIN MY . . .
Rappers & Their Signature Accessories.

1. Bobcat—Davy Crockett hat
2. Cappadonna—baseball bat
3. Eazy-E—locs and Compton hat
4. Flavor Flav—clock
5. Fresh Kid Ice—sling
6. Ice-T—wifey Darlene
7. Kool Moe Dee—Porsche sunglasses
8. Kwamé—polka dot shirt
9. Luke—ass
10. Mobb Deep—sickles
11. Prime Minister Pete Nice—cane
12. Professor X—staff
13. Ras Kass—toothpick
14. Redman—tissue in his nose
15. Slick Rick—eye patch, mouth full of good teeth
16. Treach—macheté, masterlock

15 Rappers Who Have Been Photographed In The Buff Or In Their Drawers.

1. **Big Daddy Kane***
   EXPOSED IN: Madonna's *Sex* book (Warner Books, 1992).
2. **Digital Underground**
   EXPOSED IN: The uncensored version of the video for "Return Of The Crazy One" (Tommy Boy, 1993).
3. **DMX**
   EXPOSED IN: The slammin' motion picture *Belly* (Artisan Entertainment, 1998).
4. **Doctor Dré & Ed Lover**
   EXPOSED IN: The pages of their *Naked Under Our Clothes* book (Simon & Schuster, 1996).
5. **Foxy Brown**
   EXPOSED IN: The video for "Firm Biz" (Aftermath, 1997).
6. **MC Hammer**
   EXPOSED IN: The video for "Pumps And A Bump" (Giant, 1994).
7. **Lauryn Hill**
   EXPOSED ON: The cover of the December 1995 *Rap Pages*.
8. **Kool Keith**
   EXPOSED ON: The cover of *Sex Style* (Funky Ass, 1997).
9. **Kwamé**
   EXPOSED IN: The March 9, 1990's pay-per-view *Rap Mania* concert—where he dropped his pants.
10. **Lil' Kim**
    EXPOSED ON: The cover of April 1997 *Paper*.
11. **Redman**
    EXPOSED IN: *ego trip* #9 photographed sitting on the toilet.
12. **Son Doobie**
    EXPOSED IN: The X-rated video *Son Doobie, Porn King* (Vivid, 1995).
13. **2Pac**
    EXPOSED IN: Photograph by David LaChapelle posing in a bathtub.
14. **Vanilla Ice**
    EXPOSED IN: Madonna's *Sex* book (Warner Books, 1992).
15. **Whodini**
    EXPOSED AT: Live shows worldwide—rap's first full-scale exhibitionists.

*We're still trying to forget the infamous *Playgirl* pictorial.

IT'S GOOD TO BE THE KING: Son Doobie busts loose in his sin-ematic debut.

IN FULL GEAR.

THE NEEDLE & THE DAMAGE DONE:
Tattoos That Make An Impression.

1. **Busta Rhymes:** The names of his sons, T'Ziah and the late Tahiem II, encircled by elaborate markings that represent truth, strength and wealth on his left arm.

2. **DMX:** "One Love, Boomer," in homage to his first and favorite dog, on his back.

3. **Eve:** Paw prints between her breasts.

4. **Foxy Brown:** A fox face and "Inga" (her birth name) on her right shin; Chinese characters on her left and right arms and above her left breast. (Translated, the latter roughly means "with love.")

5. **Lil' Cease:** A portrait of The Notorious B.I.G. based on the July, 1995 cover of *The Source* magazine on his left bicep; "I Love My Family" on his back.

6. **LL Cool J:** A crowned microphone with "Mr. Smith" running through it on his right bicep.*

7. **Master P, Silkk The Shocker & C-Murder:** A portrait of their late brother Kevin Miller on each's left bicep.

8. **Keith Murray:** Several gravestones representing the memories of deceased loved ones on his chest.

9. **The Notorious B.I.G.:** Phrases from Psalm 27 on his right forearm.

10. **2Pac:** "Thug Life" across his abdomen.

*Inspired his rival, Canibus, to get the same tattoo.

You Gotta Reckon With Fashion.

1. "Beeds On A String"—Jungle Brothers (Warner Bros., 1989)
2. "Bike Tights"—Rob Base & DJ E-Z Rock (Funky Base, 1994)
3. "Converse"—Busy Bee (Uni, 1988)
4. "Figaro Chain"—LA The Darkman (Supreme Team, 1998)
5. "Get It Right (Put On Your Bally Shoes)"—YZ (Tuff City, 1990)
6. "Gold"—Nice & Smooth (Fresh, 1989)
7. "Gortex"—Sir Mix-A-Lot (Def American, 1989)
8. "Gucci Time"—Schoolly D (Schoolly D, 1985)
9. "In Full Gear"—Stetsasonic (Tommy Boy, 1988)
10. "My Adidas"—Run-D.M.C. (Profile, 1986)
11. "My Filas"—Fresh Gordon (Tommy Boy, 1986)
12. "Nike"—Heavy D (Uptown, 1987)
13. "Pumps And A Bump"—MC Hammer (Giant, 1994)
14. "Put Your Filas On"—Schoolly D (Schoolly D, 1986)
15. "Tennis Shoe Pimpin"—40 Thevz (Mercury, 1997)
16. "Wu-Wear: The Garment Renaissance"—RZA featuring Method Man & Cappadonna (Big Beat, 1996)

Products Slick Rick Plugs In "La Di Da Di" (Reality, 1985).*

1. Oil Of Olay.
2. Gucci underwear.
3. Johnson's baby powder.
4. Polo cologne.
5. Bally shoes.
6. Kangol.

*In the order they're mentioned.

Leave My Jheri Curl Alone.

1. Barry B
   (The Get Fresh Crew)
2. Eazy-E
3. MC Eiht
4. Fearless Four
5. Full Force
6. Hi-C
7. Ice Cube
8. Kurtis Blow
9. The L.A. Dream Team

Good Hair.

1. Bizzy Bone
2. B-Real (Cypress Hill)
3. Busta Rhymes
4. C & H (Dru Down)
5. Crime Boss
6. Dres
7. Dru Down
8. Ice-T
9. DJ Quik
10. Snoop Doggy Dogg
11. Special Ed

Cock-Diesel Rap Dudes.

1. Boo-Yaa T.R.I.B.E.
2. D.M.C.
3. DMX
4. Freddie Foxxx
5. Ganksta Nip
6. Grandmaster Melle Mel
7. LL Cool J
8. Sticky Fingaz (Onyx)
9. Treach (Naughty By Nature)

Short But Funky.

1. Buckshot (Black Moon)
2. Bushwick Bill
3. Canibus
4. Daddy-O
5. Das EFX
6. Jermaine Dupri
7. Eazy-E
8. Mobb Deep
9. Money B
   (Digital Underground; Raw Fusion)
10. Onyx
11. Phife Dawg (A Tribe Called Quest)
12. Ras Kass
13. Shortie No Mass
14. Too $hort*

*Not that short, but included out of respect.

IN FULL GEAR.

6 Feet High & Rising.

1. EPMD
2. Ghostface Killah
3. Inspectah Deck
4. Jay-Z
5. King Sun
6. KRS-One
7. Method Man
8. Q-Tip
9. Redman
10. Rock (Heltah Skeltah)
11. Will Smith

Skinny & Proud.

1. Beastie Boys
2. Flavor Flav
3. J-Treds
4. Kurious
5. Kurupt
6. Kwamé
7. Mic Geronimo
8. Opio (Souls Of Mischief)
9. Silkk The Shocker
10. Skinny Boys
11. Slim Kid Tré (The Pharcyde)
12. Snoop Doggy Dogg

Rap Heavyweights (Literally).

1. Big Punisher
2. Biz Markie
3. Boo-Yaa T.R.I.B.E.
4. Buddha Monk
5. Chubb Rock
6. Diamond D
7. E-40
8. Eightball
9. Fat Boys
10. Fat Joe
11. Heavy D
12. Ms. Melodie
13. The Notorious B.I.G.
14. Pudgee Tha Phat Bastard
15. Skull Duggery
16. 2-Bigg MC

Go See The Dentist.

1. Biz Markie
2. Charlie Brown (Leaders Of The New School)*
3. Delite (Stetsasonic)
4. Heavy D
5. Luke
6. Nas
7. Ol' Dirty Bastard
8. Tom J (Knucklehedz)
9. Too $hort
10. Yukmouth

*Author of the lyric: "Brown skin, curly hair, mashed-up teeth" from "Spontaneous (13 MC's Deep!)" (Elektra, 1993).

The *ego trip* Fashion Awards.

1. **Treacherous Old School Costume Award: The Never Mind The Bollocks Look.**
   Sure, hip hop's early '80s excursions from BX parks to downtown clubs allowed b-boys and new wave white liberals to dance to the same drummer's beat. Unfortunately, some brothers got shafted in the cross-cultural fashion exchange when they traded their sheepskins and Kangols for black leather quasi-punk-S&M-bondage get-ups that Dre from OutKast wouldn't touch with a ten foot polecat.

2. **Gods Of Invention Award: Dapper Dan & Shirt Kings.**
   Uptown's high fashion bootleg godfather and Jamaica, Queens' cotton canvas royalty pioneered this hip hop clothing mogul shit in manners strictly street: Dan, by surreptitiously sewing designer names into custom made gear for the fresh and fly to flaunt (witness various album and 12" single covers for Eric B. & Rakim and Big Daddy Kane); Shirt Kings, by emblazoning graf style graphics onto long sleeve tees—ideal for Q-borough drug dealers to pose in for photos while displaying their hard-earned grip. For the ghetto by the ghetto. And always fabulous.

3. **I Shouldn't Have Worn It Award: Big Daddy Kane.**

   On more than one occasion, hip hop heads have sat around the campfire and debated the exact moment in which the career and credibility of Big Daddy Kane came tumblin' down. It was The Suit, baby—the extra snug purple paisley ensemble with matching vest and slacks that King Asiatic sported in the star-studded video for Heavy D's "Don't Curse" (Uptown, 1991). With his arm in a sling, Kane looked like an out-of-work pimp with a morning hangover. From that moment on, the magic was gone.

4. **"You Say, 'Oh No, You Bitch-Ass Promo'" Award: The Ugly XXXL-Sized T-Shirt.**
   For the freshest in fat man *haute couture* look no further than your standard promotional T-shirt. Given away free and coming in dimensions that fit comfy on a beached sperm whale, this graphically-challenged tee—prominently sporting your (least) favorite rapper's butt-ugly logo—transforms the wearer into a walking billboard and makes grown-ass adults look like lil' seeds rockin' big mama and poppa's garments. But like the song says, the shirts is freeeeeee, but the crack costs money—oh yeah!

5. **"Girl, You Know It's True (Ooh, Child—You're A Mess!)" Award: Foxy Brown & Lil' Kim.**
   Speech coaches and stylists beware. Not only have these dueling divas been known to mangle the pronunciation of many an exotic fashion designer's name, but they've also got at least

IN FULL GEAR.

one unforgivable fashion *faux pas* on their permanent records: wearing identical outfits on the inner sleeves of their respective debut albums. Definitely an ill no-no.

6. **Greatest Fashion Moment In A Music Video Award: "All The Way To Heaven"—Doug E. Fresh & The Get Fresh Crew (Reality, 1986).**
Although his partner Slick Rick had just bounced from The Get Fresh Crew for Def Jam solo riches, the Original Human Beat Box kept his head up and revenge on his mind. The closing moments to the always freshly-dipped Harlem-bred brother's debut video features a showdown sequence in which a pair of his beloved Bally sneakers bucks down a pair of lace-less shell-toed Adidas. To this day, the question remains: Was Doug E. Doug's dis of Run-D.M.C. the big payback for Run's brother Russell Simmons taking his old friend away?

7. **Eatin' Right Award: Rappers Who Literally Blow Up.**
All rappers aspire to live large. But by the looks of their rapidly-expanding waistlines once they drop platinum platters, some hungry emcees must feel that the key to life is money, power and lots of turkey bacon. They might blow up, but they won't go to Jenny Craig.

8. **Keep It In The Closet Award: Played-Out Gear You Wouldn't Be Caught Dead Wearing Today.**
Cross Colours, 8-Ball jackets, Troop, Apple Jack hats, inside-out Starter jackets, dolphin earrings, polka dot shirts. If any of these items are presently in your daily wardrobe, it's time to reconsider any previous prejudices and put Calvin Klein on your behind.

9. **Return Of The Doo Rag Award: Jay-Z.**
Jigga's our nigga. In addition to possessing the mind capacity of a young Butch Cassidy, Brooklyn's finest proudly insists on rocking that staple of hooligan head wear—the doo rag—like it's going out of style, all without ever endorsing set-trippin' or speed-knots. You're a good man, Shawn Carter.

10. **Tommy Field Nigger Award: Rappers Owning Their Own Clothing Lines.**
When unofficial Hilfiger spokesman Grand Puba rhymed, "If Tommy [Hilfiger] ain't givin' loot, I'll be the fuck if I wear it," in 1995, the rap world listened and learned. No longer content to rock name brands for the other man, every rapper and his cousin has begun promoting his own line of gear for mass consumption. Yes, now you too can pay designer fees for the promotional T-shirts that industry fucks like us get for free. Suckers!

STUNTS, BLUN

TS & HIP HOP.

TALK LIKE SEX:
Freakiest Songs About Doin' The Nasty.

1. "Behind The Bush"—Jungle Brothers(Idlers, 1988)
2. "Freaks Of The Industry"—Digital Underground (Tommy Boy, 1990)
3. "Freaky Tales"—Too $hort (Jive, 1989)
4. "Froggy Style"—Hi-C (Skanless, 1991)
5. "Gangster Of Love"—Geto Boys (Rap-A-Lot, 1989)
6. "How Do U Want It"—2Pac featuring K-Ci & Jojo (Death Row, 1996)
7. "I'd Rather Fuck You"—N.W.A (Ruthless, 1991)
8. "I'm A Ho"—Whodini (Jive, 1986)
9. "Knockin' Boots"—Candyman (Epic, 1990)
10. "Me So Horny"—2 Live Crew (Luke, 1989)
11. "Secret Fantasies"—Tim Dog featuring Kool Keith (Ruffhouse, 1991)
12. "Sex"—Ice-T (Sire, 1987)
13. "Sex Style"—Kool Keith (Funky Ass, 1997)
14. "Take It Off"—Spoonie Gee (Tuff City, 1987)
15. "Tres Equis"—Cypress Hill (Ruffhouse, 1991)
16. "Wild Thang"—2 Much (Warlock, 1988)

DISHONORABLE MENTION:
"Wide Open"—LeShaun (Tommy Boy, 1993):
A song about sticking fingers up someone's butt.

IT'S ON FIRE TONIGHT:
Songs About The Dangers Of Not Practicing Safe Sex.

1. "Down W/HIV"—Gregory D (RCA, 1992)
2. "Go See The Doctor"—Kool Moe Dee (Rooftop, 1986)
3. "HIV Positive"—Choice (Rap-A-Lot, 1992)
4. "Jimmy"—Boogie Down Productions (Jive, 1988)
5. "KK Punanni"—Movement Ex (Columbia, 1990)
6. "Let's Talk About Sex"—Salt-N-Pepa (Next Plateau, 1990)
7. "Look Who's Burnin'"—Ice Cube (Priority, 1991)
8. "Mr. Bozak"—EPMD (Def Jam, 1990)
9. "Nasty Hoes"—Sadat X, Fat Joe & Diamond D (EastWest, 1996)
10. "Ooh Shit"—Master P (No Limit, 1992)
11. "Pissin' Razor Blades"—Bust Down (Luke, 1991)
12. "Protect Yourself"—Fat Boys (Tin Pan Apple, 1987)
13. "Pubic Enemy"—A Tribe Called Quest (Jive, 1990)
14. "Raincoat"—Domino (Outburst, 1993)
15. "The Rubbers Song"—The Pharcyde (GRP, 1994)
16. "Safe Sex"—Erick Sermon (Def Jam, 1993)
17. "Too Hot"—Coolio (Tommy Boy, 1995)
18. "Use A Condom (Reggae Jam)"—MC Mitchski (Ski, 1988)
19. "V.D. Woman"—Gregory D & DJ Mannie Fresh (Yo, 1989)
20. "Who's Fuckin' Who"—2 Live Crew (Luke, 1991)

DR. FEELGOOD:
Kool Keith's Favorite Places To Pleasure Himself In Public.

1. Macy's Department Store fitting room.
2. Yankee Stadium concession stand . . .
3. . . . and in the crowd.
4. Across the street from Madison Square Garden.
5. Sbarro.
6. Gray's Papaya.
7. Downstairs at BBQ.
8. In the vocal booth of certain, different studios.
9. Polygram Records.

Other things that former Ultramagnetic MC and rap legend Kool Keith enjoys doing is coming up with wacky aliases (i.e., Rhythm X, Big Willie Smith, Dr. Octagon, Dr. Dooom, etc.), dyeing women's panties different custom-made colors and fantasizing about mating different animals with each other. Needless to say, he's our kind of nigga.

STUNTS, BLUNTS & HIP HOP.

BUST-A-RHYME:
The Essential Likwit Tit-ography.

1. "I Got It Bad Y'all"—King Tee featuring Tha Alkaholiks (Capitol, 1993)
   J-Ro: "They softer than a hooker's chest."

2. "Bullshit"—Tha Alkaholiks (Loud, 1993)
   J-Ro: "I hate big tits . . . Bullshit!"

3. "Freestyle Ghetto"—King Tee featuring Xzibit, Breeze & Tha Alkaholiks (Capitol, 1994)
   J-Ro: "J-Ro the titty fiend."

4. "Let It Out"—Tha Alkaholiks (Loud, 1995)
   J-Ro: "I love hips, tits and rap hits."

5. "Hit And Run"—Tha Alkaholiks featuring Xzibit (Loud, 1995)
   E-Swift: "Staring at your chest/ And I can only guess/ Lord have mercy/ What's up under that Adidas dress."

6. "Hit And Run"—Tha Alkaholiks featuring Xzibit (Loud, 1995)
   J-Ro: "Her name was Nina/ Or Tina/ Or was it Regina?/ Fuck it/ The bitch with the tig ol' bitties and the boomin' bass."

7. At the end of "Flashback"—Tha Alkaholiks (Loud, 1995)
   J-Ro: "And remember this . . . you cannot escape the power of the twwwooos.*

8. "The Next Level"—Tha Alkaholiks featuring Diamond D (Loud, 1995)
   J-Ro: "Every time I come home I got 50 messages/ I only call back the girls with big, big, breasteses/ I got biddies in all the major cities/ The safest way to have sex is right between the twwwooos."

9. "Plastic Surgery"—Xzibit featuring Ras Kass & Saafir (Loud, 1996)
   Xzibit: "If you want it done right/ Nigga come see this/ Maybe even send your bitch/ We can fix them tits/ From a C cup to a double-D cup/ Make them big shits/ Dr. Likwit twwwooos."

10. "Feel The Real"—Tha Alkaholiks (Loud, 1997)
    J-Ro: "You blessed with a fat ass with no ripples/ Twwwooos big like hippos/ It's the Liks, Liks, baby, baby on them nipples."

11. "All Night"—Tha Alkaholiks (Loud, 1997)
    J-Ro: "It goes down like/ One, twwwooo, three."

*Amongst members of the Likwit crew, "twos" (pronounced "twwwooos") mean breasts. But don't tell anybody.

GIRLS, GIRLS, GIRLS, GIRLS, IT'S GIRLS WE DO ADORE . . .

69 Songs Dedicated To That Special Lady.

1. "Annie Mae"—Warren G featuring Nate Dogg (Def Jam, 1997)
2. "Bedie Boo"—Dana Dane (Profile, 1990)
3. "Belly Dancin' Dina"—Jungle Brothers (Warner Bros., 1989)
4. "Betty Boop"—Kings Of Swing (Bum Rush, 1990)
5. "Black Sarah"—Land Of Da Lost (Lic N Shot, 1998)
6. "Blow Job Betty"—Too $hort (75 Girls, 1985)
7. "Bonita Applebum"—A Tribe Called Quest (Jive, 1990)
8. "Carousel Chanel"—Cool C (Atlantic, 1990)
9. "Cheri"—Nice & Smooth (RAL, 1994)*
10. "Cindy"—Gregory D & DJ Mannie Fresh (Yo, 1989)
11. "Cleopatra"—Indo G (Relativity, 1998)
12. "Dear Yvette"—LL Cool J (Def Jam, 1985)
13. "Donna"—Larry Larr (Ruffhouse, 1991)
14. "Fast Peg"—LL Cool J (Def Jam, 1989)
15. "Faye"—Stetsasonic (Tommy Boy, 1986)
16. "Hawaiian Sophie"—The Jaz (EMI, 1989)
17. "Heidi Hoe"—Common (Relativity, 1992)
18. "Ho Happy Jackie"—AZ (EMI, 1995)
19. "Iesha"—Another Bad Creation (Motown, 1991)
20. "Jane"—EPMD (Fresh, 1988)
21. "Jenifa (Taught Me)"—De La Soul (Tommy Boy, 1988)
22. "Judy"—Whodini (MCA, 1991)
23. "Kanday"—LL Cool J (Def Jam, 1987)
24. "Latoya"—Just-Ice (Fresh, 1986)
25. "Linda"—Bobcat (Arista, 1989)
26. "Lisa Lipps"—Cru (Def Jam, 1997)
27. "Lola From The Copa"—MC Lyte (First Priority, 1991)
28. "Lolita"—Mighty MC's (Straight Up, 1988)
29. "Lori"—Twin Hype (Profile, 1989)
30. "Luke's Sheila"—Luke (Luke, 1997)
31. "Mahogany"—Eric B. & Rakim (MCA, 1990)
32. "Maria"—Wu-Tang Clan (Loud, 1997)
33. "Mary Go Round"—Cool C (Atlantic, 1989)
34. "Mary, Mary"—Run-D.M.C. (Profile, 1988)
35. "Melissa"—MC Serch (Warlock, 1986)
36. "Miss Elaine"—Run-D.M.C. (Profile, 1988)

STUNTS, BLUNTS & HIP HOP.

37. "Miss Terry"—Brotherhood Creed (Gasoline Alley, 1992)
38. "Mona Lisa"—Slick Rick (Def Jam, 1988)
39. "Ms. Crabtree"—Hoodratz (Epic, 1993)
40. "Nikole"—Kurious (Columbia, 1994)
41. "Nina"—Dana Dane (Maverick, 1995)
42. "Oh! Veronica"—Glamour Girls (Pop Art, 1986)
43. "Once A Dawg (Janine 2)"—AMG (Select, 1991)
44. "Paula & Janet"—Too $hort (Jive, 1990)
45. "Renee"—Lost Boyz (Universal, 1996)
46. "Renee-Renee"—K-Solo (Atlantic, 1990)
47. "Rita"—Class A Felony (Mercury, 1993)
48. "Roxanne, Roxanne"—U.T.F.O. (Select, 1984)
49. "Sally"—Stetsasonic (Tommy Boy, 1988)
50. "Sally And Dee"—Sir Fresh & DJ Critical (Ultra, 1987)
51. "Sally Got A One Track Mind"—Diamond D (Chemistry, 1992)
52. "Sandee"—J.V.C. Force (Idlers, 1990)
53. "Shakiyla"—Poor Righteous Teachers (Profile, 1990)
54. "Shana"—The Jaz (EMI, 1989)

55. "Sharane"—Mic Geronimo (Blunt, 1995)
56. "She's Not Just Another Woman (Monique)"—Biz Markie (Cold Chillin', 1989)
57. "Sonia"—Luke (Luke, 1992)
58. "Speaking Of A Girl Named Suzy"—Stetsasonic (Tommy Boy, 1990)
59. "Stronjay"—O.C. (Payday, 1997)
60. "Suzi Wants To Be A Rock Star"—Professor Griff (Luke, 1990)
61. "Tanya's Freakin' Me"—Little Shawn (Capitol, 1992)
62. "A Thing Named Kim"—Biz Markie (Cold Chillin', 1989)
63. "3 Brothers And Yvonne"—Black, Rock & Ron (RCA, 1989)
64. "Tudy Fruity Judy"—T La Rock (Fresh, 1987)
65. "Understand Me Vanessa (Vanessa Yo)"—Anttex (Tuff City, 1991)
66. "Veronica"—Bad Boys featuring K Love (Starlite, 1985)
67. "Veronica"—Onyx (Def Jam, 1998)
68. "X-Rated Lynn"—Gee & Jay (Mob, 1988)
69. "Yvette"—Grandmaster Caz (Tuff City, 1984)

*Your man Smooth B sings on this joint.

THE LOVE MOVEMENT:*
Rap Love.

1. Apache & Nikki D
2. Hurby "Luvbug" Azor & Salt (Salt-N-Pepa)
3. Brother J & Queen Mother Rage
4. Buffy (Fat Boys) & Queen Pen
5. Everlast & Tairrie B
6. KRS-One & Ms. Melodie
7. Kurupt & Foxy Brown
8. Lil' Rodney Cee (Funky 4 + 1; Double Trouble) & Angie B. (Sequence)
9. Marley Marl & Dimples D
10. The Notorious B.I.G. & Charli Baltimore
11. The Notorious B.I.G. & Lil' Kim
12. Prince Markie Dee & (old school) Pepa (Salt-N-Pepa)
13. Erick Sermon & Hurricane G
14. Special Ed & one of the Safari Sisters (Y'know, those dancing girls for Queen Latifah)
15. Spyder-D & Sparky D
16. Treach & (now school) Pepa (Salt-N-Pepa)
17. Van Silk & The Original Spinderella
18. Young Zee & Rah Digga (Flipmode Squad)

Rap/Celebrity Love.

19. Adrock (Beastie Boys) & Molly Ringwald
20. Adrock (Beastie Boys) & Ione Skye
21. B-Real (Cypress Hill) & Carmen Electra
22. Left Eye & André Rison
23. LL Cool J & Kidada Jones
24. MCA (Beastie Boys) & Madonna
25. Q-Tip & Angie Martinez
26. 2Pac & Kidada Jones
27. 2Pac & Salli Richardson
28. Vanilla Ice & Madonna
29. Will Smith & Jada Pinkett

Rap/R&B Love.

30. Butterfly (Digable Planets) & Coko (SWV)
31. C-Murder & Monica
32. Dr. Dre & Michel'le
33. Dre (OutKast) & Erykah Badu
34. Ed Lover & Lelee (SWV)
35. Ma$e & Brandy
36. The Notorious B.I.G. & Faith Evans
37. Gipp (Goodie Mob) & Joi

*Past and present.

STUNTS, BLUNTS & HIP HOP.

A Teenage Love.

1. "Butta-Few-Co"—Kwest Tha Madd Lad (American, 1996)
2. "Jail Bait"—Busy Bee (Pan Disc, 1992)
3. "She Was Only 16"—The Click (Sick Wid It, 1995)
4. "6Teen"—Audio Two (First Priority, 1990)
5. "13 And Good"—Boogie Down Productions (Jive, 1992)
6. "Young Girl Bluez"—Biz Markie (Cold Chillin', 1993)

Women Russell Simmons Wishes He Could Have Dated Before He Got Married.*

1. Pussy Galore (from the James Bond film, *Goldfinger*)
2. Pamela Anderson
3. Paulina Porizkova
4. Pamela Dennis
5. Penny Baker
6. Patti Reynolds (*Playboy* Playmate)
7. Patti Hanson
8. Pam Grier
9. Peggy Lipton
10. Peta Wilson
11. Pam Johnson (my next door neighbor growing up in Hollis, Queens)
12. Pia Zadora
13. Penny Marshall
14. Pam Dawber
15. Peaches (as in Peaches & Herb)
16. Patricia Arquette
17. Priscilla Presley
18. Patricia Ford (*Playboy* Playmate)
19. Pat Benatar
20. Patricia Velasquez
21. Paula Abdul

*Says Russell: "I thought I would give you my list beginning with the letter 'P.' It seemed like a good place to start."

Russell Simmons is the Berry Gordy of hip hop. From producing and managing Run-D.M.C. to co-founding Def Jam Records to putting his mack hand down on the regular to becoming a happily married mogul, he remains extra large and in charge like Heatwave—always and forever.

CAN'T TRUSS IT:
23 Sneaky Tales About Infidelity.

1. "Ain't No Nigga"—Jay-Z featuring Foxy Brown (Roc-A-Fella, 1996)
2. "Betcha Got A Dude On The Side"—Star Quality & Class (R&R, 1982)
3. "Big Ole Butt"—LL Cool J (Def Jam, 1989)
4. "Cake & Eat It Too"—Nice & Smooth (RAL, 1991)
5. "Cheatin' Girl"—Steady B (Pop Art, 1986)
6. "Cheat On You"—Ma$e (Bad Boy, 1997)
7. "Chick On The Side"—Salt-N-Pepa (Next Plateau, 1986)
8. "Hey Love"—Sun King-D Moët (Zakia, 1987)
9. "Hush Hush Tip"—N-Tyce (Wild Pitch, 1994)
10. "I Didn't Mean To"—Casual (Jive, 1994)
11. "If I Took Your Boyfriend"—The Click (Jive, 1995)
12. "I'll Take Her"—Ill Al Skratch (Mercury, 1994)
13. "I'll Take Your Man"—Salt-N-Pepa (Next Plateau, 1988)
14. "I Shouldn't Have Done It"—Slick Rick (Def Jam, 1991)
15. "Just A Friend"—Biz Markie (Cold Chillin', 1989)
16. "Me & My Crazy World"—Lost Boyz (Universal, 1997)
17. "My Homeboy's Girlfriend"—Eightball (Suave House, 1998)
18. "Da Nex Niguz"—Onyx (Def Jam, 1993)
19. "O.P.P."—Naughty By Nature (Tommy Boy, 1991)
20. "Plan B"—Master P featuring Mia X (No Limit, 1997)
21. "Somebody Else Bumped Your Girl"—Freddie Foxxx (MCA, 1989)
22. "To All The Girls"—Wyclef Jean (Ruffhouse, 1997)
23. "Treat Her Like A Prostitute"—Slick Rick (Def Jam, 1988)

RETURN OF THE "G"-STRING:
OutKast's Big Boi Puts You Up On His Favorite Atlanta Strip Clubs.

1. **The Gentleman's Club**
2. **Blue Flame**
3. **Jazzy T's**
4. **Magic City**
5. **Pleasers Club**
6. **Goosebumps**
7. **Club Nikki**
8. **Montreyes**
   You could get anything you wanted in there back in the day. It's still open, but they lost their liquor license.
9. **Foxy Lady**
   If you really want to get ghetto, you can hit that Foxy Lady—off of Moreland Avenue. But nobody go over there no more, though. Man, that thing is the bottom of the barrel, G.
10. **The Gold Club**
    If you really just want to go get you some white Zinfandel, you gotta hit that Gold Club.

In addition to being a strip club connoisseur, Big Boi is the Aquarius half of OutKast.

DJ Mister Cee Names The 10 Best Ways For DJs To Get Ass.

1. **Always have your tour laminate prominently displayed on you.**
   This way girls can see who you're down with and stuff like that. Always have those magnets—the laminate, the V.I.P. pass and stuff like that.

2. **Get to the arena early.**
   Instead of getting there at the time I needed to perform, I would always get there real early before we had to go on. That way, I could walk around the arena with my laminate and make sure people noticed me and stuff like that.

3. **Offer backstage invitations.**
   When you're doing a show and there's this girl you wanna get with, just invite her backstage. And if she got friends just be like, "Yo, come backstage with me, whatever!" That's pretty much a sure "in" for ass.
   The only thing about that, though, is that you gotta do what we used to call "preserve the puss." When you bring them backstage you gotta make sure they're not going crazy for someone else that's back there! You gotta let her know right away before you get backstage, "Don't be gettin' crazy back there, don't be trying to play me." You gotta play her close so no one else will fuck with her, but at the same time give her some space so she won't feel cluttered. Women don't like a man to be all up under them just like we don't like that. Know when to walk away—even though 9 times out of 10 you're still worried about losing that puss.

4. **Always DJ the after parties.**
   Whenever you get the opportunity, show your skills and alladat.

5. **Be persistent.**
   If you don't have no ass by the time you get to the hotel, just take a walk around the hotel lobby and just be like, "Notice me! PLEASE!" A lot of times, groups of girls come back to the hotel. Sit around with their friends, join the conversation and blend in with them. Make them feel like, "I'm down with y'all." But in the back of your mind you know you just want some ass from one of them.

6. **Play it cool.**
   There were times when I was around Scoob, Scrap and Kane and there was a bunch of girls around them. They were a little more vocal and energetic than me about their approach to women back then. So what I would do is play the quiet role, the shy boy. Girls would be attracted to that. At least one of them would be like, "Who's that?" Guaranteed. Either that or have a mad face and act like you got an attitude or something. Then girls will want to know what's going on—"Who's this person?" They find out, boom, boom, pow. Then—ASS!

7. **Always be willing to give away shit.**
   Give away mad fuckin' CDs, cassettes and shit. You see a chick, just give it to her. But you gotta make sure your picture is on whatever you give out. Your picture gotta be on it so then she can just jump on the dick.

8. **Spit game.**
   Know how to talk to women because no matter what status you think you own, you still gotta know how to talk to the puss to get the puss. You just gotta have the gift of gab and let them know that it's alright to give up some ass.

STUNTS, BLUNTS & HIP HOP.

9. **Be open-minded about locations.**
You might not be able to have your own room on tour so you might have to fuck on the terrace. You might have to fuck on the bus. You have to know how to adapt.

The place I always used to catch them with was in the bathroom. Scoob or Scrap would be in the bedroom and I'd just take the girl in the bathroom and solve the problem right there. Between that and the staircase—you know, just get it on. I remember when I first started having sex in the staircase of the hotel and told Scoob and Scrap, they were like, "Yo, that's a great idea!"

10. **Last, but not least, just say who you are.**
I'd just go, "Yo, I'm Mister Cee—Big Daddy Kane's DJ," and see if that worked. Sometimes there's guys who get some ass off some bragging shit. It may not work for all, but it works for some.

DJ Mister Cee (nicknamed "The Nasty African" for reasons that should be readily apparent) is recognized the world over for being Big Daddy Kane's longtime DJ, executive producing The Notorious B.I.G.'s Ready To Die and producing underground party records like the pervertedly funky "Shake Dat Ass Girl." He resides in Do-Or-Die Bed-Stuy, Brooklyn, baby.

Cat Got Their Tongue.

1. "All About The Pussy"—Big Ken (4th & B'way, 1992)
2. "Blac Vagina Finda"—Onyx (Def Jam, 1993)
3. "Brown Sugar"—Extra Prolific (Jive, 1994)
4. "Eatin' Pussy"—Pooh-Man (Jive, 1992)
5. "Eat This"—H.W.A. (Drive By, 1990)
6. "Fa Sho' Pussy"—Odd Squad (Rap-A-Lot, 1994)
7. "Givin' Up The Nappy Dug Out"—Ice Cube (Priority, 1991)
8. "I Need Some Pussy"—Willie D (Rap-A-Lot, 1989)
9. "Is The Pussy Still Good"—BWP (RAL, 1991)
10. "Lick The Pussy"—The Beatnuts (Relativity, 1994)
11. "Over Pussy"—JCD & The Dawg LB. (Profile, 1992)
12. "Pass The Pussy"—The A.T.E.E.M (Select, 1992)
13. "The 'P' Is Free"—Boogie Down Productions (B-Boy, 1987)
14. "'P' Is Still Free"—KRS-One (Jive, 1993)
15. "Pussy Ain't Nothin'"—Schoolly D (Jive, 1989)
16. "Pussy Ain't Shit"—Funkdoobiest (Immortal, 1995)
17. "Pussy Hound"—Rondo & Crazy Rak (High Powered, 1995)
18. "Some Bomb Azz Pussy"—Tha Dogg Pound (Death Row, 1995)
19. "Stuck On Pussy Drive"—Kool Keith (Funky Ass, 1997)
20. "Sweet Black Pussy"—DJ Quik (Profile, 1991)
21. "Wasted Pussy"—Nikki D (Def Jam, 1991)

Rocket In The Pocket.

1. "All On My Nut Sac"—Da Lench Mob (Street Knowledge, 1992)
2. "Big Black Caddy"—Grandmaster Flash & The Furious Five (Elektra, 1987)
3. "D. Control"—AMG (Select, 1991)
4. "Deez Nutz"—Kool Moe Dee (Wrap, 1994)
5. "Dick Almighty"—2 Live Crew (Luke, 1989)
6. "Dick 'Em Down"—Fresh Kid Ice (Effect, 1992)
7. "Dick On The Track"—Mystikal (No Limit, 1997)
8. "Dumb Dick (Richard)"—Kool Moe Dee (Jive, 1986)
9. "Get Off My Dick And Tell Yo Bitch To Come Here"—Ice Cube (Priority, 1990)
10. "Get Off My Log"—Milk (American, 1995)
11. "Get Off The Dick"—Ultra (Our Turn, 1996)
12. "Get The Bozack"—EPMD (Fresh, 1989)
13. "Git Off Ma Dic"—Hoodratz (Epic, 1993)
14. "Gota Let Your Nuts Hang"—Geto Boys (Rap-A-Lot, 1991)
15. "Hand On My Nutsac"—Coolio (Tommy Boy, 1994)
16. "Hed"—Noreaga featuring Nature (Penalty, 1998)
17. "Hogg Nuts"—N2Deep (Bust It, 1994)
18. "Hum Deez Nuts"—King Sun (Cold Chillin', 1994)
19. "Jimbrowski"—Jungle Brothers (Idlers, 1988)
20. "Jimmy"—Boogie Down Productions (Jive, 1988)
21. "Long Dick Chinese"—Fresh Kid Ice (Effect, 1992)
22. "Mr. Big Dick"—Schoolly D (Jive, 1988)
23. "Mr. Bozack"—EPMD (Def Jam, 1990)
24. "My Dick Is So Large"—Yaggfu Front (Mercury, 1994)
25. "My Ding-A-Ling"—Leaders Of The New School (Elektra, 1991)
26. "My Jimmy Weighs A Ton"—Jungle Brothers (Warner Bros., 1993)
27. "My Nuts"—Fat Boys (Tin Pan Apple, 1987)
28. "Nine Inches Hard"—Juice (Arista, 1995)
29. "On Da Dick"—Young Lay (Young Black Brotha, 1996)
30. "Operation CB"—Kool G Rap & DJ Polo (Cold Chillin', 1992)*
31. "Suck A Little Dick"—Gangsta Boo (Relativity, 1998)
32. "Suck My Dick"—The New 2 Live Crew (Luke, 1993)
33. "This Dick's For You"—Geto Boys (Rap-A-Lot, 1993)
34. "Worship The Dick"—Saafir (Qwest, 1994)
35. "You Can Get The Dick"—DFC (Big Beat, 1994)

*Take Note: CB stands for cock block.

Potluck.

1. BuckWeed (Wascals)
2. Buddha Monk
3. Buddha Real (b/k/a B-Real) (Cypress Hill)
4. Canibus
5. Cheba
6. Dust Brothers
7. Eddie Cheeba
8. Ganjah K.
9. Indo G
10. LA The Darkman
11. Mean Green
12. Meen Green (Western HemisFear)
13. Method Man
14. Sonny Cheeba (Camp Lo)
15. Spliff Star (Flipmode Squad)
16. Sunny Cheeba (Punk Barbarians)

STUNTS, BLUNTS & HIP HOP.

20 Dope Anti-Drug Songs.

1. "Ain't Got No Class"—Da Lench Mob (Street Knowledge, 1992)
2. "Dirty South"—Goodie Mob (LaFace, 1995)
3. "F.B.I."—Donald D (Epic, 1989)
4. "Girl"—Too $hort (75 Girls, 1985)
5. "Git Up, Git Out"—OutKast (LaFace, 1994)
6. "Jane, Stop This Crazy Thing"—MC Shan (Cold Chillin', 1986)
7. "King Heroin (Don't Mess With Heroin)"—Jazzy Jeff (Jive, 1985)
8. "Mega Blast"—Public Enemy (Def Jam, 1987)
9. "My Brother's A Basehead"—De La Soul (Tommy Boy, 1991)
10. "Night Of The Living Baseheads"—Public Enemy (Def Jam, 1988)
11. "No"—Doug E. Fresh & The New Get Fresh Crew (Bust It, 1992)
12. "Pause"—Run-D.M.C. (Profile, 1989)
13. "Say No Go"—De La Soul (Tommy Boy, 1989)
14. "Sister Morphine"—The A.T.E.E.M. (Select, 1992)
15. "Slow Down"—Brand Nubian (Elektra, 1990)
16. "Slump"—OutKast (LaFace, 1998)
17. "Sometimes I Rhyme Slow"—Nice & Smooth (RAL, 1991)
18. "Things Get A Little Easier"—Biz Markie (Cold Chillin', 1989)
19. "The Tragedy (Don't Do It)"—Super Kids (Nia, 1985)
20. "White Lines (Don't Do It)"—Grandmaster Melle Mel (Sugar Hill, 1983)

THE HIGH & MIGHTY:
Smokin' Weed Anthems.

1. "Cheeba Cheeba"—Tone-Lōc (Delicious Vinyl, 1987)
2. "How To Roll A Blunt"—Redman (Def Jam, 1992)
3. "I Can't Wake Up"—KRS-One (Jive, 1993)
4. "I Got 5 On It"—Luniz (Noo Trybe, 1995)
5. "I'm In Love With Indica" —Jungle Brothers (Warner Bros., 1993)
6. "I Wanna Get High"—Cypress Hill (Ruffhouse, 1993)
7. "Mad Izm"—Channel Live (Capitol, 1994)
8. "Married To Marijuana" —Capone-N-Noreaga (Penalty promo, 1997)
9. "Mary Jane"—Tha Alkaholiks (Loud, 1993)
10. "Pack The Pipe"—The Pharcyde (Delicious Vinyl, 1992)
11. "Smoke Buddah"—Redman (Def Jam, 1996)
12. "Stoned Is The Way Of The Walk"—Cypress Hill (Ruffhouse, 1991)
13. "Take 2 And Pass"—Gang Starr (Chrysalis, 1992)

People Ricky Powell Wishes He Could Have Gotten Zooted With.

1. Johnny Boy from *Mean Streets* at the St. Anthony Feast while watching Nancy Sinatra sing "These Boots Were Made For Walking."

2. Allen Iverson or Lew Alcindor while watching a game at the Rucker Tournament.

3. Dock Ellis, the Pittsburgh Pirate who once pitched a no-hitter on three hits of acid.

4. Julie Newmar in her Catwoman outfit.

5. Vonetta McGee, the former *Soul Train* dancer in the early '70s.

6. Bridgette Bardot at an animal rights rally.

7. Dancing Harry, Earl Monroe's boy, who used to put the whammy on opposing teams in a flamboyant matching hat and cloak.

8. Faye Dunaway in *Bonnie & Clyde*.

9. Barbarella or Cassius Clay at Playland in Times Square.

10. Broadway Joe Willie Namath on the set of Classic Sports Network while munching on some tofu dogs and watching *Football Follies*.

11. Wonder/Bionic Woman at the dog run in Washington Square Park.

12. Lou Donaldson/Pinella sitting on a stoop and whistling at girls.

13. Earl/Marilyn Monroe in the bleacher section of Yankee Stadium.

14. The chick from *Planet Of The Apes* on the beach looking at the Statue Of Liberty.

15. Duane Thomas, the former thoroughbred running back for the Cowboys in the early '70s who gave the silent treatment to his team in '71 for the whole season because he felt wrongly treated for being whatever, himself. He was cool.

ego trip columnist and photojournalist Ricky Powell is the author of Oh Snap! & The Rickford Files, *groovy overviews of some of his best work.*

Crack Attack.

1. "Close The Crackhouse"—Professor X featuring Brother J, Wise Intelligent, Big Daddy Kane, Money B (Digital Underground; Raw Fusion), Shock G & Humpty Hump (Digital Underground), Ex-Girlfriend, Chuck D, Sister Souljah, Freedom Williams, YZ, College Boyz & Two Kings In A Cipher (Polygram, 1993)
2. "Crack, Crack, Don't Do It"—The Maniacs (Zakia, 1986)
3. "Cracked Out"—Masters Of Ceremony (Strong City, 1988)
4. "Crack It Up"—Funkmaster Wizard Wiz (Tuff City, 1984)
5. "Crack Slangas"—Gregory D (RCA, 1992)
6. "Dope Man"—N.W.A (Ruthless, 1987)
7. "Get Off The Crack"—Poor Righteous Teachers (Profile, 1993)
8. "Get Your Mother Off The Crack"—Audio Two (First Priority, 1990)
9. "Ice Cream Man"—Dru Down featuring Luniz (Relativity, 1994)
10. "I Cram To Understand U"—MC Lyte (First Priority, 1988)
11. "Jane, Stop This Crazy Thing"—MC Shan (Cold Chillin', 1986)
12. "Monster Crack"—Kool Moe Dee (Rooftop, 1986)
13. "The 'P' Is Free"—Boogie Down Productions (B-Boy, 1987)
14. "Pocket Full Of Stones"—U.G.K. (Jive, 1992)
15. "Quarter Gram Pam"—Positive K (First Priority, 1987)
16. "Runnin' Out Da Crackhouse"—Spice 1 (Jive, 1993)
17. "Slow Down"—Brand Nubian (Elektra, 1990)
18. "Tales From The Crack Side"—K-Solo (Atlantic, 1990)
19. "Ten Crack Commandments"—The Notorious B.I.G. (Bad Boy, 1997)
20. "Time To Check My Crackhouse"—Master P (No Limit, 1996)

Last Call.

1. "Crack Da 40"—Mac Mall (Young Black Brotha, 1994)
2. "Do You Wanna Go To The Liquor Store"—Toddy Tee featuring Mixmaster Spade (Evejim, 1987)
3. "Drink Away The Pain (Situations)"—Mobb Deep (Loud, 1995)
4. "Drink It Up"—The Fila Fresh Crew (Comptown, 1988)
5. "40 Oz. For Breakfast"—Blackalicious (SoleSides, 1994)
6. "Hennessy"—Domino (OutBurst, 1996)
7. "Here's A Drink"—The Beatnuts (Relativity, 1997)
8. "Hip Hop Drunkies"—Tha Alkaholiks featuring Ol' Dirty Bastard (Loud, 1997)
9. "Hurricane"—The Click (Sick Wid It, 1995)
10. "Let's Get Drunk"—The Click (Sick Wid It, 1995)
11. "Mr. X & Mr. Z Drink Old Gold"—Mr. X & Mr. Z (Urban Rock, 1987)
12. "Only When I'm Drunk"—Tha Alkaholiks (Loud, 1993)
13. "On Tha Rox"—King Tee (Capitol, 1993)
14. "Tap The Bottle"—Young Black Teenagers (SOUL, 1992)
15. "Tonite"—DJ Quik (Profile, 1991)

TO MADONNA:

Rap's Lyrical Obsession With The Material Girl.

1. "At The Speed Of Life"—Xzibit (Loud, 1996)
   "Before hip hop was all about drama, anything for a dollar/ Before Kane fucked Madonna, Xzibit maintained and stayed bent like a comma."

2. "The Dream Shatterer"—Big Punisher (Loud, 1998)
   "Sometimes rhyming I blow my own mind like Nirvana/ Comma, and go the whole nine like Madonna."

3. "Have A Nice Day"—Roxanne Shanté (Cold Chillin', 1987)
   "A pioneer like Lola Falana with a name that stands big like Madonna/ Speaking of Madonna, some girls on the mic rap like virgins and get real tight."

4. "Kick The Bobo"—Prime Minister Pete Nice & Daddy Rich (Def Jam, 1993)
   "Don't sweat Madonna—Madonna got a bony ass/ If you got to pass gas, you better leave the room fast."

5. "Rock The Bells"—LL Cool J (Def Jam, 1985)
   "I'm not a virgin so I know I'll make Madonna scream."

6. "Sex Style"—Kool Keith (Funky Ass, 1997)
   "I'm on stage gettin' sucked by Madonna/ Stickin' pipes in ya ass you stop the freestyle drama."

7. "Tonight's The Night (Remix)"—Redman (Def Jam, 1994)
   "Freak funkadelic phrases cuz I choose to/ I'm fuckin' Madonna, down to Smurfette, now I'm down to Mfufu."

8. "You & Your Heroes"—Da Lench Mob (Street Knowledge, 1992)
   Shorty: "Madonna, you muthafuckin' slut/ You can show your butt and jimmy still won't get up."

HONORABLE MENTIONS:

"To My Donna"—Young Black Teenagers (SOUL, 1991)
This song was payback by The Bomb Squad for Madonna's unauthorized use of P.E.'s "Security Of The First World" (Def Jam, 1988) for her Lenny Kravitz-produced hit, "Justify My Love" (Sire, 1990).

"Keep It Together (45 King Remix)"—Madonna (Sire, 1990)
Ms. Ciccone did do it legit, however, when 45 King blessed the Material Girl with this revamp of her single.

STUNTS, BLUNTS & HIP HOP.

DAMN, IT FEELS GOOD TO SEE PEOPLE UP ON IT:
Songs About Fame.

1. "Check 'N Me Out"—Def Squad (Def Jam, 1998)
2. "Crossover"—EPMD (Def Jam, 1992)
3. "Dana Dane With Fame"—Dana Dane (Profile, 1987)
4. "Don't Even Try It"—DJ Jazzy Jeff & The Fresh Prince (Jive, 1987)
5. "Don't Let It Go To Your Head"—Brand Nubian (Arista, 1998)
6. "Elevators"—OutKast (LaFace, 1996)
7. "Everybody Knows Me"—K-Solo (Atlantic, 1990)
8. "Everybody Loves A Star"—Doug E. Fresh & The Get Fresh Crew (Reality, 1988)
9. "Get Off My Dick And Tell Yo Bitch To Come Here"—Ice Cube (Priority, 1990)
10. "Groupie Therapy"—The Pharcyde (Delicious Vinyl, 1995)
11. "I'm Not A Star"—MC Shy-D (Luke, 1987)
12. "It Wasn't Me, It Was The Fame"—EPMD (Fresh, 1989)
13. "Juicy"—The Notorious B.I.G. (Bad Boy, 1994)
14. "Life Of An Entertainer"—MC Rell & The Houserockers (Polygram, 1989)
15. "Lost Ones"—Lauryn Hill (Ruffhouse, 1998)
16. "Mr. Nobody Is Somebody Now"—Chubb Rock (Select, 1989)
17. "1-900-LLCOOLJ"—LL Cool J (Def Jam, 1989)
18. "Ring Ring Ring (Ha Ha Hey)"—De La Soul (Tommy Boy, 1991)
19. "Same Song"—Digital Underground featuring 2Pac (Tommy Boy, 1990)
20. "Show Business"—A Tribe Called Quest featuring Brand Nubian & Diamond D (Jive, 1992)
21. "Somebody For Me"—Heavy D (Uptown, 1989)
22. "Vapors"—Biz Markie (Cold Chillin', 1988)

LOONY TUNES:
Songs About Paranoia.

1. "Are You Crazy"—Tony Da Skitzo (Immortal, 1995)
2. "Cell Therapy"—Goodie Mob (LaFace, 1995)
3. "Feel Like I'm The One Who's Doin' Dope"—U.G.K. (Jive, 1992)
4. "The Ghetto's Tryin' To Kill Me"—Master P (No Limit, 1993)
5. "The Godz . . ."—Brand Nubian (Elektra, 1992)
6. "Hellucination"—Smif-N-Wessun (Nervous, 1995)
7. "Illusions"—Cypress Hill (Ruffhouse, 1995)
8. "Mind Playing Tricks On Me"—Geto Boys (Rap-A-Lot, 1991)
9. "Nightmares"—Dana Dane (Profile, 1987)
10. "Paranoia, Paranoia"—Nice & Smooth (RAL, 1991)
11. "Streets Is Watching"—Jay-Z (Roc-A-Fella, 1997)
12. "The Unseen Hand"—Souls Of Mischief (Industry, 1996)

YA SLIPPIN':
Songs About Falling Off.

1. "Cheesy Rat Blues"—LL Cool J (Def Jam, 1991)
2. "F.A.L.L.I.N. & You Can't Get Up"—Funkmaster Flex & Nine Double M (b/k/a Nine) (Warlock, 1991)
3. "Here Today, Gone Tomorrow"—Gang Starr (Chrysalis, 1990)
4. "I'm Fallin'"—Teenage Fanclub & De La Soul (Immortal, 1993)
5. "I'm Not Goin' Out Like That"—Run-D.M.C. (Profile, 1988)
6. "Mr. Pitiful"—Big Daddy Kane (Cold Chillin', 1990)
7. "Outta Here"—KRS-One (Jive, 1993)
8. "True To The Game"—Ice Cube (Priority, 1991)
9. "You Played Yourself"—Ice-T (Sire, 1989)

BEE

Hip Hop's Wonderful World Of Wax Wars.

1. **The Real Deal Roxanne Saga (Fuck All Those Imposter Roxanne Records): U.T.F.O. & The Real Roxanne vs. Roxanne Shanté; Sparky D vs. Roxanne Shanté**
   ROUND 1: "Roxanne, Roxanne"—U.T.F.O. (Select, 1984)
   ROUND 2: "Roxanne's Revenge"—Roxanne Shanté (Pop Art, 1985); "The Real Roxanne"—The Real Roxanne featuring U.T.F.O. (Select, 1985)
   ROUND 3: "Sparky's Turn (Roxanne You're Through)"—Sparky D (Nia, 1985)
   ROUND 4: "Queen Of Rox"—Roxanne Shanté (Pop Art, 1985)
   ROUND 5: "Round 1 (Uncensored)"—Roxanne Shanté vs. Sparky D (Spin, 1985)
   WINNER: Her royal badness, Roxanne Shanté.

2. **Juice Crew & Poet vs. Boogie Down Productions**
   ROUND 1: "The Bridge"—MC Shan (Bridge, 1986)
   ROUND 2: "South Bronx"—Boogie Down Productions (B-Boy, 1986)
   ROUND 3: "Kill That Noise"—MC Shan (Cold Chillin', 1987)
   ROUND 4: "The Bridge Is Over"—Boogie Down Productions (B-Boy, 1987)
   ROUND 5: "Have A Nice Day"—Roxanne Shanté (Cold Chillin', 1987); "Beat You Down"—Noel Rockwell featuring Poet (11-A, 1987)
   ROUND 6: "I'm Still #1 (Numero Uno Re-Recording)"—Boogie Down Productions (Jive, 1988)
   WINNER: The crew that's called BDP.

3. **Kool Moe Dee vs. LL Cool J**
   ROUND 1: "How Ya Like Me Now"—Kool Moe Dee (Jive, 1987)
   ROUND 2: "Jack The Ripper"—LL Cool J (Def Jam, 1988)
   ROUND 3: "Let's Go"—Kool Moe Dee (Jive, 1988)
   ROUND 4: "To Da Break Of Dawn"—LL Cool J (Motown, 1990) (Also disses MC Hammer & Ice-T)
   ROUND 5: "Death Blow"—Kool Moe Dee (Jive, 1991)
   WINNER: LL Cool J, nigga.

4. **Antoinette vs. MC Lyte**
   ROUND 1: "I Got An Attitude"—Antoinette (Next Plateau, 1987)
   ROUND 2: "10% Dis"—MC Lyte (First Priority, 1988)
   ROUND 3: "Lights Out, Party's Over" & "Watch The Gangstress Boogie"—Antoinette (Next Plateau, 1988)
   ROUND 4: "Shut The Eff Up! (Hoe)"—MC Lyte (First Priority, 1988)
   WINNER: MC Lyte—that's right, she can win a rhyme fight.

5. **J.J. Fad vs. Roxanne Shanté**
   ROUND 1: "Anotha Ho" (Also disses Sparky D, The Real Roxanne & Salt-N-Pepa) b/w "Supersonic"—J.J. Fad (Dream Team, 1987)
   ROUND 2: "Wack Itt"—Roxanne Shanté (Cold Chillin', 1988)
   ROUND 3: "Ya Goin' Down"—J.J. Fad (Ruthless, 1988)
   ROUND 4: "Skeezer"—Roxanne Shanté (Warner Bros., 1989)
   ROUND 5: "Bad Sister"—Roxanne Shanté (Cold Chillin', 1989)
   WINNER: Once again, the girl named Shanté.

6. **3rd Bass/MC Serch vs. MC Hammer**
   ROUND 1: "The Gas Face" & "The Cactus"—3rd Bass (Def Jam, 1989)
   ROUND 2: "3 Strikes 5000"—3rd Bass (Def Jam, 1990)
   ROUND 3: "Ace In The Hole"—3rd Bass (Def Jam, 1991)
   ROUND 4: "Daze In A Weak"—MC Serch (Def Jam, 1992)
   ROUND 5: "Break 'Em Off Something Proper"—MC Hammer (Giant, 1994) (Also disses Q-Tip, Redman, Dres, Rodney O & Run-D.M.C.)
   WINNER: Dem white fellas, 3rd Bass, in a relatively one-sided brawl.

7. **Compton's Most Wanted/MC Eiht vs. DJ Quik**
   ROUND 1: "Duck Sick"—MC Eiht (Orpheus, 1990)
   ROUND 2: A DJ Quik underground mix tape dis of Compton's Most Wanted.
   ROUND 3: "Def Wish"—MC Eiht (Orpheus, 1991)
   ROUND 4: "Way 2 Fonky" & "Tha Last Word"—DJ Quik (Profile, 1992) (Also disses Tim Dog)
   ROUND 5: "Def Wish II"; "Duck Sick II"; "Who's Xxxxing Who" (Also disses Tim Dog) & "Dead Men Tell No Lies"—MC Eiht (Orpheus, 1992)
   ROUND 6: "Def Wish III"—MC Eiht (Epic, 1994)
   ROUND 7: "Dollars & Sense"—DJ Quik (Death Row, 1994)
   ROUND 8: "Let You Havit"—DJ Quik (Profile, 1995)
   ROUND 9: "Def Wish IV (Tap That Azz)"—MC Eiht (Epic, 1996)
   WINNER: We can't call it. However, on "You're A Gangsta" (Arista, 1998), Quik reaches out to Eiht about one day doing a song together.

8. **Dr. Dre & Snoop Doggy Dogg vs. Luke**
   ROUND 1: "Intro" & "Fuck Wit Dre Day (And Everybody's Celebratin')"—Dr. Dre featuring Snoop Doggy Dogg (Death Row, 1992) (Also disses Tim Dog & Eazy-E)
   ROUND 2: "Dre's Momma Needs A Haircut" & "Cowards In Compton"—Luke (Luke, 1993)
   ROUND 3: "Tha Shiznit"—Snoop Doggy Dogg (Death Row, 1993)
   WINNER: Dre and his little homie Snoop (whose *still* got his back).

9. **Dr. Dre & Tha Dogg Pound vs. Eazy-E & B.G. Knocc Out & Dresta**
   ROUND 1: "Intro"; "Fuck Wit Dre Day (And Everybody's Celebratin')"—Dr. Dre featuring Snoop Doggy Dogg (Also disses Luke & Tim Dog) & "Bitches Ain't Shit"—Dr. Dre featuring Tha Dogg Pound & Jewell (Death Row, 1992)
   ROUND 2: "Puffin' On Blunts And Drankin' Tanqueray"—Dr. Dre featuring The Lady Of Rage & Tha Dogg Pound (Death Row, 1993)
   ROUND 3: The entire It's On (Dr. Dre) 187um Killa LP especially "Real Muthaphuckkin' G's"—Eazy-E featuring B.G. Knocc Out & Dresta (Ruthless, 1993)
   ROUND 4: "What Would U Do?"—Tha Dogg Pound (Death Row, 1994)
   ROUND 5: "D.P.G./K"—B.G. Knocc Out & Dresta (OutBurst, 1995)
   WINNER: Tha Dogg Pound Gangstas.

10. **Common vs. Ice Cube**
    ROUND 1: "i used to love h.e.r."—Common (Relativity, 1994)
    ROUND 2: "Westside Slaughterhouse"—Mack 10 featuring Ice Cube & WC (Priority, 1995)
    ROUND 3: "The Bitch In Yoo"—Common (Relativity, 1996)
    ROUND 4: "Hoo Bangin' (WSCG Style)"—Westside Connection (Priority, 1996)
    WINNER: Common—that's the muthafucka.

11. **Cypress Hill vs. Ice Cube**
    ROUND 1: "Throw Your Set In The Air"—Cypress Hill (Ruffhouse, 1995)
    ROUND 2: "Friday"—Ice Cube (Priority, 1995) (Cypress claimed Cube bit the hook from "Throw Your Set In The Air" on "Friday")
    ROUND 3: "No Rest For The Wicked"—Cypress Hill (Ruffhouse, 1995)
    ROUND 4: "King Of The Hill"—Westside Connection (Priority, 1996)
    ROUND 5: "Ice Cube Killa"—Cypress Hill (Ruffhouse promo, 1996)
    WINNER: Although both parties squashed beef by coming together on "Men Of Steel"—Shaquille O'Neal (Qwest, 1997), Cube was heading up the river in a boat and no paddle and Cypress was handing out verbal beatdowns.

12. **LL Cool J vs. Canibus & Wyclef Jean**
    ROUND 1: "4, 3, 2, 1"—LL Cool J featuring Method Man, Redman, Canibus & DMX (Def Jam, 1997)
    ROUND 2: "Second Round K.O."—Canibus (Universal, 1998)
    ROUND 3: "The Ripper Strikes Back"—LL Cool J (Def Jam promo, 1998)
    ROUND 4: "What's Clef Got To Do With It"—Wyclef Jean (Ruffhouse, 1998)
    ROUND 5: "Rasta Impasta"—LL Cool J (unreleased, 1998)
    WINNER: An anti-climactic draw.

Mo' Beef, Mo' Problems.

1. **Wreckx-N-Effect vs. Stetsasonic**
   ROUND 1: "Leave The Mike Smokin'"—Wreckx-N-Effect (Motown, 1989)
   ROUND 2: "Anytime, Anyplace"—Stetsasonic (Tommy Boy, 1990)
   WINNER: Just say Stet.

2. **X Clan vs. 3rd Bass**
   ROUND 1: "A Day Of Outrage, Operation Snatchback"—X Clan (4th & B'way, 1989)
   ROUND 2: "Fire & Earth (100% Natural)"—X Clan (4th & B'way, 1991)
   ROUND 3: "Herbalz In Your Mouth" & "Green Eggs & Swine"—3rd Bass (Def Jam, 1991)
   WINNER: X Clan, siseeeees! (Lumumba's revenge).

3. **Luke vs. Vanilla Ice**
   ROUND 1: "I Ain't Bullshittin' Part 2"—Luke (Luke, 1990)
   ROUND 2: "Minutes Of Power"—Vanilla Ice (SBK, 1994)
   WINNER: Cool-ass Luke.

4. **Luke vs. Kid 'N Play**
   ROUND 1: "I Ain't Bullshittin' Part 2"—Luke (Luke, 1990)
   ROUND 2: "Next Question"—Kid 'N Play (Select, 1991) (Also disses Vanilla Ice)
   ROUND 3: "Pussy Ass Kid And Hoe Ass Play (Payback Is A Mutha Fucker)"—Luke (Luke, 1992)
   WINNER: Uncle Luke does it again.

5. **3rd Bass vs. Vanilla Ice**
   ROUND 1: "Pop Goes The Weasel"—3rd Bass (Def Jam, 1991)
   ROUND 2: "Kick 'Em In The Grill" & "Ace In The Hole"—3rd Bass (Def Jam, 1991)
   ROUND 3: "The Wrath"; "Hit 'Em Hard" (Also disses Marky Mark & MC Hammer) & "Ice Man Party"—Vanilla Ice (SBK, 1994)
   WINNER: 3rd Bass. No contest.

6. **X Clan vs. Boogie Down Productions**
   ROUND 1: "Fire & Earth (100% Natural)"—X Clan (4th & B'way, 1991)
   ROUND 2: "Build & Destroy"—Boogie Down Productions (Jive, 1992)
   WINNER: The Head Humanist In Charge.

7. **N.W.A vs. Ice Cube**
   ROUND 1: "100 Miles And Runnin'"—N.W.A (Ruthless, 1990) & "Real Niggaz"—N.W.A (Ruthless, 1991)
   ROUND 2: "Alwayz Into Somethin'" & "Message To B.A."—N.W.A (Ruthless, 1991)
   ROUND 3: "No Vaseline"—Ice Cube (Priority, 1991)
   WINNER: Ice Cube, the runaway slave.

8. **Tim Dog vs. Dr. Dre & Snoop Doggy Dogg**
   ROUND 1: "Fuck Compton"; "Michel'le Conversation" & "Step To Me"—Tim Dog (Ruffhouse, 1991)
   ROUND 2: "Intro" & "Fuck Wit Dre Day (And Everybody's Celebratin')"—Dr. Dre featuring Snoop Doggy Dogg (Death Row, 1992) (Also disses Luke & Eazy-E)
   ROUND 3: "Puffin' On Blunts And Drankin' Tanqueray"—Dr. Dre featuring The Lady Of Rage & Tha Dogg Pound (Death Row, 1993)
   ROUND 4: "Bitch With A Perm"—Tim Dog (unreleased, 1993)
   WINNER: Dre and his little homie Snoop (whose got his back).

9. **Tim Dog vs. DJ Quik**
   ROUND 1: "Fuck Compton"; "DJ Quik Beat Down" & "Step To Me"—Tim Dog (Ruffhouse, 1991)
   ROUND 2: "Way 2 Fonky" & "Tha Last Word"—DJ Quik (Profile, 1992) (Also disses MC Eiht)
   WINNER: Quik... to get in a Dog's ass.

BEEF.

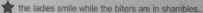

10. **House Of Pain vs. DJ Quik**
ROUND 1: "Shamrocks & Shenanigans (Remix)"—House Of Pain (Tommy Boy, 1992)
ROUND 2: "Can't Fuck Wit A Nigga"—DJ Quik featuring 2nd II None (Jive, 1993)
WINNER: Quik... to get in a white boy's ass.

11. **Pooh-Man vs. The Dangerous Crew**
ROUND 1: *Judgement Day*—Pooh-Man (Righteous, 1993) (Contains *six* dis songs against his former crew, including "Bring It To 'Em" [Target: Ant Banks] & "Studio Gangster" [Target: Spice 1])
ROUND 2: "Get In Where You Fit In"—Too $hort featuring Rappin' Ron & Ant Diddley Dog (Jive, 1993)
ROUND 3: "Fuckin' Wit Banks"—Ant Banks featuring Too $hort & Goldy (Jive, 1994)
ROUND 4: "You Done Fucked Up"—Spice 1 (Jive, 1994)
WINNER: The Dangerous Crew, beeyotch.

12. **Luniz vs. Too $hort**
ROUND 1: "Playa Hata"—Luniz (Noo Trybe, 1995)
ROUND 2: "That's Why"—Too $hort (Jive, 1996)
WINNER: None. Beef squashed. Please refer to "Funkin' Over Nuthin'"—Luniz featuring Too $hort (Noo Trybe, 1997) for more details.

13. **2Pac (a/k/a Makaveli) vs. Mobb Deep**
ROUND 1: "Hit 'Em Up"—2Pac featuring The Outlawz (Death Row, 1996) (Also disses The Notorious B.I.G., Sean "Puffy" Combs, Bad Boy Records, Lil' Cease, Lil' Kim & Chino XL)
ROUND 2: "Drop A Gem On 'Em"; "In The Long Run" (Also disses Def Squad) & Game Show Skit—Mobb Deep (Loud, 1996)
ROUND 3: "Against All Odds"—Makaveli (Also disses Nas, Dr. Dre & Sean "Puffy" Combs) & "Bomb First (My Second Reply)" —Makaveli featuring The Outlawz (Death Row, 1996) (Also disses Bad Boy Records, Jay-Z, Nas, The Notorious B.I.G. & Xzibit)
WINNER: None. 2Pac's death marked the end of this battle.

14. **Fugees vs. Jeru The Damaja**
ROUND 1: "Zealots"—Fugees (Ruffhouse, 1996)
ROUND 2: "Black Cowboys"—Jeru The Damaja (Payday, 1996)
ROUND 3: "Don't Cry Dry Your Eyes"—Fugees (Ruffhouse, 1996)
WINNER: Fugees (ha, ha, ha, ha, ha, you shouldn't test Refugees).

15. **Jeru The Damaja vs. Foxy Brown**
ROUND 1: "One Day"—Jeru The Damaja (Payday, 1996) (Also disses Sean "Puffy" Combs)
ROUND 2: "Ill Na Na"—Foxy Brown (Def Jam, 1996)
WINNER: Who cares?

16. **Redman vs. PMD**
ROUND 1: "Soopaman Luva 3"—Redman (Def Jam, 1996)
ROUND 2: "It's The Pee (Remix)"—PMD featuring Prodigy (Mobb Deep) (Relativity, 1996)
WINNER: Ditto #15.

17. **Queen Latifah vs. Foxy Brown**
ROUND 1: "Name Callin'"—Queen Latifah featuring Nikki D (Elektra, 1996)
ROUND 2: "10% Dis"—Foxy Brown (Loud, 1998)
ROUND 3: "Name Callin' Part II"—Queen Latifah (Motown promo, 1998)
WINNER: Queen Latifah. The lady's still first.

18. **Tragedy vs. Noreaga**
ROUND 1: "Blood Type"—Tragedy (Gee Street, 1998)
ROUND 2: "Halfway Thugs Pt. 2"—Noreaga (Penalty promo, 1998)
WINNER: Funkmaster Flex plays Richard Steele and stops the fight just when things were getting exciting.

GO ON, GIRLS: Roxanne Shanté and Sparky D rap 'n duke it out.

BIG MAMA SAID
KNOCK YOU OUT:
Artists Roxanne Shanté Targets On "Bite This" (Pop Art, 1985).*

1. The Real Roxanne
2. Sparky D
3. "All the other Roxannes imitatin' me."
4. Run-D.M.C.
5. Kurtis Blow
6. LL Cool J
7. Bad Boys featuring K Love

*In the order they're mentioned.

BATTLE OF THE SEXES:
16 Adversarial Male-Female Rap Duets.

1. "All Men Are Dogs"—Bandit featuring Keisha Black (London, 1995)
2. "Domestic Violence"—RZA As Bobby Digital featuring Jamie Sommers (Gee Street, 1998)
3. "Extravagant Girls"—Extravagant Girls & Symbolic Three (Public, 1986)
4. "Get Money"—Junior M.A.F.I.A. featuring The Notorious B.I.G. (Big Beat, 1995)
5. "How U Like It"—MAG featuring Gangsta Boo (Relativity, 1998)
6. "I Don't Know"—Kid 'N Play & Salt-N-Pepa (Select, 1990)
7. "I Got A Man"—Positive K featuring his damn self (Island, 1992)
8. "I'm Fly Shanté"—Roxanne Shanté featuring Steady B (Pop Art, 1986)
9. "I'm Not Havin' It"—MC Lyte featuring Positive K (First Priority, 1988)
10. "It's A Man's World"—Ice Cube featuring Yo Yo (Priority, 1990)
11. "Put It In Your Mouth"—Akinyele featuring Kia Jefferies (Stress, 1996)
12. "Suck A Little Dick"—Gangsta Boo featuring DJ Paul & Juicy J (Relativity, 1998)
13. "Walk On By"—Fat Joe featuring Charli Baltimore (Big Beat, 1998)
14. "We Don't Need It"—Junior M.A.F.I.A. (Elektra, 1996)
15. "Who Freaked Who?"—Apache featuring Nikki D (Tommy Boy, 1993)
16. "Who You Jackin?"—Masta Ace featuring Paula Perry (Delicious Vinyl, 1993)

BEEF.

6 Battles On Wax That Were Staged In The Studio.

1. **"The Battle"—Sparky D vs. The Playgirls (Nia, 1985)**
Roxanne warrior princess Sparky goes *mano a mano* with her ex-homegirls. The insults launched in this cat-fight are weaker than producer Spyder-D's flaccid Linn Drum beats.

2. **"Chi Ali vs. Vanilla Shake"—Chi Ali (Relativity, 1992)**
The adolescent Native Tongue-ster takes on a satirical version of every rapper's favorite punching bag, Vanilla Ice.

3. **"Kid vs. Play (The Battle)"—Kid 'N Play (Motown, 1990)**
A hair-raising scene from *House Party* that lives forever on record. Goosebumps, anyone?

4. **"Meth vs. Chef"—Method Man featuring Raekwon (Def Jam, 1994)**
Wu-Tang swordsmen square off in a verbal cutting contest best remembered for Rae's (perhaps intentionally) flubbed verse. Was there a fix?

5. **"Round 1 (Uncensored)"—Roxanne Shanté vs. Sparky D (Spin, 1985)**
A makeshift in-studio battle in which the participants actually do get in each other's asses. Once again, Shanté does the most damage: "They tell me all about you/ And all the niggas in Brooklyn that you screw."

6. **"Showdown"—The Furious Five Meets The Sugarhill Gang (Sugar Hill, 1981)**
Not much of a "battle" and for good reason. The Five were good sports to even allow Jersey rap puppets Sugarhill in the same studio with them.

8 Rappers Who Took It To The Stage, Sucka.

1. **King Sun vs. Ice Cube**
   Claiming that Ice Cube jacked the hook for his hit single, "Wicked," from a demo he'd submitted to him, King Sun crashed Ice Cube's October 29, 1993 concert at New York's Palladium. Invading the DJ booth, Sun got on the mic and called Cube (who'd just finished performing "True To The Game") a biter. Cube challenged Sun to come to the stage. Sun attempted to oblige, but security prevented him from making his way to the front of the audience, leaving Cube with the last word. "That's right, I'm 'Wicked!' What'chu gonna do about it?" he yelled. Jack The Rapper strikes again.

2. **KRS-One vs. PM Dawn**
   Hip hop's most infamous stage rush took place on January 13, 1992 at New York's Sound Factory during a birthday celebration for *Yo! MTV Raps'* T-Money. PM Dawn was performing when KRS-One brought the ruckus, crashing its set and literally tossing group leader Prince Be's large frame into the crowd. Kris proceeded to take over the show, performing BDP's "I'm Still #1" to an astounded crowd. The outburst had come in reaction to comments Be had made in *Details* magazine questioning Kris' "teacher" status. In the aftermath, KRS would catch a shitstorm of bad press that scrutinized how the man who penned "Stop The Violence" could resort to such uncivilized behavior. And although the beef between KRS and Be was eventually squashed, PM Dawn's career never fully recovered from the attention garnered from the unfortunate incident.

3. **LL Cool J vs. Kool Moe Dee**
   At the height of the LL Cool J/Kool Moe Dee rivalry, the two came face-to-face in, of all places, St. Louis, MI. Performing on rival tours crisscrossing the country simultaneously in 1988, LL Cool J had a rare night off and decided to check out the old school legend's show. In the midst of one of Moe Dee's songs, an animated LL briefly strutted on stage, walked by Moe and began blowing kisses to the crowd, causing bedlam in the arena. But when Moe attempted to confront him, LL was nowhere to be found. After continuing with his set, Moe later located LL standing in the audience. Moe placed the spotlight on his young

nemesis and challenged him to a battle. The offer was refused so Moe went into his card-pulling LL disfest, "Let's Go." Upon finishing the song, he slammed the mic down and claimed himself the victor.

4. **Ol' Dirty Bastard vs. Doug E. Fresh**
5. **Ol' Dirty Bastard vs. Akinyele**
6. **Ol' Dirty Bastard vs. The Roots**
   The 1998 Grammy Awards ceremony was not the first time Wu-Tang's incomparable Ol' Dirty Bastard elected to bum rush a show. In fact, by that point ODB had become legendary for snatching the spotlight away from other performers.
   At the 1995 *Vibe* Music Seminar party, Doug E. Fresh was doing his world's greatest entertainer thang when the uninvited ODB crashed the stage and refused to leave until security assisted him away. A year later at the annual How Can I Be Down? summit in Miami, ODB was invited to perform at Uncle Luke's party. Again, he refused to leave when his time was up, prompting fellow raunchy vocalist Akinyele (whose performance was to follow) to become visibly upset. The two engaged in a scuffle that led to shots being fired in the air, but no one was hurt. Finally, Dirty repeated his appearing act at a Roots show at New York's Irving Plaza in 1996. What began as Dirty's impromptu speech bigging up the group, once again degenerated into another shoving match set to shouts of disapproval from the audience.

7. **Treach vs. De La Soul**
   Angered over a lyrical reference from De La Soul's *Stakes Is High* intro (Posdnuos: "Stick to your Naughty By Nature's and your Kane"), Treach approached the stage at the group's show on September 7, 1996 at New York's Palladium. The Jersey-bred muscleman was in the midst of bear-hugging Pos when security separated the two. Claiming that Treach misinterpreted the lyric's meaning, De La and their then-labelmate later quietly mended their differences.

8. **2Pac vs. A Tribe Called Quest**
   At the historic first annual *The Source* Awards in 1994, coastal tensions were already high. Matters were made even worse when A Tribe Called Quest's acceptance speech for its Artist Of The Year award was rudely interrupted by the start of 2Pac's musical performance. Actually, Mr. Controversy wasn't at fault this time. It was the show's confused production staff (who had begun running Pac's DAT prematurely) that had cued him to hit the stage before Tip and company were through.

BEEF.

HATE ME NOW:
Sir Mix-A-Lot's 10 Signs That You're Being Player Hated.

1. Your name is Mix. John loves Kathy. Kathy fucks Mix. John slashes Mix's tires!

2. You drive a Benz. You love soul food. The four niggas standin' in the doorway at the restaurant key your shit while you're eatin'.

3. When you was broke, muthafuckas was calling you a cool-ass brotha. After your first check, you're a punk-ass sell-out!

4. Whenever you use a word with more than one syllable, they call you "Uncle Tom."

5. Your name is MC Hammer and every broke-ass, wannabe rapper hates your guts cuz yo' ass is paid.

6. When you walk in a club you can overhear women saying, "Oooh, that's him," and you overhear men saying, "Ah, I knew that nigga when he was jackin' for bus fare!"

7. You hear the famous player hater quote: "Ah, fuck him. He ain't never did nothin' for me."

8. You shake a female's hand in public and her man whips her ass in the parking lot.

9. Some hip hop magazine starts talking shit about you in order to look like their way is the way to "true rap."

10. Your song is #1 and the nine songs under you are all songs about you.

THE FINAL WORD: Remember, the biggest baller is the target of all would-be-ballers!!!

Through hits like "Baby Got Back" and "Put 'Em On The Glass," Seattle's Sir Mix-A-Lot earned fancy cars, trunk jewelry, tons o' guns and exotic women feeding him grapes well before anybody else in the rap game. And you hated him for it.

1. **"Ain't No Burner"—Street Smartz (Tru Criminal, 1996)**
   ANSWER TO: "Ain't No Nigga"—Jay-Z featuring Foxy Brown (Roc-A-Fella, 1996)

2. **"Bad Girls"—Betty Boo And Ms. Thang (Starlite, 1985)**
   ANSWER TO: "Bad Boys"—Bad Boys featuring K Love (Starlite, 1985)

3. **"E-vette's Revenge"—E-vette Money (Slice, 1986)**
   ANSWER TO: "Dear Yvette"—LL Cool J (Def Jam, 1985)

4. **"A Fly Guy"—Pebblee Poo (Profile, 1985)**
   ANSWER TO: "A Fly Girl"—Boogie Boys (Capitol, 1985)

5. **"A Fly Guy"—Sweet Trio (Tommy Boy, 1985)**
   ANSWER TO: "A Fly Girl"—Boogie Boys (Capitol, 1985)

6. **"Fuck Me Now"—Willie D (Rap-A-Lot, 1989)**
   ANSWER TO: "How Ya Like Me Now"—Kool Moe Dee (Jive, 1987)

7. **"Games Females Play"—Gigolette (Fever, 1983)**
   ANSWER TO: "Games People Play"—Sweet G (Fever, 1983)

8. **"Goya"—MC Mitchski (Ski, 1987)**
   ANSWER TO: "Latoya"—Just-Ice (Fresh, 1986)

9. **"Guys Ain't Nothing But Trouble"—Ice Cream Tee (Word Up, 1986)**
   ANSWER TO: "Girls Ain't Nothing But Trouble"—DJ Jazzy Jeff & The Fresh Prince (Word Up, 1986)

10. **"It's Mine"—Pretty Ricky & Boo-Ski (Select, 1985)**
    ANSWER TO: "It's Yours"—T La Rock & Jazzy Jay (Party Time, 1984)

11. **"L.A., L.A."—Capone-N-Noreaga featuring Mobb Deep & Tragedy (25 To Life, 1995)**
    ANSWER TO: "New York, New York"—Tha Dogg Pound featuring Snoop Doggy Dogg (Death Row, 1995)

12. **"My Filas"—Fresh Gordon (Tommy Boy, 1986)**
    ANSWER TO: "My Adidas"—Run-D.M.C. (Profile, 1986)

13. **"No Show"—Symbolic Three (Reality, 1986)**
    ANSWER TO: "The Show"—Doug E. Fresh & The Get Fresh Crew (Reality, 1985)

BEEF.

14. **"Oh! Veronica"—Glamour Girls featuring Craig G (Pop Art, 1986)**
ANSWER TO: "Veronica"—Bad Boys featuring K Love (Starlite, 1985)

15. **"One Love"—Cornega (Def Jam promo, 1998)**
ANSWER TO: "One Love"—Nas (Columbia, 1994)

16. **"She's A Skeezer"—Fresh Force (b/k/a Kid 'N Play) (Sutra, 1986)**
ANSWER TO: "My Adidas"—Run-D.M.C. (Profile, 1986)

17. **"The Show Stoppa (Is Stupid Fresh)" —Super Nature (b/k/a Salt-N-Pepa) (Pop Art, 1985)**
ANSWER TO: "The Show"—Doug E. Fresh & The Get Fresh Crew (Reality, 1985)

18. **"So You Think You Got 'Em Locked"— The PreC.I.S.E. M.C. featuring Super Lover Cee (Luke, 1991)**
ANSWER TO: "Girls I Got 'Em Locked"— Super Lover Cee & Casanova Rud (Elektra, 1988)

19. **"Sucker DJs (I Will Survive)"—Dimples D (Partytime, 1983)**
ANSWER TO: "Sucker MCs"—Run-D.M.C. (Profile, 1983)

20. **"Take Your Radio"—Steady B (Pop Art, 1985)**
ANSWER TO: "I Can't Live Without My Radio"—LL Cool J (Def Jam, 1985)

21. **"Who Been There, Who Done That?" —J-Flex (Death Row, 1996)**
ANSWER TO: "Been There Done That"— Dr. Dre (Aftermath, 1996)

22. **"Why Should I Fuck U Fa Free?"—Choclatt featuring Akinyele (Shot Callas, 1998)**
ANSWER TO: "Fuck Me For Free" —Akinyele (Stress, 1996)

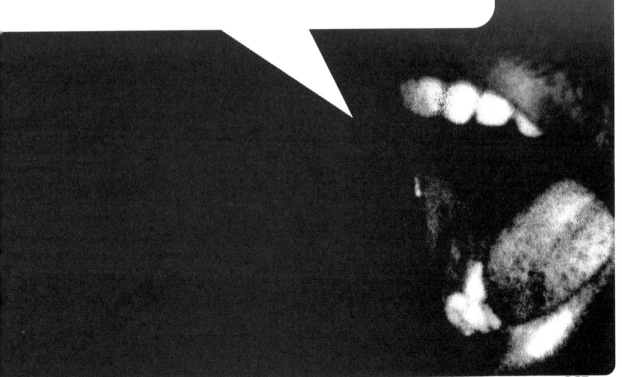

HIT 'EM UP:
5 Acts Of Random Violence Between Rappers.

1. **Above The Law vs. Ice Cube & Da Lench Mob**
   Music conventions are a great place for rappers to reach out and touch each other. Got beef? Travel 3,000 miles and settle that shit, son. That's what Eazy-E's archangels, Above The Law, did when they ran into Ice "Benedict Arnold" Cube and his Lench Mob associates at Tom Silverman's lavish summertime industry pow-wow, the 1990 New Music Seminar. The fight—which combusted into a chair-throwing frenzy before the festivities' concluding rap panel—placed rap music's acceptance at the NMS in serious jeopardy. Thankfully, cooler heads prevailed and a rap-inclusive seminar continued on for another four years.

2. **Double XX Posse vs. Live Squad**
   In 1993, at a CMJ showcase at New York club Wetlands, all hell broke loose when two of rap's toughest crews decided to tussle. This all-out brawl actually spilled out onto the Rotten Apple's mean streets outside of the club and prominent members of two other rap crews, Zhigge and The Pharcyde, got caught in the crossfire of fisticuffs.

3. **Dr. Dre vs. Dee Barnes**
   Upset over the editing of a *Pump It Up* episode in which Ice Cube dissed his former crew, N.W.A's good doctor attacked the show's host, Sista Dee, at a Bytches With Problems party in January 1991. This bitch-ass attack remains a blemish on the career of one of rap's most accomplished producers.

4. **Q-Tip vs. Wreckx-N-Effect**
   Upset over a perceived dis in Phife Dawg's lyric from A Tribe Called Quest's "Jazz (We've Got)" ("Strictly hardcore tracks/ Not a new jack swing"), Wreckx-N-Effect's thugged-out associates rushed Q-Tip on March 16, 1993 outside of a Naughty By Nature/ Run-D.M.C. concert at New York's Radio City Music Hall. In the scuffle, Tip suffered a serious eye jammie. Thankfully, two months later, the beef was officially squashed through the efforts of the Nation of Islam and Minister Conrad Muhammad.

5. **Tone-Lōc vs. Boo-Ya T.R.I.B.E.**
   During a 1991 Leaders Of The New School performance, L.A. turned into the Wild Wild West of old when cool cat Lōc lost his cool and decided to exchange bullets with Boo-Ya's band of fearless Samoans. Fortunately, no one got touched by the hot lead exchanges.

Unforgettable Video Disses.

1. **"Cowards In Compton"—Luke (Luke, 1993)**
   TARGET: Dr. Dre

2. **"Def Wish II"—Compton's Most Wanted (Orpheus, 1992)**
   TARGET: DJ Quik

3. **"Dre Day"—Dr. Dre featuring Snoop Doggy Dogg (Death Row, 1992)**
   TARGET: Eazy-E & Luke

4. **"The Gas Face"—3rd Bass featuring Zev Love X (Def Jam, 1989)**
   TARGET: MC Hammer

5. **"Get Money"—Junior M.A.F.I.A. featuring The Notorious B.I.G. (Undeas, 1995)**
   TARGET: Faith Evans (courtesy of Charli Baltimore)

6. **"Gone 'Til November (Remix)"—Wyclef Jean featuring Canibus (Ruffhouse, 1997)**
   TARGET: LL Cool J

7. **"King Of Rock"—Run-D.M.C. (Profile, 1985)**
   TARGET: The Beatles

8. **"L.A., L.A."—Capone-N-Noreaga featuring Mobb Deep & Tragedy (25 To Life, 1995)**
   TARGET: Tha Dogg Pound

9. **"No Fear"—Originoo Gunn Clappaz (Duck Down, 1996)**
   TARGETS: The Notorious B.I.G. & Foxy Brown

10. **"Pop Goes The Weasel"—3rd Bass (Def Jam, 1991)**
    TARGET: Vanilla Ice

11. **"Pump It Up (Here's The News)"—MC Hammer (Capitol, 1988)**
    TARGET: Run-D.M.C.

12. **"Rat Bastard"—Prime Minister Pete Nice & Daddy Rich (Def Jam, 1993)**
    TARGET: MC Serch

13. **"Second Round K.O."—Canibus (Universal, 1998)**
    TARGET: LL Cool J

14. **"Traveling At The Speed Of Thought"—Ultramagnetic MC's (Next Plateau, 1988)**
    TARGETS: Kool Moe Dee, LL Cool J & Slick Rick

15. **"Whoop! Whoop!"—DJ Pooh featuring Kam (Da Bomb, 1997)**
    TARGET: Ice Cube

BEEF.

Shit That Rappers Do That Gets On Fat Joe's Nerves.

1. **Not Payin' Dues.**
I don't wanna wish nobody bad, but I don't like it when muthafuckas who didn't pay dues sell records; muthafuckas who are overnight successes and don't appreciate what they got; niggas who got the momentum their way and they're sellin' mad records and they've never been through the struggle or nuthin'.

2. **Suckas Who Need Bodyguards.**
Another thing that makes me mad about rappers is when they come out and they all humble and shit. Next thing you know, they blow up and they got a lil' money and they hire a crew. They start hangin' with niggas who ain't really down wit' them like that and they start actin' like something they're not.

3. **Muthafuckas Who Don't Try To Be Themselves.**
It bothers me when rappers sound like other rappers. Yo, niggas be bitin', yo. Like how can niggas try to rap and sound just like Bone Thugs-N-Harmony? You hear Cam'Ron come out wit' that lil' fast style, the next thing you know you hear three rappers *serious-lyyyyy* tryin' to sound just like him. What the fuck do they think this is? Then you got rappers like Foxy Brown tryin' to sound like Lil' Kim all of a sudden—you know, *just like her*! It's just incredible.

4. **Forgettin' The Old School.**
Muthafuckas can throw a jam payin' tribute to all the old school artists who paved the way for us and no new rapper'll show up. Niggas don't care about them no more. Niggas is just carin' about money. Niggas overseas is studyin' our fuckin' culture more than we are. These niggas here don't even understand what we got. Today's rappers don't pay homage.

5. **Not Movin' The Crowd.**
I hate to see wack shows. Niggas back in the days used to put on a show. Back in the days there wasn't even records. Hip hop started out to see who rocked what jam the most. And niggas' names spread through word of mouth through the city. Right now niggas is like, "That's the muthafucka that I pump in my jeep deck." I'm like, "Word? Doin' a wack show like that?" I just think a performer has to let out a certain energy if you want the crowd to give you back the energy.

6. **Not Comin' With Lyrics.**
The rap game is different now. It ain't just about the lyrics no more. Right now I like the music down south, but they not into lyrics like that. Today I was in traffic and I seen a bum walkin' by wit' headphones and shit. A homeless nigga. And he was singin' like, *"It ain't my fault/ Did I do that?"*
    I guess it's just some fun shit now. Like with Noreaga, I don't think he's the best lyricist in the world. But niggas love Noreaga. And I love Noreaga. I wanna hear some Noreaga shit. But it's not about who got the deepest lyrics and shit like it used to be.

7. **Fakin' Jacks.**
The main thing that gets me upset is when rappers claim to be what they not—when they say that they thugs, they killers, they hustlers, then you look up what area they from and them niggas got no credibility whatsoever. These niggas never done shit. They all pussy. It's the whole contradiction in rap. I had to learn the hard way that rap is just entertainment. I wish rap woulda been all real—that whatever you say in your lyrics is real. But it's not. So, fuck all rappers.

After paying dues for years in New York's underground scene, Fat Joe celebrated his first gold LP with 1998's Don Cartagena. *This Boogie Down Bronx bomber talks the talk and walks the walk. And he's never been a shook one.*

52 Disses You Might Have Missed.*

"Advertisement"—King Tee (MCA, 1994)
TARGET: Luke

"A.W.O.L."—RBX (Premeditated, 1995)
TARGET: Dr. Dre

"Beat Biter"—MC Shan (Bridge, 1986)
TARGET: LL Cool J

"Beatin' Down KRS"—Butchy B (Groovy Move, 1988)
TARGET: KRS-One

"Biters In The City"—Fantasy Three (CCL, 1983)
TARGET: Crash Crew

"Brooklyn Blew Up The Bridge"—MC Mitchski (Ski, 1987)
TARGET: MC Shan

"Burning Bridges"—The UBC (EMI, 1990)
TARGET: Audio Two

"Crazy Like A Foxxx"—Freddie Foxxx (Flavor Unit, 1994)
TARGET: Ultramagnetic MC's

"Daze In A Weak (Remix)"—MC Serch (Def Jam, 1993)
TARGET: Prime Minister Pete Nice

"Diss Fe Liar"—YZ (Tuff City, 1990)
TARGET: Wise Intelligent

"Duck Alert"—Marley Marl featuring Craig G (Cold Chillin', 1988)
TARGET: Kool DJ Red Alert

"Gangstrology"—H.W.A. (Drive By, 1990)
TARGETS: N.W.A & Tairrie B.

"Get At Me"—DJ Quik (Profile, 1995)
TARGET: AMG

"Get At Me Dog"—DMX featuring Sheek (The Lox) (Def Jam, 1998)
TARGET: K-Solo

"Get Off The Rhythm"—Tony D featuring YZ (Sure Shot, 1989)
TARGETS: Big Daddy Kane, Lakim Shabazz, Gang Starr & Flavor Unit

"Going For The Throat"—Craig G (Atlantic, 1991)
TARGET: MC Shan

17. "Head Or Gut"—Illegal (Rowdy, 1993)
TARGET: Chi Ali

18. "Horse & Carriage (Remix)"—Cam'Ron featuring Big Punisher, Charli Baltimore, Silkk The Shocker & Wyclef Jean (Untertainment, 1998)
TARGET: Ma$e (courtesy of Charli Baltimore)

19. "I Get Rough"—Mikey D & The L.A. Posse (Public, 1987)
TARGET: LL Cool J

20. "I'll Wax Anybody"—Tim Dog (Ruffhouse, 1991)
TARGET: Monie Love

21. "It's All Good"—MC Hammer (Giant, 1994)
TARGET: Black Sheep

22. "It's On"—Naughty By Nature (Tommy Boy, 1993)
TARGET: Sir Mix-A-Lot

23. "Let's Start Over"—Freestyle Fellowship (Sun, 1991)
TARGET: The L.A. Dream Team

24. "Live By Yo Rep (B.O.N.E. Dis)"—Three 6 Mafia (Prophet, 1995)
TARGET: Bone Thugs-N-Harmony

25. "Man Down"—Mobb Deep featuring Big Noyd (Loud, 1996)
TARGET: Def Squad

26. "M.U.G."—O.C. featuring Freddie Foxxx (Payday, 1997)
TARGET: Boot Camp Clik

27. "New York Love (All Eyez On Sun)"—Sun Dullah (b/k/a King Sun) & Doo Wop (Tape Kingz, 1996)
TARGET: Death Row Records

28. "The Next Level"—Show & AG (Payday, 1995)
TARGET: Lords Of The Underground

29. "Nothin' To Lose (Naughty Live)"—Naughty By Nature (Tommy Boy, 1997)
TARGET: Radio personality Wendy Williams

30. "1,2,3"—Naughty By Nature featuring Lakim Shabazz & Apache (Tommy Boy, 1991)
TARGET: YZ (courtesy of Treach)

31. "Paul's Revenge"—De La Soul (Tommy Boy, 1993)
TARGET: Prince Paul

32. **"Pissin' On Your Steps"—Del The Funkeé Homosapien (Elektra, 1991)**
TARGETS: MC Hammer & Vanilla Ice

33. **"Record Haters"—E-40 (Jive, 1996)**
TARGETS: AZ & NBA forward Rasheed Wallace*

34. **"Rhyme Fighter"—Mellow Man Ace (Capitol, 1989)**
TARGET: Eazy-E

35. **"Rollin' Wit The Lench Mob"—Ice Cube (Priority, 1990)**
TARGET: KRS-One

36. **"$ad Millionaire"—Luniz (Noo Trybe, 1997)**
TARGET: Master P

37. **"Scenario (Remix)"—A Tribe Called Quest featuring Kid Hood & Leaders Of The New School (Jive, 1991)**
TARGET: Vanilla Ice (courtesy of Phife Dawg)

38. **"Sons Of 3rd Bass"—3rd Bass (Def Jam, 1989)**
TARGET: Beastie Boys

39. **"Steady Fucking"—MC Lyte (First Priority, 1993)**
TARGET: Roxanne Shanté

40. **"Thugz Cry"—Bizzy Bone (Ruthless, 1998)**
TARGET: Tomica Wright (Eazy-E's wife)

41. **"To Live & Die In L.A."—Makaveli (Death Row, 1996)**
TARGET: Dr. Dre

42. **"Toss It Up"—Makaveli (Death Row, 1996)**
TARGETS: Dr. Dre, Lil' Kim & Sean "Puffy" Combs

43. **"The Truth"—Grandmaster Melle Mel & The Furious Five (Sugar Hill, 1984)**
TARGET: Run-D.M.C.

44. **"Warm It Up Kane"—Big Daddy Kane (Cold Chillin', 1989)**
TARGET: Mr. Magic

45. **"Whatever"—Jeru The Damaja (Payday, 1996)**
TARGET: Blahzay Blahzay

46. **"What We Go Through"—Warren G featuring Mr. Malik, Perfec & Bad Azz (Def Jam, 1997)**
TARGET: LL Cool J (courtesy of Warren G)

47. **"Whoop! Whoop!"—DJ Pooh featuring Kam (Da Bomb, 1997)**
TARGET: Ice Cube

48. **"Worldwide"—Royal Flush (Blunt, 1997)**
TARGET: Tha Dogg Pound

49. **"The Wrong Nigga To Fuck Wit"—Ice Cube (Priority, 1991)**
TARGET: Wreckx-N-Effect

50. **"Yo Baby"—Grandmaster Flash & The Furious Five (Elektra, 1988)**
TARGETS: Beastie Boys, LL Cool J, Run-D.M.C. & Whodini

51. **"You Ain't Shit"—Tim Dog (Ruffhouse, 1991)**
TARGETS: Kid 'N Play, Kwamé, Young MC & MC Hammer ("A wack-ass rapper, but a dope-ass dancer.")

52. **"You Better Ask Somebody"—Yo Yo featuring Ice Cube (EastWest, 1993)**
TARGET: Roxanne Shanté

*Excludes the entire Ultramagnetic MC's catalog because their disses travel faster than the speed of thought.

BEEF.

9 IN THE CHAMBER:
Dis Songs That Were Never Commercially Released.

1. **"Big Momma Thang (Original Version)"—Lil' Kim**
   TARGET: 2Pac

2. **"Can-I-Bitch"—Truck Turner**
   TARGET: Canibus

3. **"Death Row Killers"—Snoop Doggy Dogg**
   TARGET: Suge Knight

4. **"Friends"—Jeru The Damaja**
   TARGET: Gang Starr Foundation

5. **"A Million And One Questions (Original Remix)"—Jay-Z**
   TARGETS: Foxy Brown, Sean "Puffy" Combs & various industry player haters

6. **"Never Personal (Fuck Nas)"—Cormega**
   TARGET: Nature

7. **"The Set Up"—The Lady Of Rage featuring Heather B. & Nikki D**
   TARGET: Foxy Brown (courtesy of Heather B.)

8. **"Top Ten List"—Masta Ace**
   TARGET: Fat Joe

9. **"What's All This Hey Ho Shit?"—YZ**
   TARGET: Treach (Naughty By Nature)

Makaveli's Most Venomous Unreleased Dis Records.

1. **"Bad Boy Killaz"**
   TARGETS: Bad Boy Records & Mobb Deep

2. **"Money On My Mind"**
   TARGETS: Mobb Deep, Jay-Z & Dr. Dre

3. **"My Lil' Homies"**
   TARGETS: Junior M.A.F.I.A. & LL Cool J

4. **"When We Ride On Our Enemies"**
   TARGETS: Fugees, Mobb Deep, Da Brat & Bad Boy Records

5. **"Why You Turn On Me"**
   TARGETS: Radio personality Wendy Williams & Havoc (Mobb Deep)

The ego trip Shit List.

1. Shark niggas.
2. "Funny" magazines and writers.
3. Incompetent publicists who can't communicate our ideas properly to their artists.
4. Rap, an unorganized mess, that nothing—not even this book—can clean up properly.
5. People who make false promises.
6. Sleazy magazine publishers.
7. Fake-ass music industry fucks.
8. Rudolph Giuliani.
9. Conniving exotic dancers.
10. Everything else you can possibly think of.

THE REAL

NESS.

CONCRETE JINGLES:
Songs About The Projects.

1. "The Bridge"—MC Shan (Bridge, 1986)
2. "In The PJs"—Big Daddy Kane (MCA, 1994)
3. "Life In The Projects"—U.T.F.O. (Jive, 1991)
4. "Livin In The Project"—Juvenile (Cash Money, 1997)
5. "No Wonduh (The Projects)"—Diamond D (Mercury, 1997)
6. "Once Upon A Time In The Projects"—Ice Cube (Priority, 1990)
7. "On In The Projects"—OFTB (Big Beat, 1992)
8. "Project Hallways"—Mobb Deep (4th & B'way, 1993)
9. "Project Ho"—MC Shan (Cold Chillin', 1987)
10. "Projects"—Wu-Tang Clan (Loud, 1997)
11. "The Projects"—The Dead (4.5.14, 1998)
12. "The Projects"—Pooh-Man (Jive, 1992)
13. "Where I'm From"—Jay-Z (Roc-A-Fella, 1998)

WHITEY, TAKE NOTE: Beastie Boys' "Live At P.J.'s" (Capitol, 1992) is not about the projects.

JAILHOUSE RAP:
Albums That Were Released While The Artists Or Group Members Were Incarcerated.

1. *Ain't No Love*—Pooh-Man (In-A-Minute, 1994)
2. *Behind Bars*—Slick Rick (Def Jam, 1994)
3. *Da Dirty 30*—Cru (Def Jam, 1997): Mighty Ha
4. *F.B.I.*—The Dayton Family (Relativity, 1996): Bootleg
5. *Intoxicated Demons* The EP—The Beatnuts (Relativity, 1993): Fashion (b/k/a Al Tariq)
6. *Lifers Group*—Lifers Group (Hollywood BASIC, 1991)
7. *Living Proof*—Lifers Group (Hollywood BASIC, 1993)
8. *Me Against The World*—2Pac (Interscope, 1995)*
9. *Off Parole*—Rappin' 4-Tay (Chrysalis, 1996)
10. *The Ruler's Back*—Slick Rick (Def Jam, 1991)
11. *The War Report*—Capone-N-Noreaga (Penalty, 1997): Capone**
12. *Xorcist*—X-Raided (Black Market, 1996)***

*The first artist with an album to hit #1 while he was in the joint.
**Originally met partner, Noreaga, years before while both were serving bids.
***Vocals were recorded over the phone while X-Raided was incarcerated, where he remains today.

THE REALNESS.

12 Pieces Of Suggested "Evidence" That 2Pac Is Still Alive.

1. Photographs were never released of 2Pac in the hospital in Las Vegas after the reported "shooting."

2. Despite a plethora of lyrics in which he rhymes about being "buried" upon his demise, 2Pac's body was allegedly "cremated" the day after his "death." Funeral services were canceled in both Los Angeles and Atlanta, and there was no viewing of his body.

3. In the video for the song, "I Ain't Mad At Cha" (Death Row, 1996), released shortly after his "death," 2Pac is presciently portrayed as an angel in heaven, thus suggesting that when he created the video he had already planned to stage his own "demise."

4. For *Don Killuminati: The 7 Day Theory* (Death Row, 1996), released two months after his "death," 2Pac adopted the alias Makaveli in homage to Niccolo Machiavelli, the late-15th century/early-16th century Italian political philosopher. Machiavelli's treatise, *The Prince*, advocates the faking of one's own death as a means of combating one's enemies.

5. The title, *The 7 Day Theory*, reflects the chronology of 'Pac's staged "death." 2Pac was "shot" on September 7, and survived on the 7th, 8th, 9th, 10th, 11th, 12th, and "died" on the 13th.

6. At the conclusion of *The 7 Day Theory*, 2Pac is shot dead, also foreshadowing his own real-life "assassination."

7. In the video for "To Live & Die In L.A." (Death Row, 1996), 2Pac is wearing the newest edition of the Nike Air Jordans. However, the shoes were not released by Nike until November—two months after his "death" in September. Also, in the video for "Toss It Up" (Death Row, 1996), 2Pac sports a pair of Penny Hardaway sneakers which were also not available until after the time of his "death."

8. In the photograph for the ad promoting Fatal's *In The Line Of Fire* (Relativity, 1998), Fatal and 2Pac are seen hugging in an unspecified location that resembles an exotic locale (perhaps Cuba), thus supporting the theory that 2Pac is in exile.

9. On 2Pac's *Greatest Hits* (Death Row, 1998), 'Pac states, "Rest in peace to my nigga, Biggie Smalls," at the opening of "God Bless The Dead." 2Pac, however, was supposedly "murdered" six months before The Notorious B.I.G.'s death.

10. Bay Area rapper Richie Rich's *Seasoned Veteran* (Def Jam, 1996), was released on the same day as *The 7 Day Theory*. On the 2Pac duet, "Niggas Done Changed," 2Pac rhymes, "I've been shot and murdered/ Can't tell you how it happened word for word/ But best believe that niggas gonna get what they deserve." These lyrics suggest that 2Pac had planned his "death" to occur by the time of *Seasoned Veteran*'s release.

11. Bone Thugs-N-Harmony's *The Art Of War* (Relativity, 1997) features a 2Pac duet entitled "Thug Luv." At the conclusion of Bizzy Bone's verse (1:15 into the song), his voice can be heard in the background chanting, "He's alive, he's alive, he's alive."

12. Real niggas don't die.

Bönz Malone's Real Nigga Rules 4 Life.

1. Anyone who will get you killed is your enemy.
2. Real niggas study conventional wisdom.
3. Real niggas shun conventional wisdom.
4. The last "a" in "gangsta" is for amateurism.
5. Potential threats don't speak.
6. Power is not what you can have done, it's what you can get done despite opposition and resistance.
7. Success is a journey, not a destination.
8. To become truly great, help others achieve greatness.
9. Real niggas build themselves into commodities by lifting with their heads, which builds the mind.
10. Real niggas don't have to keep it real, they keep it to themselves.

While herb new jack rap journalists come and go, Ambassador Bönz Malone remains a made man. You wanna great read? Give him an hour plus a pen and a pad. His acclaimed works have appeared in Vibe, The Source and Spin, and he is the screenwriter and co-star of the award-winning motion picture, Slam.

NIGGA PLEASE:
99 "Nigga" Songs.

1. "Ain't No Nigga"—Jay-Z featuring Foxy Brown (Roc-A-Fella, 1996)
2. "All These Niggaz Crazy"—DJ DMD (Inner Soul, 1997)
3. "Alotta Niggas"—Ice-T (Rhyme Syndicate, 1996)
4. "Another Nigger In The Morgue"—Geto Boys (Rap-A-Lot, 1991)
5. "Another Wild Nigger From The Bronx"—Fat Joe (Relativity, 1993)
6. "Anti-Nigger Machine"—Public Enemy (Def Jam, 1990)
7. "Bang On Niggas"—Dosia (Awol, 1998)
8. "Black Nigga Killa"—Eazy-E (Ruthless, 1998)
9. "Broke Ass Niggas"—Grandmaster Melle Mel & Scorpio (Str8 Game, 1997)
10. "Broke Niggaz"—Luniz featuring Knucklehead & Eclipse (Noo Trybe, 1995)
11. "Bronx Nigga"—Tim Dog (Ruffhouse, 1991)
12. "But Can You Kill The Nigger In You?"—Chuck D (Mercury, 1996)
13. "Check For A Nigga"—Cappadonna (Razor Sharp, 1998)
14. "Clinic Niggaz"—Above The Law (Tommy Boy, 1998)
15. "Crazy Lil' Nigga"—Bloods & Crips (Dangerous, 1993)
16. "Daddy Called Me Niga Cause I Likeded To Rhyme"—Young Black Teenagers (MCA, 1991)
17. "Dat's My Nigga"—Maestro Fresh Wes (LMR, 1994)
18. "The Day The Niggaz Took Over"—Dr. Dre featuring Daz Dillinger, Snoop Doggy Dogg & RBX (Death Row, 1992)
19. "Definition Of A Thug Nigga"—2Pac (Epic, 1993)
20. "Die Nigger Die"—Schoolly D (Capitol, 1991)
21. "Dog Ass Nigga"—Gregory D (RCA, 1992)
22. "Down Goes Anotha Nigga"—B.G. Knocc Out & Dresta (OutBurst, 1995)
23. "Down With My Nigga"—Paradise (Epic, 1992)
24. "Eclipsin' Niggas"—Punk Barbarians (Lethal, 1996)
25. "Field Nigguhz In A Huddle"—Professor Griff (Lethal, 1998)
26. "Fly Nigga Hill Figga"—M.O.P. (Relativity, 1998)
27. "Flypn' Nygaz Like Ounces"—JT The Bigga Figga (Get Low, 1995)
28. "4 Nigg's In 1"—The Hard Boyz (Big Beat, 1996)
29. "Tha Frustrated Nigga"—Jeru The Damaja (Avatar, 1995)
30. "Fuck Dat Nigga"—Richie Rich (Shot, 1996)
31. "Fuck Nigga"—The New 2 Live Crew (Luke, 1993)
32. "Gimme Your Shit Nigga"—Schoolly D (Ruffhouse, 1994)
33. "Highest Niggaz In The Industry"—Luniz featuring E-40 & B-Legit (Noo Trybe, 1997)
34. "House Nigga's"—Boogie Down Productions (Jive, 1990)
35. "House Niggas Bleed Too"—Paris (Scarface, 1992)
36. "How Many Niggas Wanna Get With This"—Sinister (Interscope, 1994)
37. "I Ain't The Nigga"—The Coup (Wild Pitch, 1993)
38. "I Don't Wanna Be Called Yo Niga"—Public Enemy (Def Jam, 1991)
39. "I'm That Type Of Nigga"—The Pharcyde (Delicious Vinyl, 1992)
40. "Jeep Ass Niguh"—Masta Ace (Delicious Vinyl, 1993)
41. "Knockin' Niggaz Off"—Das EFX (EastWest, 1995)
42. "Let My Niggas Out Tha Pen"—Mad CJ Mac (Rap-A-Lot, 1995)
43. "Live Nigga Rap"—Nas featuring Mobb Deep (Columbia, 1996)

THE REALNESS.

44. "Made Niggas"—Mack 10 featuring Master P & Mystikal (Hoo Bangin', 1998)
45. "Made Niggaz"—2Pac featuring The Outlawz (Death Row, 1997)
46. "Mafia Niggaz"—Marvaless (Awol, 1998)
47. "My Kinda Nigga"—Heather B. featuring M.O.P. (EMI, 1996)
48. "My Kinda Nigga Part II"—M.O.P. featuring Heather B. (Relativity, 1998)
49. "My Nigga's Crazy"—Indo G (Relativity, 1998)
50. "Nann Nigga"—Trick Daddy featuring Trena (Slip-N-Slide, 1998)
51. "New Niggas"—The Legion (Mercury, 1994)
52. "Next Niggas Ho"—3X Krazy (Noo Trybe, 1997)
53. "Nickel Slick Nigga"—Who Am I? (Ruthless, 1991)
54. "Nigga Bridges"—Onyx (Def Jam, 1993)
55. "Nigga Code"—Original Flavor (Atlantic, 1993)
56. "Nigga For Hire"—Hard Knocks (Wild Pitch, 1992)
57. "Nigga Nigga Nigga"—Skull Duggery (No Limit, 1996)
58. "Niggas And Flies"—Geto Boys (Rap-A-Lot, 1996)
59. "Niggas Bleed"—The Notorious B.I.G. (Bad Boy, 1997)
60. "Niggas Come In All Colors"—L.A. Posse (Atlantic, 1991)
61. "Niggas Don't Give A Fuck"—Tha Dogg Pound (Epic, 1993)
62. "Nigga Sings The Blues"—Spice 1 (Jive, 1994)
63. "The Nigga Ya Love To Hate"—Ice Cube (Priority, 1990)
64. "Niggaz And Jewz"—Blood Of Abraham (Ruthless, 1993)
65. "Niggaz Make The Hood Go Round"—MC Eiht (Epic, 1994)
66. "Niggaz My Height Don't Fight"—Eazy-E (Ruthless, 1992)
67. "Niggonometry"—Canibus (Universal, 1998)
68. "Nigguz Will Be Nigguz"—Papa Chuk (Pendulum, 1994)
69. "Nuttin' Ass Nigga"—E-40 (Sick Wid It, 1993)
70. "Prodigy Of A Nigga"—Duce Duce (Delicious Vinyl, 1995)
71. "Real Niggas"—C-Bo (Awol, 1998)
72. "Real Niggas"—Mac Dre (Romp, 1997)
73. "Real Niggaz"—Jay-Z featuring Too $hort (Roc-A-Fella, 1997)
74. "Real Niggaz"—N.W.A (Ruthless, 1990)
75. "Real Niggaz Don't Die"—N.W.A (Ruthless, 1991)
76. "Real Niggaz Makin' Noise"—Indo G & Lil' Blunt (Luke, 1994)
77. "Real Niggaz Up"—Heather B. (EMI, 1996)
78. "Rich Niggaz"—Juvenile (Cash Money, 1998)
79. "Rules 4 Real Nigga$"—Scarface (Rap-A-Lot, 1998)
80. "Scared Lil' Nigga"—Da Lench Mob (Priority, 1994)
81. "Shame On A Nigga"—Wu-Tang Clan (Loud, 1993)
82. "Still The Same Nigga"—MC Ren (Ruthless, 1996)
83. "St. Louis Niggas"—JCD & The Dawg LB. (Profile, 1992)
84. "Strictly 4 My N.I.G.G.A.Z . . ."—2Pac (Interscope, 1993)
85. "Sucka Nigga"—A Tribe Called Quest (Jive, 1993)
86. "Super Nigga"—King Tee featuring DJ Pooh & Rashad (MCA, 1994)
87. "Super Nigga"—Sylk Smoov (PWL America, 1991)
88. "Super Nigga"—Yall So Stupid (Rowdy, 1993)
89. "...er Nigger"—Schoolly D (Jive, 1989)
90. "Tha Triflin' Nigga"—King Tee (Capitol, 1991)
91. "That's The Nigga"—Mystikal (No Limit, 1998)
92. "The Wrong Nigga To Fuck Wit"—Ice Cube (Priority, 1991)
93. "Trigga Happy Aggin'"—Geto Boys (Rap-A-Lot, 1989)
94. "Trill Ass Nigga"—U.G.K. (Jive, 1992)
95. "We Be Dem Niggaz"—Pizzo (Awol, 1998)
96. "What A Niggy Know?"—K.M.D. (Elektra, 1994)
97. "Where's My Niggas At"—Hurricane (Grand Royal, 1995)
98. "Will A Nigga Make It"—Indo G (Relativity, 1998)
99. "Ya'll Niggas Ain't Ready"—Def Squad (Def Jam, 1998)

HONORABLE MENTION: *"Real Niggaz Do Real Things"—The Notorious B.I.G. (unreleased, 1995)

WHO ARE YOU CALLIN' A . . .
99 "Bitch" Songs.

1. "Ain't No Bitch In My Blood"—Indo G (Relativity, 1988)
2. "Ain't That A Bitch"—Kam (EastWest, 1993)
3. "Anotha Dead Bitch"—Reality (Revolutionary, 1997)
4. "Baby By The Wrong Bitch"—U.D.I. (Bay Rider, 1998)
5. "Bad Ass Bitch"—2 Live Crew (Luke, 1989)
6. "Be Mai Bitch"—AMG (Select, 1995)
7. "Da Bichez"—Jeru The Damaja (Payday, 1994)
8. "Big Bitch"—JCD & The Dawg LB. (Profile, 1992)
9. "B.I.T.C.H."—Passion (MCA, 1996)
10. "Bitch Betta Have My Money"—AMG (Select, 1991)
11. "Bitch Betta Have My Money"—Ja Rule (Def Jam, 1998)
12. "The Bitch Blues (Life Experiences)"—Prince Paul (WordSound, 1996)
13. "Bitches Ain't Shit"—Dr. Dre featuring Tha Dogg Pound, Snoop Doggy Dogg & Jewell (Death Row, 1992)
14. "Bitches Can't Ride For Free"—Damu Ridas (Dangerous, 1995)
15. "Bitches From Eastwick"—The Lox (Bad Boy, 1998)
16. "Bitches 2"—Ice-T (Sire, 1991)
17. "Bitchez"—The D.O.C. (Giant, 1996)
18. "Bitch Get A Job"—LB's (Livin' Large, 1992)
19. "The Bitch Girl I Hate"—Poison Clan (Luke, 1990)
20. "Bitch Haven"—Sylk Smoov (PWL America, 1991)
21. "Bitch I'm Through"—Jayo Felony (Def Jam, 1995)
22. "The Bitch In Yoo"—Common (Relativity, 1996)
23. "A Bitch Iz A Bitch"—N.W.A (Ruthless, 1989)
24. "Bitch Wit A Good Rap"—Sylk Smoov (PWL America, 1991)
25. "Black Beauty & The Bitch"—Professor Griff (Lethal, 1998)
26. "Booga Bandit Bitch"—Just-Ice (Fresh, 1987)
27. "Break-A-Bitch College"—Eightball & MJG (Suave

28. Brick Town Bitches —Diezzle Don & Tha Govener (Contract, 1995)
29. "Can't Trust No Bitch"—Dosia (Awol, 1998)
30. "Cave Bitch"—Ice Cube (Priority, 1993)
31. "Charge It 2 A Bitch"—Havoc & Prodeje (G.W.K., 1994)
32. "Check The Bitch"—Kool G Rap (Cold Chillin', 1996)
33. "Check Yo Bitch"—Pistol (Street Flavor, 1995)
34. "Crazybitchmadness"—The Conscious Daughters (Scarface, 1993)
35. "Djary Of A Mad Bitch"—Boss (Def Jam, 1993)
36. "Do Yo Bitch Got Luv"—Pistol (Street Flavor, 1995)
37. "Don't Give A Bitch An Inch"—O.C.U. (Kapone, 1991)
38. "Don't Need U Bitch"—Disco Rick (Luke, 1992)
39. "Don't Trust A Bitch"—Poetic Hustla'z (Relativity, 1997)
40. "Drunk Bitches"—Vell Bakardy (Wild West, 1995)
41. "Explanation Of A Mad Bitch"—Boss (DJ West, 1992)
42. "Fake Hair Wearin' Bitch"—No Face (RAL, 1990)
43. "Fat Bitches"—Kausion (Lench Mob, 1995)
44. "4 Star Bitch"—Big Ken (4th & B'way, 1992)
45. "Freaky Bitches"—Luke (Luther Campbell, 1996)
46. "Fuck A Bitch Cuz I'm Paid"—Master P (No Limit, 1992)
47. "Gangsta Bitch"—Apache (Tommy Boy, 1993)
48. "Gangsta Bitch"—Master P (No Limit, 1998)
49. "Gangsta Bitch"—Ram Squad (Bank, 1997)
50. "Get Off My Dick And Tell Yo Bitch To Come Here"—Ice Cube (Priority, 1990)
51. "Get That Bitch"—Da Organization (Wrap, 1997)
52. "I Ain't Yo Bitch"—Babygirl (Popular, 1997)
53. "I'm A Playa (Bitch)"—Penthouse Players Clique (Sire, 1992)
54. "I Rather Give You My Bitch"—Suga Free (Island, 1997)
55. "I Remember That Freak Bitch (From The Club)"—Cypress Hill (Ruffhouse, 1998)
56. "Irresistable Bitch"—Def Dames (Sedona, 1991)
57. "Just Cause I Called You A Bitch"—Rappin' 4-Tay (Chrysalis, 1994)
58. "Letter To The Bitch"—Derrick D. (Memphis International, 1997)
59. "Life Ain't Nothing But A Bitch"—Indo G & Lil' Blunt (Luke, 1994)
60. "Life Is A Bitch"—Magic (No Limit, 1998)
61. "Life's A Bitch"—Mac Dre (Romp, 1997)
62. "Life's A Bitch"—Nas featuring AZ (Columbia, 1994)
63. "Life's A Bitch"—Pudgee Tha Phat Bastard (Giant, 1993)
64. "Mackin' To Slob Bitches"—Bloods & Crips (Dangerous, 1993)
65. "Mai Sista Izza Bitch"—Boss (Def Jam, 1993)
66. "Me & My Bitch"—MC Eiht (Epic, 1997)
67. "Me & My Bitch"—The Notorious B.I.G. (Bad Boy, 1994)
68. "My Bitch"—Bushwick Bill (Ichiban, 1998)
69. "My Bitch"—The Delinquents (Priority, 1997)
70. "Nasty Bitch"—Bust Down (Luke, 1991)

72. "The Ole Bitch-U-Worryz"—Professor Griff (Lethal, 1998)
73. "One Less Bitch"—N.W.A (Ruthless, 1991)
74. "1-900-B-I-T-C-H-E-S"—H.W.A. (Drive By, 1990)
75. "Out Of Pocket Bitch"—Mac Vo (Relativity, 1995)
76. "Out Of Town Bitches"—Kane & Abel (No Limit, 1998)
77. "Out To The Bitches"—Pooh-Man (In-A-Minute, 1992)
78. "Pack Bitch"—Boogie (Relativity, 1994)
79. "Pimpinabitch"—Juvenile (Cash Money, 1997)
80. "Punk-Bitch Game"—Geto Boys (Rap-A-Lot, 1991)
81. "Queen Bitch"—Lil' Kim (Big Beat, 1996)
82. "Ratha Be Ya Bitch"—2Pac (Death Row, 1996)
83. "Ruthless Bitch"—Tairrie B. (MCA, 1990)
84. "Sick As A Bitch"—Black Czer (Relativity, 1994)
85. "Silly Bitch"—Tim Dog (Ruffhouse, 1993)
86. "Skanlezz Azz Bytchez"—Celly Cel (Sick Wid It, 1996)
87. "Sophisticated Bitch"—Public Enemy (Def Jam, 1987)
88. "Tell Ya 'Bout A Bitch"—JCD & Dawg LB. (Profile, 1992)
89. "Tramp Bitch"—Potna Duece (Profile, 1994)
90. "Trust No Bitch"—Penthouse Players Clique (Ruthless, 1992)
91. "Trust No Bitch"—Radio featuring Darq & Roc Chill (Interscope, 1994)
92. "Ugly Bitches"—Coolio (Tommy Boy, 1994)
93. "Uh! Real Bitch"—Awol (Bootstrap, 1994)
94. "U's A Bitch"—Compton's Most Wanted (Orpheus, 1992)
95. "Welfare Bitches"—Willie D (Rap-A-Lot, 1989)
96. "What Could Be Better Bitch"—Son Of Bazerk (MCA, 1991)
97. "When I Getta Bitch"—Sylk Smoov (PWL, 1991)
98. "Why I Gotta Be A Bitch"—Pooh-Man (In-A-Minute, 1994)
99. "Wonda Why They Call U Bitch"—2Pac (Death Row, 1996)

NBC:
Nigga-Bitch Connection.

1. "Bichasniguz"—Onyx (Def Jam, 1993)
2. "Bitch Ass Nigga"—Mobb Deep (4th & B'way, 1993)
3. "Bitch Made Nigga"—Shazzy (Elektra, 1993)
4. "Bitch Made Nigga Killa"—MC Ren (Ruthless, 1996)
5. "Bitch Made Niggas"—Family Ties featuring Kedash (Big Baller, 1998)
6. "Bitch Made Niggaz"—Marvaless (Awol, 1998)
7. "For All My Niggaz & Bitches"—Snoop Doggy Dogg featuring Tha Dogg Pound & The Lady Of Rage (Death Row, 1993)
8. "Niggas And Bitches"—Jayo Felony (Def Jam, 1995)

THE REALNESS.

MONEY IN THE BANK:
Freddie Foxxx's 10 Tips For Playing Ceelo.

1. **To Avoid Problems, Always Make The Rules Before You Start Gambling.**
A lot of times people try to make up extra rules to the game. To me, if the dice hits your foot and stops and you win, it's just as bad as if the dice hits your foot and it stops and you lose.

2. **Don't Over-Bet.**
I think ceelo's a dope way to come up. You just throw your nuts on the table, man. Sometimes you can rock, sometimes you can't. Don't over-bet, though. If the bank allows you to, start off low. See how the dice feel. Get a good roll in.

3. **See Who The Big Bettors Are.**
Feel out the circle. Try to shoot somewhere close to the big bettors. The way I like to play is I either like to shoot right after or right before the dealer shoots again. I don't wanna shoot in the middle wit' all them other cats.
    One time I was playin' wit' Treach and some cats from North Carolina. It was during the *19 Naughty III* album. This high roller dude comes into the game. He got alligator shoes on. He was throwin' hundred dollar bills on the floor. I rocked him for like maybe $3,000. Rocked him sweet. He dressed me for another week. Treach was laughin' his ass off cuz dude was talkin' a lot of shit. When I finished wit' that muthafucka he needed a bus ticket. And then we got on stage, we rocked and I left.

4. **Don't Get Into Games Where There's Too Many Guys.**
If there's like three guys shootin', I'm down. But I'll sit back and watch and let everybody get their money down before I get into the game.

5. **Make 'Em *Roll* The Dice.**
See, a lot of dudes try to put the dice a certain way and roll 'em. Some dudes don't roll the dice, they drop the dice. Don't let your opponent drop the dice. Some dudes shoot on carpet or hard floor. Hard floor to me is better. I can kill somebody on a carpet, though, because you don't get as much bounce. You gotta watch the weight of the dice.

6. **Don't Let Cats Just Jump In A Game.**
Say there's about six guys shootin' and there's $120 in the bank and you the seventh guy and you wanna get in. You can't come in the circle from right there and say, "Yo, stop the bank. I wanna shoot for that $120." I wouldn't allow it. He might be the lucky one to take all your money.

7. **Watch For Cheaters.**
I don't cheat so I really wouldn't know too many ways of cheatin'. You can have funny dice. But then again, after a while, you can't shoot that too long. The worst shit I ever did was one time I was playin' ceelo wit' six dudes and I lost all my money. So I waited 'til I found out who won all the money and I took all the money. Cuz I got pissed off and I was bein' a sore loser that day. So I robbed everybody. It wasn't a stick-up wit' no guns or nuthin'. It was strictly "Foxxx will kick me in my fuckin' head." But then I felt guilty after a while because I was cool wit' everybody there, so I gave the money back.

8. **Play Against Intoxicated Opponents.**
I don't get high, but I don't mind playin' against a drunk muthafucka. I'll give him a handful of ones and shit and he won't know the difference. A hustle is what it is.

9. **The Only Law That Matters Is The Law Of The Streets.**
I ain't never seen a rule that tells a muthafucka when you up quit. If that's how you wanna play, that becomes a principle thing. If you dealin' wit' a cat on the street and he wanna get a chance to win his money back, you might have to fight your way out the block. It comes back down to your skills.

10. **It's Strictly Luck.**
There's no way somebody can tell me, "I'm a roll ceelo three times in a row." Bullshit. It's strictly luck. If anybody tells you anything other than that, it's bullshit.

Freddie Foxxx is one of hip hop's most furious microphone annihilators. Don't test your luck with him.

BANGIN' ON WAX:

13 Gang-Related Rhymes.

1. "Act A Fool"—King Tee (Capitol, 1988)
"If you wanna roll, just wear neutral colors/ If anybody asks you, just tell 'em you're my brother."

2. "Anti-Nigger Machine"—Public Enemy (Def Jam, 1990)
Chuck D: "Went to Cali a rally was for a brother's death/ It was the fuzz who shot him and not the Bloods or Cuz."

3. "Colors"—Ice-T (Warner Bros., 1988)
"But my true mission is just revenge, you ain't my set, you ain't my friend/ Wear the wrong color your life could end, homicide is my favorite binge."

4. "The Day The Niggaz Took Over"—Dr. Dre featuring Daz Dillinger, Snoop Doggy Dogg & RBX (Death Row, 1992)
Dr. Dre: "Bloods, Crips on the same squad/ Wit' the éses helpin', nigga it's time to rob and mob."

5. "4th Chamber"—The Genius featuring Ghostface Killah, Killah Priest & RZA (Geffen, 1995)
Killah Priest: "Throw up signs like a Crip and throw all types of fit/ I'll leave 'em split like ass cheeks and rag pussy lips."

6. "Fuckin' Wit Uh House Party"—WC (Payday, 1998)
"I feel like a straight mark walkin' in the house gettin' punked by niggas too young to get in Magic Mountain/ So I roll back on 'em right on the spot, told 'em, 'Fuck your set!'/ That's when I heard the music stop."

7. "Hip Hop Drunkies"—Tha Alkaholiks featuring Ol' Dirty Bastard (Loud, 1997)
J-Ro: "Your lyrics are loners/ My styles are wild like G's,

DON'T MAKE THEM ANGRY:

8 Rappers With Certified Handskills.

1. Big Mike
2. E-A-Ski
3. Freddie Foxxx
4. Grandmaster Melle Mel
5. Just-Ice
6. K-Solo
7. Melachi The Nutcracker
8. Willie D

THE BIG BANG THEORY:

Rap Artists Who've Survived Shootings.

1. Beanie Siegel
2. Big Noyd
3. B-Real
4. Bushwick Bill
5. Capone
6. Dr. Dre
7. Dresta
8. Fat Joe
9. Ghostface Killah
10. Krumb Snatcha
11. LV
12. Ol' Dirty Bastard
13. Shyne
14. Slick Rick

THE REALNESS.

cholos and stoners."

8. "Hole In The Head"—Cypress Hill (Ruffhouse, 1991)
B-Real: "But this vato's rollin' up and they stickin' up the flag, he jumps out with the sag/ 'Hey, where you from, homes?' It's on, he sees him reachin' for his chrome, buckshot to the dome."

9. "Mathematics (Esta Loca)"—Noreaga (Penalty, 1998)
"Hey, yo, my family is half-Latin King, half-God Body/ Half-Blood and half-Ñeta, so nigga, *wepa.*"

10. "My Summer Vacation"—Ice Cube (Priority, 1991)
"Bust a cap and outta there in a hurry/ Wouldn't you know, a drive-by in Missouri."

11. "Runnin'"—The Pharcyde (Delicious Vinyl, 1995)
Fat Lip: "I can recall Crip niggas throwin' 'C's in my face down the hall or kickin' it in the back of the school eatin' chicken at three/ Wonderin', 'Why is everybody always pickin' on me?'"

12. "Super Nigga"—King Tee featuring DJ Pooh & Rashad (MCA, 1994)
Pooh: "I'm here to rid the city of the wack-ass groups, them wack-ass lyrics wit' them wack-ass loops/ They fakin' like gangstas, turn into a Crip tonight, they don't faze me cuz we can still fight."

13. "We Run N.Y."—Redman featuring Hurricane G (Def Jam, 1994)
Redman: "Eager as a nigga wantin' my shit to dub/ Cuz my shit be bangin' like the Crips and Bloods."

How About Some Hardcore Parodies?

1. "Afro Connections At A Hi 5 (In The Eyes Of The Hoodlum)"—De La Soul (Tommy Boy, 1991)
2. "Am Gon T' Jail"—Hawd Gankstuh Rappuh Emsees Wid Ghatz (WordSound, 1996)
3. "The Bullshit"—Jeru The Damaja (Payday, 1995)
4. "J.O.B.–Das What Dey Is!"—Prince Paul (WordSound, 1996)
5. "Pork"—The Pharcyde (Delicious Vinyl, 1993)
6. "Rapper's Delight"—CB4 (Hi-C, Daddy-O & Kool Moe Dee) (MCA, 1992)
7. "Slaughtahouse"—Masta Ace (Delicious Vinyl, 1993)
8. "Straight Out Of Locash"—CB4 (Hi-C & Daddy-O) (MCA, 1992)
9. "Sweat Of My Balls"—CB4 (Hi-C & Daddy-O) (MCA, 1992)
10. "U Mean I'm Not"—Black Sheep (Mercury, 1991)

WHEN WE REMINISCE OVER YOU:
10 Forgotten Guest Vocal Appearances
By The Notorious B.I.G....

1. "All Men Are Dogs (Remix)"—Bandit also featuring Pudgee Tha Phat Bastard, Snagglepuss, Positive K, Raggedy Man, Grand Daddy I.U. & Grand Puba (London, 1995)
2. "Buddy X (Remix)"—Neneh Cherry (Hut, 1996)
3. "Bust A Nut"—Luke (Luther Campbell, 1996)
4. "For My Niggaz"—Red Hot Lover Tone also featuring Prince Poetry (Organized Konfusion) & M.O.P. (Select, 1995)
5. "Jam Session"—Heavy D & Troo-Kula (MCA, 1994)

6. "Keep Your Hands High"—Tracey Lee (Universal, 1997)
7. "This Time Around"—Michael Jackson (Epic, 1995)
8. "Who's The Man"—Doctor Dré & Ed Lover also featuring King Just & Todd One (Relativity, 1994)
9. "You Can't Stop The Reign"—Shaquille O'Neal (Interscope, 1996)
10. "Young G's Perspective"—Blackjack also featuring DSP & Snakes (Junior M.A.F.I.A.) (Penalty, 1996)

PALLADIUM
BACKSTAGE

THE REALNESS.

... & 10 Forgotten Guest Vocal Appearances By 2Pac.

1. "Call It What U Want"—Above The Law also featuring Money B (Ruthless, 1992)
2. "Dusted 'N Disgusted"—E-40 also featuring Spice 1 & Mac Mall (Sick Wid It, 1995)
3. "Gotta Get Mine"—MC Breed (Ichiban, 1993)
4. "Jealous Got Me Strapped"—Spice 1 (Jive, 1994)
5. "Niggas Done Changed"—Richie Rich (Def Jam, 1996)
6. "#1 With A Bullet"—Raw Fusion (Hollywood BASIC, 1991)
7. "P.Y.T. (Playa Young Thugs)"—Smooth (Jive, 1995)
8. "Skank Wit' U"—Don Jagwarr (Priority, 1994)
9. "Slipping Into Darkness (Remix)"—Funky Aztecs (Raging Bull, 1995)
10. "We Do This"—Too $hort also featuring MC Breed & Father Dom (Jive, 1995)

PEACEFUL JOURNEY: Pac, Puff and B.I.G. at the New Music Seminar, Manhattan, 1993.

BACKSTAGE

Rappers Who Have At One Time Announced Their Retirements.

1. Diamond D
2. Jay-Z
3. LL Cool J
4. Master P*
5. Public Enemy
6. Show**
7. Too $hort

*Retired from solo work, but still appears on many No Limit releases.
**The D.I.T.C. producer/emcee retired from rhyming, not from making hot-ass beats.

Mobb Deep's Back Catalog Of Unreleased Gems.

1. "The Bridge '94"
2. "Cop Hell"
3. "Crime Connection" featuring Cormega
4. "Everyday Gunplay"
5. "First Day Of Spring" featuring Tragedy
6. "In The Long Run"
7. "Patty Shop" featuring Big Noyd
8. "Q.U."
9. "Rep The Q.B.C."
10. Hostage Skit (Havoc soothingly explains to a gagged hostage why he must kill him as Al Green's "For The Good Times" plays in the background.)
11. Game Show Skit (Like the "$20 Sack Pyramid" skit from Dr. Dre's *The Chronic*, this interlude uses the game show format to crack jokes about Tupac Shakur, with whom the group had beef with at the time.)
12. "Take It In Blood"
13. "True Lies"
14. "We About To Get Hectic"
15. "Young Luv"

It Gets No Realer Than This.

1. "Down For The Real"—Brand Nubian (Elektra, 1994)
2. "I'm Real"—Kris Kross (Ruffhouse, 1993)
3. "It's All Real"—Bone Thugs-N-Harmony (Ruthless, 1997)
4. "It's Real"—Paris (Priority, 1994)
5. "Iz He 4 Real"—Redman (Def Jam, 1996)
6. "Keep It On The Real"—3XKrazy (Noo Trybe, 1997)
7. "Keep It Real"—Apache (Flavor Unit, 1993)
8. "Keep It Real"—Jamal (Rowdy, 1995)
9. "Keep It Real"—Lost Boyz (Universal, 1996)
10. "Keep It Real"—Miilkbone (Capitol, 1995)
11. "Keep It Real"—PHD (Tuff City, 1993)
12. "Keep It Real"—Sylk-E. Fine featuring Too $hort (RCA, 1998)
13. "Keep It Real"—Timbaland featuring Ginuwine (Blackground, 1998)
14. "Keep It Real"—Young Bleed (No Limit, 1998)
15. "Keep It Real . . . Represent"—Kool Keith (Funky Ass, 1997)
16. "Keep Shit On The Real"—Champ MC (EastWest, 1994)
17. "Reality (Killin' Every Nigga In Sight)"—Black Moon (Nervous, 1994)
18. "Real Live Shit"—Real Live (Big Beat, 1996)
19. "The Realness"—Group Home featuring Smiley The Ghetto Child & Jack The Ripper (Payday, 1995)
20. "Represent The Real Hip Hop"—KRS-One featuring Das EFX (Jive, 1995)
21. "Return Of The Real"—Ice-T (Rhyme Syndicate, 1996)
22. "The Shit Is Real"—Fat Joe (Relativity, 1993)
23. "Shit Iz Real"—Black Moon (Nervous, 1993)
24. "Shit's Real"—Mic Geronimo (Blunt, 1995)
25. "Stay Real"—Erick Sermon (Def Jam, 1993)
26. "What's Real"—Sir Mix-A-Lot (American, 1994)
27. "What's The Real"—Kurious featuring Casual (Columbia, 1994)
28. "You Can't Front (Shit Is Real)"—Diamond D featuring Sadat X & Lord Finesse (Chemistry, 1993)

THE REALNESS.

Gone But Not Forgotten . . .

Angel Duster
B Doggs (Wreckx-N-Effect)
Bigga B
Big L
Big T (Almighty RSO)
Billy 167
Boo (Graveyard Shift)
Buffy (a/k/a The Human Beatbox) (Fat Boys)
Caine 1
Charizma
Cliff 159
Colt MPC
Cowboy (Furious Five)
Darryl C. (Crash Crew)
Dean BYB
Disco King Mario
Doctor Rock (Force MD's)
Dondi
Eazy-E
Harry Fobbs
Freaky Tah (Lost Boyz)
Funkenklein
Grandmaster Flowers
DJ Junebug
Kalonee
Kid Hood
Kid Panama
Killer Black (Mobb Deep)
Kist Cia
Masterdon
Mercury (Force MD's)
Kevin Miller
Mr. Cee (RBL Posse)

The Notorious B.I.G.
Rudy Pardee (The L.A. Dream Team)
Paul C.
Pimp Daddy
Pinkhouse
Lesley Pitts
Prince Messiah
Pumpkin
Rock (Almighty RSO)
Rockafella
Sane
Scientifik
Scott La Rock
Seagram
Seus
Shy 147
Sin UA
Smily 149
Stretch (Live Squad)
Subroc (K.M.D.)
Sugar Shaft (X Clan)
TCD (Force MD's)
Tombstone (Graveyard Shift)
Top Cat 126
DJ Train
T-Rex 131
MC Trouble
Trouble T-Roy (Heavy D & The Boyz)
2Pac
VE
Whiz Kid
Yella (UNLV)

RAC

Prominent Five Percent Rappers.

1. Big Daddy Kane
2. Brand Nubian
3. Busta Rhymes
4. Divine Styler
5. King Sun
6. K.M.D.
7. Knowledge (Digable Planets)
8. Movement Ex
9. Poor Righteous Teachers
10. Rakim
11. Sir Ibu
12. The World Famous Supreme Team
13. Wu-Tang Clan

HONORABLE MENTION: C&C Music Factory clock puncher/mic wrecker, Freedom Williams. Peace, brother. Keep makin' 'em sweat.

Stay Black.

1. Blac Haze
2. Blac Monks
3. Black A.G.
4. Blackalicious
5. Black Attack
6. Black By Demand
7. Black Eyed Peas
8. Blackface
9. Blackjack
10. Black Menace
11. Black Moon
12. Black Mophia Clan
13. Black Rob
14. Black, Rock & Ron
15. Black Sheep
16. Black Star
17. Blak Czer
18. Gangsta Blac
19. Joe Blakk
20. Pitch Black
21. Positively Black
22. Rich Black (Da Beatminerz)
23. Rufus Blaq

How Can I Be Black?

1. **Al Skratch is "The Black Mandingo"**
ON: "I'll Take Her"—Ill Al Skratch (Mercury, 1994)

2. **Canibus is "The Black Cyrano de Bergerac"**
ON: "Let's Ride"—Canibus (Universal, 1998)

3. **Cappadonna is "The Black Idi Amin"**
ON: "If It's Alright With You"—Cappadonna featuring U-God (Epic, 1998)

4. **Cold 187um & KM.G are both "The Black Superman"**
ON: "Black Superman"—Above The Law (Ruthless, 1994)

5. **Ghostface Killah is "The Black Jesus"**
ON: "Ice Water"—Raekwon featuring Ghostface Killah & Cappadonna (Loud 1995)

6. **Heltah Skeltah are "The Black Fonzirelliz"**
ON: "The Black Fonzirelliz"—Heltah Skeltah (Duck Down, 1998)

7. **Jay-Z is "The Black Scorcese"**
ON: "Pre-Game"—Sauce Money featuring Jay-Z (Def Jam, 1998)

8. **Master P is "The Black Sylvester Stallone"**
ON: "You Don't Wanna Go To 2 War"—Mia X featuring Master P (No Limit, 1997)

9. **M.F. Grimm is "The Black Ted Turner" & "The Black Vincent Price"**
ON: "Emotions"—M.F. Grimm (Dolo, 1996)

10. **Keith Murray is "The Black Indiana Jones"**
ON: "Dangerous Ground"—Keith Murray (Jive, 1997)

11. **The Notorious B.I.G. is "The Black Frank White"**
ON: "Get Money"—Junior M.A.F.I.A. featuring The Notorious B.I.G. (Undeas, 1995)

12. **Raekwon is "The Black Lex Luthor"**
ON: "Spot Rusherz"—Raekwon featuring Ghostface Killah (Loud, 1995)
Raekwon is "The Black Trump"
"Incarcerated Scarfaces"—Raekwon (Loud, 1995)

13. **Rakim is "The Black Michaelangelo"**
ON: "No Omega"—Eric B. & Rakim (MCA, 1990)

14. **Redman is "The Black Jack The Ripper"**
ON: "Rock Da Spot"—Redman (Def Jam, 1996)

15. **Royal Flush is "The Black Ebenezer"**
ON: "I Can't Help It"—Royal Flush (Blunt, 1997)

16. **Silkk The Shocker is "The Black Frank Nitty"**
ON: "Weed & Money"—Master P featuring Silkk The Shocker (No Limit, 1997)

17. **Smooth B is "The Black Blake Carrington"**
ON: "Early To Rise"—Nice & Smooth (Fresh, 1989)

18. **Tragedy is "The Black Moses"**
ON: "Calm Down"—Capone-N-Noreaga featuring Tragedy & Nas (Penalty promo, 1997)

19. **Wyclef Jean is "The Black Abraham"**
ON: "Rumble In The Jungle"—Fugees featuring John Forté, A Tribe Called Quest & Busta Rhymes (Mercury, 1997)

20. **Xzibit is "The Black John McClane"**
ON: "Killin' It"—Tha Alkaholiks featuring Xzibit (Loud, 1997)
Xzibit is "The Black Bruce Willis"
ON: "3 Card Molly"—Xzibit featuring Ras Kass & Saafir (Loud, 1998)

Stretch Armstrong's Most Embarrassing Moments As A White DJ In The Rap Game.

1. Seeing a dude rockin' a ridiculous amount of beads (Zulu Nation beads, to be exact) behind the wheels of steel right before a Lord Finesse show at the Muse in 1992. I asked him if he was Mike Smooth (Finesse's DJ at the time). It turned out to be Afrika Islam. Definitely embarrassing.
2. DJing for Nas on my radio show (89 Tech Nine, NYC) and playing a fresh, brand new instrumental of Large Professor's remix of Gang Starr's "Gotta Get Over." It was a test pressing so the record skipped and Nas sonned me. He told me, "You better get it on time, kid." I was mortified.
3. Being called MC Serch.
4. Noreaga calling me an "albino ostrich" on the air during my prime time slot on Hot 97.
5. Buying a dope pair of suede, navy blue Adidas, only to find out they were bootlegs.
6. The list you're reading now.

If you're still paying attention, you deserve mad props. That's right, Stretch Armstrong—the star of rap radioland's The Stretch Armstrong Show—*is white. And to be perfectly honest, we're more embarrassed by this list than he is.*

GHETTO SUPER PASS:
White Rappers... & Their Black Affiliations.

1. Bas Blasta (Nice & Smooth *and* Kid)
2. Blood Of Abraham (Eazy-E)
3. Chilly Tee (The Bomb Squad)
4. Eminem (Dr. Dre; The Outsidaz)
5. Everlast (Ice-T)
6. Brian Austin Green (The Pharcyde)
7. Kid Panic (The Bomb Squad)
8. Knucklehedz (EPMD)
9. Miilkbone (Naughty By Nature)
10. Powder (Bone Thugs-N-Harmony)
11. Remedy (Wu-Tang Clan)
12. Tairrie B. (Eazy-E)
13. Young Black Teenagers (The Bomb Squad)

AIN'T THE DEVIL HAPPY?
White Mainstream Media Darlings.

1. Beastie Boys
2. Biz Markie
3. Busta Rhymes
4. Cypress Hill
5. De La Soul
6. Missy Elliott
7. Lauryn Hill
8. Kool Keith
9. PM Dawn
10. Public Enemy
11. DJ Shadow
12. DJ Spooky
13. Timbaland
14. Wu-Tang Clan (especially Ol' Dirty Bastard)
15. Wyclef Jean

10 Remarkably Racist Recordings.

1. "Bichasbootleguz"—Onyx (Def Jam, 1993)
2. "Black Korea"—Ice Cube (Priority, 1991)
3. "Buck Tha Devil"—Da Lench Mob (Street Knowledge, 1992)
4. "Cave Bitch"—Ice Cube (Priority, 1991)
5. "Chinese Delivery"—Shazzy (Elektra, 1990)
6. "Dark Skin Girls"—Del The Funkeé Homosapien (Elektra, 1991)
7. "Go To Hail (Skit)"—Black Sheep (Mercury, 1991)
8. "Horny Lil' Devil"—Ice Cube (Priority, 1991)
9. "Illegal Aliens"—Convicts (Rap-A-Lot, 1991)
10. "Shanghai"—Cam'Ron (Untertainment, 1998)

20 Colorful Songs About Racism.

1. "Black And White"—Master P (No Limit, 1998)
2. "Blackman Can't Catch A Cab"—U.T.F.O. (Jive, 1991)
3. "Clear Blue Skies"—Juggaknots (Fondle 'Em, 1996)
4. "Erase Racism"—Kool G Rap & DJ Polo featuring Biz Markie & Big Daddy Kane (Cold Chillin', 1990)
5. "A Fight"—Apache (Tommy Boy, 1993)
6. "Fuck The KKK"—Willie D (Rap-A-Lot, 1989)
7. "Hate"—Organized Konfusion (Priority, 1997)
8. "The Hatred"—Chubb Rock (Select, 1992)
9. "Human Race"—White Boys (Tin Pan Apple, 1988)
10. "Nature Of The Threat"—Ras Kass (Priority, 1996)
11. "Pollywanacraka"—Public Enemy (Def Jam, 1990)
12. "Prejudice"—Original Concept (Def Jam, 1988)
13. "Race War"—Ice-T (Rhyme Syndicate, 1993)
14. "The Racist"—Boogie Down Productions (Jive, 1990)
15. "Social Narcotics"—MC Serch (Def Jam, 1992)
16. "Soul Controller"—Grand Puba (Elektra, 1992)
17. "Stop Racism"—Tony D (4th & B'way, 1991)
18. "That's What I Like (No Cream In My Coffee)"—Cooly Live (RCA, 1992)
19. "United Snakes Of America"—Movement Ex (Columbia, 1990)
20. "White Man'z World"—Makaveli (Death Row, 1996)

RACE.

Of The World Famous Beat Junkies Name The Top 5 Reasons Why Asian Hip Hop DJs Cut So Fresh.

5. After many years of watching Mr. Miyagi doing his "wax on, wax off" techniques, we decided to try it with records.
4. Fat Asians aren't good at martial arts (except for Arsenio's main man, Sammo Hung).
3. Our parents gave us two options: a lowered Civic/Acura or turntables.
2. We Can't Rap For Shit!!! (Except for a chosen few . . .)
1. Due to many years of using chopsticks, our dexterity is perfect for DJing!!!

Additional reporting by DJ C-Los of Fat Beats, CA.

California spin doctors Rhettmatic and Babu got more cuts than muthafuckin' Benihana. (Ha ha ha! Get it? Benihana! They're Asian!) Along with the rest of The World Famous Beat Junkies, they are amongst the sharpest turntable technicians to ever speak with their hands.

THOSE AMAZIN' ASIANS: Q-Bert (left) and Shortkut of the Invisibl Skratch Piklz on *The Shiggar Fraggar Show!*, 1998.

COP HELL:
28 Scathing Songs About Racist Punk Police.

1. "Batterram"—Toddy Tee (Evejim, 1985)
2. "The Beast Within"—King Of Chill & The Alliance Of MC's (b/k/a Alliance) (Super Tronics, 1985)
3. "Black And Blue"—Brand Nubian (Elektra, 1992)
4. "Black Cop"—KRS-One (MCA, 1993)
5. "Coffee, Donuts & Death"—Paris (Scarface, 1992)
6. "Crooked Cops"—D-Shot featuring E-40 & B-Legit (Sick Wid It, 1992)
7. "Crooked Officer"—Geto Boys (Rap-A-Lot, 1993)
8. "Dirty Cop Named Harry"—Hard Knocks (Wild Pitch, 1992)
9. "Duck Da Boyz"—Strickly Roots (Friends Connections, 1993)
10. "Fuck Tha Police"—N.W.A (Ruthless, 1988)
11. "Get The Fuck Out Of Dodge"—Public Enemy (Def Jam, 1990)
12. "Good Cop/Bad Cop"—Blahzay Blahzay (Mercury, 1996)
13. "Illegal Search"—LL Cool J (Def Jam, 1990)
14. "In The Line Of Duty"—Eightball & MJG (Suave House, 1995)
15. "Just A Friendly Game Of Baseball"—Main Source (Wild Pitch, 1991)
16. "Looking Through The Eye Of A Pig"—Cypress Hill (Ruffhouse, 1998)
17. "One Time Gaffled Em Up"—Compton's Most Wanted (Orpheus, 1990)
18. "One Time's Got No Case"—Sir Mix-A-Lot (American, 1992)
19. "Pigs"—Cypress Hill (Ruffhouse, 1991)
20. "Probable Cause"—Brand Nubian (Arista, 1998)
21. "Protect & Serve"—U.G.K. (Jive, 1994)
22. "Punk Police"—Mac Dre (Young Black Brotha, 1992)
23. "Sa Prize (Part 2)"—N.W.A (Ruthless, 1990)
24. "Say Hi To The Bad Guy"—Ice Cube (Priority, 1992)
25. "Souljah's Revenge"—2Pac (Interscope, 1993)
26. "Sound Of Da Police"—KRS-One (Jive, 1993)
27. "Time For Us To Defend Ourselves"—MC Shan (Cold Chillin', 1990)
28. "Who Killed Jane"—EPMD (Def Jam, 1992)

RACE.

¡VIVA LOS RHYMES!
Top 10 Lyrical Mexican References.

1. "To Live & Die In L.A."—Makaveli (Death Row, 1996)
"It wouldn't be L.A. without Mexicans/ Black love, Brown pride in the sets again."

2. "Who Dem Niggas"—Tha Alkaholiks featuring Threat (Loud, 1993)
J-Ro: " '93 Mandingo, I got my own lingo/ My Mexican homie told me never trust a gringo."

3. "A Million And One Questions"—Jay-Z (Roc-A-Fella, 1997)
"What you doin' in L.A. with Filipinos and éses/ Latinos in Chevys down by Pico with Fredrico?"

4. "Black And White"—Master P (No Limit, 1998)
"And all the money can't change the color of your skin/ Why so many Blacks and Mexicans in the pen?"

5. "Show & Prove"—Big Daddy Kane featuring Big Scoob, Sauce Money, Shyheim, Jay-Z & Ol' Dirty Bastard (MCA, 1994)
Kane: "Look inside my rap book at every text, my man/ And see that I got more essays [éses] than a Mexican."

6. "Ice Water"—Raekwon featuring Ghostface Killah & Cappadonna (Loud, 1995)
Ghostface: "Move like a bunch of Mexicans with bandanas."

7. "Guantanamera"—Wyclef Jean featuring Lauryn Hill (Ruffhouse, 1997)
Lauryn: "Parents came from Cuba, part Mexican/ Pure sweet, dons fell to her feet."

8. "Cold World"—The Genius featuring Inspectah Deck (Geffen, 1995)
"Similar to hit men who pull out tecs and then/ Drop those who crack like tacos from Mexicans."

9. "Watcha Gonna Do"—Jayo Felony featuring Method Man & DMX (Def Jam, 1998)
DMX: "I got more homes than an ése."

10. "Keep Tha Peace"—Kam (EastWest, 1995)
"Now they say it's on wit' the éses, right? But I know Chicano pride/ I can't buy it when I hear that's the enemy cuz I'm knowin' deep down they some kin to me."

NATIVE TONGUES:
Notable Bilingual Rap Songs.

1. "Asi Es La Vida"—The Latin Empire (Culebra, 1991)
2. "Blow Your Mind"—Redman (Def Jam, 1992)*
3. "Change The Beat"—Fab 5 Freddy (Celluloid, 1982)
4. "De Corazon"—Hurricane G (H.O.L.A., 1997)
5. "Disco Dream"—Mean Machine (Sugar Hill, 1981)
6. "Doin' Damage In My Native Language"—Zimbabwe Legit (Hollywood BASIC, 1992)
7. "Firme Hina"—Proper Dos (Skanless, 1992)
8. "Hermana Tan Linda"—Hen-Gee & Evil-E (Pendulum, 1991)
9. "Hip Hop Junkies (Spanish Version)"—Nice & Smooth (RAL, 1991)
10. "It's Nasty (Genius Of Love)"—Grandmaster Flash & The Furious Five (Sugar Hill, 1981)
11. "Latin Lingo"—Cypress Hill (Ruffhouse, 1991)
12. "Le Bien, Le Mal"—Guru featuring MC Solaar (Chrysalis, 1993)
13. "Long Island Wildin'"—De La Soul featuring SDP & Takagi Kan (Tommy Boy, 1993)
14. "Mentirosa"—Mellow Man Ace (Capitol, 1989)
15. "Papi Chulo (Spanish)"—Funkdoobiest (Buzz Tone, 1997)
16. "Phonkie Melodia"—Tha Mexakinz (Mad Sounds, 1994)
17. "Sang Fezi"—Wyclef Jean featuring Lauryn Hill (Ruffhouse, 1997)
18. "Shape Shifters"—Key Kool & Rhettmatic featuring Saafir (Up Above, 1995)
19. "Spanglish"—Spanish Fly & The Terrible Two (Enjoy, 1981)
20. "Spanish Flavor"—Mesanjarz Of Funk (Atlantic, 1993)
21. "Top Notch"—Kurious featuring Kadi, Psycho Les & Lucien (Columbia, 1994)
22. "Vida Mia"—Doug E. Fresh & The New Get Fresh Crew (Bust It, 1992)
23. "Ya Estuvo"—Kid Frost (Virgin, 1990)

*Hear him freak it in Korean!

22 Interracial Rap Groups.

1. Blahzay Blahzay
2. Charizma & Peanut Butter Wolf
3. Cold Crush Brothers
4. Company Flow
5. Compton's Most Wanted*
6. Cypress Hill
7. Delinquent Habits
8. Digital Underground
9. Dilated Peoples
10. Disposable Heroes Of Hiphoprisy
11. Downtown Science
12. Fantastic Five
13. Fearless Four
14. Funkdoobiest
15. Jurassic 5
16. Killarmy
17. Lootpack
18. Mad Flava
19. Raw Fusion
20. 7A3
21. 3rd Bass
22. Tuff Crew

*First album only.

22 Biracial Rap Artists.

1. Apldap (Black Eyed Peas) (African-American/Filipino)
2. AZ (African-American/Dominican)
3. Big Noyd (African-American/Puerto Rican)
4. Bizzy Bone (African-American/Italian)
5. Black Attack (African-American/Jewish)
6. Charli Baltimore (African-American/German)
7. Dres (African-American/Puerto Rican)
8. Fresh Kid Ice (Jamaican/Chinese)
9. Kid (Kid 'N Play) (Jamaican/Caucasian)
10. Kid Capri (African-American/Italian)
11. Johnny "J" (African-American/Mexican)
12. Lateef (African-American/Puerto Rican)
13. Linque (African-American/Chinese)
14. Lyrics Born (Japanese/Italian)
15. Mad Rapper (African-American/Puerto Rican)
16. Noreaga (African-American/Puerto Rican)
17. Peter Gunz (African-American/Caucasian)
18. Professor Griff (African-American/Native American)
19. QDIII (African-American/Caucasian)
20. Roxanne Shanté (African-American/Cuban)
21. Taboo (Black Eyed Peas) (Native American/Mexican)
22. Terminator X (African-American/German)

RACE.

★ red, white, tan, black, yellow or brown, it really doesn't matter we can all get down.

Cypress Hill's Sen Dog Gives Props To His Cuban Heroes.

1. **My Mom & Dad**
   I give props to my mom and dad for getting out of a Communist situation. My dad did five years in the fuckin' pen out there for nuthin'. And my mom somehow raised four kids by herself to the point where we were able to get out of there. If it wasn't for them, I wouldn't be here right now.

2. **Celia Cruz**
   She's from the same part of Cuba we're from, Pinar del Rio. I admire the accomplishments that Celia has made in the music world. She's like the Queen of Cuba. They shoulda given her the damn island and let her fuckin' fix that place up.

3. **Tony Perez**
   Growing up, I liked the Cincinnati Reds because first baseman Tony Perez was Cuban. I liked the Boston Red Sox cuz of Luis Tiant being Cuban. I used to pull for whoever had a Cuban player on their team. The Dodgers were cool, but if the Big Red Machine ever came to town, you best believe I was tryin' to have my parents buy me tickets behind Tony Perez at first base.

   By the way, I think it's really fucked that we haven't put Tony Perez in the Hall of Fame yet. And the only reason they haven't put him in yet is because he didn't talk English good. But he was there to play baseball and win games for the Cincinnati Reds. And if Peter Ueberroth or whoever at *Sports Illustrated* don't like that, they can stick it, man.

4. **José Canseco**
   He wasn't born in Cuba. But he's been around for awhile and we're at a point right now where there's not too many Cuban baseball players consistently coming to play in the Majors.

5. **Orlando (a/k/a El Duque) & Livan Hernandez**
   When somebody asks me to do something and there's a game on, I say, "No, I'm gonna watch the Yankees play because El Duque is pitchin'." Believe you me, I don't miss a game when that brother pitches. And that's because of the whole thing that he and his brother had to go through which is common for Cuban folks—to have to go in a raft through shark-infested waters and dehydration and escape the country. My mom and dad and me didn't have to go through that, but my cousins and aunts and a bunch of people I know did. Anybody who makes it through that should be commended, man. Cuz only like 10% of the people make it. There's a lot of Cubans at the bottom of that ocean or in a shark's belly.

Sen Dog is a charter member of Cypress Hill, who with hits like, "How I Could Just Kill A Man," "Insane In The Brain" and "Throw Your Set In The Air" are, arguably, the most successful interracial hip hop group of all-time. Sen also clocks overtime as frontman of his rock band, SX-10.

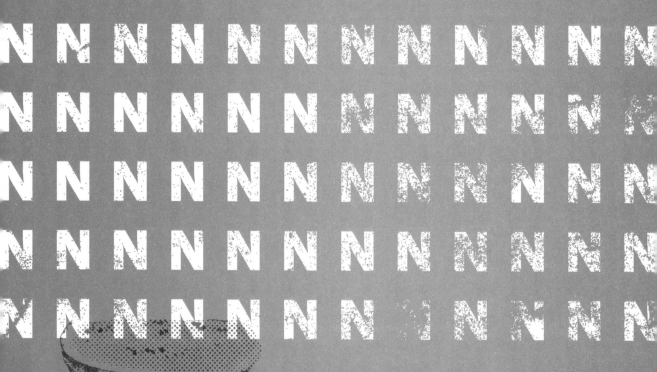

FOR THE REAL NIGGA IN YOU:
Of Times The "N" Word Appears On N.W.A's Albums.

1. *Straight Outta Compton* (Ruthless, 1988): 42
2. *100 Miles And Runnin'* EP (Ruthless, 1990): 105
3. *Efil4zaggin* (Ruthless, 1991): 249

RACE.

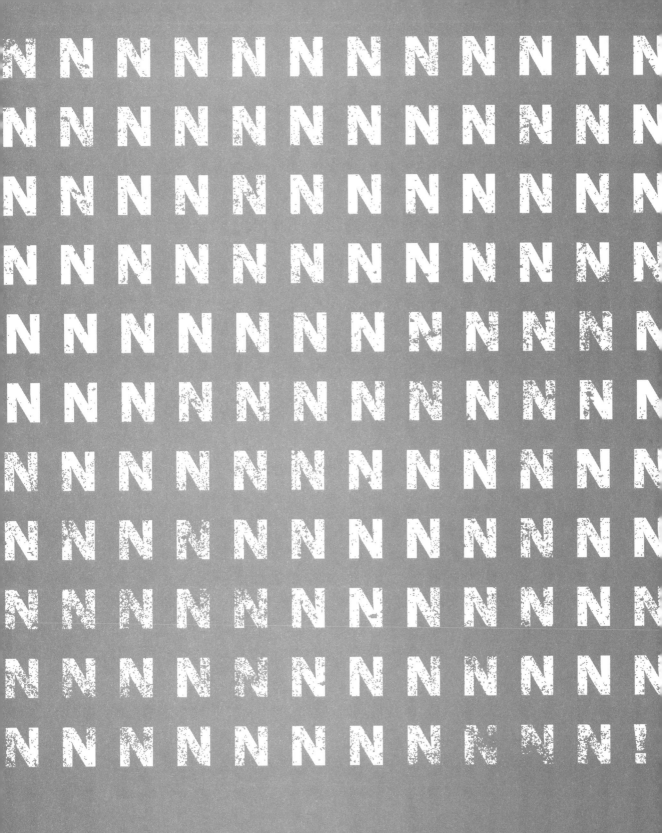

AWAR

First 10 Gold Rap Singles.

1. "The Breaks"—Kurtis Blow (Mercury, 1980) (certified 8/19/80)
2. "Rapture"—Blondie (Chrysalis, 1981) (certified 3/27/81)
3. "Planet Rock"—Afrika Bambaataa & The Soul Sonic Force (Tommy Boy, 1982) (certified 9/16/82)
4. "The Show"—Doug E. Fresh & The Get Fresh Crew (Reality, 1985) (certified 2/27/86)
5. "Parents Just Don't Understand"—DJ Jazzy Jeff & The Fresh Prince (Jive, 1988) (certified 2/24/89)
6. "Me, Myself And I"—De La Soul (Tommy Boy, 1989) (certified 6/27/89)
7. "I'm That Type Of Guy"—LL Cool J (Def Jam, 1989) (certified 7/24/89)
8. "Self-Destruction"—Stop The Violence Movement (Jive, 1989) (certified 8/2/89)
9. "Me So Horny"—2 Live Crew (Luke Skyywalker, 1989) (certified 12/14/89)
10. "Mentirosa"—Mellow Man Ace (Capitol, 1990) (certified 7/13/90)

First 10 Gold Rap Albums.

1. *Run-D.M.C.*—Run-D.M.C. (Profile, 1984) (certified 12/17/84)
2. *Fat Boys*—Fat Boys (Sutra, 1984) (certified 5/6/85)
3. *Fat Boys Are Back*—Fat Boys (Sutra, 1985) (certified 1/9/86)
4. *Paid In Full*—Eric B. & Rakim (4th & B'way, 1987) (certified 12/4/87)
5. *Dana Dane With Fame*—Dana Dane (Profile, 1987) (certified 1/21/88)
6. *The 2 Live Crew Is What We Are*—2 Live Crew (Luke Skyywalker, 1986) (certified 5/13/88)
7. *Coming Back Hard*—Fat Boys (Tin Pan Apple, 1988) (certified 8/24/88)
8. *Strictly Business*—EPMD (Fresh, 1988) (certified 11/9/88)
9. *Power*—Ice-T (Sire, 1988) (certified 11/22/88)
10. *Rock The House*—DJ Jazzy Jeff & The Fresh Prince (Jive, 1987) (certified 12/1/88)

First 10 Platinum Rap Singles.*

1. "Wild Thing"—Tone-Lōc (Delicious Vinyl, 1988) (double platinum, first certified 2/3/89)
2. "Funky Cold Medina"—Tone-Lōc (Delicious Vinyl, 1989) (certified 5/9/89)
3. "Push It"—Salt-N-Pepa (Next Plateau, 1987) (certified 10/13/89)
4. "It Takes Two"—Rob Base & DJ E-Z Rock (Profile, 1988) (certified 12/28/89)
5. "Bust A Move"—Young MC (Delicious Vinyl, 1989) (certified, 1/12/90)
6. "Just A Friend"—Biz Markie (Cold Chillin', 1989) (certified 4/12/90)
7. "The Humpty Dance"—Digital Underground (Tommy Boy, 1989) (certified 4/23/90)
8. "Expression"—Salt-N-Pepa (Next Plateau, 1989) (certified 5/25/90)
9. "Ice Ice Baby"—Vanilla Ice (SBK, 1990) (certified 10/29/90)
10. "Knockin' Boots"—Candyman (Epic, 1990) (certified 12/18/90)

*Many early classics like "Rapper's Delight"—Sugarhill Gang (Sugar Hill, 1979) and "The Message"—Grandmaster Flash & The Furious Five (Sugar Hill, 1982) moved crazy units but were never certified.

First 10 Platinum Rap Albums.

1. *Raising Hell*—Run-D.M.C. (Profile, 1986) (triple platinum, first certified 7/15/86)
2. *Licensed To Ill*—Beastie Boys (Def Jam, 1986) (eight-times platinum, first certified 2/2/87)
3. *King Of Rock*—Run-D.M.C. (Profile, 1985) (certified, 2/18/87)
4. *Bigger And Deffer*—LL Cool J (Def Jam, 1987) (double platinum, first certified 8/11/87)
5. *Crushin'*—Fat Boys (Tin Pan Apple, 1987) (certified 9/16/87)
6. *Radio*—LL Cool J (Def Jam, 1985) (certified 4/19/88)
7. *Tougher Than Leather*—Run-D.M.C. (Profile, 1988) (certified 7/19/88)
8. *He's The DJ, I'm The Rapper*—DJ Jazzy Jeff & The Fresh Prince (Jive, 1988) (triple platinum, first certified 7/21/88)
9. *How Ya Like Me Now*—Kool Moe Dee (Jive, 1987) (certified 11/14/88)
10. *Let's Get It Started*—MC Hammer (Capitol, 1988) (certified 4/17/89)

AWARDS.

Rap Artists With The Most Platinum Albums.*

1. Ice Cube, 6 (five solo, one as a member of N.W.A)
2. LL Cool J, 6
3. Too $hort, 6
4. Beastie Boys, 5
5. MC Hammer, 5
6. Will Smith, 4 (one solo, three as part of DJ Jazzy Jeff & The Fresh Prince)
7. 2Pac, 4

*As of January 1, 1999.

THE NOT-SO-SWEET 16:
Major Hip Hop Artists Who Have Never Had A Gold Album.

1. Above The Law
2. The entire Bootcamp Clik
3. Brand Nubian
4. Chubb Rock
5. The entire Hieroglyphics Crew
6. Jungle Brothers
7. Kool G Rap & DJ Polo
8. Nice & Smooth
9. Poor Righteous Teachers
10. Schoolly D
11. Special Ed
12. Steady B
13. Stetsasonic
14. Ultramagnetic MC's
15. U.T.F.O.
16. Yo Yo

MORE AND MORE HITS: LL, a Slaytanic Rick Rubin and a bunch of CBS Records execs throw their hands in the air for Mr. Smith's gold (and eventually platinum) *Radio* in 1986.

Grammy Award-Winning Hip Hop Artists By Year.

1. **DJ Jazzy Jeff & The Fresh Prince**
Best Rap Performance—"Parents Just Don't Understand," 1988

2. **Young MC**
Best Rap Performance—"Bust A Move," 1989

3. **MC Hammer**
Best Rap Solo Performance; Best Rhythm & Blues Song—"U Can't Touch This"; Best Music Video Long Form—*Please Hammer Don't Hurt 'Em The Movie*, 1990

4. **Quincy Jones featuring Big Daddy Kane, Ice-T, Kool Moe Dee & Grandmaster Melle Mel**
Best Rap Performance By A Duo Or Group—"Back On The Block," 1990

5. **DJ Jazzy Jeff & The Fresh Prince**
Best Rap Performance By A Duo Or Group—"Summertime," 1991

6. **LL Cool J**
Best Rap Solo Performance—"Mama Said Knock You Out," 1991

7. **Arrested Development**
Best New Artist; Best Rap Performance By A Duo Or Group—"Tennessee," 1992

8. **Sir Mix-A-Lot**
Best Rap Solo Performance—"Baby Got Back," 1992

9. **Digable Planets**
Best Rap Performance By A Duo Or Group—"Rebirth Of Slick (Cool Like Dat)," 1993

10. **Dr. Dre**
Best Rap Solo Performance—"Let Me Ride," 1993

11. **Queen Latifah**
Best Rap Solo Performance—"U.N.I.T.Y.," 1994

12. **Salt-N-Pepa**
Best Rap Performance By A Duo Or Group—"None Of Your Business," 1994

13. **Coolio**
Best Rap Solo Performance—"Gangsta's Paradise," 1995

14. **Method Man featuring Mary J. Blige**
Best Rap Performance By A Duo Or Group—"I'll Be There For You/You're All I Need To Get By," 1995

15. **Naughty By Nature**
Best Rap Album—*Poverty's Paradise*, 1995

16. **Bone Thugs-N-Harmony**
Best Rap Performance By A Duo Or Group—"Tha Crossroads," 1996

17. **Fugees**
Best R&B Performance By A Duo Or Group With Vocal—"Killing Me Softly With His Song"; Best Rap Album—*The Score*, 1996

18. **LL Cool J**
Best Rap Solo Performance—"Hey Lover," 1996

19. **Puff Daddy & Faith Evans featuring 112**
Best Rap Performance By A Duo Or Group—"I'll Be Missing You," 1997

20. **Puff Daddy & The Family**
Best Rap Album—*No Way Out*, 1997

21. **Will Smith**
Best Rap Solo Performance—"Men In Black," 1997

22. **Beastie Boys**
Best Rap Performance By A Duo Or Group—"Intergalactic"; Best Alternative Music Performance—*Hello Nasty*, 1998

23. **Lauryn Hill**
Best New Artist; Album Of The Year; Best R&B Album—*The Miseducation Of Lauryn Hill*; Best R&B Song; Best Female R&B Vocal Performance—"Doo Wop (That Thing)," 1998

24. **Jay-Z**
Best Rap Album—*Vol. 2 . . . Hard Knock Life*, 1998

25. **Will Smith**
Best Rap Solo Performance—"Gettin' Jiggy Wit It," 1998

AWARDS.

Rap Recipients Of MTV Music Video Awards By Year.

1. **DJ Jazzy Jeff & The Fresh Prince**
   Best Rap Video—"Parents Just Don't Understand," 1989

2. **MC Hammer**
   Best Rap Video; Best Dance Video—"U Can't Touch This," 1990

3. **LL Cool J**
   Best Rap Video—"Mama Said Knock You Out," 1991

4. **Arrested Development**
   Best Rap Video—"Tennessee," 1992

5. **Arrested Development**
   Best Rap Video—"People Everyday," 1993

6. **Salt-N-Pepa featuring En Vogue**
   Best R&B Video—"Whatta Man," 1994

7. **Snoop Doggy Dogg featuring The Dramatics**
   Best Rap Video—"Doggy Dogg World," 1994

8. **Dr. Dre**
   Best Rap Video—"Keep Their Heads Ringin'," 1995

9. **Coolio**
   Best Dance Video—"1, 2, 3, 4 (Sumpin' New)," 1996;
   Best Video From A Film—"Gangsta's Paradise," 1996

10. **Fugees**
    Best R&B Video—"Killing Me Softly With His Song," 1996

11. **The Notorious B.I.G.**
    Best Rap Video—"Hypnotize," 1997

12. **Puff Daddy & Faith Evans featuring 112**
    Best R&B Video—"I'll Be Missing You," 1997

13. **Will Smith**
    Best Video From A Film—"Men In Black," 1997

14. **Puff Daddy & The Family featuring The Lox, Lil' Kim, The Notorious B.I.G. & Fuzzbubble**
    Viewers' Choice—"It's All About The Benjamins (Rock Remix)," 1998

15. **Will Smith**
    Best Rap Video—"Gettin' Jiggy Wit It," 1998;
    Best Male Video—"Just The Two Of Us," 1998

16. **Wyclef Jean**
    Best R&B Video—"Gone 'Til November," 1998

13 Artists Chubb Rock Felt Deserved Grammy Recognition. From The Composition, "And The Winner Is ...(The Grammys)"—Chubb Rock Featuring Hitman Howie Tee (Select, 1989).*

1. Run-D.M.C.
2. LL Cool J
3. Kool Moe Dee
4. Heavy D
5. Eric B.**
6. Dana Dane
7. Salt-N-Pepa
8. Whodini
9. Whistle
10. Chubb Rock
11. Kid 'N Play
12. Big Daddy Kane
13. Biz Markie

*In the order they're mentioned.
**The God Rakim was mysteriously omitted.

BLACK RAGE: [illegible] Flavor Flav and The [illegible] screamed on The [illegible] February 22, [illegible]

New Music Seminar & Supermen DJ Battle Winners By Year.

1. Whiz Kid (New York City), 1981
2. Grandmixer D.ST (New York City), 1982
3. Afrika Islam (Los Angeles), 1983
4. DJ Cheese (Philadelphia), 1984
5. Easy G Rockwell (Original Concept) (New York City), 1985
6. DJ Jazzy Jeff (Philadelphia), 1986
7. DJ Cash Money (Philadelphia), 1987
8. DJ Scratch (New York City), 1988
9. DJ Miz (Philadelphia), 1989
10. DJ Steve D (New York City), 1990
11. DJ Supreme (Washington D.C.), 1991
12. Mixmaster Mike (San Francisco), 1992*
13. DJ 8-Ball (San Francisco), 1993
14. DJ Noise (Denmark), 1994

*Denotes the commencement of Supermen Productions' sponsorship of the battle.

New Music Seminar & Supermen MC Battle Winners By Year.

1. Busy Bee (New York City), 1985
2. Grandmaster Caz (New York City), 1986
3. Grandmaster Melle Mel (New York City), 1987
4. Mikey D (New York City), 1988
5. Freshco (Philadelphia), 1989
6. Kid Jazz (New York City), 1990
7. MC Serge (Cleveland), 1991
8. Supernatural (New York City), 1993
9. Judgemental (Chicago), 1994

NOTE: In 1992, there was only a DJ battle and no MC battle.

Technics DMC DJ Competition Winners By Year.

1. 1986 World: DJ Cheese (US)
2. 1987 World: Chad Jackson (UK)
3. 1988 World: DJ Cash Money (US)
4. 1989 World: Cutmaster Swift (UK); US: DJ Aladdin (Los Angeles)
5. 1990 World: DJ David (Germany); US: Baby G (Texas)
6. 1991 World: DJ David (Germany); US: Q-Bert (San Francisco)
7. 1992 World: Rocksteady DJs (Q-Bert, Mixmaster Mike, DJ Apollo) (US); US: Rocksteady DJs (Q-Bert, Mixmaster Mike, DJ Apollo) (San Francisco)
8. 1993 World: The Dream Team (Q-Bert, Mixmaster Mike) (US); US: DJ Rectangle (Los Angeles)
9. 1994 US-East Coast: DJ Ghetto (Philadelphia); US-West Coast: Shortkut (San Francisco)
10. 1994–1995 World: Roc Raida (US); US: Roc Raida (New York City)*
11. 1995 US-East Coast: Mista Sinista (New York City); US-West Coast: Babu (Los Angeles)
12. 1995–1996 US: Swamp (Cleveland)*
13. 1996 World: DJ Noise (Denmark)
14. 1997 World: A-Trak (Canada); US: DJ Slyce (New Jersey)
15. 1998 World: DJ Craze (US); US: DJ Craze (Miami)

*These victories took place during the end of one year and the start of the next.

AWARDS.

5 Most Underrated Hip Hop Artists.

1. **U.G.K.**
   Jay-Z knows, fool—U.G.K. is the lick. Since 1992, the duo of Bun B and Pimp C have quietly carved out their own innovative down south niche through a series of consistently enjoyable LPs. True underground kings from deep in the heart of Texas.

2. **M.O.P.**
   Perhaps the reason the Mash Out Posse's Lil' Fame and Billy Danze scream so passionately on the mic is because no one's hearing them. After four power-packed releases, it's difficult to comprehend why. DJ Premier loves this group and so should you.

3. **Likwit Crew (Tha Alkaholiks, King Tee & Xzibit)**
   They've got rhymes. They've got beats. They've paid dues. They're Westside rap specialists content to spray infectious and inebriated verses in the land of gangstas. Plus, they've spawned promising talent such as Defari, Lootpack and others. Sober up and listen, you dummies.

4. **D.I.T.C. (AG, Big L, Buckwild, Diamond D, Fat Joe, Lord Finesse, O.C. & Show)**
   Once simply a crew of talented Bronx and Uptown rhyming and beatmaking pals, Diggin' In The Crates is now a certified supergroup, albeit seemingly one that only a small, devoted hip hop fanship gives props to. You know that ain't right.

5. **The Beatnuts**
   For years, Corona, Queens' Latin kings of decadence have been the Big Apple's answer to Cypress Hill, but with a wider range of subject matter (i.e., hoes and booze as well as violence and weed). It'll take a nation of frat boys to wake up and smell the Hennessy for them to get their due.

5 Most Overrated Hip Hop Artists.

1. **All second generation Wu-Tangers**
   Clan in the front. Keep the killer B-teamers in the back.

2. **Foxy Brown**
   Style-over-substance glamour girl has reached multi-platinum heights unknown to deserving veteran femme favorites like MC Lyte and Queen Latifah.

3. **Canibus or Ras Kass (take your pick)**
   A good lyricist who has yet to master the art of making good records.

4. **Spice 1**
   East Bay gangsta has been shooting creative blanks for years.

5. **Digital Underground**
   One hot debut album, one decent follow-up EP and far too much bullshit thereafter.

Slept-On Albums For Dat Ass.

1. **Ain't A Damn Thang Changed—WC And The MAAD Circle (Priority, 1991)**
Before Coolio embarked on his fantastic voyage to the top of the charts, he was Dub C's first lieutenant in this first rate Cali underground battalion. Things done changed, but this gangsta platter still kicks ass.

2. **Ass, Gas Or Cash (No One Rides For Free)—K-Dee (Lench Mob, 1994)**
Pimpin' ain't easy, even when you're Ice Cube's protegé. Guest appearances from Morris Day and Bootsy Collins couldn't prevent the album (whose artwork is memorable for its backdrop of swimming sperm) from comin' up short like an unproductive ho. Fo' sho.

3. **Convicts—Convicts (Rap-A-Lot, 1991)**
Big Mike shines in his pre-Geto Boys, pre-solo career with an LP of songs like "Fuck School," "Woop Her Ass" and "I Love Boning."

4. **Crazy Noize—Stezo (Fresh, 1989)**
This former EPMD dancer had horrible taste in threads (witness his shredded denim-look on the album cover), but decent mic skills and great taste in beats. Crazy slept-on.

5. **Criminal—Scientifik (Definite, 1994)**
A criminally underrated underground effort featuring production from Diamond D, Buckwild and RZA. Tragically, the Bostonian was killed in a car accident in 1998.

6. **Da Dirty 30—Cru (Def Jam, 1997)**
A wildly entertaining collection of South Bronx old school energy and tasteless comedy that somehow got lost in the Def Jam shuffle.

7. **Enigma—Keith Murray (Jive, 1996)**
The most beautifullest thing in this world? Mr. Murray's second album, jive turkeys.

8. **Fadanuf Fa Erybody—Odd Squad (Rap-A-Lot, 1994)**
The only hip hop group to showcase a blind emcee (Rob Quest), Houston's Odd Squad also featured foul-mouthed emcee/crooner, Devin. Scarface has called Fadanuf the best album ever released on Rap-A-Lot. A-ight, then.

9. **From Pyramids To Projects—Two Kings In A Cipher (Bahia, 1991)**
Future Bad Boy Hitmen Deric "D-Dot" Angelettie and Ron "Amen-Ra" Lawrence say it loud: they're Afrocentric and they're proud (and they've got hot beats).

10. **Fruits Of Nature—UMC's (Wild Pitch, 1991)**
An eclectic, perpetually overlooked post-D.A.I.S.Y. Age jewel in the rough. Forget the image of the group sparring with a bizarre puppet in its "Blue Cheese" video and drift away to the funky fresh beats of this Shaolin never-never land.

11. **Girls I Got 'Em Locked—Super Lover Cee & Casanova Rud (Elektra, 1988)**

AWARDS.

A forgotten gem from hip hop's golden era. Funky dope maneuvers and rapid-fire lyrics straight outta Astoria, Queens.

12. *Livin' Proof*—**Group Home (Payday, 1995)**
From sequencing to interludes to the actual tracks, this shamefully neglected LP remains one of DJ Premier's finest top-to-bottom production efforts. Low budget environments striving for perfection.

13. *Never Dated*—**Milk (American, 1995)**
Shrill Audio Two frontman goes solo with incredible, ear-shattering results. Timeless moment: a special guest appearance on "Spam" from Beastie Boy Adrock.

14. *The New World Order*—**Poor Righteous Teachers (Profile, 1996)**
Newark's Five Percent mainstays came with a hot fourth album (complete with guest shots from KRS-One and the Fugees) at the point in which most groups kick the bucket. A well-balanced program anchored by the anthemic "Gods, Earths And 85ers," featuring rap lion king Nine.

15. *Play Witcha Mama*—**Willie D (Ichiban, 1994)**
Misunderstood Geto Boy-on-the-run broke away from the Rap-A-Lot family and paid the price commercially but not artistically. Bolstered by tunes like "Shit Is Real (My Mind's Still Playin' Tricks On Me)," "I Wanna Fuck Your Mama" and the Ice Cube-guested title track, *Play Witcha Mama* is arguably Willie's finest solo effort.

16. *Retaliation, Revenge And Get Back*—**Daz Dillinger (Death Row, 1998)**
The last man standing on Death Row never had a chance. Label kingpin Suge Knight's incarceration helped relegate this promising album to tax write-off status.

17. *Slaughtahouse*—**Masta Ace (Delicious Vinyl, 1993)**
An exceptional concept album that outwitted old Juice Crew fans expecting more rhyming with Biz.

18. *Straight From The Basement Of Kooley High!*—**Original Concept (Def Jam, 1988)**
Kooley High's fun-filled pastiche of juvenile jokery featured future *Yo! MTV Raps* host Doctor Dré and sidekick T-Money. However, it couldn't help but be overshadowed by the release of two of the greatest albums of all-time from labelmates P.E. (*It Takes A Nation Of Millions To Hold Us Back*) and Slick Rick (*The Great Adventures Of Slick Rick*).

19. *Vagina Diner*—**Akinyele (Interscope, 1993)**
Two tons of boasts, freaky tales and wicked wordplay. Plus, it's the only complete LP production from Large Professor outside of Main Source's *Breaking Atoms*.

20. *We Could Get Used To This*—**Alliance (First Priority, 1988)**
We could've gotten used to more from this super superb Brooklyn trio, who basked in the shadow of higher profile labelmates Audio Two and MC Lyte.

The *ego trip* Achievement Awards.

1. **The Sammy Davis Jr. Thrill Me Award: Doug E. Fresh**
After splitting with partner Slick Rick, the Original Human Beatbox displayed his unparalleled versatility and willingness to please absolutely everybody in the world. Doug E. dabbled in go-go ("I'm Gettin' Ready"), bilingual rap ("Vida Mia"), religion ("All The Way To Heaven"), ragga-rhythm ("Freaks"), abortion ("Abortion"), starred in a feature film (*Let's Get Bizzee*), briefly joined the Hammer family (1992's *Doin' What I Gotta Do*) and continued to rock one of hip hop's forgotten cornerstones, the harmonica, in concert. Whew!

2. **Worst Rap Industry Trend Of The Late '90s: Shipping (Fool's) Gold**
Hip hop's got more plaque than the Cavity Creeps (y'know, those indentured Black dudes that got busy on your pearly whites). But, alas, all that glitters ain't gold. Today, it is common industry practice for record labels to rig sales results based on advanced hype and pre-orders—not actual units moved. Blockbuster first week showings make way for the motherlode: a bunch of little fucking trophies that don't really impress anyone but your doting aunt and local chickenheads. Stop shamming: a lot of you Reynolds rappers are going bronze.

3. **Hypocritter Award: Jimmy "The Girlies I Like Are Underage . . ." Page**
Led Zeppelin's pasty hoochie coochie man sued Philly Gucci coochie man Schoolly D for unauthorized usage of "Kashmir" on Schoolly's "Signifying Rapper" after hearing it in the Abel Ferrara film, *Bad Lieutenant*. Years later, the suddenly rap-friendly Page flipped the script for some of that *Godzilla* scrilla by making the unlistenable "Come With Me" (a/k/a "Kashmir '98—I Like That") with Puff Daddy.

4. **Iron Man Endurance Award: Freddie Foxxx**
Despite recording one album (1989's overlooked *Freddie Foxxx Is Here*) and guest spots on records by Kool G Rap, Naughty By Nature and Boogie Down Productions, former Eric B. & Rakim bodyguard Funkmaster Freddie Foxxx might have wound up a forgotten footnote in hip hop history. But in one of the most surprising and inspiring career turnarounds around, Foxxx, fueled by heralded collaborations with O.C., Gang Starr and M.O.P., has muscled his way to the vanguard of the contemporary underground hip hop scene. Backpackers beware, he carries a full pack.

5. **Mr. Potential Underachiever Award: Method Man**
Wu-Tang's most charismatic industry party bumrusher has skills, respect and more female fans than the Blackstreet Usher Boys. He's also got two enjoyable, commercially-proven albums that still, unfortunately, only hint at his true artistic capabilities. Meth appears best off when keeping it Stapleton Projects grimy (as "Bring The Pain" and "Dangerous Ground" demonstrate) and staving off "Judgement Day's" runaway Trans Euro-Express. Get back, get back, get back to where you once belonged.

AWARDS.

6. **Steve Harvey Overachiever Award: Noreaga**
Not blessed with the lyrical sophistication of a Rakim, Queens, NY's most unorthodox rhyme peddler spits non-sensical, riddle-filled verses that have made him the perennial people's choice. "Ay yo, we light a candle/ Run laps around the English Channel/ Neptunes, I got a cocker spaniel," Nore growls on his phenomenal hit single, "SuperThug." Mo' lyrics of fury please.

7. **You Can Take The Nigga Out Of The Ghetto (And The Album Title) Award: *Only Built 4 Cuban Linx . . . —* Raekwon (Loud, 1995)**
The actual title of Rae's Wu Gambino masterwork is *Only Built 4 Cuban Linx Niggas*. Betcha didn't know that. But contrary to the title, Rae was wrong. This was the Wu's most universally revered anthology of street corner wisdom.

8. **The Moment We Feared Award: Q-Tip With The Beastie Boys At Madison Square Garden, 1998**
A Tribe Called Quest had announced its retirement preceeding the commencement of the Beasties' Hello Nasty Tour, for which Quest filled the opening band slot. During the Beasties' closing set, Q-Tip was invited on stage to rock his spot on "Get It Together," his duet with the group. The Abstract (apparently high off of the adrenaline rush of his homecoming performance), electrified the capacity caucasian crowd with some Jim Jones-esque revisionist history. Gushily, he stated, "If it weren't for the Beastie Boys, hip hop wouldn't be in the glory that it's in today." Hallelujah—(white) kids hear this!

9. **Worst Lyrical Switch-Up In The Face Of 50,000 White People: KRS-One At The 1997 Tibetan Freedom Concert, Randall's Island, NY**
In the midst of performing his jeep-slammer, "MC's Act Like They Don't Know," KRS acted like we didn't know that the song contained the lyrics, "Now they got white kids calling themselves 'niggers.'" Conveniently enough, the Blastmaster—between chucking autographed tennis balls into the crowd like a deranged Black John McEnroe—had the wits about him to stop the song before uttering these hurtful words at the sea of appreciative honky tonk boys and girls. Now tell us, what the fuck was he supposed to do?

10. **Most Entertaining Hip Hop Characteristic Of All-Time Award: The Preposterous Rap Rumor**
From Big Daddy Kane confessing to Barbara Walters that he had AIDS on *20/20* to Rakim serving time for dope dealing on Riker's Island to Suge Knight getting stabbed in the neck with a chicken bone in prison to Lauryn Hill declaring that her white fans don't matter, the rap rumor mill just keeps on churning out the he-said-she-said fodder. More outrageous than a Busta Rhymes costume change, rap gossip continues to provide hours of amusing water cooler conversation. Keep on talking . . . shit.

BONUS B

The B-Side Wins Again.

1. **"The Bridge"—MC Shan (Bridge, 1986)**
   B-SIDE OF: "Beat Biter"

2. **"Bring The Noise"—Public Enemy (Def Jam, 1987)**
   B-SIDE OF: "Are You My Woman?"—Black Flames

3. **"Broken Language"—Smoothe Da Hustler featuring Trigger Tha Gambler (Profile, 1996)**
   B-SIDE OF: "Hustlin'"

4. **"Buck Whylin'"—Terminator X featuring Chuck D & Sister Souljah (RAL, 1991)**
   B-SIDE OF: "Wanna Be Dancin'"—Terminator X featuring Celo (Casino Brothers)

5. **"A Chorus Line"—Ultramagnetic MC's (Next Plateau, 1989)**
   B-SIDE OF: "Traveling At The Speed Of Thought (Hip House Mix)"

6. **"DWYCK"—Gang Starr featuring Nice & Smooth (Chrysalis, 1992)**
   B-SIDE OF: "Take It Personal"

7. **"How I Could Just Kill A Man"—Cypress Hill (Ruffhouse, 1991)**
   B-SIDE OF: "The Phuncky Feel One"

8. **"It's Not A Game"—Pete Rock & CL Smooth (Elektra, 1994)**
   B-SIDE OF: "Lots Of Lovin'"

9. **"Jack The Ripper"—LL Cool J (Def Jam, 1987)**
   B-SIDE OF: "Going Back To Cali"

10. **"J. Beez Comin' Through"—The Jungle Brothers (Warner Bros., 1990)**
    B-SIDE OF: "What 'U' Waitin' '4'?"

11. **"King Tim III (Personality Jock)"—Fatback (Spring, 1979)**
    B-SIDE OF: "You're My Candy Sweet"

12. **"Let's Go"—Kool Moe Dee (Jive, 1988)**
    B-SIDE OF: "Respect"

13. **"A Million And One Questions"—Jay-Z (Roc-A-Fella, 1997)**
    B-SIDE OF: "The City Is Mine"

14. **"Rebel Without A Pause"—Public Enemy (Def Jam, 1987)**
    B-SIDE OF: "You're Gonna Get Yours"

15. **"Roxanne, Roxanne"—U.T.F.O. (Select, 1984)**
    B-SIDE OF: "Hangin' Out"

16. **"Sherm Stick"—Jayo Felony (JMJ, 1994)**
    B-SIDE OF: "Niggas And Bitches"

17. **"6 'N The Mornin'"—Ice-T (Techno-Hop, 1986)**
    B-SIDE OF: "Dog'n The Wax"

18. **"Supersonic"—J.J. Fad (Dream Team, 1987)**
    B-SIDE OF: "Anotha Ho"

19. **"Top Billin'"—Audio Two (First Priority, 1987)**
    B-SIDE OF: "Make It Funky"

20. **"Wrath Of Kane"—Big Daddy Kane (Cold Chillin', 1988)**
    B-SIDE OF: "I'll Take You There (Remix)"

BONUS BEATS.

The Dubwiser Selects
The 10 Worst Rap-Reggae Songs Of All-Time.

At its best, reggae mixed with hip hop can sound like a family reunion. Think of records like KRS-One and Shabba Ranks' "The Jam" (Epic, 1991) or Doug E. Fresh and Papa San's amazing live performances. But at its worst, "ragga-rap" sounds like a listless mutant hybrid, a laboratory accident spawned in an urban marketing meeting. Here are some of the most tragic missteps in a long, undistinguished tradition.

1. **"Make Way For The Indian"—Apache Indian featuring Tim Dog (Island, 1994)**
The man who brought you "Fuck Compton" licks shots for the raja!

2. **"Tell Me"—Beenie Man featuring Angie Martinez (VP Records, 1998)**
Good song + remix with well-known radio personality who wants to be a rapper ≠ a hit tune.

3. **"Original Man"—Capleton featuring Q-Tip (Def Jam, 1997)**
Hey, even The Prophet can have a bad day.

4. **"Straight From Queens"—LL Cool J featuring Lieutenant Stitchie (Def Jam, 1993)**
Lieutenant Loves Cool J's funky flow on this forgotten gem from *14 Shots To The Dome*.

5. **"Two Bredrens"—Shabba Ranks featuring Chubb Rock (Epic, 1995)**
A song that's every bit as beautiful as a friendship between two men who aren't afraid to show that they care about each other—just one human being to another.

6. **"Jump (Dessork Mix)"—Kris Kross featuring Super Cat (Ruffhouse, 1992)**
Daddy Mack/Mack Daddy meet Don Dada in this historic cultural event.

7. **"Who You Are"—Yankee B featuring Big Punisher & Reign (Gee Street, 1998)**
Pun's line—"Why niggas bluff like they raggamuff?"—kinda says it all.

8. **"Life Of A Shortie"—Vicious featuring Shyheim (Epic, 1994)**
Even scarier than the movie *KIDS*.

9. **"Roll 'Em Up"—Vanilla Ice (SBK, 1994)**
The Ice Beast shows his versatility with an effortless segue from Cameo-'do to raggamuff mop top. And rastas do be blazing their hootie-mack!

10. **"Dead End Street"—Mad Cobra featuring Geto Boys (Columbia, 1993)**
Kingston meets Houston inna doo-doo stylee.

BONUS LIFETIME ACHIEVEMENT AWARD: Mad Lion & Snow (tie)
Making Average Dollars Lifting Irie Otherman Notions and Stylish Nordic Octaroon Wildman. Yes, Jah!

THIRD RUNNER-UP: Wyclef Jean
Copping Leftovers Everywhere for Free (C.L.E.F.). Check the Refugee's verse on "Here We Go"—Khadejia featuring Product (Loud, 1998) on which the Haitian Sensation lifted verbatim from Spragga Benz's hit tune, "We No Like" (Xtra Large, 1997).

The Dubwiser is the don dada of reggae knowledge. In between his extensive interviews with the genre's elite, he enjoys lounging at home listening to rare 45s on his old school juke box—seen!

DOWN WITH THE KING OF POP:
Rappers Who've Collaborated With Michael Jackson.

1. **A+ (Wreckx-N-Effect):**
   "She Drives Me Wild" (Epic, 1991)

2. **John Forté:**
   "2 Bad (Refugee Camp Mix)" (Epic, 1997)

3. **Heavy D:**
   "Jam" (Epic, 1991)

4. **The Notorious B.I.G.:**
   "This Time Around" (Epic, 1995)

5. **Shaquille O'Neal:**
   "2 Bad" (Epic, 1995)

6. **Treach:**
   "Scream (Naughty By Nature Remix)" (Epic, 1995)

HONORABLE MENTIONS: Run-D.M.C. recorded an unreleased song with big Mike about the dangers of crack for the *Bad* LP. LL Cool J also joined forces with Jacko for *Dangerous*, but again, the material was left in the can somewhere in a vault in Neverland.

(DON'T) COME TOGETHER:
Worst Rap-Rock Collabos Of All-Time.

1. "Come With Me"—Puff Daddy & Jimmy Page (Epic, 1998)
2. "Lethal"—U.T.F.O. featuring Anthrax (Select, 1987)
3. "Radio Song"—R.E.M. featuring KRS-One (Warner Bros., 1991)
4. "Street Rock"—Kurtis Blow featuring Bob Dylan (Mercury, 1986)*
5. "Step Right In"—Dog Eat Dog featuring RZA (Roadrunner, 1996)
6. "War"—Bone Thugs-N-Harmony, Henry Rollins, Tom Morello & Flea (Dreamworks, 1998)
7. "Fame 90"—David Bowie featuring Queen Latifah (EMI, 1990)
8. "This Means War!!"—Busta Rhymes featuring Ozzy Osbourne (Elektra, 1998)
9. "Big 12 Inch"—The Don featuring Ted Nugent (RAL, 1991)**
10. "The Omen"—DMX featuring Marilyn Manson (Def Jam, 1998)

*Also the worst use ever of "Seven Minutes Of Funk"—The Whole Darn Family (Soul International, 1976).
**Your man The Nuge not only plays guitar but rhymes on this abomination.

RAP THIS WAY:
Rap Covers Of Rock Songs.

1. "Alone Again Naturally"—Biz Markie (Cold Chillin', 1991)
2. "Big Girls Don't Cry"—MC Lyte (First Priority, 1988)
3. "Do Wah Diddy"—2 Live Crew (Luke Skyywalker, 1988)
4. "Hit Me With Your Best Shot"—Antoinette (Next Plateau, 1989)
5. "Iron Man"—Sir Mix-A-Lot featuring Metal Church (Def American, 1988)
6. "Louie Louie"—Fat Boys (Tin Pan Apple, 1988)
7. "Magic Carpet Ride"—Grandmaster Flash & The Furious Five featuring John Kay of Steppenwolf (Elektra, 1988)
8. "Mary Mary"—Run-D.M.C. (Profile, 1988)
9. "Norwegian Wood"—PM Dawn (Gee Street, 1993)
10. "Pretty Woman"—2 Live Crew (Luke, 1989)
11. "Should I Stay Or Should I Go"—Mack 10 featuring Ice Cube (Priority, 1998)
12. "Shout (Rap Version)"—Craig G (Pop Art, 1985)
13. "Takin' Care Of Business"—Kurtis Blow (Mercury, 1980)
14. "They're Coming To Take Me Away (Ha Haa)"—Biz Markie (Prism, 1986)
15. "The Twist"—Fat Boys & Chubby Checker (Tin Pan Apple, 1988)
16. "Twist And Shout"—Salt-N-Pepa (Next Plateau, 1988)
17. "Walk This Way"—Run-D.M.C. featuring Aerosmith (Profile, 1986)
18. "Wipeout!"—Fat Boys & The Beach Boys (Tin Pan Apple, 1987)

BONUS BEATS.

5 Rock 'N Roll Memories
From Cee-Lo Of The Goodie Mob.

1. Black Stones & Blondie.
When I first heard "Miss You" from the Rolling Stones, I thought they were Black. I used to love "Miss You." I used to hear it on the radio all the time. This was at a time when there wasn't necessarily rap like we know it now. Like Blondie's "Rapture" is most definitely one of the first rap cadences I ever heard. I had heard them do "Heart Of Glass" too. But that "Rapture" song used to have an eerie kind of vibe to me. It was kinda ill.

2. The Glamorous Life.
Later on, I used to like "The Look Of Love" by ABC. That's like the first 45 I bought. But then I got into Billy Idol and that Poison "Talk Dirty To Me"-type of era—the glam rock look wit' Twisted Sister and Quiet Riot. I forgot their last names, but there was a Carlos and a Kevin in Quiet Riot. My name is Carlos and my cousin's name is Kevin. So I used to be like, "Well, I'm the guitar player Carlos," and we would lip-synch to "Cum On Feel The Noize."

At the time, a lot of the Iron Maiden artwork was tuff. That's some childhood shit I remember. They were big at one time wit' those T-shirts. Did I have an Iron Maiden shirt? Nah. I may have had a Wham T-shirt . . . nah, that was a joke, man. I could never fuck wit' them. I never did go that far.

3. Hellraiser.
The biggest impression rock had on me was this backward masking seminar I went to like in '84. It was at a church in Atlanta. They played Led Zeppelin's "Stairway To Heaven," Queen's "Another One Bites The Dust" and AC/DC's "Highway To Hell" backwards. They had a slide machine and they were showin' the album covers, like the one where Angus Young from AC/DC had the horns in his hat.

I was scared to death. I actually snatched my rock posters down in my room after that, you know what I'm sayin'? But before that, I remember my mother wouldn't

let me get the Mötley Crüe *Shout At The Devil* album. She happened to be all-the-way religious. So I was like, "No, they not sayin', 'Shout *wit'* the Devil.' They sayin', 'Shout *at* the Devil.'" But, still, they had the pentagram on the damn album cover.

4. Punk Rock Rap.
I'm a rapper by profession and a punk rocker in spirit. Punk rock is the equivalent of hip hop because it's rebellious, it's expressive, it's a big "fuck you" to the system. So I guess that's why I was attracted to it—because it was just wild. Wit' me stage-divin' I just let myself go. It's just fun, man.

My first stage-divin' was done on a tour in '97. Actually, one night in New York at Roseland nobody caught me when I stage dove. I ain't no lil' fella, so usually I like to let the crowd know I'm comin' out there. But this time I was just back near the drum riser diggin' the Fishbone set. And I just took off. I jumped and nobody caught me. But I didn't hit the ground hard or anything. I got right up, moshed a lil' bit and I was out of there.

5. The Lizard King.
I was lookin' at the Doors movie and there's a part where Jim Morrison's walkin' in a club. He's gonna meet Andy Warhol, and Velvet Underground's "Venus In Furs" is playin'. And it sounded like some type of alien sound. I was like, "Damn, what the hell is that?" I thought it was a Doors song. But I ended up likin' a lot of the Velvet Underground's and the Doors' music. But it was really Jim Morrison's personality that I liked. I'm actually like a cult fan of his. He's a cool white boy to me. And Val Kilmer sure acted it out too. Jim Morrison reminds me of me.

If Cee-Lo, one-fourth of southern specialists Goodie Mob, could assemble his own dream rock 'n roll band, the line-up would go as follows: Jim Morrison (lead singer); Tommy Lee, Alex Van Halen or John Bonham (drums); Flea (bass) and Eddie Van Halen, Eric Clapton or Jeff Beck (guitar). Let it roll, baby, roll.

Songs That End With Explosions.

1. "Audio X"—Cypress Hill featuring Barron Ricks (Ruffhouse, 1998)
2. "Blowin' Up The Spot"—Gang Starr (Chrysalis, 1994)
3. "Blow Your Mind (Remix)"—Redman (Def Jam, 1992)
4. "Born 2 Be A Soldier"—Mystikal featuring Master P & Silkk The Shocker (No Limit, 1997)
5. "Follow The Leader"—Eric B. & Rakim (Uni, 1988)
6. "Get At Me Dog"—DMX featuring Sheek (The Lox) (Def Jam, 1998)
7. "I Ain't No Joke"—Eric B. & Rakim (4th & B'way, 1987)
8. "I'm A Soldier"—Silkk The Shocker featuring Master P, Fiend, C-Murder, Mystikal, Mac, Skull Duggery, Big Ed & Mia X (No Limit, 1998)
9. "I'm Blowin' Up"—Kool Moe Dee (Jive, 1989)
10. "Louder Than A Bomb"—Public Enemy (Def Jam, 1988)
11. "Older Gods"—Wu-Tang Clan (Loud, 1997)
12. "Quiet On Tha Set"—Big Punisher, Fat Joe & Cuban Link (Priority, 1998)
13. "Raise The Roof"—Public Enemy (Def Jam, 1987)
14. "She's On It"—Beastie Boys (Def Jam, 1985)
15. "Show & Prove"—Big Daddy Kane featuring Big Scoob, Sauce Money, Shyheim, Jay-Z & Ol' Dirty Bastard (MCA, 1994)

Can't Get Enough... Of That Monkey Stuff!

1. *A Constipated Monkey*—Kurious (Columbia, 1994)
2. "Gorilla"—C.E.B. (Ruffhouse, 1993)
3. "Gorillapimpin'"—Above The Law (Tommy Boy, 1996)
4. "Guerillas Ain't Gangstas"—Da Lench Mob (Jive, 1993)
5. "Guerillas In Tha Mist"—Da Lench Mob (Street Knowledge, 1992)
6. "Guerillas In The Mist"—Paris (Scarface, 1992)
7. "Let Da Monkey Out"—Redman (Def Jam, 1998)
8. "Monkey Off My Back"—Yall So Stupid (Rowdy, 1993)
9. "Monkey On My Back"—C.E.B. (Ruffhouse, 1993)
10. "Planet Of Da Apes"—Da Lench Mob (Priority, 1994)
11. "Put The Monkey In It"—Daz Dillinger & Soopafly (Tommy Boy, 1997)
12. "Primates In Stitches"—The Future Sound (EastWest, 1992)

25 Bumpin' Car Songs.

1. "Benz Or Beamer"—OutKast (Tommy Boy, 1995)
2. "The Boomin' System"—LL Cool J (Def Jam, 1990)
3. "Born To Roll"—Masta Ace (Delicious Vinyl, 1993)
4. "Carhoppers"—Positive K (Island, 1992)
5. "Cars"—Kool G Rap & DJ Polo (Cold Chillin', 1988)
6. "Cars"—Masta Ace (INC, 1998)
7. "Cars With The Boom"—L'Trimm (Atlantic, 1988)
8. "Crazy 'Bout Cars"—Doug E. Fresh & The Get Fresh Crew (Reality, 1988)
9. "Cutlass, Monte Carlo's & Regals"—Big Tymers (Cash Money, 1998)
10. "Dippin'"—King Tee (MCA, 1994)
11. "Driveby Miss Daisy"—Compton's Most Wanted (Orpheus, 1991)
12. "Fuck My Car"—U.G.K. (Jive, 1996)
13. "If It Ain't A Caddy (It Ain't A Car)"—Double J (4th & B'way, 1991)
14. "Jeep Ass Niguh"—Masta Ace (Delicious Vinyl, 1993)
15. "Jeeps, Lex Coups, Bimaz & Benz"—Lost Boyz (Universal, 1996)
16. "Let Me Ride"—Dr. Dre (Death Row, 1992)
17. "My Hooptie"—Sir Mix-A-Lot (Def American, 1989)
18. "On Them Thangs"—Mack 10 (Priority, 1995)
19. "Rolling In My '64"—Pistol (Ruthless, 1994)
20. "Sittin' On Chrome"—Masta Ace (Delicious Vinyl, 1995)
21. "Six Tray"—Freestyle Fellowship (4th & B'way, 1993)
22. "Sobb Story"—Leaders Of The New School (Elektra, 1991)
23. "Two Dope Boyz (In A Cadillac)"—OutKast (LaFace, 1996)
24. "Westside Story"—Yo Yo (EastWest, 1993)
25. "You're Gonna Get Yours"—Public Enemy (Def Jam, 1987)

BONUS BEATS.

Cover art from De La Soul's "Millie Pulled A Pistol On Santa" (Tommy Boy, 1991)

HO! HO! HO!

ego trip's 15 Favorite Goddamn Christmas Songs.

1. "Christmas Fuckin' Day"—Luke (Luke, 1994)
2. "Christmas In Hollis"—Run-D.M.C. (Profile, 1987)
3. "Christmas Rappin'"—Kurtis Blow (Mercury, 1979)
4. "Dana Dane Is Coming To Town"—Dana Dane (Profile, 1987)
5. "Let The Jingle Bells Rock"—Sweet Tee (Profile, 1987)
6. "Merry Muthafuckin' Christmas"—Eazy-E (Ruthless, 1992)
7. "The Night Before Christmas"—Cutmaster D.C. (Zakia, 1985)
8. "Rappin' Christmas"—The Cold Crew (Profile, 1982)
9. "Santa Claus Goes Straight To The Ghetto"—Snoop Doggy Dogg (Death Row, 1996)
10. "Santa Is A B-Boy"—Whistle (Select, 1985)
11. "Santa's Beat Box"—Cutmaster D.C. (Zakia, 1986)
12. "Santa's Groove"—Lightning Rich, Big John & The Maniacs (Slice, 1985)
13. "Santa's Rap"—Treacherous Three (Atlantic, 1984)
14. "Santa's Rap Party"—Super J (Sound Of New York USA, 1980)
15. "Season's Greetings"—Sound On Sound Productions (Reflection, 1980)

DELICIOUS VINYL:
50 Songs With Food Titles.

1. "Beef"—Boogie Down Productions (Jive, 1990)
2. "Beef Pattie"—U.T.F.O. (Jive, 1991)
3. "Blue Cheese"—UMC's (Wild Pitch, 1991)
4. "Brown Sugar"—Extra Prolific (Jive, 1994)
5. "Candy And Cream"—Concentration Camp II (C-Loc, 1998)
6. "Can-O-Corn"—Coolio (Tommy Boy, 1994)
7. "Cappucino"—MC Lyte (First Priority, 1988)
8. "Cold Cuts"—Kool G Rap & DJ Polo (Cold Chillin', 1988)
9. "Cookies-N-Cream"—Screwball (Hydra, 1998)
10. "Cooky Puss"—Beastie Boys (Rat Cage, 1983)
11. "Cornbread"—Freestyle Fellowship (4th & B'way, 1993)
12. "Don't Drink The Milk"—Chubb Rock (Select, 1992)
13. "Fish"—Ghostface Killah featuring Cappadonna & Raekwon (Razor Sharp, 1996)
14. "Fish Heads"—Alliance (Atlantic, 1988)
15. "4 Chicken Wings And Rice"—Nine (Profile, 1996)
16. "Fried Chicken"—Ice-T (Sire, 1991)
17. "Funky Lemonade"—Chi Ali (Relativity, 1992)
18. "Green Eggs And Swine"—3rd Bass (Def Jam, 1991)
19. "Greens, Cornbread & Cabbage" —Kane & Abel (No Limit, 1998)
20. "Ham 'N Eggs"—A Tribe Called Quest (Jive, 1990)
21. "Hoe Cakes"—The Afros (Def Jam, 1990)
22. "Hot Fudge"—Busta Rhymes (Elektra, 1996)
23. "Hot Potato"—Freestyle Fellowship (4th & B'way, 1993)
24. "Ice Cream"—Raekwon featuring Method Man, Ghostface Killah & Cappadonna (Loud, 1995)
25. "I Like Cherries"—Audio Two (First Priority, 1988)
26. "Ketchup On My Hotdog" —Section 8 Mob (Dark City, 1994)
27. "Kibbles & Bits"—JCD & The Dawg LB. (Profile, 1992)
28. "Lobster & Scrimp"—Timbaland featuring Jay-Z (Blackground, 1998)
29. "Milk"—Parental Advisory (MCA, 1993)
30. "Milky Cereal"—LL Cool J (Def Jam, 1991)
31. "More Cheese"—Tru Bash (Bashton, 1997)
32. "No Bones In Ice Cream" —Nice & Smooth (Fresh, 1990)
33. "Oreo Cookie"—Alliance (First Priority, 1987)
34. "Pass The Pickle"—Prime Minister Pete Nice & Daddy Rich (Def Jam, 1993)
35. "Peaches"—OutKast (LaFace, 1994)
36. "Peas Porridge"—De La Soul (Tommy Boy, 1991)
37. "Pig Feet"—Fat Boys (Tin Pan Apple, 1988)
38. "Potato Chip"—The Dayton Family (Relativity, 1995)
39. "Poundcake"—Harmony (Virgin, 1990)
40. "Puddin' Pie"—Laquan (4th & B'way, 1990)
41. "Sandwiches (I Got A Feeling)" —Count Bass D (Hoppoh, 1995)
42. "Soda Pop"—Tha Alkaholiks featuring Field Trip (Loud, 1993)
43. "Soul Food"—Def Jef (Delicious Vinyl, 1991)
44. "Spam"—Milk (American, 1995)
45. "Spring Water"—LA The Darkman (Supreme Team, 1998)
46. "Sweet Potato Pie"—Domino (OutBurst, 1993)
47. "Time To Make The Doughnuts" —Class A Felony (Mercury, 1993)
48. "Verbal Milk"—X Clan (4th & B'way, 1990)
49. "Whipped Cream, Nuts & Cherries" —Goldy (Jive, 1994)
50. "Who Stole My Last Piece Of Chicken?"—Organized Konfusion (Hollywood BASIC, 1991)

BONUS BEATS.

Songs By Common With Food Titles.

1. "Food For Funk" (Relativity, 1997)
2. "Orange Pineapple Juice" (Relativity, 1994)
3. "Puppy Chow" (Relativity, 1992)
4. "Two Scoops Of Raisins" (Relativity, 1992)
5. "Watermelon" (Relativity, 1994)

MAMA'S IN THE KITCHEN:

Mia X's Creole Shrimp & Crabmeat Stew Recipe.

INGREDIENTS:

2 pounds of shrimp
2 containers of lump crabmeat
1 large onion (yellow onion preferred)
2 whole garlic cloves
2 large green bell peppers
1 green onion (scallions)
Fresh thyme
Parsley flakes
Cayenne pepper
Garlic powder
Onion powder
1 stick of margarine
2 cans of whole tomatoes
1 jar of your favorite tomato sauce
1 cup of water
1 teaspoon of sugar

INSTRUCTIONS:

1. Peel, wash and de-vein the shrimp.
2. Wash all vegetables and cut very fine.
3. In a sturdy pot, combine shrimp, crab, vegetables, spices, 1/2 stick of margarine, 1 cup of water and tomatoes.
4. Stir over medium fire.
5. Onions will appear translucent.
6. Shrimp will turn slightly orange while cooking.
7. Add salt, pepper, garlic powder, onion powder, parsley, thyme and cayenne pepper according to taste.
8. Continue to sauté. After 20 minutes, lower fire and add tomato sauce and remaining margarine.
9. Add one teaspoon of sugar to cut tartness of tomato sauce.
10. Stir occasionally.
11. Cover pot and allow to simmer, tasting every now and then, adding any spices according to taste.

This recipe serves six and is great over white or brown rice and pasta.

Mia X, the saucy queen of the No Limit tank, has been cooking since she was nine years old. But whether she's in the kitchen, on stage or in the studio knockin' out tasty albums like Unlady Like *and* Mama Drama, *this mama's always serving up the hot stuff.*

BROOKLYN KEEPS ON TAKIN' IT:
50 BK Big-Ups.

1. "Back To Brooklyn"—Prince Markie Dee (Columbia, 1992)
2. "B..B..B..Bklyn"—Ms. Melodie (Jive, 1989)
3. "The Big East"—Masta Ace (Delicious Vinyl, 1993)
4. "Boogie Down Bronx/BK Connection"—Nice & Smooth (Street Life, 1997)
5. "Borough Check"—Digable Planets (Pendulum, 1994)
6. "Brooklyn"—MC Lyte (First Priority, 1993)
7. "Brooklyn Battles"—Masta Ace (Cold Chillin', 1990)
8. "Brooklyn Blew Up The Bridge"—MC Mitchski (Ski, 1987)
9. "Brooklyn Bounce"—Daddy-O (Island, 1993)
10. "Brooklyn, Brooklyn"—Barsha (Virgin, 1990)
11. "Brooklyn Pride"—Lordz Of Brooklyn (American, 1995)
12. "Brooklyn-Queens"—3rd Bass (Def Jam, 1989)
13. "Brooklyn Rocks The Best"—Cutmaster D.C. (Zakia, 1986)
14. "Brooklyn's Finest"—Jay-Z featuring The Notorious B.I.G. (Roc-A-Fella, 1996)
15. "Brooklyn's In The House"—Cutmaster D.C. (Zakia, 1985)
16. "Brooklyn Story"—Unity 2 (Reprise, 1990)
17. "Brooklyn Style"—Choice MCs with Fresh Gordon (Rocky, 1985)
18. "Brooklyn Style . . . Laid Out"—Big Daddy Kane (MCA, 1994)
19. "Brooklyn To L.A."—Doctor Ice (Jive, 1989)
20. "Brooklyn Took It"—Jeru The Damaja (Payday, 1994)
21. "Brooklyn To T-Neck"—Das EFX (EastWest, 1992)
22. "The Brooklyn Uptown Connection"—Ill Al Skratch (Mercury, 1994)
23. "Brooklyn Zoo"—Ol' Dirty Bastard (Elektra, 1995)
24. "Brooklyn Zoo II (Tiger Crane)"—Ol' Dirty Bastard featuring Ghostface Killah (Elektra, 1995)
25. "Brownsville"—M.O.P. (Relativity, 1996)
26. "Brownsville"—Queen Latifah (Motown, 1998)
27. "Brownsville II Long Beach"—Heltah Skeltah featuring Tha Dogg Pound (Duck Down, 1998)
28. "Bucktown"—Smif-N-Wessun (Nervous, 1994)
29. "The Bush"—Special Ed (Profile, 1989)
30. "Crooklyn"—Crooklyn Dodgers (MCA, 1994)
31. "Do Or Die Bed Sty"—Divine Sounds (Reality, 1986)
32. "East NY Theory"—Group Home featuring Brainsick Mob (Tape Kingz, 1996)
33. "A Flower Grows In Brooklyn"—Positive K (Island, 1992)
34. "Fort Greene (S)killz"—Dana Dane (Maverick, 1995)
35. "Go Brooklyn 1"—Stetsasonic (Tommy Boy, 1987)
36. "Go Brooklyn 3"—Stetsasonic (Tommy Boy, 1991)
37. "Hello Brooklyn (B-Boy Bouillabaisse)"—Beastie Boys (Capitol, 1989)
38. "The Hill That's Real"—Lil' Fame (4th & B'way, 1992)
39. "Kickin' 4 Brooklyn"—MC Lyte (First Priority, 1988)
40. "Lost In Brooklyn"—Down South (Big Beat, 1994)
41. "Madina Passage"—John Forté (Ruffhouse, 1998)
42. "Medina's In Da House"—Blahzay Blahzay (Mercury, 1996)
43. "The Place Where We Dwell"—Gang Starr (Chrysalis, 1992)
44. "The Planet"—Gang Starr (Chrysalis, 1994)
45. "Took Place In East New York"—Stetsasonic (Tommy Boy, 1991)
46. "Return Of The Crooklyn Dodgers"—Crooklyn Dodgers '95 (MCA, 1995)
47. "Up On Prospect"—Hillfiguz (Dolo, 1996)
48. "Where Brooklyn At?"—DJ Mister Cee (Tape Kingz, 1995)
49. "Where I'm From"—Jay-Z (Roc-A-Fella, 1997)
50. "Wild Cowboys In Bucktown"—Originoo Gunn Clappaz (Duck Down, 1996)

WHITE PEOPLE TAKE NOTE: "No Sleep Til Brooklyn" by the Beastie Boys is about touring, not Brooklyn.

BONUS BEATS.

NUTHIN' BUT A "CPT" THANG:
Songs About Compton.

1. "Born & Raised In Compton"—DJ Quik (Profile, 1991)
2. "Compton & Watts"—B.G. Knocc Out & Dresta (OutBurst, 1995)
3. "Compton Bomb"—MC Eiht (Epic, 1994)
4. "Compton Cyco"—MC Eiht (Epic, 1994)
5. "Compton Forever"—Toddy Tee (Thump, 1995)
6. "Compton 4 Death"—MC Eiht (Epic, 1997)
7. "Compton 4 Life"—Compton's Most Wanted (Orpheus, 1992)
8. "Compton Hoe"—B.G. Knocc Out & Dresta (OutBurst, 1995)
9. "Compton Hoochies"—Hi-C (Skanless, 1991)
10. "Compton's In The House"—N.W.A (Ruthless, 1988)
11. "Compton's Lynchin'"—Compton's Most Wanted (Orpheus, 1991)
12. "Compton Swangin'"—B.G. Knocc Out & Dresta (OutBurst, 1995)
13. "It's A Compton Thang"—Compton's Most Wanted (Orpheus, 1990)
14. "Jus Lyke Compton"—DJ Quik (Profile, 1992)
15. "Live From Compton Saturday Night"—MC Ren (Ruthless, 1996)
16. "Raised In Compton"—Compton's Most Wanted (Orpheus, 1991)
17. "Real Compton City G's"—Eazy-E featuring B.G. Knocc Out & Dresta (Ruthless, 1993)
18. "Straight Outta Compton"—N.W.A (Ruthless, 1988)
19. "This Is Compton"—Compton's Most Wanted (Orpheus, 1990)
20. "Voyage To Compton"—MC Ren (Ruthless, 1998)
21. "Ya Better Bring A Gun"—King Tee featuring Mixmaster Spade (Techno Hop, 1987)

10 Reasons Why Will Smith Loves Miami.*

1. It's a place where he can really let go.
2. Every day is like Mardi Gras because everybody is partying hard (i.e., no work, all play).
3. Every time the ladies pass by Will they call out his name in adulation.
4. Most enjoyable is that said ladies are of all races and ages with real sweet faces.
5. More half-dressed ladies can be found on the Miami strip singing the praises of his music.
6. Hot, *mami*-packed meringue clubs are conveniently located right off the beach.
7. Even more international ladies come out the woodwork and when he's driving around in his drop-top Bentley they jock Will.
8. There's plenty of Dominican women with cinnamon tans.
9. He really enjoys taking long walks on the beach and drawing hearts in the sand with his true honey-bun. (Peace, Jada.)
10. If he's lucky, Will sees his main man Sly Stallone at clubs.

*Based on the international smash hit "Miami" (Columbia, 1997).

Give Me Body.

1. "Ankle Blues"—Da Lench Mob (Street Knowledge, 1992)
2. "Bang Your Head"—Gravediggaz (Gee Street, 1994)
3. "Belly Of The Beast"—Lifers Group (Hollywood BASIC, 1991)
4. "Big Mouth"—Whodini (Jive, 1984)
5. "Black Eyes And Chalk White Lips"—K-9 Posse (Arista, 1991)
6. "Blood On My Hands"—O.C.U. (Kapone, 1991)
7. "Brain"—Jungle Brothers (Gee Street, 1997)
8. "Cross My Heart"—Killah Priest (Geffen, 1998)
9. "Elbow Room"—Hurricane (Grand Royal, 1995)
10. "Eyes Are The Soul"—MC Lyte (First Priority, 1991)
11. "Finger On The Trigger"—Indo G & Lil' Blunt (Luke, 1994)
12. "Going For The Throat"—Craig G (Atlantic, 1991)
13. "Hair Or Weave"—Bobby Jimmy & The Critters (Priority, 1989)
14. "Hickey's On Your Chest"—Lil' Shawn (Capitol, 1992)
15. "Hit Me On The Hip"—Kid Sensation (Ichiban, 1996)

Give Me Bodily Functions.

1. "I Gotta Call Earl"—King Tee (Capitol, 1993)
2. "I'm Shittin' On 'Em"—Funkdoobiest (Immortal, 1993)
3. "Niggas Bleed"—The Notorious B.I.G. (Bad Boy, 1997)
4. "P Upon A Tree"—Run-D.M.C. (Profile, 1990)
5. "Rest In Piss"—Brotha Lynch Hung (Black Market, 1995)
6. "Room To Breathe"—Downtown Science (Def Jam, 1991)
7. "She Swallowed It"—N.W.A (Ruthless, 1991)
8. "Somebody Farted"—Bobby Jimmy & The Critters (Priority, 1989)
9. "Tears"—Da King & I (Rowdy, 1993)
10. "'U' Make Me Sweat"—Jungle Brothers (Warner Bros., 1989)

FUNKY TECHNICIANS:
8 Songs About Body Odor.

1. "The Dragon"—Biz Markie (Cold Chillin', 1989)
2. "I'm Funky"—Bobby Jimmy & The Critters (Priority, 1989)
3. "I Stink 'Cause I'm Funky"—Funk Master Wizard Wiz (Tuff City, 1985)
4. "A Little Bit Of Soap"—De La Soul (Tommy Boy, 1989)
5. "Stank Breath"—Chunky A (MCA, 1989)
6. "Underarms"—Grandmaster Flash & The Furious Five (Elektra, 1987)
7. "Wash Your Ass"—Convicts (Rap-A-Lot, 1991)
8. "You Stink"—Captain Rock (Nia, 1985)

BONUS BEATS.

16. "Lend Me An Ear"—The D.O.C. (Atlantic, 1989)
17. "Let Your Backbone Slide"—Maestro Fresh Wes (LMR, 1989)
18. "Lisa Lipps"—Cru (Def Jam, 1997)
19. "No Nose Job"—Digital Underground (Tommy Boy, 1991)
20. "Pat Your Foot"—Hurricane (Grand Royal, 1995)
21. "Pump Your Fist"—Kool Moe Dee (Jive, 1989)
22. "Strictly Snappin' Necks"—EPMD (Fresh, 1989)
23. "Suspect Chin Music"—Method Man featuring Street Life (Def Jam, 1998)
24. "Take It To Ya Face"—Naughty By Nature (Tommy Boy, 1993)
25. "Tip Of The Tongue"—Mad Skillz (Big Beat, 1996)
26. "Toe To Toe"—Kid 'N Play (Select, 1990)
27. "Tooth 4 A Tooth"—Bustin' Melonz (Continuum, 1994)
28. "Understanding The Inner Mind's Eye"—Leaders Of The New School (Elektra, 1991)
29. "Windpipe"—Wu-Tang Clan featuring RZA, Ol' Dirty Bastard & Ghostface Killah (Def Jam, 1998)
30. "You Must Be Out Of Your Fuckin' Mind"—Fat Joe featuring Apache & Kool G Rap (Relativity, 1993)

Butt . . . Of Course!

1. "A.F.D. (Ass For Days)"—Domino (Outburst, 1993)
2. "Baby Got Back"—Sir Mix-A-Lot (Rhyme Cartel, 1992)
3. "Back That Azz Up"—Juvenile featuring Mannie Fresh & Lil Wayne (Cash Money, 1998)
4. "Big Booty"—Ultramagnetic MC's (Wild Pitch, 1993)
5. "Big Ole Butt"—LL Cool J (Def Jam, 1989)
6. "Da Booty"—A Tribe Called Quest (Jive, 1998)
7. "Tha Booty Up"—AMG (Select, 1991)
8. "Bounce That Azz"—Down South Hustlers (No Limit, 1995)
9. "Bust Dat Ass"—King Tee featuring Tha Alkaholiks (Capitol, 1993)
10. "Bust Dat Ass"—Onyx (Def Jam, 1993)
11. "Comin' For Datazz"—Gang Starr (Chrysalis, 1994)
12. "A Day In The Life Of My Asspipe"—Kwest Tha Madd Lad (American, 1996)
13. "Dazzey Duks"—Duice (Bellmark, 1992)
14. "Dunkie Butt"—12 Gauge (Street Life, 1994)
15. "Face Down Ass Up"—Luke (Luke, 1990)
16. "Feminine Fatt"—Leaders Of The New School (Elektra, 1991)
17. "Give Me Tha Ass"—The Beatnuts (Relativity, 1997)
18. "Lick My Ass"—Kool Keith (Funky Ass, 1997)
19. "Move Them Butts"—DJ Magic Mike And The Royal Posse (Magic, 1994)
20. "Rock 'Dat Ass"—B.O.X. (PWL, 1991)
21. "Rump Shaker"—Wreckx-N-Effect (MCA, 1992)
22. "Shake Dat Ass, Girl"—Mister Cee (Tape Kingz, 1995)
23. "Shake Your Booty"—Public Enemy (Def Jam, 1998)
24. "Shake Your Rump"—Beastie Boys (Capitol, 1989)
25. "Shit Pit!"—Odd Squad (Rap-A-Lot, 1994)
26. "Shorty's Got A Fat Ass"—Fat Joe (Relativity, 1993)
27. "Soft Shoe Booty"—King Sun (Profile, 1990)
28. "Stick Da Butt Out"—Rough House Survivors (Relativity, 1992)
29. "Tootsie Roll"—69 Boyz (Rip-It, 1994)
30. "Wakeupscratchyobutt!!!"—Kwamé (Atlantic, 1992)

BONUS BEATS.

A Few Of Biz Markie's Favorite Things.*

1. My Godzilla doll that blows fire and talks.
2. My AFX Slot Car Race Track.
3. My Rock 'Em Sock 'Em Robots.
4. My collection of action figures, especially Action Jackson, Muhammad Ali and Mr. T.
5. My Atari, Coleco Vision and Pong video games.
6. My 20 freestanding video games.
7. My *Frankenstein Jr.* cartoon videos.
8. My *Fat Albert* and *Wheelie & The Chopper Bunch* lunch boxes.
9. My collection of karate movie posters.
10. My original pair of blue & white Pumas.
11. My Japanese Mothra doll that spits a caterpillar web.
12. My "Take Me To The Mardi Gras" Bob James 12" single (It's without the bells. It's just the beat at first and then it comes into the bells. A lot of people don't even know, but "Mardi Gras" is a live record. It's on CTI. I guess it was a fluke cuz I never seen nobody else with it.)
13. The rest of my 12" promo single collection—especially "Misdemeanor"—Foster Sylvers, "Johnny The Fox"—Thin Lizzy, "Mister Magic"—Grover Washington Jr. and "Stiletto"—Billy Joel. (My 12" collection is out of this world. There's only a couple niggaz that can mess with me on the twelve inches.)
14. My collection of every version of "Get Out Of My Life Woman."
15. My John Travolta record with the break.
16. My white label promos of all of James Brown's albums.
17. My collection of Wacky Packs.
18. My *Welcome Back Kotter* and *Good Times* trading cards.
19. My Reggie Jackson candy bar wrapper.
20. My collection of *Mad* magazines.
21. My collection of every board game ever made.
22. My Barbie doll collection. (My treasure. I got them from the beginning, like from Marilyn Monroe days to now. I got different races from different countries and all that.)

*In no particular order.

When it comes to collecting rare pieces of pop culture paraphernalia, nobody beats the Diabolical Biz Markie. The creator of "Pickin' Boogers," "Vapors" and "Just A Friend" maintains two homes—one to house his vast range of collectibles and one to live in—but says, "I'm, like, a basic person."

1. Bill Adler And The Biz

2. Afu-Ra And The Biz

3. Alchemist And The Biz

4. Harry Allen And The Biz

5. Baby Paul And The Biz

6. Big Daddy Kane And The Biz

7. Big Punisher And The Biz

8. Big Shug And The Biz

9. Black Star And The Biz

———— And The Biz.

Masta (neé, *Master*) Ace's masterpiece, "Me And The Biz" (Cold Chillin', 1990), not only pioneered the short-lived genre of ventriloquism rap, but spawned the spiffy Biz Markie puppet pictured here. Don't ask us how we got our hands on him. Don't ask us if he's up for sale. And don't ask us why too-cool-for-school rap dudes get giddier than Webster on Wacko Jacko's lap at the very sight of him. Just pucker up when the *ego trip* Biz-Cam is in your town and say, "Government cheese!"

BONUS BEATS.

10. Cappadonna And The Biz

11. Daddy-O & Dyme And The Biz

12. Dead Prez And The Biz

13. El-P And The Biz

14. Eminem And The Biz

15. DJ Evil Dee And The Biz

16. Fat Joe And The Biz

17. Freddie Foxxx And The Biz

18. Bobbito Garcia And The Biz

19. Abélla Gomez Gotay (The Bike-Riding Hottie From Redman's "I'll Bee Dat" Video) And The Biz

20. Greg Nice And The Biz

21. Guru And The Biz

22. Haze And The Biz

23. Heather B. And The Biz

24. Mike Heron And The Biz

25. Kaves And The Biz

26. Kool Keith And The Biz

27. Krayzie Bone And The Biz

28. Lootpack And The Biz

29. Mac Mall And The Biz

30. Angie Martinez And The Biz

31. Debi Mazar And The Biz

32. M.O.P. And The Biz

33. Mr. Len And The Biz

34. Mr. Serv On And The Biz

35. Mr. Walt And The Biz

36. Ninety-9 And The Biz

37. Noreaga, Musolini & Maze And The Biz

38. Peanut Butter Wolf And The Biz

39. Percee P And The Biz

40. Pharoahe Monch And The Biz

41. Ricky Powell And The Biz

42. DJ Premier And The Biz

43. Prince Paul And The Biz

44. R.A. The Rugged Man And The Biz

45. A Kid Called Roots And The Biz

46. Scaramanga And The Biz

47. Schoolly D And The Biz

48. Shabaam Sahdeeq & Shazam And The Biz

49. Special K And The Biz

50. Tash And The Biz

51. Teflon And The Biz

52. Too Poetic And The Biz

53. Too $hort And The Biz

54. Wise And The Biz

55. Xzibit And The Biz

BONUS BEATS.

YOU JUST FOUND ELEVEN:
Bonus Moments
On CD & Wax That You Might Have Missed.

1. *Autobiography Of Mistachuck*—**Chuck D (Mercury, 1996)**
   At 9:22 of track number 12 on the CD, the distorted voice of Mistachuck lists his "10 Resentments Of The Industry" for four minutes and some seconds over cosmically sloppy organ runs.

2. *The Beatnuts*—**The Beatnuts (Relativity, 1995)**
   The 'Nuts' first full-length effort concludes 6:37 into the final CD track with an enormous burp.

3. *Diezzle Don & Tha Govener*—**Diezzle Don & Tha Govener (Lockdown, 1995)**
   1:50 into the final track of this Brick City duo's smoked-out debut reveals a bonus song, "Ill Funk Flow," featuring a funky intro from none other than fellow Jerseyite, Redman.

4. *Do You Want More?!!!??*—**The Roots (Geffen, 1994)**
   At 7:50 of track 16, "The Unlocking," the crew's resident human beatbox extraordinaire, Rahzel, does his spectacular kung-fu movie impersonation.

5. *Dr. Octagonecologyst*—**Dr. Octagon (Bulk, 1996)**
   6:44 into track 19 of the original Bulk Recordings edition of the CD reveals an excerpt from the film *Cabin Boy* and an untitled bonus song (later identified on the Dreamworks reissue as "halfsharkalligatorhalfman").

6. *Here To Save You All*—**Chino XL (American, 1996)**
   Selecting track 60 on Chino's overpacked punchline debut reveals a skit composed of tasteless Nicole Brown Simpson jokes that is more memorable than the album itself.

7. *"It's A Demo"*—**Kool G Rap & DJ Polo (Cold Chillin', 1986)**
   And ya don't stop: the instrumental version of this Marley Marl-produced classic concludes with G Rap's a cappella voice purposely repeating the song's title on the vinyl's inner groove, as the needle endlessly skips.

8. *Life After Death*—**The Notorious B.I.G. (Bad Boy, 1997)**
   The second pressings of this posthumous double CD contain an interview with Biggie (conducted in Los Angeles in the weeks preceeding his murder) that may be found at the end of Disc 1. During this 11-minute, 25-second conversation, Biggie discusses his thoughts in the aftermath of Tupac Shakur's death, his hopes of squashing any remaining tensions in the East Coast-West Coast feud and, most lamentably, his ambition to retire early and comfortably from the toils of the rap game.

9. *"Me Myself & I," "Ain't Hip To Be Labeled A Hippie" & "What's More" b/w "Me Myself & I (Oblapos Remix)" & "Brain Washed Follower"*—**De La Soul (Tommy Boy, 1988)**
   Hip hop's first and only "three-sided" single. Side B of the vinyl is pressed with side-by-side grooves of alternating programs. Depending on where you drop the needle, you'll either hear "Me Myself & I (Oblapos Remix)" or "Brain Washed Follower."

10. *My Field Trip To Planet 9*—**Justin Warfield (Qwest, 1993)**
    Bonus moments out the ying-yang. At the 1:30 mark of track 16, producer Prince Paul leaves an answering machine message for Justin in which he accuses Warfield of "biting his rhymes." This is immediately followed by a return message from Warfield pretending that he's Prince Paul. (Get it? He's biting his style, so he's calling back as Paul). *This* is followed by the jarring sound of the phone-being-left-off-the-hook and Warfield's voice informing us that, "The record's over." *This* is in turn followed by the bubbling of bongwater accompanied by Indian sitar music and the soothing sounds of ocean waves. At 7:16 it all mercifully comes to a close with the sound of a needle being dragged across a record. We've painstakingly detailed all of this for you so that you never have to experience it yourself.

11. *Sex Style*—**Kool Keith (Funky Ass, 1997)**
    4:58 into track 17 unveils a bonus cut of additional salaciousness set to the beat from EPMD's "You're A Customer."

CHAR

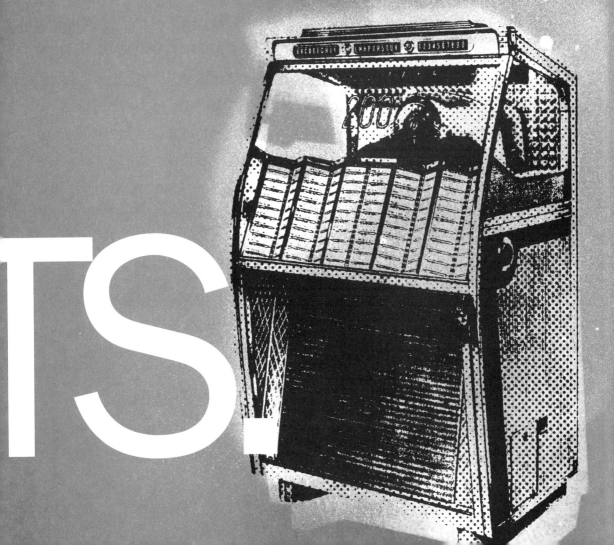

TS.

What you have before you is a juggernaut: two sets of lists—singles and albums—which, in our modest opinions, consist of the greatest and/or most impactful rap music ever bestowed upon mankind. We'd like to tell you that this *ego trip* hit parade has been tabulated through painstaking methods of super scientifical precision; that we inspected *Billboard* chart positions and Soundscan digits; mined the playlists of the most influential club, on-air and mix tape spin doctors and polled sage-like b-boy yogi's from regions throughout the globe for their infinite wisdom. But then we'd be filling your little hip hop-hungry craniums with a buncha mambajahambo.

Okay, granted, we *have* employed some methods to the madness of putting this puppy together. Some of you fuddy-duddies may notice that the chart years herein don't always correspond with the release years listed in the rest of the book. That's because we've made considerations for a recording's year of impact (i.e., if it was released near the end of one year and carried over into the next). We've also allotted just 15 smash hits for our singles chart for 1979 and condensed the first half of the '80s on our albums charts due to the sparingness of releases during these periods. (That's right, crumbsnatchers: there was a time when there *weren't* more rap records than you could listen to.)

Otherwise, in the words of Positive K, it's all gravy! We've handpicked 40 singles and 25 LPs for each year for the cheap thrill of showing you just how much rap we know about and forcing our tastes down your collective throats. Read it and weep. And if you don't like it, go write your own goddamn book.

CHARTS.

Hip Hop's Greatest Singles By Year.

1979

1. "Rapper's Delight"—Sugarhill Gang (Sugar Hill)
2. "Superappin'"—Grandmaster Flash & The Furious Five (Enjoy)
3. "Christmas Rappin'"—Kurtis Blow (Mercury)
4. "Rappin' And Rocking The House"—Funky 4 + 1 (Enjoy)
5. "We Rap More Mellow"—The Younger Generation (b/k/a Grandmaster Flash & The Furious Five) (Brass)
6. "Rhymin' And Rappin'"—Paulette & Tanya Winley (Winley)
7. "Funk You Up"—Sequence (Sugar Hill)
8. "To The Beat, Y'all"—Lady B (T.E.C.)
9. "MC Rock"—Jazzy 4MCs (Razzberri Rainbow)
10. "Lady D"—Lady D (Reflection)
11. "Street Talk (Madame Rapper)"—Funky Constellation (Funky Constellation)
12. "Wack Rap"—Solid C, Bobby D & Kool Drop (Wackie's)
13. "Spiderap"—Ron Hunt (Reflection)
14. "Rapper's Delight" b/w "Rocker's Choice"—Xanadu & Sweet Lady (Joe Gibbs Music)
15. "King Tim III (Personality Jock)"—Fatback (Spring)

1980

1. "The Breaks"—Kurtis Blow (Mercury)
2. "High Powered Rap"—Disco Dave & The Force Of The 5 MC's (b/k/a Crash Crew) (Mike & Dave)
3. "Spoonin' Rap"—Spoonie Gee (Sound Of New York, USA)
4. "Love Rap" b/w "New Rap Language"—Spoonie Gee & Treacherous Three (Enjoy)
5. "The Body Rock"—Treacherous Three (Enjoy)
6. "Zulu Nation Throwdown Volume 1"—Afrika Bambaataa & The Cosmic Force (Winley)
7. "Freedom"—Grandmaster Flash & The Furious Five (Sugar Hill)
8. "Adventures Of Super Rhyme (Rap)"—Jimmy Spicer (Dazz)
9. "Vicious Rap"—Tanya Winley (Winley)
10. "Zulu Nation Throwdown Volume 2"—Afrika Bambaataa & The Soul Sonic Force (Winley)
11. "Monster Jam"—Sequence featuring Spoonie Gee (Sugar Hill)
12. "8th Wonder"—Sugarhill Gang (Sugar Hill)
13. "At The Party"—Treacherous Three (Enjoy)
14. "Raptivity"—Ronnie Gee (Reflection)
15. "How We Gonna Make The Black Nation Rise?"—Brother D (Clappers)
16. "And You Don't Stop"—T.J. Swann (Express)
17. "Rap, Bounce, Rockskate"—Trickeration (Sound Of New York)
18. "Super Rappin' No. 2"—Grandmaster Flash & The Furious Five (Enjoy)
19. "Philosophy Rappin' Spree"—Super 3 (Delmar International)
20. "Big Apple Rappin' (National Rappin' Anthem)"—Spyder-D (Newtroit)
21. "Rappin' All Over"—The Younger Generation (b/k/a Grandmaster Flash & The Furious Five) & The Marvelous 3 (Brass)
22. "The Ultimate Rap"—Nice & Nasty 3 (Holiday)
23. "Do You Like That Funky Beat (Ah, Beat Beat)"—Kool Kyle The Starchild & The Disco Dolls (Enjoy)
24. "Let's Rock"—Harlem World Crew (Tay-ster)
25. "Rapper's Convention"—Harlem World Crew (Tay-ster)
26. "The Rappin' Spree"—The Jazzy Three (New City)
27. "Scoopy Rap"—Scoopy (Sound Of New York, USA)
28. "Party People"—Rappermatical 5 (Dynamite)
29. "T.S.O.B."—Master Jay & Michael Dee (The Sound Of Brooklyn)

30. "Move To The Groove"—Disco Four (Enjoy)
31. "Santa's Rap Party"—Super J (Sound Of New York, USA)
32. "More Ounce (Rap)"—Bobby/Demo (Scorpio)
33. "Willie Rap"—Willie Wood & The Willie Wood Crew (Sound Of New York, USA)
34. "CC Crew"—CC Crew (Golden Flamingo)
35. "Family Rap"—Family (Sound Of New York, USA)
36. "Get Up (And Go To School)"—Pookey Blow (Tri-State)
37. "Rhapazooty In Blue"—Sicle Cell & Rhapazooty (Showstoppers)
38. "Rappin' With Mr. Magic"—Mr. Magic (Magic)
39. "Young Ladies"—Lonnie Love (b/k/a Mr. Hyde) (Nia)
40. "Searchin' Rap"—Bon Rock & The Rhythm Rebellion (Reelin' & Rockin')

1981

1. "Jazzy Sensation (Bronx Version)"—Afrika Bambaataa & The Jazzy 5 (Tommy Boy)
2. "Feel The Heartbeat"—Treacherous Three (Enjoy)
3. "The Adventures Of Grandmaster Flash On The Wheels Of Steel"—Grandmaster Flash (Sugar Hill)
4. "That's The Joint"—Funky 4 + 1 (Sugar Hill)
5. "Catch The Beat"—T Ski Valley (Grand Groove)
6. "Genius Rap"—Dr. Jeckyll & Mr. Hyde (Profile)
7. "Rappin' Ain't No Thang"—Boogie Boys featuring Kool Ski, Kid Delight & Disco Dave (Mike & Dave)
8. "Can I Get A Soul Clap, Fresh Out The Pack"—Grand Wizard Theodore & The Fantastic Five (Soul Wax)
9. "It's Nasty (Genius Of Love)"—Grandmaster Flash & The Furious Five (Sugar Hill)
10. "Pump Me Up"—Trouble Funk (Jam)
11. "Spoonie Is Back"—Spoonie Gee (Sugar Hill)
12. "Girls Of The World"—Just Four (Grand Groove)
13. "Disco Dream"—Mean Machine (Sugar Hill)
14. "Put The Boogie In Your Body"—Treacherous Three (Enjoy)
15. "Birthday Party"—Grandmaster Flash & The Furious Five (Sugar Hill)
16. "Life On The Planet Earth"—Pee Wee Mel & Barry B (12 Star)
17. "Maximus Party"—T.J. Swann, Pee Wee Mel & Swann Controllers (Express)
18. "We Want To Rock"—Crash Crew (Sugar Hill)
19. "Get The Party Jumpin'"—Solo Sound (Express)
20. "Positive Life"—Lovebug Starski & The Harlem World Crew (Tay-ster)
21. "The Big Throwdown"—South Bronx (Dakar)
22. "Rock The Message Rap"—Grandmaster Chilly T & Stevie G (12 Star)
23. "It's Rockin' Time"—Kool Kyle The Starchild (Enjoy)
24. "Real Rocking Groove"—Chapter Three (Grand Groove)
25. "Do It, Do It"—Disco Four (Enjoy)
26. "Spanglish"—Spanish Fly & The Terrible Two (Enjoy)
27. "Never Let Go"—T Ski Valley (Grand Groove)
28. "Death Rap"—Margo's Kool Out Crew (Heavenly Star)
29. "Tricky Tee Rap"—Troy Rainey (Heavenly Star)
30. "Doctor Love & Sister Love Rap"—Doctor Love & Sister Love (Heavenly Star)
31. "Gangster Rock"—Land Of Hits Orchestra (Golden Flamingo)
32. "Get Fly"—T.J. Swann & Company (Express)
33. "School Days"—Busy Bee (Master Five)
34. "Smurf Trek"—Chapter Three (Grand Groove)
35. "A Heartbeat Rap"—Sweet G (West End)
36. "Calling Doctor Ice"—Doctor Ice (Enjoy)
37. "Apache"—Sugarhill Gang (Sugar Hill)
38. "Rapture"—Blondie (Chrysalis)
39. "Super Jay Love Theme"—Super Jay (Hitmakers Of America)

CHARTS.

40. "To The Beat Y'all"—Sangria (Reel To Reel)

1982

1. "The Message"—Grandmaster Flash & The Furious Five (Sugar Hill)
2. "Planet Rock"—Afrika Bambaataa & The Soul Sonic Force (Tommy Boy)
3. "Rockin' It"—Fearless Four (Enjoy)
4. "Flash To The Beat (Live)"—Grandmaster Flash & The Furious Five (Bozo Meko)
5. "Weekend"—Cold Crush Brothers (Elite)
6. "Making Cash Money"—Busy Bee (Sugar Hill)
7. "Looking For The Perfect Beat"—Afrika Bambaataa & The Soul Sonic Force (Tommy Boy)
8. "It's Magic"—Fearless Four (Enjoy)
9. "Change The Beat"—Fab 5 Freddy (Celluloid)
10. "Buffalo Gals"—Malcolm McLaren & The World Famous Supreme Team (Island)
11. "The Bubble Bunch"—Jimmy Spicer (Mercury)
12. "Yes We Can Can"—Treacherous Three (Sugar Hill)
13. "Do You Want To Rock (Before I Let Go)"—Funky 4 + 1 (Sugar Hill)
14. "Funk Box Party"—Masterdon Committee (Enjoy)
15. "Flash To The Beat"—Grandmaster Flash & The Furious Five (Sugar Hill)
16. "Standing On The Top"—Super 3 (Delmar International)
17. "Mt. Airy Groove (Rap Version)"—Pieces Of A Dream (Elektra)
18. "Jam To Remember"—Just Four (Grand Groove)
19. "Country Rock & Rap"—Disco Four (Enjoy)
20. "Space Cowboy"—Jonzun Crew (Tommy Boy)
21. "Message II (Survival)"—Grandmaster Melle Mel & Duke Bootee (Sugar Hill)
22. "Funky Soul Makossa"—Nairobi featuring Awesome Foursome (Streetwise)
23. "Breaking Bells (Take Me To The Mardi Gras)"—Crash Crew (Sugar Hill)
24. "The Grandmixer Cuts It Up"—Grandmixer D.ST & The Infinity Rappers (Celluloid)
25. "Magic's Wand"—Whodini (Jive)
26. "Scorpio"—Grandmaster Flash & The Furious Five (Sugar Hill)
27. "We're At The Party"—Disco Four (Profile)
28. "Daydreamin'"—Kurtis Blow (Mercury)
29. "The Bottom Line"—South Bronx (Rissa Chrissa)
30. "Getting Over"—Kool Kyle The Starchild (Frills)
31. "We Want To Get Down"—Mr. Sweety "G" (Mike & Dave)
32. "I Believe In The Wheel Of Fortune"—Tanya & Paulette Winley (Winley)
33. "Betcha Got A Dude On The Side"—Star Quality & Class (R&R)
34. "Missy Missy Dee"—Missy Dee & The Melody Crew (Universal Record Co.)
35. "Boogie Feelin' Rap"—Sweet G (Queens Constance)
36. "The Micstro"—Radiance featuring Prize (Ware)
37. "Touch The Rock (Rhythm Rap Rock Revival)—Count Coolout (Boss)
38. "Check It Out"—Wayne & Charlie The Rappin' Dummy (Sugar Hill)
39. "Sexual Rapping"—T Ski Valley (TSMP)
40. "Junior Wants To Play"—Bon Rock & Cotton Candy (Tommy Boy)

1983

1. "It's Like That" b/w "Sucker MC's"—Run-D.M.C. (Profile)
2. "White Lines (Don't Do It)"—Grandmaster Melle Mel (Sugar Hill)
3. "Beat Bop"—K-Rob vs. Rammelzee (Tartown)
4. "Play That Beat Mr. DJ (Lesson 1: The Payoff Mix)" b/w "Lesson 2: The James Brown Mix"—Double Dee & Steinski (Mastermix promo)
5. "Money (Dollar Bill, Y'all)"—Jimmy Spicer (Spring)

6. "It's Your Rock"—Fantasy Three (Specific)
7. "2, 3 Break"—The B-Boys (Vintertainment)
8. "Hard Times" b/w "Jam Master Jay"—Run-D.M.C. (Profile)
9. "Games People Play"—Sweet G (Fever)
10. "Action"—Treacherous Three (Sugar Hill)
11. "New York, New York"—Grandmaster Flash & The Furious Five (Sugar Hill)
12. "On The Radio"—Crash Crew (Sugar Hill)
13. "Beat Box" b/w "Moments In Love"—Art Of Noise (ZTT)
14. "Fresh"—Fresh 3 MC's (Profile)
15. "You Gotta Believe" b/w "Lovebug Starski Live At The Fever"—Lovebug Starski (Fever)
16. "Sucker DJs (I Will Survive)"—Dimples D (Party Time)
17. "Play That Beat Mr. DJ"—G.L.O.B.E. & Whiz Kid (Tommy Boy)
18. "Problems Of The World Today"—Fearless Four (Elektra)
19. "Break Dance-Electric Boogie"—West Street Mob (Sugar Hill)
20. "Cooky Puss"—Beastie Boys (Rat Cage)
21. "Haunted House Of Rock"—Whodini (Jive)
22. "It's Life (You Gotta Think Twice)"—Rockmaster Scott & The Dynamic Three (Reality)
23. "Jam On Revenge (The Wikka-Wikka Song)"—Newcleus (Sunnyview)
24. "King Of The Beat"—Pumpkin (Profile)
25. "Renegades Of Funk"—Afrika Bambaataa & The Soul Sonic Force (Tommy Boy)
26. "We Are Known Emcees (We Turn Parties Out)"—Crash Crew (Sugar Hill)
27. "The Big Beat"—Spoonie Gee (Tuff City)
28. "No Sell Out"—Malcolm X (Music by Keith LeBlanc) (Tommy Boy)
29. "Street Justice"—The Rake (Profile)
30. "Get Into The Mix"—DJ Divine (West End)
31. "Rock The House" b/w "Cuttin' Herbie"—The B-Boys (Vintertainment)
32. "Punk Rock Rap"—Cold Crush Brothers (Tuff City)
33. "All Night Long (Waterbed)"—Kevie Kev (a/k/a Waterbed Kev) (Sugar Hill)
34. "You've Got The Power To Get High On Yourself"—South Bronx Movement (Positive Juice)
35. "Games Females Play"—Gigolette (Fever)
36. "Watch The Closing Doors"—I.R.T. (Interboro Rhythm Team) (RCA)
37. "Cuts It Up"—T Ski Valley (Grand Groove)
38. "To The Max"—Rickey G & The Everlasting Five (Capo)
39. "Bad Times (I Can't Stand It)"—Captain Rapp (Magic Disc)
40. "Dog Talk"—K-9 Corps featuring Pretty C (Capitol)

1984

1. "It's Yours"—T La Rock & Jazzy Jay (Partytime)
2. "I Need A Beat"—LL Cool J (Def Jam)
3. "Rock Box"—Run-D.M.C. (Profile)
4. "Roxanne, Roxanne"—U.T.F.O. (Select)
5. "Friends" b/w "Five Minutes Of Funk"—Whodini (Jive)
6. "Roxanne's Revenge"—Roxanne Shanté (Pop Art)
7. "8 Million Stories" b/w "AJ Scratch"—Kurtis Blow (Mercury)
8. "One For The Treble (Fresh)"—Davy DMX (Tuff City)
9. "Fresh, Fly, Wild & Bold"—Cold Crush Brothers (Tuff City)
10. "Hey DJ"—The World Famous Supreme Team (Island)
11. "Freaks Come Out At Night"—Whodini (Jive)
12. "Fat Boys" b/w "Human Beat Box"—Disco 3 (b/k/a Fat Boys) (Sutra)
13. "What People Do For Money"—Divine Sounds (Specific)
14. "Unity"—Afrika Bambaataa & James Brown (Tommy Boy)

CHARTS.

15. "The Main Event"—Freddy B & The Mighty Mic Masters (Tuff City)
16. "Jailhouse Rap"—Fat Boys (Sutra)
17. "Jam On It"—Newcleus (Sunnyview)
18. "Beat Street Breakdown"—Grandmaster Melle Mel (Atlantic)
19. "Step Off"—The Furious Five featuring Cowboy, Grandmaster Melle Mel & Scorpio (Sugar Hill)
20. "Basketball"—Kurtis Blow (Mercury)
21. "Megamix II (Why Is It Fresh?)"—Grandmixer D.ST (Celluloid)
22. "Hip Hop On Wax Volume 1"—Chuck Chillout (Vintertainment)
23. "Hip Hop On Wax Volume 2"—Kool DJ Red Alert (Vintertainment)
24. "Can You Feel It?"—Fat Boys (Sutra)
25. "Don's Groove"—Donald D (Elektra)
26. "Here Comes That Beat!"—Pumpkin & The Profile All-Stars (Profile)
27. "Just Having Fun"—Doug E. Fresh featuring DJs Chill Will & Barry Bee (Enjoy)
28. "Original Human Beat Box"—Doug E. Fresh (Vintertainment)
29. "Turning You On"—Treacherous Three (Sugar Hill)
30. "Masters Of The Scratch"—Master O.C. & Krazy Eddie featuring Peso & Tito of the Fearless Four & Main Attraction (Next Plateau)
31. "Fast Life" b/w "A.M./P.M."—Dr. Jeckyll & Mr. Hyde (Profile)
32. "That's Life"—Cutmaster D.C. (Airport)
33. "Cosmic Blast"—Captain Rock (Nia)
34. "Hollywood's Message"—DJ Hollywood (H.I.K.I.M.-Ali)
35. "Starski Live At The Fever Pt. II"—Lovebug Starski (Fever)
36. "What Are We Gonna Do?"—Ultimate 3 MC's (Partytime)
37. "Funky Breakdown"—Awesome Foursome (Partytime)
38. "Games Of Life"—Just Four (Express)
39. "I'm Somebody Else's Guy"—Frederick "MC Count" Linton (Vinyl Dreams)
40. "Paid The Cost To Be The Boss"—Masterdon Committee (Enjoy)

1985

1. "The Show" b/w "La Di Da Di"—Doug E. Fresh & The Get Fresh Crew (Reality)
2. "P.S.K." b/w "Gucci Time"—Schoolly D (Schoolly D)
3. "Rock The Bells"—LL Cool J (Def Jam)
4. "King Of Rock"—Run-D.M.C. (Profile)
5. "Marley Marl Scratch"—Marley Marl featuring MC Shan (Nia)
6. "I Can't Live Without My Radio"—LL Cool J (Def Jam)
7. "Fresh Is The Word"—Mantronix featuring MC Tee (Sleeping Bag)
8. "(Nothing Serious) Just Buggin'"—Whistle (Select)
9. "Brooklyn's In The House"—Cutmaster D.C. (Zakia)
10. "Just Say Stet"—Stetsasonic (Tommy Boy)
11. "Bite This"—Roxanne Shanté (Pop Art)
12. "Larry's Dance Theme"—Grandmaster Flash (Elektra)
13. "Girls"—The B-Boys (Vintertainment)
14. "Girls Pt. 2"—The B-Boys (Vintertainment)
15. "Queen Of Rox"—Roxanne Shanté (Pop Art)
16. "King Kut"—Word Of Mouth featuring DJ Cheese (Beauty & The Beat)
17. "A Fly Girl"—Boogie Boys (Capitol)
18. "Batterram"—Toddy Tee (Evejim)
19. "Girl"—Too $hort (75 Girls)
20. "If I Ruled The World"—Kurtis Blow (Mercury)
21. "Together Forever (Krush Groove 4)"—Run-D.M.C. (Profile)
22. "Bad Boys"—Bad Boys featuring K Love (Starlite)

23. "It's The Beat"—Hollis Crew (Def Jam)
24. "Rock Hard"—Beastie Boys (Def Jam)
25. "Veronica"—Bad Boys featuring K Love (Starlite)
26. "The Roof Is On Fire" b/w "Request Line"—Rockmaster Scott & The Dynamic Three (Reality)
27. "Hollywood's World"—DJ Hollywood (Abdull-Akbar)
28. "Def Jam" b/w "Cold Chillin' In The Spot"—Jazzy Jay (Def Jam)
29. "The Show Stoppa (Is Stupid Fresh)"—Super Nature (b/k/a Salt-N-Pepa) (Pop Art)
30. "Sparky's Turn (Roxanne You're Through)"—Sparky D (Nia)
31. "The Tragedy (Don't Do It)"—Super Kids (Nia)
32. "Just Call Us Def" b/w "Fly Shanté"—Steady B featuring Roxanne Shanté (Pop Art)
33. "I Want You" b/w "Dangerous"—LL Cool J (Def Jam)
34. "Needle To The Groove"—Mantronix (Sleeping Bag)
35. "Shout (Rap Version)"—Craig G (Pop Art)
36. "Itchin' For A Scratch"—Force MD's (Atlantic)
37. "She's On It"—Beastie Boys (Def Jam)
38. "Johnny The Fox"—Tricky Tee (Sleeping Bag)
39. "2, 3 Break (Part II-The Sequel)"—DJ Born Supreme Allah (Vintertainment)
40. "Funkbox 2"—Masterdon Committee (Profile)

1986

1. "Eric B. Is President" b/w "My Melody"—Eric B. & Rakim (Zakia)
2. "My Adidas" b/w "Peter Piper"—Run-D.M.C. (Profile)
3. "The Bridge"—MC Shan (Bridge)
4. "South Bronx"—Boogie Down Productions (B-Boy)
5. "Ego Trippin'"—Ultramagnetic MC's (Next Plateau)
6. "Hold It Now, Hit It"—Beastie Boys (Def Jam)
7. "It's A Demo" b/w "I'm Fly"—Kool G Rap & DJ Polo (Cold Chillin')
8. "Make The Music With Your Mouth Biz"—Biz Markie (Prism)
9. "Go Stetsa I"—Stetsasonic (Tommy Boy)
10. "Latoya"—Just-Ice (Fresh)
11. "Cold Gettin' Dumb"—Just-Ice (Fresh)
12. "Def Fresh Crew"—Roxanne Shanté featuring Biz Markie (Pop Art)
13. "It's The New Style" b/w "Paul Revere"—Beastie Boys (Def Jam)
14. "6 'N The Mornin'"—Ice-T (Techno-Hop)
15. "My Mic Sounds Nice"—Salt-N-Pepa (Next Plateau)
16. "Play This Only At Night"—Doug E. Fresh & The Get Fresh Crew (Reality)
17. "Freaky Tales"—Too $hort (Jive)
18. "Girls Ain't Nothing But Trouble"—DJ Jazzy Jeff & The Fresh Prince (Word Up)
19. "Pee-Wee's Dance"—Joeski Love (Vintertainment)
20. "It's My Beat"—Sweet Tee & DJ Jazzy Joyce (Profile)
21. "Brooklyn Rocks The Best"—Cutmaster D.C. (Zakia)
22. "Nightmares"—Dana Dane (Profile)
23. "Coast To Coast"—Word Of Mouth featuring DJ Cheese (Profile)
24. "One Love"—Whodini (Jive)
25. "Knowledge Me" b/w "Can U Feel It"—Original Concept (Def Jam)
26. "All The Way To Heaven" b/w "Nuthin'"—Doug E. Fresh & The Get Fresh Crew (Reality)
27. "Do Or Die Bed Sty"—Divine Sounds (Reality)
28. "Everlasting Bass"—Rodney O & Joe Cooley (Egyptian Empire)
29. "Funky Beat"—Whodini (Jive)
30. "It's Like That, Y'all"—Sweet Tee & DJ Jazzy Joyce (Profile)
31. "Payback's A Mutha"—King Tee (Techno-Hop)

CHARTS.

32. "Bust It"—DBL Crew (Urban Rock)
33. "Faye" b/w "4 Ever My Beat"—Stetsasonic (Tommy Boy)
34. "Jane, Stop This Crazy Thing" b/w "Cocaine"—MC Shan (Cold Chillin')
35. "Go See The Doctor"—Kool Moe Dee (Rooftop)
36. "Style (Peter Gunn Theme)"—Grandmaster Flash (Elektra)
37. "Mr. Big Stuff"—Heavy D & The Boyz (Uptown)
38. "Bang Zoom (Let's Go-Go)"—The Real Roxanne featuring Hitman Howie Tee (Select)
39. "Bring The Beat Back"—Steady B (Pop Art)
40. "Woppit"—B. Fats (Posse)

1987

1. "Top Billin'"—Audio Two (First Priority)
2. "Rebel Without A Pause"—Public Enemy (Def Jam)
3. "The Bridge Is Over"—Boogie Down Productions (B-Boy)
4. "It's My Thing" b/w "You're A Customer"—EPMD (Fresh)
5. "Raw"—Big Daddy Kane (Prism)
6. "Bring The Noise"—Public Enemy (Def Jam)
7. "Nobody Beats The Biz"—Biz Markie (Prism)
8. "I Know You Got Soul"—Eric B. & Rakim (4th & B'way)
9. "Public Enemy No. 1" b/w "Timebomb"—Public Enemy (Def Jam)
10. "Just Rhymin' With Biz"—Big Daddy Kane featuring Biz Markie (Prism)
11. "Do The James"—Super Lover Cee & Casanova Rud (Citi-Beat)
12. "I'm Bad"—LL Cool J (Def Jam)
13. "Funky"—Ultramagnetic MC's (Next Plateau)
14. "Boyz-N-The Hood"—Eazy-E (Ruthless)
15. "Holy War (Live)"—Divine Force (Yamak-ka)
16. "Saturday Night"—Schoolly D (Schoolly D)
17. "I Ain't No Joke"—Eric B. & Rakim (4th & B'way)
18. "I Cram To Understand U"—MC Lyte (First Priority)
19. "Dope Man"—N.W.A (Ruthless)
20. "Going Way Back"—Just-Ice (Fresh)
21. "Have A Nice Day"—Roxanne Shanté (Cold Chillin')
22. "Pickin' Boogers"—Biz Markie (Prism)
23. "Tramp" b/w "Push It"—Salt-N-Pepa (Next Plateau)
24. "Poetry"—Boogie Down Productions (B-Boy)
25. "Rikers Island" b/w "Rhyme Time"—Kool G Rap & DJ Polo (Cold Chillin')
26. "Jimbrowski"—Jungle Brothers (Idlers)
27. "Small Time Hustler"—Dismasters (Urban Rock)
28. "The Overweight Lover's In The House"—Heavy D & The Boyz (Uptown)
29. "The Godfather"—Spoonie Gee (Tuff City)
30. "Bustin' Loose" b/w "Do It, Do It" & "Oreo Cookie"—Alliance (First Priority)
31. "I Got An Attitude"—Antoinette (Next Plateau)
32. "Take It Off"—Spoonie Gee (Tuff City)
33. "Last Night"—Kid 'N Play (Select)
34. "This Cut's Got Flavor" b/w "Puttin' On The Hits"—Latee (Wild Pitch)
35. "Use Me (Before I Let Go)"—Steady B (Jive)
36. "Sexy"—Masters Of Ceremony (Strong City)
37. "Suicide"—Busy Bee (Strong City)
38. "My Mic Is On Fire"—Lord Shafiyq (NUWR)
39. "New Generation"—Classical Two (Rooftop)
40. "We Want Some Pussy!!"—2 Live Crew (Luke Skyywalker)

1988

1. "It Takes Two"—Rob Base & DJ E-Z Rock (Profile)
2. "Paid In Full (Seven Minutes Of Madness Remix)"—Eric B. & Rakim (4th & B'way)
3. "Ain't No Half Steppin'"—Big Daddy Kane (Cold Chillin')
4. "My Philosophy"—Boogie Down Productions (Jive)
5. "Run's House" b/w "Beats To The Rhyme"—Run-D.M.C. (Profile)
6. "Don't Believe The Hype"—Public Enemy (Def Jam)
7. "The Symphony"—Marley Marl featuring Masta Ace, Craig G, Kool G Rap & Big Daddy Kane (Cold Chillin')
8. "Plug Tunin'"—De La Soul (Tommy Boy)
9. "You Gots To Chill"—EPMD (Fresh)
10. "Vapors"—Biz Markie (Cold Chillin')
11. "Keep Risin' To The Top"—Doug E. Fresh & The Get Fresh Crew (Reality)
12. "Strong Island"—J.V.C. Force (B-Boy)
13. "The Biz Is Goin' Off"—Biz Markie (Cold Chillin')
14. "The 900 Number"—45 King (Tuff City)
15. "Jack Of Spades" b/w "I'm Still #1 (Numero Uno Re-Recording)"—Boogie Down Productions (Jive)
16. "Microphone Fiend"—Eric B. & Rakim (Uni)
17. "10% Dis"—MC Lyte (First Priority)
18. "Sally" b/w "DBC Let The Music Play"—Stetsasonic (Tommy Boy)
19. "Because I Got It Like That"—Jungle Brothers (Idlers)
20. "Jenifa (Taught Me)" b/w "Potholes In My Lawn"—De La Soul (Tommy Boy)
21. "Caught Up (Remix)"—Chubb Rock featuring Hitman Howie Tee (Select)
22. "Wild Thang"—2 Much (Warlock)
23. "Droppin' Science"—Marley Marl featuring Craig G (Cold Chillin')
24. "Going Back To Cali" b/w "Jack The Ripper"—LL Cool J (Def Jam)
25. "Road To The Riches"—Kool G Rap & DJ Polo (Cold Chillin')
26. "Get Retarded"—MC EZ & Troup (Fresh)
27. "Talkin' All That Jazz"—Stetsasonic (Tommy Boy)
28. "Wrath Of My Madness" b/w "Princess Of The Posse"—Queen Latifah (Tommy Boy)
29. "Paper Thin"—MC Lyte (First Priority)
30. "Step Up Front"—Positive K (First Priority)
31. "I Pioneered This"—MC Shan (Cold Chillin')
32. "Dope Rhymes" b/w "Chillin'" & "Wild Pitch"—Chill Rob G (Wild Pitch)
33. "Do This My Way"—Kid 'N Play (Select)
34. "Super-Casanova"—Super Lover Cee & Casanova Rud (DNA International)
35. "Hit 'Em With This" b/w "Unfinished Business"—Antoinette (Next Plateau)
36. "Bass"—King Tee (Capitol)
37. "Supersonic"—J.J. Fad (Dream Team)
38. "Posse On Broadway"—Sir Mix-A-Lot (Def American)
39. "Versatility"—Supreme Nyborn (Payroll)
40. "Gittin' Funky"—Kid 'N Play (Select)

1989

1. "Fight The Power"—Public Enemy (Motown)
2. "So Wat Cha Sayin'"—EPMD (Fresh)
3. "Children's Story"—Slick Rick (Def Jam)
4. "I Got It Made"—Special Ed (Profile)
5. "Hey Young World" b/w "Mona Lisa"—Slick Rick (Def Jam)
6. "Just A Friend"—Biz Markie (Cold Chillin')
7. "Smooth Operator" b/w "Warm It Up, Kane"—Big Daddy Kane (Cold Chillin')
8. "Buddy (Native Tongue Decision)"—De La Soul featuring Jungle Brothers, A Tribe Called Quest & Monie Love (Tommy Boy)

CHARTS.

9. "Straight Outta Compton"—N.W.A (Ruthless)
10. "Funky Dividends"—Three Times Dope (Arista)
11. "It's Funky Enough"—The D.O.C. (Ruthless)
12. "Express Yourself" b/w "A Bitch Iz A Bitch"—N.W.A (Ruthless)
13. "Eazy-er Said Than Dunn"—Eazy-E (Ruthless)
14. "Me So Horny"—2 Live Crew (Luke)
15. "The Gas Face"—3rd Bass featuring Zev Love X (Def Jam)
16. "It's My Turn" b/w "To The Max"—Stezo (Fresh)
17. "Big Ole Butt"—LL Cool J (Def Jam)
18. "Words I Manifest (Remix)"—Gang Starr (Wild Pitch)
19. "Doowutchyalike"—Digital Underground (Tommy Boy)
20. "Ya Bad Chubbs"—Chubb Rock featuring Hitman Howie Tee (Select)
21. "A Good Combination"—Positive K (First Priority)
22. "In Control Of Things" b/w "Thinking Of A Master Plan"—YZ & G Rock (Diversity)
23. "Steppin' To The A.M."—3rd Bass (Def Jam)
24. "Think" b/w "Atom"—Main Source (Actual)
25. "Hey Ladies" b/w "Shake Your Rump"—Beastie Boys (Capitol)
26. "Early To Rise" b/w "More And More Hits"—Nice & Smooth (Fresh)
27. "Cha Cha Cha"—MC Lyte (First Priority)
28. "Court Is Now In Session"—Chill Rob G (Wild Pitch)
29. "Knock 'Em Out, Sugar Ray"—MC Sugar Ray & Stranger D (b/k/a Double XX Posse) (Def City)
30. "You Played Yourself"—Ice-T (Sire)
31. "Self Destruction"—Stop The Violence Movement (Jive)
32. "Why Is That?"—Boogie Down Productions (Jive)
33. "Dance For Me" b/w "Inside Out"—Queen Latifah (Tommy Boy)
34. "Pay Ya Dues"—Low Profile (Priority)
35. "Droppin' It"—The Bizzie Boyz (Payroll)
36. "Bust A Move"—Young MC (Delicious Vinyl)
37. "Ain't Sayin Nothin"—Divine Styler featuring The Scheme Team (Rhyme Syndicate)
38. "The Rhythm"—Kwamé The Boy Genius featuring A New Beginning (Atlantic)
39. "The Glamorous Life"—Cool C (Atlantic)
40. "Wild Thing"—Tone-Lōc (Delicious Vinyl)

1990

1. "Welcome To The Terrordome"—Public Enemy (Def Jam)
2. "Bonita Applebum"—A Tribe Called Quest (Jive)
3. "The Humpty Dance"—Digital Underground (Tommy Boy)
4. "Jingling Baby (Remixed And Still Jingling)"—LL Cool J (Def Jam)
5. "Funky For You" b/w "No Bones In Ice Cream"—Nice & Smooth (Fresh)
6. "Gold Digger"—EPMD (Def Jam)
7. "Just To Get A Rep" b/w "Who's Gonna Take The Weight?"—Gang Starr (Chrysalis)
8. "Can I Kick It?" b/w "When The Papes Come"—A Tribe Called Quest (Jive)
9. "Looking At The Front Door"—Main Source (Wild Pitch)
10. "Love's Gonna Get 'Cha (Material Love)"—Boogie Down Productions (Jive)
11. "Streets Of New York"—Kool G Rap & DJ Polo (Cold Chillin')
12. "In The Ghetto"—Eric B. & Rakim (MCA)
13. "Brothers Gonna Work It Out"—Public Enemy (Def Jam)
14. "Around The Way Girl"—LL Cool J (Def Jam)
15. "J.Beez Comin' Through"—Jungle Brothers (Warner Bros.)
16. "AmeriKKKa's Most Wanted" b/w "Once Upon A Time In The Projects"—Ice Cube (Priority)
17. "Buck Whylin'"—Terminator X featuring Chuck D & Sister Souljah (Def Jam)
18. "Freaks Of The Industry"—Digital Underground (Tommy Boy)

19. "Call Me D-Nice"—D-Nice (Jive)
20. "Treat 'Em Right"—Chubb Rock (Select)
21. "Product Of The Environment (Remix)" b/w "3 Strikes 5000"—3rd Bass (Def Jam)
22. "Your Mom's In My Business"—K-Solo (Atlantic)
23. "To Da Break Of Dawn"—LL Cool J (Motown)
24. "Strictly For The Ladies"—Lord Finesse & DJ Mike Smooth (Wild Pitch)
25. "Rock Dis Funky Joint"—Poor Righteous Teachers (Profile)
26. "Murder Rap"—Above The Law (Ruthless)
27. "I'm The Magnificent (The Magnificent Remix)" b/w "Ready 2 Attack"—Special Ed (Profile)
28. "Peachfuzz"—K.M.D. (Elektra)
29. "Who's The Mack?"—Ice Cube (Priority)
30. "Spellbound"—K-Solo (Atlantic)
31. "Ruff Rhyme (Back Again)" b/w "Played Like A Piano"—King Tee (Capitol)
32. "Funkin' Lesson"—X Clan (Island)
33. "La Raza"—Kid Frost (Virgin)
34. "Nod Your Head To This"—Kings Of Swing (Virgin)
35. "Me And The Biz"—Masta Ace (Cold Chillin')
36. "Executive Class"—Double XX Posse (Mel-O)
37. "The Mission"—Special Ed (Profile)
38. "The Boomin' System"—LL Cool J (Def Jam)
39. "Untouchable"—Above The Law (Ruthless)
40. "The Originators"—The Jaz featuring Jay-Z (EMI)

1991

1. "Mind Playing Tricks On Me"—Geto Boys (Rap-A-Lot)
2. "Check The Rhime"—A Tribe Called Quest (Jive)
3. "O.P.P."—Naughty By Nature (Tommy Boy)
4. "Shut 'Em Down (Pete Rock Remix)"—Public Enemy (Def Jam)
5. "How I Could Just Kill A Man"—Cypress Hill (Ruffhouse)
6. "Slow Down"—Brand Nubian (Elektra)
7. "Just Hangin Out" b/w "Live At The Barbeque"—Main Source (Wild Pitch)
8. "Summertime"—DJ Jazzy Jeff & The Fresh Prince (Jive)
9. "All For One"—Brand Nubian (Elektra)
10. "I Got To Have It"—Ed O.G & Da BULLDOGS (PWL)
11. "Ain't No Future In Yo' Frontin'"—MC Breed (Ichiban)
12. "Rampage"—EPMD featuring LL Cool J (Def Jam)
13. "Hip Hop Junkies"—Nice & Smooth (RAL)
14. "Flavor Of The Month"—Black Sheep (Mercury)
15. "Ring Ring Ring (Ha Ha Hey)"—De La Soul (Tommy Boy)
16. "Steady Mobbin'" b/w "No Vaseline"—Ice Cube (Priority)
17. "Sobb Story"—Leaders Of The New School (Elektra)
18. "Growin' Up In The Hood"—Compton's Most Wanted (Orpheus)
19. "Fuck Compton"—Tim Dog (Ruffhouse)
20. "Same Song"—Digital Underground featuring 2Pac (Tommy Boy)
21. "Jiggable Pie"—AMG (Select)
22. "Poor Georgie"—MC Lyte (First Priority)
23. "Be A Father To Your Child"—Ed O.G & Da BULLDOGS (PWL)
24. "Dress Code"—WC And The MAAD Circle (Priority)
25. "Step In The Arena" b/w "Check The Technique"—Gang Starr (Chrysalis)
26. "Shakiyla"—Poor Righteous Teachers (Profile)
27. "A Rollerskating Jam Named 'Saturdays'"—De La Soul featuring Q-Tip (Tommy Boy)
28. "Case Of The P.T.A."—Leaders Of The New School (Elektra)

CHARTS.

29. "Nitty Gritty (Remix)" b/w "Plumskinzz"—K.M.D. (Elektra)
30. "Sleepin' On My Couch"—Del The Funkeé Homosapien (Elektra)
31. "Fugitive"—K-Solo (Atlantic)
32. "Mahogany"—Eric B. & Rakim (MCA)
33. "Bad To The Bone"—Kool G Rap & DJ Polo (Cold Chillin')
34. "Bitch Betta Have My Money"—AMG (Select)
35. "25 Ta Life"—D-Nice (Jive)
36. "Tonight"—DJ Quik (Profile)
37. "Come On, Let's Move It"—Special Ed (Profile)
38. "O.G. Original Gangster" b/w "Bitches 2"—Ice-T (Sire)
39. "Who Me?"—K.M.D. (Elektra)
40. "Throw Your Hands In The Air" b/w "Do My Thang"—Raw Fusion (Hollywood BASIC)

1992

1. "The Choice Is Yours (Revisited)"—Black Sheep (Mercury)
2. "DWYCK"—Gang Starr featuring Nice & Smooth (Chrysalis)
3. "They Want EFX"—Das EFX (EastWest)
4. "Deep Cover"—Dr. Dre featuring Snoop Doggy Dogg (Epic)
5. "T.R.O.Y. (They Reminisce Over You)"—Pete Rock & CL Smooth (Elektra)
6. "Scenario"—A Tribe Called Quest featuring Leaders Of The New School (Jive)
7. "Fakin' The Funk (Remix)"—Main Source featuring Neek The Exotic (Wild Pitch)
8. "Punks Jump Up To Get Beat Down"—Brand Nubian (Elektra)
9. "Half Time"—Nas (Columbia)
10. "Crossover" b/w "Brothers From Brentwood L.I."—EPMD (Def Jam)
11. "Jump Around"—House Of Pain (Tommy Boy)
12. "Poppa Large (East Coast Remix)"—Ultramagnetic MC's (Mercury)
13. "Mic Checka (Remix)" b/w "Jussumen (Remix)"—Das EFX (EastWest)
14. "Blow Your Mind" b/w "How To Roll A Blunt"—Redman (Def Jam)
15. "Uptown Anthem"—Naughty By Nature (MCA)
16. "Juice (Know The Ledge)"—Eric B. & Rakim (MCA)
17. "Head Banger"—EPMD featuring K-Solo & Redman (Def Jam)
18. "Jazz (We've Got)"—A Tribe Called Quest (Jive)
19. "Everything's Gonna Be Alright (Ghetto Bastard)"—Naughty By Nature (Tommy Boy)
20. "Ill Street Blues"—Kool G Rap & DJ Polo (Cold Chillin')
21. "Who Got Da Props?"—Black Moon (Nervous)
22. "Gangsta Bitch"—Apache (Tommy Boy)
23. "Hand On The Pump"—Cypress Hill (Ruffhouse)
24. "Zulu War Chant"—Afrika Bambaataa Presents Time Zone (Planet Rock)
25. "360° (What Goes Around)"—Grand Puba (Elektra)
26. "Best Kept Secret" b/w "Freestyle (Yo, That's That Shit)"—Diamond D (Chemistry)
27. "Just Like Compton"—DJ Quik (Profile)
28. "Not Gonna Be Able To Do It"—Double XX Posse (Big Beat)
29. "Straighten It Out"—Pete Rock & CL Smooth (Elektra)
30. "One To Grow On"—UMC's (Wild Pitch)
31. "So What'cha Want"—Beastie Boys (Grand Royal)
32. "La Schmoove"—Fu-Schnickens featuring Phife Dawg (A Tribe Called Quest) (Jive)
33. "Fat Pockets (Remix)"—Show & AG (Payday)
34. "Fudge Pudge"—Organized Konfusion featuring O.C. (Hollywood BASIC)
35. "Age Ain't Nothin' But A #"—Chi Ali (Relativity)
36. "Mistadobalina"—Del The Funkeé Homosapien (Elektra)
37. "Don't Sweat The Technique"—Eric B. & Rakim (MCA)
38. "Final Frontier"—MC Ren (Ruthless)

39. "Baby Got Back"—Sir Mix-A-Lot (Def American)
40. "Back To The Hotel"—N2Deep (Profile)

1993

1. "Nuthin' But A 'G' Thang"—Dr. Dre featuring Snoop Doggy Dogg (Death Row)
2. "Protect Ya Neck"—Wu-Tang Clan (Wu-Tang)
3. "Come Clean"—Jeru The Damaja (Payday)
4. "Passin' Me By"—The Pharcyde (Delicious Vinyl)
5. "Tonight's Da Night"—Redman (Def Jam)
6. "I Get Around"—2Pac featuring Shock G & Money B (Interscope)
7. "Award Tour"—A Tribe Called Quest featuring Trugoy (De La Soul) (Jive)
8. "Throw Ya Gunz"—Onyx (Def Jam)
9. "Fuck Wit Dre Day (And Everybody's Celebratin')"—Dr. Dre featuring Snoopy Doggy Dogg (Death Row)
10. "Time 4 Sum Aksion"—Redman (Def Jam)
11. "Method Man"—Wu-Tang Clan (Loud)
12. "Outta Here"—KRS-One (Jive)
13. "Electric Relaxation"—A Tribe Called Quest (Jive)
14. "93 'Til Infinity"—Souls Of Mischief (Jive)
15. "On The Run (Dirty Untouchable Remix)"—Kool G Rap & DJ Polo (Cold Chillin')
16. "Slam"—Onyx (Def Jam)
17. "Streiht Up Menace"—MC Eiht (Jive)
18. "How About Some Hardcore"—M.O.P. (Select)
19. "Otha Fish"—The Pharcyde (Delicious Vinyl)
20. "Party And Bullshit"—The Notorious B.I.G. (Uptown)
21. "Make Room"—Tha Alkaholiks (Loud)
22. "Gotta Get Mine"—MC Breed featuring 2Pac (Ichiban)
23. "Reign Of The Tec"—The Beatnuts (Relativity)
24. "That's How It Is (Remix)"—Casual (Jive)
25. "Flow Joe"—Fat Joe (Relativity)
26. "Sound Of Da Police" b/w "Hip Hop vs. Rap"—KRS-One (Jive)
27. "Breakadawn"—De La Soul (Tommy Boy)
28. "Two Brothers With Checks (San Francisco, Harvey)" b/w "One, Two, One, Two"—Ultramagnetic MC's (Wild Pitch)
29. "I'm Outta Here" b/w "You Can't Front (The Shit Is Real)"—Diamond D (Chemistry)
30. "I Didn't Mean To"—Casual (Jive)
31. "Chief Rocka"—Lords Of The Underground (Elektra)
32. "Walk Like A Duck"—Kurious (Columbia)
33. "Crooked Officer"—Geto Boys (Rap-A-Lot)
34. "What's Next?"—Leaders Of The New School (Elektra)
35. "Getto Jam"—Domino (Outburst)
36. "Grand Groove (Remix)"—Intelligent Hoodlum (A&M)
37. "Keep Ya Head Up"—2Pac (Interscope)
38. "Off & On (Remix)"—Trends Of Culture (Mad Sounds)
39. "Insane In The Brain" b/w "When The Shit Goes Down"—Cypress Hill (Ruffhouse)
40. "Hit It From The Back"—Mobb Deep (4th & B'way)

1994

1. "Flava In Ya Ear"—Craig Mack (Bad Boy)
2. "Gin And Juice"—Snoop Doggy Dogg (Death Row)
3. "C.R.E.A.M."—Wu-Tang Clan (Loud)
4. "Juicy" b/w "Unbelievable"—The Notorious B.I.G. (Bad Boy)
5. "Bring The Pain"—Method Man (Def Jam)

CHARTS.

6. "Time's Up"—O.C. (Wild Pitch)
7. "i used to love h.e.r."—Common (Relativity)
8. "I Got Cha Opin (Remix)" b/w "Reality (Killin' Every Nigga In Sight)"—Black Moon (Nervous)
9. "The Most Beautifullest Thing In This World"—Keith Murray (Jive)
10. "Black Superman"—Above The Law (Ruthless)
11. "It Ain't Hard To Tell"—Nas (Columbia)
12. "Bucktown" b/w "Let's Git It On"—Smif-N-Wessun (Nervous)
13. "Nappy Heads (Remix)"—Fugees (Ruffhouse)
14. "D. Original"—Jeru The Damaja (Payday)
15. "Mass Appeal"—Gang Starr (Chrysalis)
16. "The World Is Yours"—Nas (Columbia)
17. "Player's Ball"—OutKast (LaFace)
18. "I Seen A Man Die"—Scarface (Rap-A-Lot)
19. "Supa Star"—Group Home (Payday)
20. "Murder Was The Case"—Snoop Doggy Dogg (Death Row)
21. "Money In The Ghetto"—Too $hort (Jive)
22. "Afro Puffs"—The Lady Of Rage featuring Snoop Doggy Dogg (Death Row)
23. "Can It Be All So Simple"—Wu-Tang Clan (Loud)
24. "Mad Izm"—Channel Live featuring KRS-One (Capitol)
25. "How Many MC's . . ."—Black Moon (Nervous)
26. "Rockafella (Remix)"—Redman (Def Jam)
27. "Can't Wait"—Redman (Def Jam)
28. "Buck Em Down (Remix)" b/w "Murder MC's"—Black Moon (Nervous)
29. "Ego Trippin' (Part Two)"—De La Soul (Tommy Boy)
30. "Diary Of A Madman"—Gravediggaz featuring Shabazz The Disciple & Killah Priest (Gee Street)
31. "Crooklyn"—Crooklyn Dodgers (MCA)
32. "Southernplayalisticadillacmuzik"—OutKast (LaFace)
33. "Thuggish Ruggish Bone"—Bone Thugs-N-Harmony (Relativity)
34. "Ice Cream Man"—Dru Down featuring Luniz (Relativity)
35. "Get Down (Remix)"—Craig Mack featuring Q-Tip (Bad Boy)
36. "On And On"—Shyheim (Virgin)
37. "Game Recognize Game"—JT The Bigga Figga featuring Mac Mall (Get Low)
38. "Captain Save A Hoe"—E-40 featuring The Click (Sick Wid It)
39. "Where My Homiez"—Ill Al Skratch (Mercury)
40. "Regulate"—Nate Dogg & Warren G (Death Row)

1995

1. "Shook Ones Pt. II"—Mobb Deep (Loud)
2. "One More Chance (Stay With Me Remix)"—The Notorious B.I.G. (Bad Boy)
3. "I Got 5 On It"—Luniz (Noo Trybe)
4. "Brooklyn Zoo"—Ol' Dirty Bastard (Elektra)
5. "Big Poppa" b/w "Who Shot Ya?"—The Notorious B.I.G. (Bad Boy)
6. "I'll Be There For You/You're All I Need To Get By"—Method Man featuring Mary J. Blige (Def Jam)
7. "Get Money"—Junior M.A.F.I.A. featuring The Notorious B.I.G. (Big Beat)
8. "I'm Bout It, Bout It"—TRU featuring Mia X (No Limit)
9. "Broken Language"—Smoothe Da Hustler featuring Trigger Tha Gambler (Profile)
10. "Incarcerated Scarfaces" b/w "Ice Cream"—Raekwon (Loud)
11. "MC's Act Like They Don't Know"—KRS-One (Jive)
12. "Sprinkle Me"—E-40 featuring Suga T (Jive)
13. "Danger"—Blahzay Blahzay (Mercury)
14. "West Up!"—WC And The MAAD Circle featuring Mack 10 & Ice Cube (Payday)
15. "Last Dayz"—Onyx (Def Jam)

16. "New York, New York"—Tha Dogg Pound featuring Snoop Doggy Dogg (Death Row)
17. "Player's Anthem"—Junior M.A.F.I.A. featuring The Notorious B.I.G. (Big Beat)
18. "Playa Playa"—Big Mike (Rap-A-Lot)
19. "Foe Life"—Mack 10 (Priority)
20. "How High"—Redman & Method Man (Def Jam)
21. "Criminology" b/w "Glaciers Of Ice"—Raekwon (Loud)
22. "Sound Bwoy Bureill"—Smif-N-Wessun featuring Starang Wondah (Nervous)
23. "I Like It (I Wanna Be Where You Are)"—Grand Puba (Elektra)
24. "Next Level"—Show & AG (Payday)
25. "1st Of Tha Month"—Bone Thugs-N-Harmony (Relativity)
26. "Give It 2 You (Remix)"—Da Brat (So So Def)
27. "Runnin'" b/w "Drop"—The Pharcyde (Delicious Vinyl)
28. "DAAAM!"—Tha Alkaholiks (Loud)
29. "Liquid Swords"—The Genius (Geffen)
30. "Livin' Proof"—Group Home (Payday)
31. "Return Of The Crooklyn Dodgers"—Crooklyn Dodgers '95 (MCA)
32. "Real Hip Hop"—Das EFX (EastWest)
33. "Braggin' Writes"—J-Live (Raw Shack)
34. "Whutcha Want?"—Nine (Profile)
35. "Jeeps, Lex Coups, Bimaz & Benz"—Lost Boyz (Universal)
36. "Shimmy Shimmy Ya"—Ol' Dirty Bastard (Elektra)
37. "In My Lifetime" b/w "Can't Get Wit That"—Jay-Z (Roc-A-Fella)
38. "Tear Da Club Up (Da Real)"—Three 6 Mafia (Prophet)
39. "Boriquas On Da Set"—Frankie Cutlass featuring Doo Wop, Fat Joe, Ray Boogie & True God (Relativity)
40. "My Kinda Moves"—Q-Ball & Curt Cazal (VZQ)

1996

1. "Elevators (Me & You)"—OutKast (LaFace)
2. "Dead Presidents" b/w "Ain't No Nigga"—Jay-Z (Roc-A-Fella)
3. "Killing Me Softly With His Song"—Fugees (Ruffhouse)
4. "Can't Knock The Hustle"—Jay-Z featuring Mary J. Blige (Roc-A-Fella)
5. "Woo Hah!! Got You All In Check"—Busta Rhymes (Elektra)
6. "Cell Therapy"—Goodie Mob (LaFace)
7. "Bow Down"—Westside Connection (Priority)
8. "Get Money (Remix)"—Junior M.A.F.I.A. featuring The Notorious B.I.G. (Big Beat)
9. "No Time" b/w "Queen Bitch"—Lil' Kim featuring Puff Daddy (Undeas)
10. "Drop A Gem On 'Em"—Mobb Deep (Loud)
11. "Buy You Some"—Too $hort featuring Erick Sermon (Jive)
12. "Daytona 500"—Ghostface Killah featuring Raekwon, Cappadona & The Force MD's (Razor Sharp)
13. "Ready Or Not"—Fugees (Ruffhouse)
14. "Ya Playin' Yaself"—Jeru The Damaja (Payday)
15. "Hell On Earth (Front Lines)"—Mobb Deep (Loud)
16. "Stakes Is High" b/w "The Bizness"—De La Soul (Tommy Boy)
17. "Hay"—Crucial Conflict (Pallas)
18. "Shadowboxin'" b/w "4th Chamber"—The Genius (Geffen)
19. "Fu-Gee-La" b/w "How Many Mics"—Fugees (Ruffhouse)
20. "Tried By 12"—The East Flatbush Project featuring DeS (10/30 Uproar)
21. "Put It In Your Mouth"—Akinyele featuring Kia Jefferies (Stress)
22. "California Love"—2Pac featuring Dr. Dre (Death Row)
23. "Paparazzi"—Xzibit (Loud)
24. "Leflaur Leflah Eshkoshka"—The Fab 5 (Duck Down)

CHARTS.

25. "Tha Crossroads"—Bone Thugs-N-Harmony (Relativity)
26. "Po Pimp"—Do Or Die featuring Johnny P & Twista (Rap-A-Lot)
27. "Funkorama"—Redman (Interscope)
28. "L.A., L.A."—Capone-N-Noreaga featuring Mobb Deep & Tragedy (25 To Life)
29. "8 Steps To Perfection" b/w "Vital Nerve"—Company Flow (Official)
30. "No"—Chuck D (Mercury)
31. "Brownsville" b/w "Stick To Ya Gunz"—M.O.P. (Relativity)
32. "Motherless Child"—Ghostface Killah featuring Raekwon (Razor Sharp)
33. "Bout It, Bout It II"—Master P featuring Mia X (No Limit)
34. "Fakin' Jax"—Inl (Soul Brother)
35. "Worldwide"—Royal Flush (Blunt)
36. "Father Time"—Saukrates (Day)
37. "Lyrical Tactics" b/w "Shine"—Mr. Voodoo (Fortress)
38. "Recognize & Realize (Part 1)"—Big Noyd featuring Prodigy (Mobb Deep) (Tommy Boy)
39. "Get Me Home"—Foxy Brown featuring Blackstreet (Def Jam)
40. "Crush" b/w "Official"—Big Shug (Payday)

1997

1. "It's All About The Benjamins (Remix)"—Puff Daddy featuring The Lox, Lil' Kim & The Notorious B.I.G. (Bad Boy)
2. "Mo Money Mo Problems"—The Notorious B.I.G. featuring Ma$e & Puff Daddy (Bad Boy)
3. "Hypnotize"—The Notorious B.I.G. (Bad Boy)
4. "Put Your Hands Where My Eyes Can See"—Busta Rhymes (Elektra)
5. "Off The Books"—The Beatnuts featuring Big Punisher & Cuban Link (Relativity)
6. "Who You Wit"—Jay-Z (Qwest)
7. "Been Around The World"—Puff Daddy featuring Ma$e & The Notorious B.I.G. (Bad Boy)
8. "Deja Vu (Uptown Baby)"—Lord Tariq & Peter Gunz (Codeine)
9. "Money, Power & Respect"—The Lox featuring Lil' Kim & DMX (Bad Boy)
10. "Feel So Good"—Ma$e featuring Kelly Price (Bad Boy)
11. "Triumph"—Wu-Tang Clan (Loud)
12. "4, 3, 2, 1"—LL Cool J featuring Method Man, Redman, Canibus & DMX (Def Jam)
13. "How Ya Do Dat"—Young Bleed featuring Master P & C-Loc (No Limit)
14. "T.O.N.Y. (Top Of New York)"—Capone-N-Noreaga featuring Tragedy (Penalty)
15. "You Know My Steez"—Gang Starr (Noo Trybe)
16. "Hail Mary"—Makaveli featuring The Outlawz (Death Row)
17. "Crush On You (Remix)"—Lil' Kim featuring Lil' Cease (Undeas)
18. "The Rain (Supa Dupa Fly)"—Missy Elliott (EastWest)
19. "Phone Tap"—Nas, Foxy Brown, AZ & Nature (Aftermath)
20. "Guantanamera"—Wyclef Jean featuring Lauryn Hill (Ruffhouse)
21. "Whateva Man"—Redman featuring Erick Sermon (Def Jam)
22. "Hip Hop Drunkies"—Tha Alkaholiks featuring Ol' Dirty Bastard (Loud)
23. "Universal Magnetic"—Mos Def (Rawkus)
24. "Whoop! Whoop!"—DJ Pooh featuring Kam (Big Beat)
25. "It's Been A Long Time"—Rakim (Universal)
26. "Soul On Ice (Remix)"—Ras Kass (Priority)
27. "Smile"—Scarface featuring 2Pac & Johnny P (Rap-A-Lot)
28. "Metal Thangz"—Street Smartz featuring O.C. & Pharoahe Monch (Organized Konfusion) (Tru Criminal)
29. "Fortified Live"—Reflection Eternal featuring Mos Def & Mr. Man (Da Bush Babees) (Rawkus)
30. "Da Joint"—EPMD (Def Jam)
31. "Wild For Da Night"—Rampage featuring Busta Rhymes (Elektra)
32. "Hoodlum"—Mobb Deep featuring Big Noyd & Rakim (Loud)
33. "Step Into A World (Rapture's Delight)"—KRS-One (Jive)

34. "Da Dip"—Freak Nasty (HardHood)
35. "Day One"—D.I.T.C. (D.I.T.C.)
36. "Gettin' Closer To God"—Krumb Snatcha (Mass In Action)
37. "Burban & Impalas"—Big Mike (Rap-A-Lot)
38. "The Body Rock"—Mos Def, Tash & Q-Tip (Rawkus)
39. "Tired Of Ballin'"—Tela (Suave House)
40. "Visualize"—Mr. Complex (Raw Shack)

1998

1. "Hard Knock Life (Ghetto Anthem)"—Jay-Z (Roc-A-Fella)
2. "SuperThug"—Noreaga (Penalty)
3. "Still Not A Player"—Big Punisher featuring Joe (Loud)
4. "Ruff Ryders' Anthem"—DMX (Def Jam)
5. "Rosa Parks"—OutKast (LaFace)
6. "Get At Me Dog"—DMX featuring Sheek (The Lox) (Def Jam)
7. "It Ain't My Fault"—Silkk The Shocker featuring Mystikal (No Limit)
8. "Can I Get A . . . "—Jay-Z featuring Amil & Ja Rule (Roc-A-Fella)
9. "Money Ain't A Thang"—Jermaine Dupri featuring Jay-Z (So So Def)
10. "Ha"—Juvenile (Cash Money)
11. "Make 'Em Say Unngh!"—Master P featuring Fiend, Silkk The Shocker, Mia X & Mystikal (No Limit)
12. "I'll Bee Dat!"—Redman (Def Jam)
13. "Doo Wop (That Thing) b/w "Lost Ones"—Lauryn Hill (Ruffhouse)
14. "N.O.R.E."—Noreaga (Penalty)
15. "Tru Master"—Pete Rock featuring Inspectah Deck & Kurupt (Loud)
16. "Dangerous"—Busta Rhymes (Elektra)
17. "Full Cooperation"—Def Squad (Def Jam)
18. "Second Round K.O."—Canibus (Universal)
19. "Whatcha Gonna Do"—Jayo Felony featuring Method Man & DMX (Def Jam)
20. "Victory" b/w "Been Around The World (Remix)"—Puff Daddy (Bad Boy)
21. "Hope I Don't Go Back"—E-40 (Sick Wid It)
22. "Ebonics"—Big L (Fat Beats)
23. "What U See Is What U Get"—Xzibit (Loud)
24. "The Man Right Chea"—Mystikal (No Limit)
25. "Still A G Thang"—Snoop Doggy Dogg (No Limit)
26. "357" b/w "Pull It"—Cam'Ron (Untertainment)
27. "They Don't Dance No Mo'"—Goodie Mob (LaFace)
28. "Horse & Carriage"—Cam'Ron featuring Ma$e (Untertainment)
29. "Cha Cha Cha"—Flipmode Squad (Elektra)
30. "Work The Angles"/"The Main Event"/"Triple Optics"—Dilated Peoples (ABB)
31. "M. I. A."—Missin' Linx (Fat Beats)
32. "Find A Way"—A Tribe Called Quest (Jive)
33. "What You Want"—Ma$e featuring Total (Bad Boy)
34. "We Can Freak It"—Kurupt featuring Baby S (A&M)
35. "Do For Love"—2Pac (Interscope)
36. "Where Dem Dollas At"—Gangsta Boo featuring DJ Paul & Juicy J (Relativity)
37. "Here We Come"—Timbaland featuring Magoo & Missy Elliott (Atlantic)
38. "The Actual" b/w "Priceless"—All City (MCA)
39. "Cheapskate"—Sporty Thievz (Ruffhouse)
40. "The Anthem" / "Lost Art" / "Likwit Fusion"—Lootpack (Stones Throw)

CHARTS.

FEATURED PLATTERS:
Hip Hop's Greatest Albums By Year.

1979–1985

1. *Run-D.M.C.*—Run-D.M.C. (Profile, 1984)
2. *Radio*—LL Cool J (Def Jam, 1985)
3. *Wild Style* Soundtrack—Various Artists (Animal, 1983)
4. *Live Convention '82*—Various Artists (Disco Wax, 1982)
5. *Live Convention '81*—Various Artists (Disco Wax, 1981)
6. *Fat Boys*—Fat Boys (Sutra, 1984)
7. *Escape*—Whodini (Jive, 1984)
8. *King Of Rock*—Run-D.M.C. (Profile, 1985)
9. *Treacherous Three*—Treacherous Three (Sugar Hill, 1984)
10. *The Album*—Mantronix (Fresh, 1985)
11. *D'Ya Like Scratchin'* EP—Malcolm McLaren & The World Famous Supreme Team (Island, 1982)
12. *The Big Break Rapper Party*—Various Artists (Sound Of New York, USA, 1980)
13. *Fat Boys Are Back*—Fat Boys (Sutra, 1985)
14. *Don't Stop Rappin'*—Too $hort (75 Girls, 1983)
15. *Crash Crew*—Crash Crew (Sugar Hill, 1984)
16. *Raw, Uncut & X-Rated*—Too $hort (75 Girls, 1985)
17. *The Message*—Grandmaster Flash & The Furious Five (Sugar Hill, 1982)
18. *Ego Trip*—Kurtis Blow (Mercury, 1984)
19. *Players*—Too $hort (75 Girls, 1983)
20. *Whodini*—Whodini (Jive, 1983)
21. *8th Wonder*—Sugarhill Gang (Sugar Hill, 1981)
22. *The Champagne Of Rap*—Dr. Jeckyll & Mr. Hyde (Profile, 1985)
23. *Def Mix Volume 1*—Roxanne Shanté & Various Artists (Pop Art, 1985)
24. *Kurtis Blow*—Kurtis Blow (Mercury, 1980)
25. *Sugarhill Gang*—Sugarhill Gang (Sugar Hill, 1979)

1986–1987

1. *Raising Hell*—Run-D.M.C. (Profile, 1986)
2. *Criminal Minded*—Boogie Down Productions (B-Boy, 1987)
3. *Licensed To Ill*—Beastie Boys (Def Jam, 1986)
4. *Paid In Full*—Eric B. & Rakim (4th & B'way, 1987)
5. *Yo! Bum Rush The Show*—Public Enemy (Def Jam, 1987)
6. *Bigger And Deffer*—LL Cool J (Def Jam, 1987)
7. *Saturday Night-The Album*—Schoolly D (Schoolly D, 1987)
8. *2 Live Crew Is What We Are*—2 Live Crew (Luke Skyywalker, 1986)
9. *Born To Mack*—Too $hort (Jive, 1986)
10. *Down By Law*—MC Shan (Cold Chillin', 1987)
11. *Hot, Cool & Vicious*—Salt-N-Pepa (Next Plateau, 1986)
12. *Kool & Deadly (Justicizms)*—Just-Ice (Fresh, 1987)
13. *Back In Black*—Whodini (Jive, 1986)
14. *Dana Dane With Fame*—Dana Dane (Profile, 1987)
15. *Oh My God!*—Doug E. Fresh & The Get Fresh Crew (Reality, 1986)
16. *Rock The House*—DJ Jazzy Jeff & The Fresh Prince (Word Up, 1987)
17. *Back To The Old School*—Just-Ice (Fresh, 1986)
18. *On Fire*—Stetsasonic (Tommy Boy, 1986)
19. *Dynamite*—Masters Of Ceremony (4th & B'way, 1987)

20. *How Ya Like Me Now*—Kool Moe Dee (Jive, 1987)
21. *Schoolly D*—Schoolly D (Schoolly D, 1986)
22. *Rhyme Pays*—Ice-T (Sire, 1987)
23. *What's My Name*—Steady B (Jive, 1987)
24. *The Godfather*—Spoonie Gee (Tuff City, 1987)
25. *Got To Be Tough*—MC Shy D (Luke Skyywalker, 1987)

1988

1. *It Takes A Nation Of Millions To Hold Us Back*—Public Enemy (Def Jam)
2. *Straight Outta Compton*—N.W.A (Ruthless)
3. *The Great Adventures Of Slick Rick*—Slick Rick (Def Jam)
4. *Strictly Business*—EPMD (Fresh)
5. *By All Means Necessary*—Boogie Down Productions (Jive)
6. *Long Live The Kane*—Big Daddy Kane (Cold Chillin')
7. *Critical Beatdown*—Ultramagnetic MC's (Next Plateau)
8. *Follow The Leader*—Eric B. & Rakim (Uni)
9. *Goin' Off*—Biz Markie (Cold Chillin')
10. *Straight Out The Jungle*—Jungle Brothers (Idlers)
11. *Eazy-Duz-It*—Eazy-E (Ruthless)
12. *Tougher Than Leather*—Run-D.M.C. (Profile)
13. *Lyte As A Rock*—MC Lyte (First Priority)
14. *He's The DJ, I'm The Rapper*—DJ Jazzy Jeff & The Fresh Prince (Jive)
15. *In Control, Volume 1*—Marley Marl (Cold Chillin')
16. *A Salt With A Deadly Pepa*—Salt-N-Pepa (Next Plateau)
17. *Road To The Riches*—Kool G Rap & DJ Polo (Cold Chillin')
18. *The World's Greatest Entertainer*—Doug E. Fresh & The Get Fresh Crew (Reality)
19. *In Full Gear*—Stetsasonic (Tommy Boy)
20. *Move Somthin'*—2 Live Crew (Luke Skyywalker)
21. *Girls I Got 'Em Locked*—Super Lover Cee & Casanova Rud (Elektra)
22. *Life Is . . . Too $hort*—Too $hort (Jive)
23. *Act A Fool*—King Tee (Capitol)
24. *2 Hype*—Kid 'N Play (Select)
25. *Pure Righteousness*—Lakim Shabazz (Tuff City)

1989

1. *3 Feet High And Rising*—De La Soul (Tommy Boy)
2. *Paul's Boutique*—Beastie Boys (Capitol)
3. *Done By The Forces Of Nature*—Jungle Brothers (Warner Bros.)
4. *It's A Big Daddy Thing*—Big Daddy Kane (Cold Chillin')
5. *No One Can Do It Better*—The D.O.C. (Ruthless)
6. *Grip It! On That Other Level*—Geto Boys (Rap-A-Lot)
7. *The Cactus Album*—3rd Bass (Def Jam)
8. *As Nasty As They Wanna Be*—2 Live Crew (Luke)
9. *Nice & Smooth*—Nice & Smooth (Fresh)
10. *The Biz Never Sleeps*—Biz Markie (Cold Chillin')
11. *Unfinished Business*—EPMD (Fresh)
12. *All Hail The Queen*—Queen Latifah (Tommy Boy)
13. *Walking With A Panther*—LL Cool J (Def Jam)
14. *Youngest In Charge*—Special Ed (Profile)
15. *Ride The Rhythm*—Chill Rob G (Wild Pitch)
16. *We're In This Together*—Low Profile (Priority)

CHARTS.

17. *Eyes On This*—MC Lyte (First Priority)
18. *Original Stylin'*—Three Times Dope (Arista)
19. *Crazy Noize*—Stezo (Fresh)
20. *Ghetto Music: The Blueprint Of Hip Hop*—Boogie Down Productions (Jive)
21. *The Iceberg/Freedom Of Speech . . . Just Watch What You Say*—Ice-T (Rhyme Syndicate)
22. *Controversy*—Willie D (Rap-A-Lot)
23. *Big Tyme*—Heavy D & The Boyz (Uptown)
24. *SWASS*—Sir Mix-A-Lot (Def American)
25. *The Boy Genius Featuring A New Beginning*—Kwamé (Atlantic)

1990

1. *AmeriKKKa's Most Wanted*—Ice Cube (Priority)
2. *One For All*—Brand Nubian (Elektra)
3. *Fear Of A Black Planet*—Public Enemy (Def Jam)
4. *100 Miles And Runnin'* EP—N.W.A (Ruthless)
5. *Business As Usual*—EPMD (Def Jam)
6. *Mama Said Knock You Out*—LL Cool J (Def Jam)
7. *Let The Rhythm Hit 'Em*—Eric B. & Rakim (MCA)
8. *Wanted: Dead Or Alive*—Kool G Rap & DJ Polo (Cold Chillin')
9. *People's Instinctive Travels And The Paths Of Rhythm*—A Tribe Called Quest (Jive)
10. *Step In The Arena*—Gang Starr (Chrysalis)
11. *Edutainment*—Boogie Down Productions (Jive)
12. *Livin' Like Hustlers*—Above The Law (Ruthless)
13. *To The East, Blackwards*—X Clan (Island)
14. *Kill At Will* EP—Ice Cube (Priority)
15. *Funky Technician*—Lord Finesse & DJ Mike Smooth (Wild Pitch)
16. *Short Dog's In The House*—Too $hort (Jive)
17. *Legal*—Special Ed (Profile)
18. *Sex Packets*—Digital Underground (Tommy Boy)
19. *At Your Own Risk*—King Tee (Capitol)
20. *Tell The World My Name*—K-Solo (Atlantic)
21. *Holy Intellect*—Poor Righteous Teachers (Profile)
22. *Take A Look Around*—Masta Ace (Cold Chillin')
23. *This Is An EP Release*—Digital Underground (Tommy Boy)
24. *It's A Compton Thang*—Compton's Most Wanted (Orpheus)
25. *Call Me D-Nice*—D-Nice (Jive)

1991

1. *Efil4zaggin*—N.W.A (Ruthless)
2. *The Low End Theory*—A Tribe Called Quest (Jive)
3. *Breaking Atoms*—Main Source (Wild Pitch)
4. *De La Soul Is Dead*—De La Soul (Tommy Boy)
5. *Death Certificate*—Ice Cube (Priority)
6. *Cypress Hill*—Cypress Hill (Ruffhouse)
7. *A Wolf In Sheep's Clothing*—Black Sheep (Mercury)
8. *Quik Is The Name*—DJ Quik (Profile)
9. *Mr. Scarface Is Back*—Mr. Scarface (Rap-A-Lot)
10. *Soul Clap* EP—Show & AG (Payday)
11. *Derelicts Of Dialect*—3rd Bass (Def Jam)
12. *Bitch Betta Have My Money*—AMG (Select)
13. *All Souled Out* EP—Pete Rock & CL Smooth (Elektra)

14. *A Future Without A Past . . .*—Leaders Of The New School (Elektra)
15. *Naughty By Nature*—Naughty By Nature (Tommy Boy)
16. *Ain't A Damn Thing Changed*—Nice & Smooth (RAL)
17. *Apocalypse '91 . . . The Enemy Strikes Black*—Public Enemy (Def Jam)
18. *Fruits Of Nature*—UMC's (Wild Pitch)
19. *I Wish My Brother George Was Here*—Del The Funkeé Homosapien (Elektra)
20. *We Can't Be Stopped*—Geto Boys (Rap-A-Lot)
21. *Penicillin On Wax*—Tim Dog (Ruffhouse)
22. *Mr. Hood*—K.M.D. (Elektra)
23. *Straight Checkn 'Em*—Compton's Most Wanted (Epic)
24. *Organized Konfusion*—Organized Konfusion (Hollywood BASIC)
25. *To Whom It May Concern...*—Freestyle Fellowship (Sun)

1992

1. *The Chronic*—Dr. Dre (Death Row)
2. *In God We Trust*—Brand Nubian (Elektra)
3. *Daily Operation*—Gang Starr (Chrysalis)
4. *Whut? Thee Album*—Redman (Def Jam)
5. *Stunts, Blunts & Hip Hop*—Diamond D (Chemistry)
6. *Bizarre Ride II The Pharcyde*—The Pharcyde (Delicious Vinyl)
7. *Check Your Head*—Beastie Boys (Grand Royal)
8. *Mecca And The Soul Brother*—Pete Rock & CL Smooth (Elektra)
9. *Runaway Slave*—Show & AG (Payday)
10. *Dead Serious*—Das EFX (EastWest)
11. *Guerillas In Tha Mist*—Da Lench Mob (EastWest)
12. *Business Never Personal*—EPMD (Def Jam)
13. *The Predator*—Ice Cube (Priority)
14. *Way 2 Fonky*—DJ Quik (Profile)
15. *Blue Funk*—Heavy D & The Boyz (Uptown)
16. *Reel To Reel*—Grand Puba (Elektra)
17. *The Skills Dat Pay Da Bills*—Positive K (Island)
18. *Shorty The Pimp*—Too $hort (Jive)
19. *Music To Driveby*—Compton's Most Wanted (Epic)
20. *Sex And Violence*—Boogie Down Productions (Jive)
21. *Too Hard To Swallow*—U.G.K. (Jive)
22. *Spice 1*—Spice 1 (Jive)
23. *Can I Borrow A Dollar?*—Common (Relativity)
24. *House Of Pain*—House of Pain (Tommy Boy)
25. *Don't Stop 'Til We Major*—JT The Bigga Figga (Get Low)

1993

1. *Enter The Wu-Tang (36 Chambers)*—Wu-Tang Clan (Loud)
2. *Midnight Marauders*—A Tribe Called Quest (Jive)
3. *Doggystyle*—Snoop Doggy Dogg (Death Row)
4. *Buhlōōne Mind State*—De La Soul (Tommy Boy)
5. *Enta Da Stage*—Black Moon (Nervous)
6. *Return Of The Boom Bap*—KRS-One (Jive)
7. *Intoxicated Demons* The EP—The Beatnuts (Relativity)
8. *Bacdafucup*—Onyx (Def Jam)
9. *The Four Horsemen*—Ultramagnetic MC's (Wild Pitch)
10. *Tha Triflin' Album*—King Tee (Capitol)

CHARTS.

11. *21 & Over*—Tha Alkaholiks (Loud)
12. *93 'Til Infinity*—Souls Of Mischief (Jive)
13. *Slaughtahouse*—Masta Ace (Delicious Vinyl)
14. *The World Is Yours*—Mr. Scarface (Rap-A-Lot)
15. *You Better Ask Somebody*—Yo Yo (EastWest)
16. *No Need For Alarm*—Del The Funkeé Homosapien (Elektra)
17. *Till Death Do Us Part*—Geto Boys (Rap-A-Lot)
18. *Get In Where You Fit In*—Too $hort (Jive)
19. *Black Sunday*—Cypress Hill (Ruffhouse)
20. *Comin' Out Hard*—Eightball & MJG (Suave House)
21. *Federal*—E-40 (Sick Wid It)
22. *Vagina Diner*—Akinyele (Interscope)
23. *Organix*—The Roots (Remedy)
24. *Here Come The Lords*—Lords Of The Underground (Pendulum)
25. *Represent*—Fat Joe (Relativity)

1994

1. *Illmatic*—Nas (Columbia)
2. *Ready To Die*—The Notorious B.I.G. (Bad Boy)
3. *Southernplayalisticadillacmuzik*—OutKast (LaFace)
4. *The Sun Rises In The East*—Jeru The Damaja (Payday)
5. *The Beatnuts*—The Beatnuts (Relativity)
6. *Resurrection*—Common (Relativity)
7. *6 Feet Deep*—Gravediggaz (Gee Street)
8. *Stress: The Extinction Agenda*—Organized Konfusion (Hollywood BASIC)
9. *Hard To Earn*—Gang Starr (Chrysalis)
10. *Ill Communication*—Beastie Boys (Grand Royal)
11. *Somethin' Serious*—Big Mike (Rap-A-Lot)
12. *Tical*—Method Man (Def Jam)
13. *Creepin On Ah Come Up* EP—Bone Thugs-N-Harmony (Ruthless)
14. *Do You Want More?!!!??!*—The Roots (Geffen)
15. *The Diary*—Scarface (Rap-A-Lot)
16. *IV Life*—King Tee (Capitol)
17. *The Mailman* EP—E-40 (Sick Wid It)
18. *Dare Iz A Darkside*—Redman (Def Jam)
19. *On The Outside Looking In*—Eightball & MJG (Suave House)
20. *Fadanuf Fa Erybody*—Odd Squad (Rap-A-Lot)
21. *Super Tight . . .*—U.G.K. (Jive)
22. *Explicit Game*—Dru Down (C-Note)
23. *Playaz N The Game*—JT The Bigga Figga (Get Low)
24. *We Come Strapped*—Compton's Most Wanted (Epic)
25. *A Constipated Monkey*—Kurious (Columbia)

1995

1. *Only Built 4 Cuban Linx . . .*—Raekwon (Loud)
2. *The Infamous*—Mobb Deep (Loud)
3. *Liquid Swords*—The Genius (Geffen)
4. *Return To The 36 Chambers: The Dirty Version*—Ol' Dirty Bastard (Elektra)
5. *Coast II Coast*—Tha Alkaholiks (Loud)
6. *Soul Food*—Goodie Mob (LaFace)
7. *Me Against The World*—2Pac (Interscope)

8. *Livin' Proof*—Group Home (Payday)
9. *Dah Shinin'*—Smif-N-Wessun (Nervous)
10. *KRS-One*—KRS-One (Jive)
11. *Dogg Food*—Tha Dogg Pound (Death Row)
12. *Safe & Sound*—DJ Quik (Profile)
13. *2000*—Grand Puba (Elektra)
14. *In A Major Way*—E-40 (Sick Wid It)
15. *Curb Servin'*—WC And The MAAD Circle (Payday)
16. *E. 1999 Eternal*—Bone Thugs-N-Harmony (Ruthless)
17. *Jealous One's Envy*—Fat Joe (Relativity)
18. *Mack 10*—Mack 10 (Priority)
19. *Operation Stackola*—Luniz (Noo Trybe)
20. *True*—TRU (No Limit)
21. *Labcabincalifornia*—The Pharcyde (Delicious Vinyl)
22. *On Top Of The World*—Eightball & MJG (Suave House)
23. *Down And Dirty*—The Click (Sick Wid It)
24. *Dwellin' In Tha Labb*—JT The Bigga Figga (Get Low)
25. *Lifestylez Ov Da Poor & Dangerous*—Big L (Columbia)

1996

1. *Reasonable Doubt*—Jay-Z (Roc-A-Fella)
2. *Ironman*—Ghostface Killah (Razor Sharp)
3. *Hell On Earth*—Mobb Deep (Loud)
4. *ATLiens*—OutKast (LaFace)
5. *The Score*—Fugees (Ruffhouse)
6. *Muddy Waters*—Redman (Def Jam)
7. *Firing Squad*—M.O.P. (Relativity)
8. *Stakes Is High*—De La Soul (Tommy Boy)
9. *Psychoanalysis (What Is It?)*—Prince Paul (WordSound)
10. *The Don Killuminati: The 7 Day Theory*—Makaveli (Death Row)
11. *Enigma*—Keith Murray (Jive)
12. *Dr. Octagonecologyst*—Dr. Octagon (Bulk)
13. *The Coming*—Busta Rhymes (Elektra)
14. *All Eyez On Me*—2Pac (Death Row)
15. *Bow Down*—Westside Connection (Priority)
16. *Hard Core*—Lil' Kim (Big Beat)
17. *Illadelph Halflife*—The Roots (Geffen)
18. *Wrath Of The Math*—Jeru The Damaja (Payday)
19. *Tha Hall Of Game*—E-40 (Sick Wid It)
20. *Nocturnal*—Heltah Skeltah (Duck Down)
21. *Ridin' Dirty*—U.G.K. (Jive)
22. *The Resurrection*—Geto Boys (Rap-A-Lot)
23. *At The Speed Of Life*—Xzibit (Loud)
24. *Ice Cream Man*—Master P (No Limit)
25. *The Final Tic*—Crucial Conflict (Universal)

1997

1. *Life After Death*—The Notorious B.I.G. (Bad Boy)
2. *The War Report*—Capone-N-Noreaga (Penalty)
3. *Wu-Tang Forever*—Wu-Tang Clan (Loud)

CHARTS.

4. *The Carnival*—Wyclef Jean featuring Refugee Allstars (Ruffhouse)
5. *Stone Crazy*—The Beatnuts (Relativity)
6. *Unpredictable*—Mystikal (No Limit)
7. *No Way Out*—Puff Daddy & The Family (Bad Boy)
8. *Ghetto D*—Master P (No Limit)
9. *Supa Dupa Fly*—Missy Elliott (EastWest)
10. *Unlady Like*—Mia X (No Limit)
11. *In My Lifetime, Vol. 1*—Jay-Z (Roc-A-Fella)
12. *Sex Style*—Kool Keith (Funky Ass)
13. *Funcrusher Plus*—Company Flow (Rawkus)
14. *When Disaster Strikes . . .*—Busta Rhymes (Elektra)
15. *Harlem World*—Ma$e (Bad Boy)
16. *The Art Of War*—Bone Thugs-N-Harmony (Ruthless)
17. *The 18th Letter The Book Of Life*—Rakim (Universal)
18. *Back In Business*—EPMD (Def Jam)
19. *Jurassic 5 EP*—Jurassic 5 (Rumble)
20. *Tru 2 Da Game*—TRU (No Limit)
21. *Jewelz*—O.C. (Payday)
22. *The Untouchable*—Scarface (Rap-A-Lot)
23. *Based On A True Story*—Mack 10 (Priority)
24. *Da Dirty 30*—Cru (Def Jam)
25. *Accept Your Own & Be Yourself (The Black Album)*—No I.D. (Relativity)

1998

1. *Moment Of Truth*—Gang Starr (Noo Trybe)
2. *Aquemini*—OutKast (LaFace)
3. *Vol. 2 . . . Hard Knock Life*—Jay-Z (Roc-A-Fella)
4. *The Miseducation Of Lauryn Hill*—Lauryn Hill (Ruffhouse)
5. *First Family 4 Life*—M.O.P. (Relativity)
6. *Still Standing*—Goodie Mob (LaFace)
7. *It's Dark And Hell Is Hot*—DMX (Def Jam)
8. *Doc's Da Name 2000*—Redman (Def Jam)
9. *N.O.R.E.*—Noreaga (Penalty)
10. *Capital Punishment*—Big Punisher (Loud)
11. *El Niño*—Def Squad (Def Jam)
12. *MP Da Last Don*—Master P (No Limit)
13. *Life In 1472*—Jermaine Dupri (So So Def)
14. *Charge It 2 Da Game*—Silkk The Shocker (No Limit)
15. *Da Game Is To Be Sold, Not To Be Told*—Snoop Doggy Dogg (No Limit)
16. *Retaliation, Revenge And Get Back*—Daz Dillinger (Death Row)
17. *My Balls And My Word*—Young Bleed (No Limit)
18. *400 Degreez*—Juvenile (Cash Money)
19. *The Shadiest One*—WC (Payday)
20. *The Element Of Surprise*—E-40 (Sick Wid It)
21. *. . . a s.w.a.t. healin' ritual*—Witchdoctor (Interscope)
22. *Lost*—Eightball (Suave House)
23. *Life Or Death*—C-Murder (No Limit)
24. *The Dude*—Devin (Rap-A-Lot)
25. *Full Scale EP*—Show & AG (D.I.T.C.)

THE MONKEY

CADEMY

The Monkey Academy, main library, basement level, room 1971 with the crappy plumbing (b/k/a the ego trip office). New York City, March 5, 1999.

THE MONKEY ACADEMY.

THE MONKEY ACADEMY.

Items On The Cover Of *ego trip's Book Of Rap Lists.*

1. **Harry Allen**
   Media Assassin. Word.

2. **"Anatomy Of An Ass-Whipping (Kwest Fucks L-Smooth's Shit Up At NYC MC Battle, 1990)"—Kwest Tha Madd Lad (Ill Labels, 1993)**
   Promo only green vinyl of Tommy Kwest's freestylin' fandango.

3. **Beastie Boys paper coffee cups (Grand Royal, 1998)**
   Promo item for *Hello Nasty.* That's right, it makes no sense.

4. **Beastie Boys Tour book (Def Jam, 1987)**
   Souvenir photo book from the Licensed To Ill Tour.

5. **Beat Street one sheet (Orion, 1984)**
   Lobby poster for seminal hip hop goes Hollywood film.

6. **"Biz Is Goin' Off"—Biz Markie (Cold Chillin', 1988)**
   Classic psychedelic 12" sleeve from the Diabolical.

7. **Biz Markie puppet (Cold Chillin', 1990)**
   From the cover and video of Masta Ace's "Me And The Biz" single.

8. **Break Dancing: Step-By-Step Instructions (Beekman House, 1984)**
   Fun-filled photo book by Jim Sullivan and Lori Calicott, featuring the fancy footwork of Felix Castro, Peter Garcia and Javier Gonzales, amongst others.

9. **Busta Rhymes posterboard (Elektra, 1998)**
   Snipe ad for *E.L.E.: Extinction Level Event.*

10. **Busta Rhymes "spirit hand" (Elektra, 1997)**
    Promo item for the "Put Your Hands Where My Eyes Can See" single.

11. **"Children's Story"—Slick Rick (Def Jam, 1989)**
    Autographed 12" copy of Ricky's classic tale.

12. **Crash Crew—Crash Crew (Sugar Hill, 1983)**
    Debut LP from one of the old school's great ensembles.

13. **Cypress Hill slipmat (Ruffhouse, 1995)**

Promo item for *III (Temples Of Boom)*

14. **Death Mix Live!—Afrika Bambaataa (Winley, 1983)**
    Ultra rare original pressing of Bam and Jazzy Jay's live recording at the Bronx's James Monroe High School. Autographed on the back by both of 'em.

15. **De La Soul poster (Rock On, circa 1989)**
    Concert poster announcing the trio's performance in Germany at Saga Billetcenter.

16. **De La Soul T-shirt (Tommy Boy, 1989)**
    Glow-in-the-dark mail-order T-shirt for *3 Feet High And Rising.*

17. **Disco 3 poster (Saturn Disco, 1984)**
    Concert poster announcing a performance of the future Fat Boys in Brooklyn.

18. **Do Or Die slipmat (Neighborhood Watch, 1996)**
    Promo item for *Picture This.*

19. **ego trip (ego trip Publications, 1998)**

THE MONKEY ACADEMY.

Double-sized "lucky" #13 issue of the greatest magazine of all time.

20. **EPMD poster (Fresh, 1988)**
Promo poster for Erick and Parrish's debut, *Strictly Business*.

21. **Eminem posterboard (Aftermath, 1999)**
Snipe ad for "My Name Is..." 12" single.

22. **Extra Prolific comic book (Jive, 1994)**
Promo for *Like It Should Be*.

23. **Fugees passport (Columbia, 1996)**
Invitation for a boat party for *The Score*.

24. **Fugees snippet cassette (Ruffhouse, 1997)**
Promo package in the form of a milk carton.

25. **Funky 4 + 1 poster (Sugar Hill, circa 1981)**
Point-of-sales promo.

26. **The Genius skateboard (Wu-Tang Hardgood Co., 1998)**
Licensed GZA-design skateboard deck (Kevin Taylor version) from discontinued "Wu-Tang Racing Team Series."

27. **"Go Stetsa I"—Stetsasonic (Tommy Boy, 1986)**
Rare 12" of a Brooklyn anthem.

28. **MC Hammer doll (Mattel, 1991)**
"Boom box™ makes real rap sounds!" One of two versions created.

29. **Harlem World posterboard (All Out, 1999)**
Snipe ad for *The Movement*.

30. **"Have A Nice Day"—Roxanne Shanté (Cold Chillin', 1987)**
Hard-to-find 12" with picture sleeve from the baddest lady to ever rock a mic.

31. **Haze "Bauhaus" chair (1995)**
Limited-edition art chair created by graf artist/designer Eric Haze.

32. **Ice-T with Body Count poster (Vatican, 1992)**
Concert poster announcing performance in Houston. Silkscreened by artist Frank Kozik.

33. **Jungle Brothers poster (Gee Street, 1997)**
Point-of-sales poster for *Raw Deluxe*.

34. **Jungle Brothers press kit (Gee Street, 1997)**
Electronic press kit for *Raw Deluxe* in the form of a package of meat.

35. **K.M.D./RIF Productions T-Shirt (Elektra, 1991)**
Promo shirt for *Mr. Hood*.

36. **"Let's Rock"—Harlem World Crew (Tay-ster, 1980)**
Rare 12" old school gem.

37. **LL Cool J Kangol (Def Jam, 1987)**
Promo item for *Bigger And Deffer*.

38. **Lordz Of Brooklyn pizza box (Ventrue, 1995)**
Promo box for the Italian stallions from Bay Ridge.

39. **Lost Boyz frisbee (Universal, 1997)**
Promo item for *Love, Peace & Nappiness*.

40. **Luke "spirit hand" (Luke, 1997)**
Promo item for the "Raise The Roof" single.

41. **Master P doll (No Limit Toys, 1998)**
Squeeze him and you too can make him say, "Unngh!"

42. **Money Mark action figure (Mo' Wax Toys, 1998)**
Promo item of the Beastie Boys' keyboardist for his sophomore album, *Push The Button*.

43. **Naughty By Nature posterboard (Arista, 1999)**
Snipe ad for *Nature's Fury*.

44. **Oaktown's 3.5.7. longbox (Capitol, 1991)**
Discontinued packgage for *Fully Loaded*.

45. **Paris longbox (Scarface, 1992)**
Discontinued package for *Sleeping With The Enemy*.

46. **Public Enemy platinum plaque (Def Jam, 1988)**
RIAA certified sales award commerating the more than one million copies sold of *It Takes A Nation Of Millions To Hold Us Back* (a/k/a "The Greatest Rap Album Of All Time," dammit).

47. **Public Enemy poster (Def Jam, 1987)**
Point-of-sales poster for *Yo! Bum Rush The Show*.

48. **"Raptivity"—Ronnie Gee (Reflection, 1980)**
Rare old school 12" best known for its introduction: "Warning—the Surgeon General of Chilltown, New York has determined that the sounds you are about to hear can be devastating to your ear."

49. **"Rap War" (*New York Post*, 1997)**
March 10th edition of tabloid announcing the death of The Notorious B.I.G.

50. **Ras Kass "Kass" slipmat (Priority, 1996)**
Promo item for *Soul On Ice*. One of a set of two.

51. **RC-M50JW (JVC, circa 1980)**
Ghetto blaster with programmable "multi music scanner," variable "electronic echo," aggravating bass, devastating treble. Too bad it doesn't work anymore.

52. **Recording reel (private collection, 1995)**
Autographed by The Pharcyde. Featured on the cover of *Rap Pages'* May issue.

53. **Run-D.M.C T-shirt (Profile, 1986)**
T-shirt promoting *Raising Hell*.

54. **RZA posterboard (Gee Street, 1998)**
Snipe ad for *RZA As Bobby Digital*.

55. ***Sittin' On Chrome*—Masta Ace (Delicious Vinyl, 1995)**
Limited-edition promo-only vinyl LP with silver coating.

THE MONKEY ACADEMY.

56. **SL-1200MK2 turntables (Technics, circa 1989)**
The direct drive mechanism. The lasting durability. The foundation, son.

57. **"Smokin' Cheeba Cheeba"— Harlem Underground Band (Winley, 1976)**
Rare old school breakbeat sampled by the likes of Eric B. & Rakim, Boogie Down Productions and countless others.

58. **Snoop Doggy Dogg poster (Death Row, 1993)**
Poster for *Doggystyle*.

59. ***Son Doobie, Porn King* video (Vivid, 1995)**
(a/k/a *Vivid Raw 6*) Son Doobie's nearly buck-nekkid, boxer briefs-wearin' pornographic debut that he'd been threatening to make for years. He warned you.

60. **Souls Of Mischief canteen (Jive, 1995)**
Promo item for *No Man's Land*.

61. **"Spoiled Milk"—Milk (American, 1994)**
Promo only yellow vinyl copy.

62. **Stack of speakers (Rawkus, 1997)**
Set piece from the video for Mos Def, Tash & Q-Tip's "The Body Rock" constructed by artist/director Skwerm.

63. **"Step In The Arena"—Gang Starr (Chrysalis, 1991)**
Long-out-of-print 12".

64. **Stones Throw slipmat (Stones Throw, 1998)**
Promo item for Bay Area indie record label.

65. **Sway & King Tech longbox (Giant, 1991)**
Discontinued package for *Concrete Jungle*.

66. **"Thug 4 Life" (*The Village Voice*, 1996)**
Week of September 24th cover story memorializing the late Tupac Shakur.

67. ***Treacherous Three*—Treacherous Three (Sugar Hill, 1984)**
Debut LP from one of hip hop's greatest groups.

68. **UNKLE action figure (Mo' Wax Toys, 1998)**
Designed by Futura 2000 to promote UNKLE's *Psyence Fiction* featuring DJ Shadow, Kool G Rap and Mike D (Beastie Boys).

69. **"Watch Roger Do His Thing"— Main Source (Actual, 1990)**
Rare second single from the mad scientist and two (Canadian) brothers with checks.

70. **WC poster (Payday, 1998)**
Point-of-sales poster for *The Shadiest One*.

71. ***Yo! MTV Raps* sign (circa 1990)**
Set piece from the music channel's top-rated and highly influential program.

Sacha Jenkins

Sacha Jenkins—much like rap great KRS-One—is hip hop. Sachy-Sach, his sister Dominique, and their artistically inclined, Haitian-born mom-dukes, Monart, moved to Astoria, Queens, NY from Silver Springs, MD in the summer of 1977. Their Philadelphia, PA–reared, filmmaking/Emmy Award–winning pop-dukes, Horace, was already living up in NYC at the time (100th Street & Central Park West, to be exact. . . . blocks away from the infamous Rock Steady Park). During the school week, young Sacha spent his post three o'clock days playing stickball and skelly. Then. . .

1980: Sacha was blessed by an elder with an instrument of destruction that would forever change his life. "PK," a local subway scrawler with some inter-borough celebrity, handed the young boy a very juiced-up Pilot magic marker.

1988: Inspired by the *International Graffiti Times* (a rag published by aerosol legend Phase 2 and David Schmidlap), Sacha would put together *Graphic Scenes & X-plicit Language*—a zine dedicated to, yep, graf. And poetry. And anti–Gulf War rants. And humor. And towards the end, in 1991, music.

1992: *Beat Down*, America's *first* hip hop newspaper, is launched by Sacha and a childhood friend. Ten issues in, Sacha and childhood friend have a falling out. Bye bye, Black bird.

June, 1994: *ego trip* magazine is born.

1996: Sacha writes for *Vibe, Rolling Stone* and *Spin*. He gets a Writer-At-Large then Music Editor gig at *Vibe*.

Present: In his spare time, Sacha likes to play guitar, collect *Planet Of The Apes* action figures and listen to rap that isn't wack. He's a Leo.

Elliott Wilson

In the summer of 1992, armed with his worthless La Guardia Community College Associate Arts Degree, mulatto-born Elliott Wilson attempted to connect with *The Source* to no avail. Frustrated and full of half-Black rage, Wilson vowed to one day show his smarmy colleagues in the world of hip hop journalism what a tragic mistake they had made.

Befriending fellow W.C. Bryant High School alum Sacha Jenkins and L.C.C. student Haji Akhigbade, Wilson became the Music Editor of the duo's burgeoning rap news paper, *Beat Down*. After the trio disbanded in the fall of '93, Wilson encouraged Jenkins to give the publishing game another shot and the seasoned salt-and-pepper duo began to conceptualize *ego trip*.

Wilson soon realized, however, that one cannot eat off props alone. When not contributing toward ground breaking *ego trip* scriptures, he actively freelanced for *Vibe, Rap Pages, Rap Sheet, Time Out New York* and *Paper*. In 1995, he endured a brief-but-successful stint as an Associate Editor at *CMJ New Music Report* where he solidified the indie rock trade rag's hip hop coverage.

But it was in 1996 that he would enjoy a particularly sweet payback when he was wooed from *CMJ* to become *The Source*'s Music Editor. During his two-year tenure, he helped propel the already established publication to the country's top-selling music title.

From Q-borough underachiever to Big Willie publishing mogul and now author, Elliott Jesse Wilson Jr. is a living testament that dreams can and *do* come true.

Chairman Mao

Toiling for years as a truck-driving production assistant on the New York commercial filmmaking scene, New York University graduate Chairman Mao needed direction. An aspiring DJ, his addiction to acquiring wax had depleted his bank account. But in 1992, his chance meeting with an ambitious young publishing entrepreneur/film intern named Sacha Jenkins introduced an absurd solution to these fiscal woes—entering the world of music journalism! Mao began contributing to Jenkins' *Beat Down* magazine in exchange for complimentary promotional copies of hip hop records. He couldn't believe his luck.

Mao eventually exploited this writing scam so well that

THE MONKEY ACADEMY.

he actually began earning rent money with his new vocation. While becoming a fundamental cog within Jenkins' and partner Elliott Wilson's next publishing foray, *ego trip*, Mao enlightened *Rolling Stone*, *Spin*, *Entertainment Weekly* and *Vibe* with his critical musings. Amongst his most noteworthy assignments: his guest editorship for *Rap Pages'* acclaimed DJ Issue in April of 1996 and his profile of The Notorious B.I.G. in April of 1997 for the cover of *The Source* shortly before the rapper's untimely death.

Currently *ego trip's* Editor-In-Chief and a *Vibe* Writer-At-Large, Mao still can't believe he possesses a job that doesn't require him to sweep floors and chauffeur ad agency assholes. When not clocking long-but-gratifying hours at *et's* NYC HQ, he can be found in a record store near you digging for archival additions to his now 20,000-piece strong record library.

Gabriel Alvarez

Gabriel Alvarez was a long-haired, 20-year-old, L.A.-born Mexican with glasses trying to find a job in 1991. The odds were against him. Nobody wanted him. The only alternative? Intern for *gratis* at the latest magazine acquisition of *Hustler* publishing magnate Larry Flynt. *Film Threat* was a cool, anti-Hollywood, punk rock–type rag that gave the mainstream film press the kind of kick in the ass it needed. Alvarez quickly elevated to the position of Associate Editor.

Two years later, however, it was time to move on and Alvarez began working for another Flynt publication. *Rap Pages* was a hip hop mag that needed new creative energies to help it realize its potential. As Managing Editor, Alvarez expelled plenty of blood, sweat and tears and featured special graffiti, DJ and breakdance issues that intrigued a growing readership. Another three years later, though, it was time to roll the dice again.

His next job opportunity came in 1996 in the enticing form of *ego trip*, an amazingly creative magazine outta New York City, that made him an offer he couldn't refuse: a Managing Editor position demanding lots of hard work but no money. Displaying the sage decision-making skills that have guided his entire career, Alvarez immediately packs his bags and heads for the Rotten Apple. He begins freelancing extensively for *The Source* and *Vibe*. His status as an important critical voice grows. He even cuts his hair. He couldn't be happier. Or more broke.

Brent Rollins

Alternately known as Asparagus, Prima, Gor-gee, Half-Black, Kinda-Black, Brent Billions or Milton Reese (depending on the time of day), Brent Rollins, *et's* full-time Art Director and part-time scribe, is the original "Afrocentric-Asian, half-man/half-amazin'."

But whatever he's called, he's called often by the entertainment biz. Before graduating from UCLA with a BFA, Rollins had the fortunate opportunity to cut his teeth designing logos for films like Spike Lee's *Mo' Better Blues* and John Singleton's *Boyz N The Hood* as well as interning at Fattal And Collins Design & Advertising. He punctuated his college career by creating graphics for a FOX Network variety show, revamping the identity for TV's historic *Soul Train* and studying for a French exam all during his senior finals week. *C'est incroyable!*

However, it was his subsequent two-year bid (1994–1996) as Art Director for *Rap Pages* magazine which honed Rollins' talents. Since then, he's serviced clients such as Miramax Films, ICM, A&M, Mo' Wax and SoleSides Records. Along the way, he's also created art for The Pharcyde, The Notorious B.I.G., Gang Starr, Sir Menelik, Black Star and The Refugee Project charity organization. Between maintaining the 24/7 grind that has put food on his table and made his mom proud, the design veteran continues to champion the maligned and forgotten genre of "weirdo-rap."

Big time.

13 More Ways To Educate & Civilize Your Ass.*

1.   2.   3.   4.   5.   6.

7.   8.   9.   10.   11.   12.

1. NAS: Beatnuts! Beatminerz! Prong! Jeru! Violent Femmes! Chris Keefe!
2. METHOD MAN: Sick Of It All! Blues Explosion! Bob Power!
3. SMIF-N-WESSUN: Evel Knievel! Mike D! D-Generation! Ol' Dirty Bastard! Orange 9mm!
4. EAZY-E: Steve Albini! Ras Kass! Diamond D!
5. CYPRESS HILL: Raekwon! Kyuss! Shelter! Kool G Rap!
6. KRS-ONE: Pharcyde! Chavez! Genius! Prince Paul! Buju Banton!
7. A TRIBE CALLED QUEST/DE LA SOUL/LARGE PROFESSOR: Voted #1 Magazine Of 1997—*Hip Hop Connection* (UK)!
8. GHOSTFACE KILLAH: Ween! Heather Hunter! R.L. Burnside! Kool Keith & Tim Dog!
9. REDMAN: Bad Brains! Mobb Deep! Todd Bridges! M.O.P.! Manowar!
10. BIGGIE: Pavement! Punky Brewster! Mr. Scarface Meets Helmet! Space Needle!
11. RAKIM: Beatnuts! Charo! Primus! Cro-Mags! Mötley Crüe vs. Cru!
12. GANG STARR: Portishead! Deftones! Simon LeBon! Big Daddy Kane! Fu-Manchu! Marley Marl! Play The Rap Game™!
13. DEF SQUAD: Double-Sized Last Issue! Big Punisher! Monster Magnet Plays Backward Messages! Adrock Talks! Noreaga Goes To The Shrink! Interracial Dating Guide!

HONORABLE MENTIONS:

"(The) world's rawest, stinkiest, laugh-out-loud funniest magazine about hip hop."—*Spin*
"If you've been missing out on *ego trip* you've been missing out on the best...hip hop magazine of any kind."—*CMJ Monthly*
"Best Defunct Music Magazine."—*New York Press*

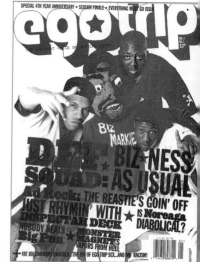

13.

*If you're gonna waste time on the internet, waste it ordering back issues at: www. .com or **PLATFORM.NET**

10 Reasons Why Rap Will Never Die.

10. Back in the days, KRS-One knew it.
9. Asian b-boys will attack, and you don't want that.
8. Some Blacks can't jump, shoot or go to their left.
7. Keeps Latinos on the dance floor and away from stealing your hubcaps.
6. It kicks harder than Tae Bo.
5. Niggas got things to say.
4. The future: white rappers.
3. It's a postmodern continuum of the African griot culture cultivated for thousands of years through ancient civilizations and manifested within such other magnificent oral and musical traditions as African American folk songs and spirituals, gospel hymns, the Mississippi Delta blues, ragtime, big band swing, be-bop jazz, beatnik poetry, early rhythm & blues, honky tonk, zydeco, rock 'n roll, go-go, funk, reggae, soca, calypso, ska, polka, flamenco, salsa, merengue, bossa nova, bluegrass, *tejano*, fusion, death metal, industrial, glam, jungle, show tunes, campfire sing-a-longs, tuberculosis cough, synchronized quaffing, gypsy muzak, yodeling, hobo harmonica music, techno-samba, porn soundtracks, gay German disco, Aboriginal freestyle, Tourette's Syndrome, snoring, conversations with God and armpit fart noises.
2. Monkey see, monkey do.
1. You can't kill something that's already dead.